The Gallup Poll

Public Opinion 1998

Other Gallup Poll Publications Available from Scholarly Resources

The Gallup Poll: Public Opinion Annual Series

1997 (ISBN 0-8420-2597-9)	*1986* (ISBN 0-8420-2274-0)
1996 (ISBN 0-8420-2596-0)	*1985* (ISBN 0-8420-2249-X)
1995 (ISBN 0-8420-2595-2)	*1984* (ISBN 0-8420-2234-1)
1994 (ISBN 0-8420-2560-X)	*1983* (ISBN 0-8420-2220-1)
1993 (ISBN 0-8420-2483-2)	*1982* (ISBN 0-8420-2214-7)
1992 (ISBN 0-8420-2463-8)	*1981* (ISBN 0-8420-2200-7)
1991 (ISBN 0-8420-2397-6)	*1980* (ISBN 0-8420-2181-7)
1990 (ISBN 0-8420-2368-2)	*1979* (ISBN 0-8420-2170-1)
1989 (ISBN 0-8420-2344-5)	*1978* (ISBN 0-8420-2159-0)
1988 (ISBN 0-8420-2330-5)	*1972–77* (ISBN 0-8420-2129-9, 2 vols.)
1987 (ISBN 0-8420-2292-9)	*1935–71* (ISBN 0-394-47270-5, 3 vols.)

International Polls

The International Gallup Polls: Public Opinion, 1979
ISBN 0-8420-2180-9 (1981)

The International Gallup Polls: Public Opinion, 1978
ISBN 0-8420-2162-0 (1980)

The Gallup International Public Opinion Polls:
France, 1939, 1944–1975
2 volumes ISBN 0-394-40998-1 (1976)

The Gallup International Public Opinion Polls:
Great Britain, 1937–1975
2 volumes ISBN 0-394-40992-2 (1976)

The
Gallup
Poll

Public Opinion 1998

George Gallup, Jr.

SR Scholarly Resources Inc.
Wilmington, Delaware

ACKNOWLEDGMENTS

The preparation of this volume has involved the dedication, skills, and efforts of many devoted individuals, to whom I am indebted. At The Gallup Organization, gratitude is owed to James Clifton, president and CEO; Alec Gallup, co-chairman; and The Gallup Poll staff, including Frank Newport, editor-in-chief; David Moore and Lydia Saad, managing editors; Judy Nelson, operations manager; and Leslie McAneny, editor of *The Gallup Poll Monthly*. At Scholarly Resources, I would like to thank Ann M. Aydelotte, who edited, proofread, and indexed this volume; Sharon L. Beck, desktop publisher; James L. Preston, production manager; and Carolyn J. Travers, managing editor. At Type Shoppe Inc. my appreciation goes to Lydia A. Wagner and Penelope Hollingsworth for their typesetting and design expertise. Finally, I wish to thank Professor Fred L. Israel of the City College of New York for his invaluable work as the principal coordinator of this publication.

G.G., Jr.

∞ The paper used in this publication meets the minimum requirements of the American National Standard for permanence of paper for printed library materials, Z39.48, 1984.

www.scholarly.com

Scholarly Resources Inc.
104 Greenhill Avenue
Wilmington, DE 19805-1897

Library of Congress Catalog Card Number: 79-56557
International Standard Serial Number: 0195-962X
International Standard Book Number: 0-8420-2698-3

CONTENTS

THE SAMPLE

Although most Gallup Poll findings are based on telephone interviews, a significant proportion is based on interviews conducted in person in the home. The majority of the findings reported in Gallup Poll surveys is based on samples consisting of a minimum of 1,000 interviews. The total number, however, may exceed 1,000, or even 1,500, interviews, where the survey specifications call for reporting the responses of low-incidence population groups such as young public-school parents or Hispanics.

Design of the Sample for Telephone Surveys

The findings from the telephone surveys are based on Gallup's standard national telephone samples, consisting of unclustered directory-assisted, random-digit telephone samples utilizing a proportionate, stratified sampling design. The random-digit aspect of the sample is used to avoid "listing" bias. Numerous studies have shown that households with unlisted telephone numbers are different from listed households. "Unlistedness" is due to household mobility or to customer requests to prevent publication of the telephone number. To avoid this source of bias, a random-digit procedure designed to provide representation of both listed and unlisted (including not-yet-listed) numbers is used.

Telephone numbers for the continental United States are stratified into four regions of the country and, within each region, further arranged into three size-of-community strata. The sample of telephone numbers produced by the described method is representative of all telephone households within the continental United States.

Only working banks of telephone numbers are selected. Eliminating nonworking banks from the sample increases the likelihood that any sampled telephone number will be associated with a residence.

Within each contacted household, an interview is sought with the youngest man 18 years of age or older who is at home. If no man is home, an interview is sought with the oldest woman at home. This

method of respondent selection within households produces an age distribution by sex that closely approximates the age distribution by sex of the total population.

Up to three calls are made to each selected telephone number to complete an interview. The time of day and the day of the week for callbacks are varied to maximize the chances of finding a respondent at home. All interviews are conducted on weekends or weekday evenings in order to contact potential respondents among the working population.

The final sample is weighted so that the distribution of the sample matches current estimates derived from the U.S. Census Bureau's Current Population Survey (CPS) for the adult population living in telephone households in the continental United States.

Design of the Sample for Personal Surveys

The design of the sample for personal (face-to-face) surveys is that of a replicated area probability sample down to the block level in the case of urban areas and to segments of townships in the case of rural areas.

After stratifying the nation geographically and by size of community according to information derived from the most recent census, over 350 different sampling locations are selected on a mathematically random basis from within cities, towns, and counties that, in turn, have been selected on a mathematically random basis.

The interviewers are given no leeway in selecting the areas in which they are to conduct their interviews. Each interviewer is given a map on which a specific starting point is marked and is instructed to contact households according to a predetermined travel pattern. At each occupied dwelling unit, the interviewer selects respondents by following a systematic procedure that is repeated until the assigned number of interviews has been completed.

Weighting Procedures

After the survey data have been collected and processed, each respondent is assigned a weight so that the demographic characteristics of the total weighted sample of respondents match the latest estimates of the demographic characteristics of the adult population available from the U.S. Census Bureau. Telephone surveys are weighted to match the characteristics of the adult population living in households with access to a telephone. The weighting of personal interview data includes a factor to improve the representation of the kind of people who are less likely to be found at home.

The procedures described above are designed to produce samples approximating the adult civilian population (18 and older) living in private households (that is, excluding those in prisons, hospitals, hotels, religious and educational institutions, and those living on reservations or military bases)—and in the case of telephone surveys, households with access to a telephone. Survey percentages may be applied to census estimates of the size of these populations to project percentages into numbers of people. The manner in which the sample is drawn also produces a sample that approximates the distribution of private households in the United States. Therefore, survey results also can be projected to numbers of households.

Sampling Tolerances

In interpreting survey results, it should be borne in mind that all sample surveys are subject to sampling error—that is, the extent to which the results may differ from what would be obtained if the whole population surveyed had been interviewed. The size of such sampling errors depends largely on the number of interviews.

The following tables may be used in estimating the sampling error of any percentage. The computed allowances have taken into account the effect of the sample design upon sampling error. They may be interpreted as indicating the range (plus or minus the figure shown) within which the results of repeated samplings in the same time period could be expected to vary, 95 percent of the time, assuming the same sampling procedure, the same interviewers, and the same questionnaire.

Table A shows how much allowance should be made for the sampling error of a percentage. Let us say a reported percentage is 33 for a group that includes 1000 respondents. First, we go to the row headed "Percentages near 30" and then go across to the column headed "1000." The number here is 4, which means that the 33 percent obtained in the sample is subject to a sampling error of plus or minus 4 points. Another way of saying it is that very probably (95 chances out of 100) the average of repeated samplings would be somewhere between 29 and 37, with the most likely figure being the 33 obtained.

In comparing survey results in two samples, such as for men and women, the question arises as to how large must a difference between them be before one can be reasonably sure that it reflects a real difference. In Tables B and C, the number of points that must be allowed for in such comparisons is indicated. Table B is for percentages near 20 or 80, and Table C is for percentages near 50. For percentages in between, the error to be allowed for is between those shown in the two tables.

TABLE A

Recommended Allowance for Sampling Error of a Percentage

	In Percentage Points (at 95 in 100 confidence level)* Sample Size					
	1,000	750	600	400	200	100
Percentages near 10	2	3	3	4	5	7
Percentages near 20	3	4	4	5	7	9
Percentages near 30	4	4	4	6	8	10
Percentages near 40	4	4	5	6	8	11
Percentages near 50	4	4	5	6	8	11
Percentages near 60	4	4	5	6	8	11
Percentages near 70	4	4	4	6	8	10
Percentages near 80	3	4	4	5	7	9
Percentages near 90	2	3	3	4	5	7

*The chances are 95 in 100 that the sampling error is not larger than the figures shown.

TABLE B

Recommended Allowance for Sampling Error of the Difference

	In Percentage Points (at 95 in 100 confidence level)* Percentages near 20 or percentages near 80			
	750	600	400	200
Size of sample				
750	5			
600	5	6		
400	6	6	7	
200	8	8	8	10

*The chances are 95 in 100 that the sampling error is not larger than the figures shown.

TABLE C

Recommended Allowance for Sampling Error of the Difference

	In Percentage Points (at 95 in 100 confidence level)* Percentages near 50			
	750	600	400	200
Size of sample				
750	6			
600	7	7		
400	7	8	8	
200	10	10	10	12

*The chances are 95 in 100 that the sampling error is not larger than the figures shown.

Here is an example of how the tables would be used: Let us say that 50 percent of men respond a certain way and 40 percent of women also respond that way, for a difference of 10 percentage points between them. Can we say with any assurance that the 10-point difference reflects a real difference between men and women on the question? The sample contains approximately 600 men and 600 women.

Since the percentages are near 50, we consult Table C, and since the two samples are about 600 persons each, we look for the number in the column headed "600" that is also in the row designated "600." We find the number 7 here. This means that the allowance for error should be 7 points, and that in concluding that the percentage among men is somewhere between 3 and 17 points higher than the percentage among women, we should be wrong only about 5 percent of the time. In other words, we can conclude with considerable confidence that a difference exists in the direction observed and that it amounts to at least 3 percentage points.

If, in another case, men's responses amount to 22 percent and women's 24 percent, we consult Table B because these percentages are near 20. We look for the number in the column headed "600" that is also in the row designated "600" and see that the number is 6. Obviously, then, the 2-point difference is inconclusive.

GALLUP POLL ACCURACY RECORD

Presidential Elections

	Candidates	Final Gallup Survey*	Election Result*	Gallup Deviation
1996	Clinton	52.0	50.1	+1.9
	Dole	41.0	41.4	−0.4
	Perot	7.0	8.5	−1.5
1992	Clinton	49.0	43.3	+5.7
	Bush	37.0	37.7	−0.7
	Perot	14.0	19.0	−5.0
1988	Bush	56.0	53.9	+2.1
	Dukakis	44.0	46.1	−2.1
1984	Reagan	59.0	59.2	−0.2
	Mondale	41.0	40.8	+0.2
1980	Reagan	47.0	50.8	−3.8
	Carter	44.0	41.0	+3.0
	Anderson	8.0	6.6	+1.4
	Other	1.0	1.6	−0.6
1976	Carter	48.0	50.1	−2.1
	Ford	49.0	48.1	+0.9
	McCarthy	2.0	0.9	+1.1
	Other	1.0	0.9	+0.1
1972	Nixon	62.0	61.8	+0.2
	McGovern	38.0	38.2	−0.2
1968	Nixon	43.0	43.5	−0.5
	Humphrey	42.0	42.9	−0.9
	Wallace	15.0	13.6	+1.4
1964	Johnson	64.0	61.3	+2.7
	Goldwater	36.0	38.7	−2.7

1960	Kennedy	51.0	50.1	+0.9
	Nixon	49.0	49.9	−0.9
1956	Eisenhower	59.5	57.8	+1.7
	Stevenson	40.5	42.2	−1.7
1952	Eisenhower	51.0	55.4	−4.4
	Stevenson	49.0	44.6	+4.4
1948	Truman	44.5	49.5	−5.0
	Dewey	49.5	45.1	+4.4
	Wallace	4.0	2.4	+1.6
	Other	2.0	3.0	−1.0
1944	Roosevelt	51.5	53.8	−2.3
	Dewey	48.5	46.2	+2.3
1940	Roosevelt	52.0	55.0	−3.0
	Willkie	48.0	45.0	+3.0
1936	Roosevelt	55.7	62.5	−6.8
	Landon	44.3	37.5	+6.8

*To allow direct comparisons with Gallup's reported estimates, the official election results are shown as the division of the major party (or three-party) vote in thirteen of the sixteen elections, and the vote for all parties including "others" in the 1948, 1976, and 1980 contests.

Trend in Deviation
(For Each Candidate)

Elections	Average Error
1936–1948	3.6%
1952–1964	2.4%
1968–1996	1.5%
1936–1996 (Overall)	2.2%

GALLUP POLL ACCURACY RECORD

Congressional Elections
(Midterm)

	Parties	*Final Gallup Survey*	*Election Result*	*Gallup Deviation*
1994	Republican	53.5	53.5	±0.0
	Democratic	46.5	46.5	±0.0
1990	Democratic	54.0	54.1	−0.1
	Republican	46.0	45.9	+0.1
1986*				
1982	Democratic	55.0	56.1	−1.1
	Republican	45.0	43.9	+1.1
1978	Democratic	55.0	54.6	+0.4
	Republican	45.0	45.4	−0.4
1974	Democratic	60.0	58.9	+1.1
	Republican	40.0	41.1	−1.1
1970	Democratic	53.0	54.3	−1.3
	Republican	47.0	45.7	+1.3
1966	Democratic	52.5	51.9	+0.6
	Republican	47.5	48.1	−0.6
1962	Democratic	55.5	52.7	+2.8
	Republican	44.5	47.3	−2.8
1958	Democratic	57.0	56.5	+0.5
	Republican	43.0	43.5	−0.5
1954	Democratic	51.5	52.7	−1.2
	Republican	48.5	47.3	+1.2

1950	Democratic	51.0	50.3	+0.7
	Republican	49.0	49.7	−0.7
1946	Republican	58.0	54.3	+3.7
	Democratic	42.0	45.7	−3.7
1942	Democratic	52.0	48.0	+4.0
	Republican	48.0	52.0	−4.0
1938	Democratic	54.0	50.8	+3.2
	Republican	46.0	49.2	−3.2

*No final congressional survey.

Trend in Deviation
(For Each Party)

Elections	Average Error
1938–1946	3.6%
1950–1970	1.2%
1974–1994	0.5%
1938–1994 (Overall)	1.5%

CHRONOLOGY

This chronology is provided to enable the reader to relate poll results to specific events, or series of events, that may have influenced public opinion.

1997

December 1   The United Nations Global Warming Conference opens in Kyoto, Japan.

December 2   Attorney General Janet Reno declines to appoint a special prosecutor to investigate campaign fund-raising telephone calls made by Vice President Al Gore and President Bill Clinton.

December 22   President Clinton tours Bosnia after announcing that U.S. troops will remain there after the withdrawal of the current NATO peacekeeping force.

1998

On December 19 the Republican-led House of Representatives voted largely along party lines to impeach President Clinton in the Monica Lewinsky sex-and-perjury scandal. Following an eight-month inquiry by Independent Counsel Kenneth Starr, the House approved two articles of impeachment accusing Clinton of lying under oath and of obstructing justice by attempting to cover up a sexual affair with Lewinsky, a former White House intern. Clinton thus became the second president impeached in the history of the United States. Despite the scandal, Clinton

continued to maintain high public support for his job performance. Gallup Polls throughout the year showed that Americans expressed "scandal fatigue" as they criticized Starr and Congress for pressing on with their inquiries.

In other news, U.S. financial markets soared for a fourth straight year despite a currency crisis in Southeast Asia and despite major economic declines in Russia, Brazil, and Argentina. The Dow Jones Industrial Average recorded a fourth consecutive rise in excess of 20%.

January 5   President Clinton states that he will propose a balanced budget for fiscal 1999, three years earlier than previously projected.

January 7   Former White House intern Monica Lewinsky denies any connection to Paula Jones's lawsuit (which accused President Clinton of sexual improprieties while he was governor of Arkansas), or any sexual relationship with Clinton. In mid-December 1997, Lewinsky and former White House employee Linda Tripp had received subpoenas from Jones's lawyers.

January 12   Linda Tripp turns over to Whitewater prosecutors some twenty hours of taped conversations with Monica Lewinsky in which the two women discussed Lewinsky's sexual relationship with the president as well as efforts to cover it up.

January 13   Linda Tripp, wearing a concealed microphone supplied by the FBI, meets with Monica Lewinsky.

             Iraq blocks a United Nations inspection team whose mission is to investigate Baghdad's capacity for producing weapons of mass destruction.

January 16   Independent Counsel Ken Starr's investigations broaden to include accusations that President

Clinton and his assistant, Vernon Jordan, advised Monica Lewinsky to lie under oath.

January 17   Lawyers for Paula Jones interrogate Clinton in her lawsuit against the president. He denies any sexual relationship with Monica Lewinsky.

January 21   The Clinton-Lewinsky affair first makes the news.

January 26   President Clinton, in a vehement denial, protests to the public in a televised statement that he "did not have sexual relations with that woman, Miss Lewinsky," and "never told anybody to lie."

January 27   President Clinton issues a warning to Iraqi leader Saddam Hussein.

January 28   The Justice Department indicts fourteen Democratic party fundraisers in a probe of 1996 campaign finance abuses. Throughout the year, Attorney General Janet Reno refuses to seek an Independent Counsel's probe of either Clinton's or Vice President Gore's fund-raising practices.

February 23   UN Secretary General Kofi Annan secures admittance to Saddam Hussein's palaces in Iraq for arms inspections.

March 5   William Ginsburg, Monica Lewinsky's lawyer, accuses Independent Counsel Ken Starr of making, and then retracting, an offer of immunity to Lewinsky in exchange for her full testimony. Starr denies any such offer.

March 27   The Federal Drug Administration approves Viagra, a prescription pill for reversing male impotence.

April 1   In Arkansas, Paula Jones's lawyers intend to appeal after a federal district judge throws out Jones's lawsuit against Clinton.

May 4	A federal district court ruling denies President Clinton the power to invoke either executive privilege or attorney-client privilege in order to keep prosecutors from questioning his advisers.
May 11	India conducts a series of underground nuclear tests, thus raising fears of a regional arms race in South Asia.
May 18	The Justice Department files an antitrust lawsuit against the Microsoft Corporation. The trial will begin on October 19.
May 22	In a setback to Clinton, a federal district judge rules that Secret Service agents can be made to testify before the grand jury investigating charges of whether the president had illegally tried to cover up an affair with Monica Lewinsky.
June 17	The U.S. Senate rejects a proposed $516 billion nationwide settlement of smoking-related lawsuits against the tobacco industry.
July 17	Chief Justice William Rehnquist turns down a last-minute plea by the Justice Department to block testimony by Secret Service agents before the grand jury investigating the Clinton-Lewinsky affair. President Clinton is subpoenaed by Independent Counsel Starr to testify before the grand jury, but the subpoena is later withdrawn in exchange for Clinton's voluntary testimony.
July 22	President Clinton signs a bill reforming the Internal Revenue Service in the wake of complaints by taxpayers of IRS abuses.
July 24	In Washington a gunman kills two police officers in a shootout at the U.S. Capitol.
July 26	United Auto Workers end their fifty-four day strike against General Motors.

July 28	Monica Lewinsky's lawyers arrange a deal with Independent Counsel Ken Starr in which she promises to testify fully in exchange for immunity from prosecution.
July 29	Upon Starr's withdrawal of the subpoena against Clinton, the president agrees to answer questions voluntarily at the White House.
July 31	Paula Jones's lawyers attempt to reinstate her sexual harassment suit against Clinton.
August 5	Iraq forbids any on-site weapons inspections but permits some UN monitoring to continue.
August 6	Monica Lewinsky appears before the grand jury.
	The House approves a campaign reform bill, but the Senate blocks its passage.
August 7	Two deadly bombs explode at U.S. embassies in Tanzania and Kenya.
August 17	President Clinton testifies before the grand jury. He admits to a television audience in the evening that he had an inappropriate relationship with Monica Lewinsky.
September 8	Mark McGwire of the St. Louis Cardinals hits his sixty-second home run of 1998 and breaks the single-season record held by Roger Maris since 1961. McGwire will finish the season with seventy home runs.
September 9	Independent Counsel Ken Starr advises House leaders that he has information that may serve as grounds for the impeachment of Clinton.
	The United Nations states that it will not lift trade sanctions against Iraq unless that country admits on-site UN inspectors.

September 14	In defiance of the UN threat, Iraq vows that it will not cooperate with international arms inspectors.
October 5	By a vote of 21 to 16 along party lines, the House Judiciary Committee launches the impeachment process against President Clinton by proposing that Congress begin a formal investigation.
October 8	The full House of Representatives, by a partisan count of 258 to 156, votes in favor of pursuing an impeachment inquiry.
October 23	Israeli and Palestinian delegates sign the Wye Memorandum at a summit meeting in Maryland hosted by President Clinton.
October 26–31	Hurricane Mitch, the deadliest Atlantic hurricane of the twentieth century, devastates Central America.
October 29–November 7	The U.S. space shuttle *Discovery* carries out a scientific mission that includes in its crew Senator John Glenn. In 1962, then astronaut Glenn was the first American to orbit the Earth.
October 31	The United States and Great Britain threaten air strikes against Iraq as it refuses to deal further with UN arms inspectors.
November 3	Democrats gain five seats in the House in midterm elections for Congress. In exit polls, almost two-thirds of the voters reply that they do not want to see President Clinton impeached.
November 5	In a letter to the White House, the chairman of the House Judiciary Committee, Rep. Henry Hyde, asks Clinton to respond to eighty-one points taken from Independent Counsel Starr's report.
November 6	House Speaker Newt Gingrich resigns because of Republican party candidates' losses in the midterm elections for Congress. On December 19,

Gingrich's successor, Robert Livingston, also will resign after admitting to having had extramarital affairs.

November 9, 19–
December 1

The House Judiciary Committee holds hearings on the possible impeachment of President Clinton. Independent Counsel Starr testifies.

November 13

Paula Jones agrees to the sum of $800,000 in an out-of-court settlement of her lawsuit against President Clinton.

November 14

Iraq allows UN weapons inspections to resume, thus averting the launch of missile attacks against that country by the United States and Great Britain.

November 21

In less than a week after UN personnel return to their assignment, Iraq objects to a routine inspection.

November 23

Iraq objects again to UN inspections.

December 8–10

White House lawyers present President Clinton's side of the Lewinsky controversy to the House Judiciary Committee.

December 11–12

Following strict party lines, the House Judiciary Committee approves four articles of impeachment and opposes the Democrats' resolution to censure the president.

December 15

The chief UN weapons inspector reports that Iraq is not in compliance with its agreement to allow inspections.

December 16

President Clinton authorizes an air strike jointly with Great Britain against Iraq, and bombing commences.

December 19

The House of Representatives impeaches President Clinton on two articles: the charge of perjury

in his testimony to the grand jury on August 17, and the charge of obstruction of justice. Two more articles—charges of perjury in the Paula Jones deposition and abuse of power—fail to pass.

December 30   A special House committee finds that two U.S. companies have transferred sensitive satellite technology information to China.

GALLUP REGIONS

EAST

New England
Maine
New Hampshire
Vermont
Massachusetts
Rhode Island
Connecticut

Mid-Atlantic
New York
New Jersey
Pennsylvania
Maryland
Delaware
West Virginia
District of Columbia

MIDWEST

East Central
Ohio
Michigan
Indiana
Illinois

West Central
Wisconsin
Minnesota
Iowa
Missouri
North Dakota
South Dakota
Nebraska
Kansas

SOUTH

Southeast
Virginia
North Carolina
South Carolina
Georgia
Florida
Kentucky
Tennessee
Alabama
Mississippi

Southwest
Arkansas
Louisiana
Oklahoma
Texas

WEST

Mountain
Montana
Arizona
Colorado
Idaho
Wyoming
Utah
Nevada
New Mexico

Pacific
California
Oregon
Washington
Hawaii
Alaska

JANUARY 1
MOST ADMIRED MAN

Interviewing Dates: 12/18–21/97
CNN/*USA Today*/Gallup Poll
Survey #GO 120690

What man whom you have heard or read about, living today in any part of the world, do you admire most? And who is your second choice?

The following are listed in order of frequency of mention, with first and second choices combined.

Bill Clinton
Billy Graham
Pope John Paul II
Colin Powell
Jimmy Carter
Nelson Mandela
Ronald Reagan
George Bush
Michael Jordan
Bill Gates

By way of comparison, the following are the results of the 1996 audit.

Bill Clinton
Pope John Paul II
Colin Powell ⎫
Billy Graham ⎬ tie
Bob Dole ⎫
Ronald Reagan ⎬ tie
Jimmy Carter
Nelson Mandela ⎫
George Bush ⎬ tie
Michael Jordan
Norman Schwarzkopf ⎭

Note: President Bill Clinton tops the rankings in the Gallup Poll's annual Most Admired Man survey, mentioned by 14% of Americans as the man "living today in any part of the world" whom they hold in the greatest esteem. An array of religious, political, and entertainment names accounts for most of the other top mentions, with one sports figure, Michael Jordan, and one business leader, Bill Gates, placing among the top ten. No one other than Clinton, however, is named by more than 6%, a rarity in the half century of Gallup's Most Admired Man poll.

Despite the apparent shortage of dominant living heroes in American culture, two-thirds of respondents are able to name a man whom they look up to. About 10% cite someone they know (a friend or relative) as the man whom they admire most, while about one-half names a more public figure.

Ranking second to Clinton is the Reverend Billy Graham with 6%, his thirty-fourth consecutive appearance on the top ten list. Pope John Paul II is a close third, followed by Colin Powell and Jimmy Carter. Ranking from sixth through tenth are South Africa's Nelson Mandela, Ronald Reagan, George Bush, Jordan, and Gates, each named by 2% to 3%.

The Gallup Poll has tracked America's choice since 1946 and finds that in almost every year, the sitting President of the United States emerges as the Most Admired Man. The few exceptions are: the post-World War II period, when Generals Dwight Eisenhower and Douglas MacArthur surpassed President Harry Truman on the list; the height of the controversy over the Vietnam War from 1967–68, when several political figures led President Lyndon Johnson; the Watergate period from 1973–74, when Graham, Henry Kissinger, and others outpaced President Richard Nixon; and in 1980, when Pope John Paul II led politically struggling President Carter.

JANUARY 1
MOST ADMIRED WOMAN

Interviewing Dates: 12/18–21/97
CNN/*USA Today*/Gallup Poll
Survey #GO 120690

What woman whom you have heard or read about, living today in any part of the world,

do you admire most? And who is your second choice?

The following are listed in order of frequency of mention, with first and second choices combined.

Hillary Rodham Clinton
Oprah Winfrey
Barbara Bush ⎫
Margaret Thatcher ⎭ tie
Madeleine Albright
Elizabeth Dole
Maya Angelou
Janet Reno
Queen Elizabeth
Nancy Reagan

By way of comparison, the following are the results of the 1996 audit.

Mother Teresa
Hillary Rodham Clinton
Barbara Bush
Oprah Winfrey ⎫
Elizabeth Dole ⎭ tie
Margaret Thatcher
Princess Diana
Madeleine Albright ⎫
Nancy Reagan ⎭ tie
Barbra Streisand ⎫
Queen Elizabeth ⎭ tie

Note: With the death of Mother Teresa of Calcutta, Gallup's list of Most Admired Women has lost a major force. The widely revered nun of the Sisters of Charity had ranked first the previous two years, and in 1996 was mentioned by nearly one-fourth of Americans, well ahead of Hillary Rodham Clinton's 1997 first-place figure.

Oprah Winfrey now ranks second, and Barbara Bush and Margaret Thatcher tie for third, each mentioned by 5%. Rounding out the top ten are Madeleine Albright, Elizabeth Dole, Maya Angelou, Janet Reno, Queen Elizabeth, and Nancy Reagan, each mentioned by 1% to 2%.

The choice of Most Admired Woman usually has been more varied. For many years, former First Ladies held the top spot over sitting First Ladies, but in 1968 presidential candidate Robert Kennedy's wife, Ethel, won over Lady Bird Johnson.

World leaders Indira Gandhi, Golda Meir, and Margaret Thatcher have all ranked first many times.

It is a tribute to her impact that despite her death this summer, Mother Teresa receives 9% of mentions, although these are not counted in the ranking of the Most Admired Woman "living today." She has been a top contender from her earliest appearance on the list in 1979 and ranked first three times—in 1986, 1995, and 1996. Diana, Princess of Wales, is also named by 9%, representing about double the figure she received the previous year.

JANUARY 10
FEDERAL BUDGET/
GOVERNMENT SPENDING

Interviewing Dates: 1/6–7/98
CNN/*USA Today*/Gallup Poll
Survey #GO 120910

As you know, the deficit has been cut by over $260 billion since 1992, and some economists say it may be balanced as early as this year. Please tell me whether you think each of the following deserves, or does not deserve, substantial credit for this reduction in the deficit:

President Clinton?

Yes, deserves	63%
Does not deserve	32
No opinion	5

	Yes, deserves	Does not deserve	No opinion
By Politics			
Republicans	41%	56%	3%
Democrats	84	14	2
Independents	65	26	9
By Political Ideology			
Conservative	52	45	3
Moderate	69	26	5
Liberal	77	18	5

The Republicans in Congress?

Yes, deserve	54%
Do not deserve	36
No opinion	10

	Yes, deserve	Do not deserve	No opinion
By Politics			
Republicans	80%	15%	5%
Democrats	35	57	8
Independents	49	35	16
By Political Ideology			
Conservative	64	29	7
Moderate	51	39	10
Liberal	46	45	9

Good economic conditions?

Yes, deserve	77%
Do not deserve	15
No opinion	8

	Yes, deserve	Do not deserve	No opinion
By Politics			
Republicans	82%	12%	6%
Democrats	78	15	7
Independents	71	17	12
By Political Ideology			
Conservative	75	15	10
Moderate	83	11	6
Liberal	76	21	3

Tax increases enacted in 1990 and 1993?

Yes, deserve	48%
Do not deserve	39
No opinion	13

	Yes, deserve	Do not deserve	No opinion
By Politics			
Republicans	45%	44%	11%
Democrats	59	31	10
Independents	42	40	18
By Political Ideology			
Conservative	47	43	10
Moderate	49	37	14
Liberal	55	36	9

Spending controls enacted in the last few years?

Yes, deserve	65%
Do not deserve	23
No opinion	12

	Yes, deserve	Do not deserve	No opinion
By Politics			
Republicans	63%	25%	12%
Democrats	72	19	9
Independents	61	24	15
By Political Ideology			
Conservative	66	24	10
Moderate	70	20	10
Liberal	61	27	12

As you may know, President Clinton just announced that his proposed budget for 1999 will be balanced—that is, the amount of money the government spends in 1999 will equal the amount it takes in. Do you personally think the federal budget will be balanced in 1999, or will political or economic factors prevent the budget from being balanced?

Will be balanced	23%
Factors will prevent it	69
No opinion	8

	Will be balanced	Factors will prevent it	No opinion
By Politics			
Republicans	19%	77%	4%
Democrats	30	61	9
Independents	20	70	10
By Political Ideology			
Conservative	22	71	7
Moderate	22	73	5
Liberal	25	67	8

If the budget is balanced in 1999, do you think that it will stay balanced for the next several years, or not?

Yes	26%
No	63
No opinion	11

	Yes	No	No opinion
By Politics			
Republicans	27%	66%	7%
Democrats...................	33	56	11
Independents...............	21	65	14
By Political Ideology			
Conservative...............	28	63	9
Moderate.....................	25	65	10
Liberal	26	62	12

As you may know, some economists say that by 1999 the amount of money the federal government collects will be larger than the amount it spends for the first time in many years, meaning that the government will run a surplus. Assuming this happens, how do you think most of the surplus money should be used—to cut federal income taxes for most Americans; to increase spending on government programs such as Social Security, Medicare, public schools, the environment, and national defense; or to pay down the debt the government owes from previous years when the federal budget was not balanced?

Cut federal income taxes	22%
Increase spending on government programs....	43
Pay down debt	30
None; other (volunteered)	1
All (volunteered)	2
No opinion..	2

	Cut taxes	Increase spending	Pay down debt	None; other; no opinion
By Politics				
Republicans.....	30%	33%	34%	3%
Democrats	16	60	22	2
Independents ...	21	39	32	8
By Political Ideology				
Conservative ...	24	38	35	3
Moderate	23	45	30	2
Liberal.............	17	56	20	7

Note: Despite recent reports that in the next fiscal year the federal budget deficit could reach zero for the first time since 1969, the public is skeptical. According to the most recent Gallup Poll, seven in ten do not expect a balanced budget next year. And even if there is one, about six in ten doubt that it will stay balanced in the ensuing years. They give credit mostly to good economic conditions for the reduction in the deficit, although majorities also credit President Bill Clinton and, separately, the Republicans in Congress. When considering the possible uses of a budget surplus, should that occur, respondents are in no rush to cut personal income taxes. Instead, they would prefer that some top-priority programs receive added funding or that the national debt be reduced.

Sixty-nine percent think that despite Clinton's recent announcement that he would submit a balanced budget for 1999, some political or economic factors will prevent it from actually being balanced. If it is balanced, 63% believe that it will not stay that way for the next several years.

Most people (77%) give credit for the reduction in the deficit over the past few years to good economic conditions, but 63% also give Clinton credit, and 54% the Republicans in Congress. Not surprisingly, these views are directly related to partisan orientation, with 84% of Democrats but just 41% of Republicans giving credit to Clinton, and 80% of Republicans but just 35% of Democrats giving credit to the Republicans. When asked to choose who deserves more of the credit, respondents are about evenly divided, with 42% citing Clinton and 39% the Republicans in Congress.

If there should be a budget surplus, as has been suggested by some economists, 43% say that it should be used to increase spending on government programs such as Social Security and Medicare, public schools, the environment, and national defense. Another 30% say that it should be used to pay down the debt incurred by the government in previous years, when the federal budget was not balanced. Only 22% want to cut federal income taxes.

When asked to evaluate several different ways that a potential surplus could be used, respondents give the highest priorities to strengthening Social Security and Medicare, reducing the national debt, and improving public schools. Lower on the priority list are cutting federal income taxes and providing tax credits to parents for child care, while at the bottom are providing tax credits to reduce pollution and increasing spending on highway construction.

JANUARY 17
TERRY NICHOLS

Interviewing Dates: 1/6–7/98
CNN/*USA Today*/Gallup Poll
Survey #GO 120910

We have some questions about Terry Nichols, the man found guilty of helping Timothy McVeigh construct the bomb used to destroy the federal office building in Oklahoma City in 1995. As you may know, Terry Nichols was indicted for first-degree murder in the bombing, among other charges. The jury only found Nichols guilty of manslaughter, not first-degree murder, but did find him guilty of conspiracy to use a weapon of mass destruction.

Overall, do you agree or disagree with the jury's verdict in this trial?

Agree	42%
Disagree	48
No opinion	10

Do you think Terry Nichols should be sentenced to death for his role in the Oklahoma City bombing, should he be sentenced to life in prison, or should he receive a lesser sentence?

Death	45%
Life in prison	42
Lesser sentence	4
Other (volunteered)	*
No opinion	9

*Less than 1%

Regardless of how you feel about his sentence, do you think Terry Nichols was as responsible as or less responsible than Timothy McVeigh for the Oklahoma City bombing?

As responsible as McVeigh	62%
Less responsible than McVeigh	27
More responsible than McVeigh (volunteered)	2
No opinion	9

Note: As the trial judge considers the sentence he will impose on Terry Nichols for his part in the 1995 bombing of the federal building in Oklahoma City, Americans are mulling over their own ideas about the case. Before the jury announced its verdict, convicting Nichols not of first-degree murder but of conspiracy and manslaughter, respondents were convinced by a 2-to-1 majority that Nichols was guilty of the more serious charge of first-degree murder. After the verdict announcement, they now express more evenly divided views about his guilt, but they are also split over whether he should be sentenced to death or given a life sentence. Still, most believe that Nichols is as responsible for the bombing as Timothy McVeigh, the only other person charged with the crime, who was convicted of first-degree murder and sentenced to death.

According to a Gallup Poll taken in December, before the jury decision in the Nichols case, 56% believed that he was guilty of first-degree murder, while 26% thought that he was guilty of a lesser charge such as manslaughter, and another 3% thought that he was not guilty at all. After the jury announced its verdict of manslaughter, respondents expressed more divided views about the verdict in a new Gallup Poll: 42% agree with it, 48% disagree. Still, almost two-thirds say that Nichols was either as responsible as McVeigh for the Oklahoma City bombing (62%) or even more responsible (2%). Just 27% say that Nichols was less responsible.

After McVeigh was found guilty of first-degree murder last June, respondents favored giving him the death penalty by a 2-to-1 majority (61% to 31%). But after Nichols was found guilty of the lesser charge (before the jury announced that it would not recommend the death penalty), they are not so eager to invoke the death penalty: 45% think that Nichols should be sentenced to die, while 42% think that he should receive a life sentence, and another 4% want a more lenient sentence.

JANUARY 23
WHITE HOUSE INTERN CONTROVERSY

Interviewing Date: 1/21/98*
CNN/*USA Today*/ Gallup Poll
Survey #GO 121151

As you may know, there are new allegations being reported in the news today that President

*Polls conducted entirely in one evening are subject to additional error or bias not found in polls conducted over several days.

Clinton may have had an extramarital affair with an employee who worked at the White House. Clinton has denied these allegations. Have you heard the news about these allegations before now, or not?

Yes 82%
No 17
No opinion 1

Next, I'm going to describe some of the allegations being made in this matter. As I read each one, please say whether you think it is definitely true, probably true, probably not true, or definitely not true:

The allegation that Bill Clinton had an extramarital affair with an employee who worked at the White House?

Definitely true 7%
Probably true 47
Probably not true 27
Definitely not true 10
No opinion 9

	Definitely true	Probably true	Probably not true	Definitely not true*
By Sex				
Male	9%	46%	27%	10%
Female.............	5	48	27	11
By Age				
18–29 Years	6	59	28	4
30–49 Years	6	52	25	6
50 Years and Over......	8	37	29	17
By Politics				
Republicans.....	14	58	15	4
Democrats	3	35	36	16
Independents ...	5	50	28	9
By Approval of Clinton				
Approve	1	37	38	15
Disapprove......	16	67	9	2
By Awareness of Story				
Heard..............	7	48	26	10
Not Heard........	3	46	32	12

*"No opinion"—at 11% or less— is omitted.

The allegation that Bill Clinton lied under oath about having an affair with this woman?

Definitely true 8%
Probably true 41
Probably not true 28
Definitely not true 15
No opinion 8

	Definitely true	Probably true	Probably not true	Definitely not true*
By Sex				
Male	11%	40%	26%	15%
Female.............	6	42	29	14
By Age				
18–29 Years	7	48	30	11
30–49 Years	8	46	24	11
50 Years and Over......	10	33	29	21
By Politics				
Republicans.....	16	52	15	8
Democrats	4	30	37	23
Independents ...	7	44	28	12
By Approval of Clinton				
Approve	3	29	38	22
Disapprove......	20	62	10	1
By Awareness of Story				
Heard..............	9	43	26	15
Not Heard........	5	34	38	14

*"No opinion"—at 11% or less—is omitted.

The allegation that Bill Clinton participated in an effort to obstruct justice by getting this woman to lie under oath about the affair?

Definitely true 6%
Probably true 33
Probably not true 33
Definitely not true 18
No opinion 10

	Definitely true	Probably true	Probably not true	Definitely not true*
By Sex				
Male	7%	35%	33%	15%
Female	6	31	33	20
By Age				
18–29 Years	7	29	39	18
30–49 Years	4	38	30	15
50 Years and Over	8	29	33	21
By Politics				
Republicans	13	48	18	9
Democrats	1	20	44	29
Independents	6	33	34	14
By Approval of Clinton				
Approve	**	18	44	27
Disapprove	17	58	16	2
By Awareness of Story				
Heard	6	34	33	17
Not Heard	4	29	34	22

*"No opinion"— at 13% or less— is omitted.
**Less than 1%

If you were convinced that Bill Clinton lied under oath or participated in attempts to get the woman to lie under oath, would you favor or oppose an effort to impeach Clinton and remove him from office?

Favor effort 46%
Oppose effort 46
No opinion 8

	Favor effort	Oppose effort	No opinion
By Sex			
Male	47%	48%	5%
Female	46	44	10
By Age			
18–29 Years	45	50	5
30–49 Years	51	40	9
50 Years and Over	42	50	8

By Politics			
Republicans	67	28	5
Democrats	32	60	8
Independents	45	47	8
By Approval of Clinton			
Approve	29	64	7
Disapprove	78	17	5
By Awareness of Story			
Heard	49	44	7
Not Heard	36	58	6

If each of the following turned out to be true, would you consider that relevant or not relevant to Bill Clinton's character and ability to serve as president:

Bill Clinton had an extramarital affair with an employee who worked at the White House?

Relevant 45%
Not relevant 52
No opinion 3

	Relevant	Not relevant	No opinion
By Sex			
Male	48%	49%	3%
Female	42	55	3
By Age			
18–29 Years	43	57	*
30–49 Years	46	52	2
50 Years and Over	45	49	6
By Politics			
Republicans	67	31	2
Democrats	26	70	4
Independents	46	52	2
By Approval of Clinton			
Approve	26	71	3
Disapprove	80	20	*
By Awareness of Story			
Heard	47	51	2
Not Heard	37	61	2

*Less than 1%

Bill Clinton lied under oath about having an extramarital affair with this woman?

Relevant 67%
Not relevant 28
No opinion 5

	Relevant	Not relevant	No opinion
By Sex			
Male	64%	31%	5%
Female	69	26	5
By Age			
18–29 Years	71	28	1
30–49 Years	73	23	4
50 Years and Over	57	36	7
By Politics			
Republicans	86	12	2
Democrats	53	43	4
Independents	66	26	8
By Approval of Clinton			
Approve	56	40	4
Disapprove	88	8	4
By Awareness of Story			
Heard	69	27	4
Not Heard	60	37	3

Bill Clinton participated in an effort to obstruct justice by getting this woman to lie under oath about the affair?

Relevant 72%
Not relevant 24
No opinion 4

	Relevant	Not relevant	No opinion
By Sex			
Male	69%	27%	4%
Female	75	21	4
By Age			
18–29 Years	76	23	1
30–49 Years	80	16	4
50 Years and Over	63	32	5

	Relevant	Not relevant	No opinion
By Politics			
Republicans	88	9	3
Democrats	57	40	3
Independents	74	20	6
By Approval of Clinton			
Approve	61	35	4
Disapprove	92	6	2
By Awareness of Story			
Heard	75	22	3
Not Heard	62	33	5

Bill Clinton had an extramarital affair with someone before he became president?

Relevant 24%
Not relevant 72
No opinion 4

	Relevant	Not relevant	No opinion
By Sex			
Male	27%	69%	4%
Female	22	75	3
By Age			
18–29 Years	76	23	1
30–49 Years	80	16	4
50 Years and Over	63	32	5
By Politics			
Republicans	88	9	3
Democrats	57	40	3
Independents	74	20	6
By Approval of Clinton			
Approve	61	35	4
Disapprove	92	6	2
By Awareness of Story			
Heard	75	22	3
Not Heard	62	33	5

Finally, we'd like to know how bothered you would be if the following aspects of this matter were shown to be true. For each aspect please say whether, if true, it would bother

you a great deal, somewhat, not much, or not at all:

The fact that the woman with whom Bill Clinton had the alleged affair was 21 years old?

Great deal 23%
Somewhat 19
Not much 20
Not at all 36
No opinion 2

	Great deal	Some- what	Not much	Not at all*
By Sex				
Male	21%	21%	21%	35%
Female.............	24	18	19	38
By Age				
18–29 Years	17	19	22	42
30–49 Years	23	20	18	37
50 Years and Over......	27	18	21	32
By Politics				
Republicans.....	26	28	18	26
Democrats	23	13	18	45
Independents ...	21	18	24	36
By Approval of Clinton				
Approve	17	16	18	48
Disapprove......	33	26	23	18
By Awareness of Story				
Heard..............	24	19	21	35
Not Heard........	20	19	18	42

*"No opinion"—at 2% or less—is omitted.

The fact that the woman with whom Bill Clinton had the alleged affair was an employee in the White House?

Great deal 27%
Somewhat 31
Not much 16
Not at all 24
No opinion 2

	Great deal	Some- what	Not much	Not at all*
By Sex				
Male	23%	34%	17%	24%
Female.............	30	29	15	23
By Age				
18–29 Years	21	30	19	30
30–49 Years	25	38	13	22
50 Years and Over......	32	25	18	21
By Politics				
Republicans.....	36	32	17	13
Democrats	27	31	15	25
Independents ...	18	31	16	31
By Approval of Clinton				
Approve	19	28	18	33
Disapprove......	41	37	12	9
By Awareness of Story				
Heard..............	26	32	17	23
Not Heard........	29	29	13	27

*"No opinion"—at 4% or less—is omitted.

The fact that the tapes on which the woman discussed the details of her alleged affair with Clinton were made without her knowing about it, using a hidden microphone?

Great deal 39%
Somewhat 25
Not much 14
Not at all 20
No opinion 2

	Great deal	Some- what	Not much	Not at all*
By Sex				
Male	38%	24%	17%	19%
Female.............	41	25	12	20
By Age				
18–29 Years	37	21	18	23
30–49 Years	42	29	11	16
50 Years and Over......	39	21	16	22

By Politics

Republicans..... 34	26	19	19
Democrats....... 41	23	15	20
Independents... 43	25	10	20

By Approval of Clinton

Approve 43	21	13	22
Disapprove...... 34	30	18	17

By Awareness of Story

Heard.............. 40	26	15	18
Not Heard........ 39	20	10	30

*"No opinion"—at 2% or less—is omitted.

Note: Revelations that Bill Clinton may have had a sexual affair with a 21-year-old White House intern has had no immediate impact on fundamental ratings of him personally or as president. According to a Gallup Poll taken Thursday night [January 22], about one-half of the public tends to believe that the allegations concerning the affair are true, but only a small handful is convinced. Perhaps as a result, Clinton's job approval rating remains high at 62%, as does his favorability rating, also at 62%.

The poll finds that four in five Americans had heard about the alleged affair as of Wednesday evening. At the same time, only a few are convinced that the allegations—Clinton had an affair, lied about it under oath, and participated in obstructing justice by asking that the woman lie under oath—are true. The number who think that each allegation is definitely true ranges from 7% concerning the affair, to 8% concerning his perjury over the affair, and 6% concerning obstruction of justice. However, when factoring in those who believe that each charge is probably true, 54% tend to believe that the affair occurred, 49% believe that Clinton lied about it, while just 39% think that he participated in getting the woman to lie.

The public is also not convinced, at this stage, that the legal implications of the alleged affair constitute an impeachable offense. Asked whether they would favor or oppose efforts to remove Clinton from office if they were sure he either lied under oath or participated in attempts to get the woman to lie under oath, respondents are divided (at 46% in favor and 46% opposed) largely along partisan lines. Two-thirds of Republicans (67%)

compared to 45% of independents and only 32% of Democrats would favor impeachment of Clinton on these matters.

When asked about the relevance of extramarital affairs when evaluating Clinton, respondents are much more likely to dismiss actions that occurred before he became president than those that may have taken place while in office. Still, the poll finds that fewer than one-half regards extramarital affairs in either case as a relevant issue in judging Clinton's character or ability to serve as president. Forty-five percent say that his having an affair with a White House employee would be relevant, while 52% say that it would not. Far fewer (24%) think that affairs he may have had before becoming president would be relevant, but 72% say that they would not be.

In terms of the other allegations, however, Clinton may find greater public scrutiny: 67% and 72%, respectively, believe that lying about such affairs or obstructing justice in covering them up is relevant to judging Clinton in office. However, the new Gallup survey finds that people are not bothered a great deal by the fact that the woman was an employee in the White House and only 21 years old at the time. Roughly one in four respondents is bothered a great deal by either of these factors. Slightly more (39%) are greatly bothered that the audiotapes on which the woman discussed details of her alleged affair were made without her knowing about them.

JANUARY 23
THE SUPER BOWL

Interviewing Dates: 1/16–18/98
CNN/*USA Today*/Gallup Poll
Survey #GO 121034

Are you a fan of professional football, or not?

Yes, a fan... 45%
Somewhat of a fan (volunteered) 11
No 43
No opinion... 1

Can you happen to tell me the names of the two teams who will be playing in the Super Bowl this year?

Green Bay Packers and Denver Broncos 52%
Packers only 10
Broncos only.. 5
Named neither 33

Which team would you like to see win this year's Super Bowl game?

	Total	Fans only
Denver Broncos	37%	47%
Green Bay Packers........................	35	45
No preference; no opinion	28	8

Regardless of whom you favor, which team do you think will win?

	Total	Fans only
Denver Broncos	18%	18%
Green Bay Packers........................	61	77
No preference; no opinion	21	5

Which do you personally find more entertaining—the Super Bowl game itself, or the advertising commercials that run during the Super Bowl?

	Total	Fans only
Game itself.....................................	46%	68%
Commercials..................................	37	30
Don't watch game (volunteered).............................	15	1
No opinion	2	1

Note: Americans are almost evenly divided over which team they want to win the Super Bowl on Sunday [January 25]. The Denver Broncos enjoy a slight edge over the Green Bay Packers for the sentimental favorite, with 37% preferring the Broncos and 35% the Packers, while 28% express no preference. Among the one-half of the public who identify as football fans, there is also a virtual tie, with 47% choosing the Broncos and 45% the Packers, while 8% are undecided.

Regardless of which team they want to win, most people (61%) predict that the Packers will repeat as NFL champions, while just 18% predict a Bronco victory. Among fans, the prediction is even

more lopsided, with three in four expecting a Packers win. And by a 2-to-1 margin, even Broncos fans concede that defeat is likely for their team.

While the country overall has no clear favorite, its four regions have taken sides. Not surprisingly, the regions in which the respective teams are located show the greatest support for their own teams, with the Midwest favoring the Packers by 56% to 38%, and the West favoring the Broncos by about the same margin (56% to 40%). The South weighs in with majority support for the Western team at 51% for the Broncos to 39% for the Packers, while the East tilts toward the Midwestern team by 47% to 41%.

Almost six in ten men say that they are football fans, compared with about one in three women. Among those who identify as fans, there is a gender gap on the choice of a sentimental favorite that rivals the political gender gap in the 1996 presidential election. In this case, male fans prefer a Broncos victory by 50% to 42%, while female fans prefer a Packers victory by exactly the same margin—a net gap of 16 percentage points.

Despite extensive publicity surrounding the Super Bowl, at least one-third of respondents are so uninterested that they cannot name either team that will be playing. About one-half can name both teams, with an additional 10% able to cite only the Packers and 5% only the Broncos. Furthermore, for many people, what interest they have in the Super Bowl is stimulated more by the ads that run during the televised event than by the game itself. Over one-third (37%) find the ads more entertaining, compared with 46% who say the game. Indeed, the commercials have become such an attraction that even among self-declared football fans, 30% find the commercials more entertaining than the game.

JANUARY 31
PRESIDENT CLINTON

Interviewing Dates: 1/23–26; 1/28/98*
CNN/*USA Today*/Gallup Poll
Surveys #GO 121132; 121206

*Polls conducted entirely in one evening are subject to additional error or bias not found in polls conducted over several days.

Do you approve or disapprove of the way Bill Clinton is handling his job as president?

	Jan. 28, 1998	Jan. 23–24, 1998
Approve	67%	58%
Disapprove	28	36
No opinion	5	6

January 23–24, 1998

	Approve	Dis-approve	No opinion
By Sex			
Male	59%	35%	6%
Female	57	36	7
By Ethnic Background			
White	54	40	6
Nonwhite	78	16	6
Black	84	11	5
By Education			
Postgraduate	69	28	3
College Graduate	60	36	4
College Incomplete	46	47	7
No College	63	30	7
By Region			
East	66	29	5
Midwest	55	40	5
South	56	38	6
West	57	34	9
By Age			
18–29 Years	58	35	7
30–49 Years	60	33	7
50–64 Years	58	38	4
65 Years and Over	55	38	7
By Household Income			
$75,000 and Over	55	38	7
$50,000 and Over	58	36	6
$30,000–$49,999	56	42	2
$20,000–$29,999	60	34	6
Under $20,000	60	30	10
By Politics			
Republicans	30	66	4
Democrats	86	10	4
Independents	55	35	10
By Political Ideology			
Conservative	43	52	5
Moderate	65	29	6
Liberal	80	13	7
By Economic Conditions Today			
Very Good	72	23	5
Somewhat Good	60	34	6
Somewhat Poor	36	55	9
Very Poor	30	64	6

National Trend

	Approve	Dis-approve	No opinion
1998			
January 25–26	59%	37%	4%
January 24–25	60	35	5
January 23–24	58	36	6
January 16–18	60	30	10
January 6–7	59	32	9
1997			
December 18–21	56	36	8
November 21–23	61	30	9
November 6–9	59	31	10
October 27–29	59	32	9
October 3–5	55	36	9
September 25–28	58	33	9
September 6–7	61	28	11
August 22–25	60	34	6
August 12–13	61	32	7
July 25–27	58	34	8
June 26–29	55	36	9
May 30–June 1	57	35	8
May 6–7	57	35	8
April 18–20	54	37	9
March 24–26	59	35	6
February 24–26	57	33	10
January 30–February 2	60	31	9
January 10–13	62	31	7
January 3–5	58	35	7
1996			
December 9–11	58	34	8
November 21–24	58	35	7
October 26–29	54	36	10
October 2–3	57	36	7
October 1–2	58	34	8
September 7–9	60	31	9

Date			
August 30–			
September 1	60	33	7
August 23–25	53	39	8
August 16–18	52	39	9
August 5–7	57	36	7
July 25–28	58	35	7
July 18–21	57	35	8
June 27–30	52	42	6
June 18–19	58	37	5
May 28–29	53	38	9
May 9–12	55	39	6
April 25–28	56	37	7
April 9–10	54	40	6
March 15–17	52	39	9
March 8–10	54	37	9
February 23–25	53	40	7
January 26–29	52	42	6
January 12–15	46	47	7
January 5–7	42	49	9

1995

Date			
December 15–18	51	44	5
November 17–18	53	38	9
November 6–8	52	41	7
October 19–22	49	40	11
October 5–7	46	42	12
September 22–24	48	44	8
September 14–17	44	44	12
August 28–30	46	43	11
August 11–14	46	44	10
August 4–7	46	42	12
July 20–23	46	44	10
July 7–9	48	42	10
June 5–6	47	42	11
May 11–14	51	42	7
April 21–24	51	39	10
April 17–19	46	45	9
April 5–6	47	45	8
March 27–29	44	47	9
March 17–19	46	45	9
February 24–26	42	48	10
February 3–5	49	44	7
January 16–18	47	45	8

1994

Date			
December 28–30	40	52	8
December 16–18	42	53	5
December 2–5	42	50	8
November 28–29	43	49	8
November 2–6	46	46	8
October 22–25	48	46	6

Date			
October 18–19	41	52	7
October 7–9	42	52	6
September 23–25	44	51	5
September 16–18	42	50	8
September 6–7	39	54	7
August 15–16	39	52	9
August 8–9	43	48	9
July 15–17	42	49	9
July 1–3	43	48	9
June 25–28	44	47	9
June 11–12	49	44	7
June 3–6	46	47	7
May 20–22	51	42	7
April 22–24	48	44	8
April 16–18	51	41	8
March 28–30	51	42	7
March 25–27	52	41	7
March 11–13	50	41	9
March 7–8	50	42	8
February 26–28	53	41	6
January 28–30	58	35	7
January 15–17	54	38	8
January 6–8	54	38	8

1993

Date			
December 17–19	54	40	6
December 4–6	52	38	10
November 19–21	48	43	9
November 15–16	50	43	7
November 2–4	48	45	7
October 28–30	48	45	7
October 13–18	47	44	9
October 8–10	50	42	8
September 24–26	56	36	8
September 13–15	46	43	11
September 10–12	47	42	11
August 23–25	44	48	8
August 8–10	44	48	8
July 19–21	41	49	10
July 9–11	45	48	7
June 29–30	46	47	7
June 18–21	39	50	11
June 5–6	37	49	14
May 21–23	44	46	10
May 10–12	45	44	11
April 22–24	55	37	8
March 29–31	52	37	11
March 12–14	53	34	13
February 26–28	59	29	12
February 12–14	51	34	15

January 29–31	54	30	16
January 24–26	58	20	22

Please tell me if you have a favorable or un- favorable opinion of Bill Clinton, or if you have never heard of him?

	Jan. 28, 1998	Jan. 23–24, 1998
Favorable	63%	55%
Unfavorable	32	41
No opinion	5	4

*"Never heard of" is less than 1% in all surveys from 1992 through 1998.

January 23–24, 1998

	Favorable	Un- favorable	No opinion
By Sex			
Male	60%	38%	2%
Female	55	42	3
By Ethnic Background			
White	53	44	3
Nonwhite	77	19	4
Black	85	11	4
By Education			
Postgraduate	58	38	4
College Graduate	61	37	2
College Incomplete	47	52	1
No College	63	33	4
By Region			
East	64	33	3
Midwest	55	44	1
South	52	44	4
West	60	38	2
By Age			
18–29 Years	58	41	1
30–49 Years	57	40	3
50–64 Years	58	39	3
65 Years and Over	57	39	4
By Household Income			
$75,000 and Over	53	44	3
$50,000 and Over	57	41	2
$30,000–$49,999	51	47	2
$20,000–$29,999	58	40	2
Under $20,000	62	33	5
By Politics			
Republicans	27	70	3
Democrats	85	13	2
Independents	56	41	3
By Political Ideology			
Conservative	40	57	3
Moderate	65	32	3
Liberal	77	21	2

National Trend

	Favorable	Un- favorable	No opinion
1998			
January 25–26	53%	43%	4%
January 24–25	58	39	3
January 23–24	57	40	3
1997			
December 18–21	58	37	5
October 27–29	62	35	3
October 3–5	56	40	4
September 25–28	61	35	4
September 6–7	63	32	5
July 25–27	62	35	3
June 26–29	59	37	4
April 18–20	60	38	2
March 24–26	63	34	3
February 24–26	61	34	5
January 31– February 2	64	32	4
January 10–13	65	31	4
January 3–5	60	36	4
1996			
November 3–4*	56	40	4
November 2–3*	57	38	5
November 1–2*	58	37	5
October 31– November 1*	59	37	4
October 30–31*	60	37	3
October 26–29*	58	38	4
October 19–20*	59	36	5
October 18–19*	58	37	5
October 17–18*	61	34	5
October 16–17*	58	38	4

Date			
October 15–16*	58	38	4
October 14–15*	59	36	5
October 13–14*	58	36	6
October 12–13*	60	35	5
October 11–12*	62	35	3
October 5–6*	62	33	5
October 4–5*	60	34	6
October 3–4*	58	37	5
October 2–3*	60	37	3
September 27–29*	63	33	4
September 3–5*	59	35	6
September 2–4*	61	34	5
September 2–4**	62	33	5
August 30– September 1**	61	35	4
August 28–29**	60	34	6
August 16–18**	57	41	2
August 14–15**	58	37	5
August 5–7**	60	37	3
July 18–21	62	35	3
June 18–19	60	36	4
May 28–29	59	38	3
May 9–12	60	39	1
March 15–17	58	38	4
February 23–25	60	37	3
January 12–15	54	44	2
1995			
November 6–8	59	38	3
September 22–24	55	41	4
August 4–7	51	44	5
July 7–9	57	40	3
April 17–19	56	42	1
March 17–19	51	45	4
January 16–18	56	42	2
1994			
December 28–30	48	49	3
November 28–29	50	47	3
September 6–7	47	50	3
July 15–17	49	48	3
April 22–24	56	41	3
March 25–27	56	40	4
March 7–8	59	38	3
January 15–17	60	37	3
January 6–8	62	35	3
1993			
November 19–21	55	41	4
November 15–16	56	38	6
November 2–4	54	42	4
September 24–26	63	32	5
August 8–10	53	42	5
July 19–21	51	45	4
June 5–6	48	44	8
April 22–24	63	32	5
January 29–31	65	27	8
January 18–19	66	26	8
1992			
November 10–11	60	34	6

*Likely voters
**Registered voters

How confident are you in Bill Clinton's abilities to carry out his duties as president—very confident, somewhat confident, not too confident, or not at all confident?

	Jan. 25–26, 1998	Jan. 24–25, 1998	Jan. 23–24, 1998
Very confident	27%	28%	29%
Somewhat confident	35	36	36
Not too confident	19	17	16
Not at all confident	18	18	18
No opinion	1	1	1

January 23–24, 1998

	Very confident	Somewhat confident	Not too confident	Not at all confident*
By Sex				
Male	29%	37%	15%	17%
Female	28	36	18	18
By Ethnic Background				
White	26	36	18	19
Nonwhite	41	40	8	10
Black	46	38	6	9
By Education				
Postgraduate	29	38	14	15
College Graduate	30	34	16	20
College Incomplete	22	36	20	22
No College	32	37	15	15
By Region				
East	35	35	14	13
Midwest	27	40	17	16
South	23	35	19	22
West	31	36	15	17

By Age

18–29 Years 23	43	20	14
30–49 Years 27	39	18	16
50–64 Years 30	37	10	22
65 Years and Over...... 36	24	16	22

By Household Income

$75,000 and Over 28	33	18	20
$50,000 and Over 26	37	16	20
$30,000–$49,999 21	42	16	21
$20,000–$29,999 28	42	10	20
Under $20,000 42	25	20	12

By Politics

Republicans..... 12	26	26	35
Democrats 49	39	8	4
Independents ... 23	42	17	17

By Political Ideology

Conservative ... 20	29	21	30
Moderate 31	42	14	12
Liberal............. 44	40	12	4

*"No opinion"—at 4% or less—is omitted.

Note: In the aftermath of his State of the Union address last Tuesday evening [January 27], Bill Clinton's job approval jumped 8 percentage points, reaching the highest level in his presidency. Significant increases were also recorded in the president's personal favorability rating and in the level of confidence that people have in him to carry out his duties. Contrary to what might be expected, these increases were not due to Democrats rallying around the president but to Republicans and independents giving him unusually high ratings. Democrats continued to be the source of Clinton's greatest support, but this support was unchanged from what they expressed over the previous weekend.

These results suggest that the Democrats had already reached a "saturation" level of support, with about nine in ten giving the president high marks. By contrast, independents and Republicans, who initially gave Clinton much lower ratings than did Democrats, seemed to be influenced by the speech—and perhaps also by the White House strategy of criticizing Independent Counsel Kenneth Starr and the news media—to a more positive view of the president.

According to a Gallup Poll conducted the night after the State of the Union address [on January 28], 67% of the public approved of the way that Clinton was handling his job as president, compared with 59% who approved the previous weekend, but the increase was found only among Republicans and independents. Among Democrats, 88% approved of the president, the highest among the three partisan groups but no different from the earlier poll. Among independents, 65% approved, up 12 points; and among Republicans, 43% approved, also 12 points higher than the weekend numbers.

A similar pattern was found on other measures of Clinton support. Last weekend, 55% gave the president a favorable rating, but the day after the State of the Union address that number surged to 63%, an 8-point increase. Among Democrats, however, the increase was just one point (to 86%), compared with a 4-point increase among Republicans (to 29%) and a 15-point jump among independents (to 65%).

Clinton's greatest improvement came in the number of respondents who have confidence in his ability to carry out his duties as president. Over the weekend, 63% were either very or somewhat confident, compared to 36% who said they were either not too or not at all confident. After Clinton's address to the nation, they expressed confidence by a margin of 76% to 22%—a jump in confidence of 13 points overall, with the number expressing little confidence declining by 14 points.

Again, the increased ratings did not come primarily from Democrats but from Republicans and independents. Democrats continue to express the greatest confidence, with 93% in the latest poll and 88% in the weekend poll, but that 5-point increase is small by comparison with the increases recorded among the other two partisan groups. Republicans showed a jump in favorability toward Clinton of 19 points, from 36% over the weekend to 55% after his speech. Similarly, independents went from 61% to 75% favorable, up 14 points.

PRESIDENT CLINTON/ PEOPLE IN THE NEWS

Interviewing Date: 1/28/98*
CNN/*USA Today*/Gallup Poll
Survey #GO 121206

Do you approve or disapprove of the way Bill Clinton is handling his job as president?

Approve	67%
Disapprove	28
No opinion	5

Selected National Trend

	Approve	Dis- approve	No opinion
1998			
January 25–26	59%	37%	4%
January 23–24	58	36	6
January 16–18	60	30	10

Next, I'd like to get your overall opinion of some people in the news. As I read each name, please say if you have a favorable or unfavorable opinion of this person, or if you have never heard of him or her:

Bill Clinton?

Favorable	63%
Unfavorable	32
No opinion	5

Selected National Trend

	Favorable	Un- favorable	No opinion
1998			
January 25–26	53%	43%	4%
January 23–24	57	40	3

Hillary Rodham Clinton?

Favorable	61%
Unfavorable	34

*Conducted between 6 P.M. and 9 P.M. EST on the evening of January 28, the day following the State of the Union address of January 27. Polls conducted entirely in one evening are subject to additional error or bias not found in polls conducted over several days.

No opinion	4
Never heard of	1

National Trend

	Favorable	Un- favorable	No opinion; never heard of*
1998			
January 24–25	61%	33%	6%
January 23–24	60	35	5
1997			
December 18–21	56	38	6
October 27–29	61	34	5
June 26–29	51	42	7
February 24–26	51	42	7
January 31– February 2	55	39	6
January 10–13	56	37	7
1996			
October 26–29**	49	43	8
August 30– September 1†	51	43	6
August 28–29†	51	41	8
August 16–18†	47	48	5
August 5–7†	48	45	7
June 18–19	46	47	7
March 15–17	47	48	5
January 12–15	43	51	6
1995			
July 7–9	50	44	6
March 17–19	49	44	7
January 16–18	50	44	6
1994			
November 28–29	50	44	6
September 6–7	48	47	5
July 15–17	48	46	6
April 22–24	56	40	4
March 25–27	52	42	6
March 7–8	55	40	5
January 15–17	57	36	7
1993			
November 2–4	58	34	8
September 24–26	62	27	11
August 8–10	57	33	10
July 19–21	56	34	10
June 5–6	50	31	19
April 22–24	61	27	12

March 22–24..............	61	31	8
January 29–31.............	67	22	11
1992			
November 10–11	50	29	21
August 31–			
September 2............	56	26	18

*"Never heard of" is 1% or less in all surveys from 1992 through 1998.
**Likely voters
†Registered voters

Independent Counsel Kenneth Starr?

Favorable	20%
Unfavorable	38
No opinion	21
Never heard of	21

Selected National Trend

	Favorable	Unfavor-able	No opinion	Never heard of
1998				
Jan. 24–25	26%	27%	23%	24%
Jan. 23–24	24	24	23	29

Monica Lewinsky?

Favorable	13%
Unfavorable	69
No opinion	18
Never heard of	*

*Less than 1%

Selected National Trend

	Favorable	Unfavor-able	No opinion	Never heard of
1998				
Jan. 24–25	29%	49%	21%	1%
Jan. 23–24	30	50	19	1

Which of the following statements do you agree with more concerning the controversy involving Clinton and Monica Lewinsky—it is mostly the result of a right-wing conspiracy which is out to get Bill Clinton, or it is mostly the result of Clinton's own behavior?

Conspiracy	44%
Own behavior	46
Neither; other (volunteered)	4
No opinion	6

	Con-spiracy	Own behavior	Neither; other	No opinion
By Politics				
Republicans.....	15%	79%	4%	2%
Democrats	68	22	3	7
Independents ...	43	44	6	7

In general, which do you think the media are more concerned with in their coverage of the allegations about Bill Clinton and Monica Lewinsky—being certain that a news story is accurate before they report it publicly, or being the first media organization to report a news story?

Being accurate	19%
Being first	77
Neither; other (volunteered)	1
No opinion	3

	Being accurate	Being first	Neither; other; no opinion
By Politics			
Republicans	24%	72%	4%
Democrats...................	18	79	3
Independents..............	17	79	4

How do you think most journalists personally feel about President Clinton's recent troubles concerning these allegations—do you think they enjoy Clinton's difficulties, they are unhappy about the situation, or they don't much care one way or the other?

	Clinton	Reagan*
Enjoy difficulties	33%	17%
Unhappy about it	22	42
Don't care	40	34
No opinion	5	7

*Question wording, January 1987: *How do you think most journalists personally feel about President Reagan's recent troubles concerning the Iran-contra affair?*

	Enjoy difficulties	Unhappy about it	Don't care	No opinion
By Politics				
Republicans.....	29%	30%	39%	2%
Democrats.......	39	22	30	9
Independents ...	30	16	49	5

Overall, do you feel the news media have acted responsibly or irresponsibly in this matter?

Responsibly	37%
Irresponsibly	55
No opinion	8

	Responsibly	Irresponsibly	No opinion
By Politics			
Republicans	57%	38%	5%
Democrats...................	27	63	10
Independents..............	32	60	8

Note: In what ranks as a seemingly major paradox in presidential politics, the American public has given Bill Clinton the highest job approval ratings of his administration in the midst of what some observers had been calling his most serious crisis—the current White House controversy over allegations of sexual misconduct and possible obstruction of justice. The number who approve of the job that Clinton is doing is now at 67%, his highest to date. One of the surprising findings from Gallup polling conducted since the crisis became public on January 21 has been the essential stability of his approval rating at a time when some critics anticipated that it would drop dramatically. It has hovered around 60% since early in 1996. That number remained about the same in polling conducted through this past Monday [January 26] in the middle of the crisis, and then jumped to 67% in a survey taken on January 28, the night after the State of the Union address.

Several factors might account for the high ratings in the midst of the controversy. First, the public's positive feelings about the way that things are going in the country were reinforced by President Clinton on January 27 in his State of the Union address, which focused exclusively on the nation's business and made no mention of the Lewinsky allegations. Previous Gallup data have documented the extent to which the public is positive about the current economic situation in this country, and Clinton himself now receives very high marks for his stewardship of the economy. The president's speech drew positive reviews from those who watched it, and these viewers reported higher levels of confidence in Clinton's ability to lead the country after they watched the speech than before.

Second, the State of the Union address may have created the type of classic "bounce" in public opinion that has historically occurred after major domestic events that focus attention on the president, including speeches and political conventions. In 1996, for example, Clinton's job approval rating increased by 5 percentage points immediately after the State of the Union address.

Third, there has been an apparent public backlash against media coverage of the White House situation. Wednesday's Gallup Poll included several questions designed to measure public assessment of the coverage of the recent events. The results are uniformly negative. Seventy-two percent say that there has been too much coverage of the controversy, which is significantly higher than respondents' replies, for example, during the Watergate crisis in 1973 and 1974. Additionally, by a margin of 55% to 37%, the public says that the media have acted irresponsibly in their coverage of the controversy. Moreover, three-quarters of the public are convinced that the media's priority is to be the first to report a news story, rather than making certain that the story is accurate before it is published. A full one-third says that members of the media are enjoying Clinton's difficulties, about twice the number who thought this way in 1987 during Ronald Reagan's troubles over the Iran-*contra* affair.

Fourth, there are strongly negative feelings about what the public perceives to be a politically motivated independent prosecutor. By an almost 2-to-1 margin, Americans say that Independent Counsel Kenneth Starr is using the criminal justice system to try to achieve political ends, rather than conducting a fair and impartial investigation into the "legitimate issues relating to President Clinton." And perhaps as a direct result of the

highly publicized attacks on Starr delivered by Hillary Rodham Clinton on morning television talk shows this week, Starr's image has taken an abrupt negative turn. Although only about six in ten know enough about Starr to evaluate him, those who do rate him are considerably more negative than positive. At the same time, the First Lady apparently did not convince everyone that her husband is the subject of a "vast right-wing conspiracy": respondents divide equally when asked to say whether the controversy is more a result of a right-wing conspiracy or Clinton's own behavior.

Finally, former White House intern Monica Lewinsky herself has now become the most negatively evaluated player in the controversy. Almost seven in ten of those interviewed on Wednesday night say that they hold an unfavorable opinion of her, while only 13% hold a favorable one. Other measures also suggest a turning away from Lewinsky's side of the story. By a margin of 54% to 33%, the public now says that it would believe Clinton rather than Lewinsky if the two make conflicting statements about what happened. However, last weekend, the public was equally divided over which person they could believe. Also, the percentage who believe the reported allegations about sexual relations, lying under oath, and obstruction of justice on the part of the president has fallen significantly over the past week.

FEBRUARY 5
IRAQ SITUATION

Interviewing Dates: 1/30–2/1/98
CNN/*USA Today*/Gallup Poll
Survey #GO 121271

As you may know, United Nations inspectors are currently in Iraq to investigate that country's weapons-producing capacity. Iraq recently announced that it would not allow these investigations to continue at certain sites.

Asked of half sample: Which would you prefer that the United States do right now to resolve the current situation—continue to use diplomacy and sanctions to pressure Iraq into compliance with the United Nations inspections; or take military action, even if other countries don't join in the effort, to force Iraq into complying?

Continue diplomacy	52%	
Take military action	45	
Neither; other (volunteered)	2	
No opinion	1	

	Continue diplomacy	Take military action	Neither; other; no opinion
By Sex			
Male	42%	55%	3%
Female	61	35	4
By Ethnic Background			
White	52	45	3
Nonwhite	53	44	3
Black	52	44	4
By Education			
Postgraduate	58	40	2
College Graduate	60	39	1
College Incomplete	51	45	4
No College	50	46	4
By Region			
East	56	40	4
Midwest	54	43	3
South	53	42	5
West	43	55	2
By Age			
18–29 Years	41	53	6
30–49 Years	61	38	1
50–64 Years	46	52	2
65 Years and Over	57	37	6
By Household Income			
$75,000 and Over	47	50	3
$50,000 and Over	49	48	3
$30,000–$49,999	61	38	1
$20,000–$29,999	49	45	6
Under $20,000	51	47	2
By Politics			
Republicans	46	53	1
Democrats	56	42	2
Independents	53	41	6
By Political Ideology			
Conservative	46	51	3
Moderate	55	41	4
Liberal	54	44	2

Asked of half sample: Which would you prefer that the United States do right now to resolve the current situation—continue to use diplomacy and sanctions to pressure Iraq into compliance with the United Nations inspections; or take military action, along with other countries, to force Iraq into complying?

Continue diplomacy 46%
Take military action....................................... 50
Neither; other (volunteered) 2
No opinion... 2

	Continue diplomacy	Take military action	Neither; other; no opinion
By Sex			
Male..............................	36%	62%	2%
Female	55	40	5
By Ethnic Background			
White	45	52	3
Nonwhite	53	41	6
Black............................	57	35	8
By Education			
Postgraduate	63	34	3
College Graduate........	59	37	4
College Incomplete.....	43	55	2
No College..................	39	56	5
By Region			
East	52	47	1
Midwest.......................	46	48	6
South............................	47	47	6
West.............................	39	60	1
By Age			
18–29 Years................	51	45	4
30–49 Years................	43	53	4
50–64 Years................	39	59	2
65 Years and Over......	59	37	4
By Household Income			
$75,000 and Over	51	46	3
$50,000 and Over	48	49	3
$30,000–$49,999........	35	63	2
$20,000–$29,999........	48	46	6
Under $20,000............	52	42	6
By Politics			
Republicans	39	60	1
Democrats...................	50	46	4
Independents...............	48	48	4
By Political Ideology			
Conservative..............	45	51	4
Moderate....................	44	53	3
Liberal	52	44	4

Note: Americans are about evenly divided on whether the United States should continue diplomatic efforts to force Iraq's cooperation with United Nations weapons inspectors or take military action now. Still, over the past two weeks, public support for a military response has increased as men more than women, and Republicans more than independents and Democrats, have responded favorably to the Clinton administration's preparation for possible war with Iraq.

While Secretary of State Madeleine Albright travels through Europe and the Middle East, obtaining support for possible military action against Iraq, support among the U.S. public seems to be growing as well. Two weeks ago, a Gallup Poll on January 16–18 showed Americans opposed to unilateral military action by more than a 2-to-1 margin (64% to 29%). Since then, support has risen 16 percentage points, and opposition has dropped 12 points, so that now respondents tilt only slightly against war (52% to 45%). This shift in opinion could be in response to Secretary Albright's insistence that the United States has the authority and determination to act unilaterally should Saddam Hussein refuse to comply with UN resolutions.

While they oppose unilateral action, respondents tilt in favor of such action by 50% to 46% if other countries are expected to participate with the United States. This represents a slight shift in opinion from two weeks ago, when they showed a one-point margin in favor of continued diplomacy.

In general, men are more supportive of military undertakings than women. That gender gap was reflected in the Gallup Poll two weeks ago, when majorities of both men and women opposed unilateral military action, but women by a wider margin than men. The gender gap at that time was an average of 14 points as women opted for diplomacy by a margin of 70% to 22%, while men did so by only 57% to 38%.

In the current poll, women continue to prefer diplomacy, though by a reduced margin of 61% to 35%, while men have switched from a majority in favor of diplomacy to one favoring military action by 55% to 42%. Two weeks ago, there were few differences among Republicans, independents, and Democrats over the question of unilateral military action against Iraq: all three groups opposed it by margins of about 2 to 1. Since then, all three groups have become more supportive of military action, but Republicans now show majority support, while independents and Democrats still show majority opposition, although by smaller margins.

FEBRUARY 11
VOLATILITY IN PRESIDENTIAL JOB APPROVAL RATINGS—AN ANALYSIS*

Despite dire predictions that the Monica Lewinsky crisis could signal the demise of his presidency, Bill Clinton now receives the highest Gallup Poll job approval ratings of his entire administration. The historical record of the public's ratings of recent presidents, however, suggests that it is far too early to say that Clinton has successfully weathered the storm of this most recent controversy. Public approval of the job being done by a president is notoriously volatile, subject to swift change, and, for at least two presidents in the last twenty-five years, dramatically affected by scandals.

Scandals Affected Nixon and Reagan

The current situation is most reminiscent of the presidencies of Richard Nixon and Ronald Reagan, each of whose standing in the eyes of the public was driven down sharply and, in the case of Nixon, fatally, by scandal. The impact of Watergate on Richard Nixon was not immediate. The actual break-in at the Watergate complex in Washington occurred in June 1972. Nixon nevertheless went on to win a sweeping reelection victory over Democrat George McGovern in November, and to a robust presidential approval rating of 62% immediately thereafter. By January 1973, however, the criminal trial of the first set of Watergate defendants and the formation of a special Senate committee to investigate Republican campaign espionage began to have an impact.

*This analysis was written by Frank Newport, editor in chief, The Gallup Organization.

Nixon's job approval dropped to 51% in a mid-January Gallup survey.

The announcement of a historic Vietnam peace settlement on January 23 resulted in a leap in Nixon's approval rating to 67%, but it also demonstrated how short-lived the effects of such international events on public opinion can be. Nixon's surge in approval evaporated almost as quickly as it appeared. The relentless uncovering of damaging information about the Watergate scandal through the spring and summer of 1973 led to a steady deterioration in public approval of Nixon month by month. By May his rating had dropped to 44%, and by August it was at 31%, representing a 36 percentage point drop in about six months. (A year later, in August 1974 when he resigned from office, Nixon's rating was 24%.)

Ronald Reagan was the second president in recent history to see his public image damaged by a scandal, but the impact of the Iran-*contra* revelations was both more immediate and ultimately less severe than was Watergate for Nixon. The facts surrounding the Iran-*contra* affair became public in November 1986. Reagan's job approval fell from 63% in October to 47% in December, and ultimately to 43% by March 1987, representing a 20-point decline in about five months.

Bush's Free-fall the Best Known

Real-world events unrelated to scandal also often have a dramatic impact on job approval ratings, underscoring the transient nature of the public's evaluation of the presidents. The most famous drop in job approval ratings in recent presidential history was suffered by George Bush, primarily as a result of public disenchantment with the way things were going economically in the country.

Bush had a long way to fall. His late February 1991 rating of 89%, the result of the allied victory in the Persian Gulf War, remains the highest ever recorded by Gallup polling dating back to the days of Franklin Roosevelt. Bush, in fact, enjoyed such high public esteem that he was thought to be undefeatable in his bid for reelection in 1992. By the fall of 1991, however, Bush began to fall victim to continuing public perceptions of a weak U.S. economy, and by December he had a rating of only 50%. By the summer of 1992 his job approval sank as low as 29%, a crash of 60 points in a period of sixteen months.

Like Bush, Jimmy Carter was beset not by scandal but by a weak economy as well as an international crisis, which dominated his last year in office. Carter's job approval rating, limping along as low as 31% in October 1979, benefited from a classic "rally" effect after the American hostages were taken in Iran by supporters of the Ayatollah Khomeini. In January 1980, Carter's job approval rose to 58%. Over the next several months, however, he was unsuccessful in negotiating a release of the hostages, and by late June his approval rating had fallen 27 points, to 31%. In the following November, Carter was defeated for reelection by Ronald Reagan.

Potential for Change in Clinton's Job Approval Ratings

How optimistic should the White House be, given that Bill Clinton's current job approval rating of 69% is the highest of his administration— roughly as high as any rating received by either Ronald Reagan or Jimmy Carter throughout their entire administrations? The example of Watergate shows how a scandal can ultimately have a devastating effect even if its impact is not immediate. Additionally, if military action should occur in Iraq, the Nixon, Carter, and Bush years show how this type of international event can provide a short-term boost, but ultimately not a lasting one.

At the same time, despite the immediate negative impact of Iran-*contra* on Ronald Reagan, it is important to remember that this scandal did not force him from office. In addition, his job approval ratings recovered to 63% by late 1988, and a recent retrospective approval rating on Reagan was 69%. Perhaps all that can be said with certainty as the current White House crisis continues to unfold is that the potential for significant changes in Clinton's job approval is as ever-present as the polls that measure it.

FEBRUARY 13
PRESIDENT CLINTON/
CONGRESS/SATISFACTION INDEX/
PEOPLE IN THE NEWS

Interviewing Dates: 1/30–2/1/98
CNN/*USA Today*/Gallup Poll
Survey #GO 121271

Do you approve or disapprove of the way Bill Clinton is handling his job as president?

Approve 69%
Disapprove 28
No opinion 3

Selected National Trend

	Approve	Dis-approve	No opinion
1998			
January 28*	67%	28%	5%
January 25–26	59	37	4
January 24–25	60	35	5
January 23–24	58	36	6
January 16–18	60	30	10
January 6–7	59	32	9

*Based on one-night poll

How strongly would you say you approve or disapprove—very strongly, or not so strongly?

Approve 69%
  Very strongly 51
  Not so strongly 18
Disapprove 28
  Not so strongly 7
  Very strongly 21
No opinion 3

Selected National Trend

	Approve very strongly	Approve not so strongly	Dis-approve not so strongly	Dis-approve very strongly*
1997				
Jan. 31–				
Feb. 2	34%	26%	9%	22%
1996				
Jan. 12–15	26	20	17	30
1995				
Jan. 16–18	21	26	17	28
1994				
July 15–17	19	23	15	34
June 3–6	26	20	15	32

*"No opinion"—at 9% or less— is omitted.

From what you have heard, read, or remember about some of our past presidents, please tell me if you approve or disapprove of the way they handled their job as president:

John F. Kennedy?

Approve	77%
Disapprove	17
No opinion	6

	Approve	Dis-approve	No opinion
By Age			
18–29 Years	76%	17%	7%
30–49 Years	79	13	8
50–64 Years	79	18	3
65 Years and Over	72	23	5
By Politics			
Republicans	66	28	6
Democrats	93	6	1
Independents	70	19	11
By Political Ideology			
Conservative	70	23	7
Moderate	84	11	5
Liberal	80	14	6

Selected National Trend

	Approve	Dis-approve	No opinion
Nov. 15–16, 1993	78%	13%	9%
June 4–8, 1992	76	14	10
Nov. 8–11, 1990	84	9	7

Richard Nixon?

Approve	32%
Disapprove	61
No opinion	7

	Approve	Dis-approve	No opinion
By Age			
18–29 Years	29%	58%	13%
30–49 Years	30	65	5
50–64 Years	35	61	4
65 Years and Over	38	54	8
By Politics			
Republicans	40	54	6
Democrats	25	70	5
Independents	32	58	10

By Political Ideology

Conservative	38	56	6
Moderate	29	64	7
Liberal	27	68	5

Selected National Trend

	Approve	Dis-approve	No opinion
Nov. 15–16, 1993	37%	56%	7%
June 4–8, 1992	35	59	6
Nov. 8–11, 1990	32	62	6

Jimmy Carter?

Approve	65%
Disapprove	29
No opinion	6

	Approve	Dis-approve	No opinion
By Age			
18–29 Years	54%	29%	17%
30–49 Years	66	31	3
50–64 Years	69	26	5
65 Years and Over	70	26	4
By Politics			
Republicans	54	43	3
Democrats	75	19	6
Independents	63	28	9
By Political Ideology			
Conservative	56	38	6
Moderate	70	25	5
Liberal	69	24	7

Selected National Trend

	Approve	Dis-approve	No opinion
Sept. 23–25, 1994	51%	46%	3%
Nov. 15–16, 1993	45	50	5
June 4–8, 1992	48	46	6
Nov. 8–11, 1990	45	52	3

Ronald Reagan?

Approve	69%
Disapprove	29
No opinion	2

	Approve	Dis-approve	No opinion
By Age			
18–29 Years	72%	25%	3%
30–49 Years	67	32	1
50–64 Years	71	28	1
65 Years and Over	66	25	9
By Politics			
Republicans	93	6	1
Democrats	51	48	1
Independents	68	27	5
By Political Ideology			
Conservative	81	18	1
Moderate	69	29	2
Liberal	52	43	5

Selected National Trend

	Approve	Dis-approve	No opinion
Sept. 23–25, 1994	55%	44%	1%
Nov. 15–16, 1993	52	45	3
June 4–8, 1992	50	47	3
Nov. 8–11, 1990	54	44	2

George Bush?

Approve	74%
Disapprove	24
No opinion	2

	Approve	Dis-approve	No opinion
By Age			
18–29 Years	74%	24%	2%
30–49 Years	73	25	2
50–64 Years	78	21	1
65 Years and Over	72	23	5
By Politics			
Republicans	90	8	2
Democrats	66	33	1
Independents	71	27	2
By Political Ideology			
Conservative	81	18	1
Moderate	75	23	2
Liberal	63	34	3

Selected National Trend

	Approve	Dis-approve	No opinion
Sept. 23–25, 1994	58%	40%	2%
Nov. 15–16, 1993	58	40	2

Now, thinking about Congress, do you approve or disapprove of the way Congress is handling its job?

Approve	56%
Disapprove	35
No opinion	9

	Approve	Dis-approve	No opinion
By Politics			
Republicans	66%	29%	5%
Democrats	54	35	11
Independents	51	40	9
By Political Ideology			
Conservative	61	31	8
Moderate	47	44	9
Liberal	57	35	8

Selected National Trend

	Approve	Dis-approve	No opinion
1998			
January 16–18	42%	47%	11%
1997			
December 18–21	39	52	9
October 27–29	36	53	11
August 22–25	41	48	11
July 25–27	34	57	9
May 6–7	32	58	10
April 18–20	30	59	11
February 24–26	37	48	15
January 31–February 2	36	51	13
January 10–13	41	49	10

In general, are you satisfied or dissatisfied with the way things are going in the United States at this time?

Satisfied	63%
Dissatisfied	35
No opinion	2

	Satisfied	Dis-satisfied	No opinion
By Sex			
Male	70%	28%	2%
Female	57	40	3
By Ethnic Background			
White	64	34	2
Nonwhite	57	39	4
Black	61	35	4
By Education			
Postgraduate	70	30	*
College Graduate	72	27	1
College Incomplete	61	36	3
No College	60	37	3
By Region			
East	67	31	2
Midwest	69	29	2
South	56	42	2
West	63	34	3
By Age			
18–29 Years	67	32	1
30–49 Years	64	35	1
50–64 Years	59	36	5
65 Years and Over	60	35	5
By Household Income			
$75,000 and Over	70	29	1
$50,000 and Over	69	29	2
$30,000–$49,999	63	35	2
$20,000–$29,999	63	34	3
Under $20,000	55	43	2
By Politics			
Republicans	53	45	2
Democrats	75	23	2
Independents	60	37	3
By Political Ideology			
Conservative	57	41	2
Moderate	68	29	3
Liberal	66	33	1
By Approval of Clinton			
Approve	76	22	2
Disapprove	35	63	2
By Importance of Moral Values			
Critical	48	51	1
Important	69	28	3
Not Important	77	20	3

*Less than 1%

Selected National Trend

	Satisfied	Dis-satisfied	No opinion
1997			
December 18–21	50%	46%	4%
August 22–25	50	48	2
May 6–7	46	51	3
January 10–13	50	47	3
1996			
December 9–11	43	55	2
November 21–24	47	47	6
October 26–29	39	56	5
August 30–September 1	45	50	5
August 16–18	38	57	5
May 9–12	37	60	3
March 15–17	36	61	3
March 8–10	41	56	3
January 5–7	24	72	4
1995			
August 11–14	33	64	3
July 7–9	32	65	3
March 27–29	30	66	4
1994			
November 28–29	29	67	4
November 2–6	30	66	4
October 22–25	31	66	3
July 15–17	33	65	2
May 20–22	33	64	3
April 22–24	32	65	3
March 25–27	35	62	3
February 26–28	36	61	3
January 15–17	35	62	3
1993			
December 4–6	34	63	3
November 2–4	27	70	3
May 21–23	24	73	3
February 12–14	25	71	4
January 8–11	29	68	3
1992			
November 10–11	26	68	6
August 28–September 2*	22	73	5
June 12–14	14	84	2
May 7–10	20	77	3
April 20–22**	19	80	1
February 28–March 1	21	78	1

January 31–
February 2**.......... 24   75   1
January 3–6†............... 24   74   2

*Gallup/CNN/Knight-Ridder Poll
**Gallup Poll for *Newsweek*
†Registered voters

Next, I'd like your overall opinion of some people in the news. As I read each name, please say if you have a favorable or unfavorable opinion of this person, or if you have never heard of him or her:

Bill Clinton?

Favorable 65%
Unfavorable 34
No opinion 1

	Favorable	Unfavorable	No opinion
By Politics			
Republicans	32%	66%	2%
Democrats...................	91	8	1
Independents..............	64	34	2
By Political Ideology			
Conservative...............	47	51	2
Moderate.....................	72	27	1
Liberal	80	19	1

Selected National Trend

	Favorable	Unfavorable	No opinion
1998			
January 28*.................	63%	32%	5%
January 25–26.............	53	43	4
January 24–25.............	58	39	3
January 23–24.............	57	40	3

*Based on one-night poll

Hillary Rodham Clinton?

Favorable 64%
Unfavorable 34
No opinion 2

	Favorable	Unfavorable	No opinion
By Politics			
Republicans	35%	62%	3%
Democrats...................	87	12	1
Independents..............	64	33	3
By Political Ideology			
Conservative...............	46	50	4
Moderate.....................	78	22	*
Liberal	73	25	2

*Less than 1%

Selected National Trend

	Favorable	Unfavorable	No opinion
1998			
January 28*.................	61%	34%	5%
January 24–25.............	61	33	6
January 23–24.............	60	35	5

*Based on one-night poll

Al Gore?

Favorable 62%
Unfavorable 31
No opinion 7

	Favorable	Unfavorable	No opinion
By Politics			
Republicans	36%	54%	10%
Democrats...................	85	12	3
Independents..............	61	30	9
By Political Ideology			
Conservative...............	46	47	7
Moderate.....................	69	25	6
Liberal	78	16	6

Selected National Trend

	Favorable	Unfavorable	No opinion
1998			
January 24–25.............	56%	32%	12%
January 23–24.............	55	33	12

Independent Counsel Kenneth Starr?

Favorable 25%
Unfavorable 42
No opinion 14
Never heard of 19

	Favorable	Unfavor-able	No opinion	Never heard of
By Politics				
Republicans.....	40%	28%	15%	17%
Democrats	13	55	12	20
Independents ...	24	40	15	21
By Political Ideology				
Conservative ...	37	32	18	13
Moderate	21	46	12	21
Liberal	13	52	10	25

Selected National Trend

	Favorable	Unfavor-able	No opinion	Never heard of
1998				
Jan. 28*	20%	38%	21%	21%
Jan. 24–25	26	27	23	24
Jan. 23–24	24	24	23	29

*Based on one-night poll

Monica Lewinsky?

Favorable 11%
Unfavorable 66
No opinion 17
Never heard of 6

	Favorable	Unfavor-able	No opinion	Never heard of
By Politics				
Republicans.....	15%	64%	17%	4%
Democrats	8	72	14	6
Independents ...	10	63	20	7
By Political Ideology				
Conservative ...	11	63	20	6
Moderate	11	67	16	6
Liberal	10	71	13	6

Selected National Trend

	Favorable	Unfavor-able	No opinion	Never heard of
1998				
Jan. 28*	13%	69%	18%	**
Jan. 24–25	29	49	21	1
Jan. 23–24	30	50	19	1

*Based on one-night poll
**Less than 1%

Interviewing Dates: 1/24–25/98
CNN/*USA Today*/Gallup Poll
Survey #GO 121132

Do you approve or disapprove of the way Newt Gingrich is handling his job as Speaker of the U.S. House of Representatives?

Approve 46%
Disapprove 40
No opinion 14

	Approve	Dis-approve	No opinion
By Politics			
Republicans	62%	28%	10%
Democrats	40	49	11
Independents	43	44	13
By Political Ideology			
Conservative	57	35	8
Moderate	47	41	12
Liberal	29	59	12

Selected National Trend

	Approve	Dis-approve	No opinion
1998			
January 23–24	48%	41%	11%
1997			
March 24–26	25	63	12
January 3–5	27	59	14
1996			
April 9–10	33	55	12
March 11–17	31	55	14
February 12–18	35	55	10
January 8–14	33	58	9

June 5–6	37	46	17
April 17–19	37	49	14
March 27–29	37	47	16
February 24–26	36	48	16
February 3–5	38	48	14
January 16–18	39	35	26

Note: The current controversy over allegations of sexual impropriety by President Bill Clinton seems to have led, although indirectly, to an outpouring of positive feelings by the American public. Gallup Polls now report that Clinton's approval rating is the highest of his presidency; that general satisfaction with the way things are going in the country is the highest since the U.S. victory in the Persian Gulf War in 1991; and that approval of the way Congress is doing its job is the highest since Gallup first polled on this subject almost twenty-five years ago. Some observers suggest that these high ratings are related to Clinton's positive message in his State of the Union speech, which cited a major drop in violent crime, the successful bipartisan effort to achieve a balanced budget, and a booming economy.

Ironically, the sexual allegations may have acted as a catalyst for the positive ratings by stimulating people to watch the speech in the first place. A Gallup Poll of those who had viewed or listened to Clinton (conducted immediately after he finished speaking) supports this interpretation. Many people who probably would not have tuned into the speech, but did so because they were curious as to how well Clinton would handle the situation, nevertheless came away feeling more positive about him and the subjects he addressed than they had beforehand.

The spillover of these positive reactions reaches into some unlikely areas. Both First Lady Hillary Rodham Clinton and Vice President Al Gore have seen their favorability ratings soar to their highest levels since early 1993, shortly after Clinton first assumed the presidency. And Speaker of the House Newt Gingrich, long identified as one of the most unpopular political leaders in the country, now receives his highest performance rating ever, with more respondents approving than disapproving of the way that he is handling his job.

Perhaps the most unusual spillover is the more positive retrospective ratings of three former presidents. In 1993 they showed little change from the two previous ratings in 1990 and 1992. But in the latest Gallup Poll, when respondents were asked to indicate their approval or disapproval of the job performance of five former presidents, George Bush's retrospective approval rating jumped by 16 percentage points to 74%, Ronald Reagan's by 17 points to 69%, and Jimmy Carter's by 20 points to 65%. John Kennedy's approval, already at the highest level, remained constant at 77%. Only Richard Nixon's rating suffered, falling 5 points to 32%.

While recent events have produced increasingly positive ratings for most public political figures, both Independent Counsel Kenneth Starr and Monica Lewinsky have become less popular with the public over the past three weeks. When the allegations against Clinton first became public, more respondents thought that Starr was conducting a fair investigation. Today, a majority thinks that the investigation is unfair. And Starr's personal rating, which had been evenly split between favorable and unfavorable, now shows a 17-point margin in the unfavorable category. Similarly, opinion about Lewinsky has become more negative, with 50% giving her an unfavorable and 30% a favorable rating three weeks ago, compared with 66% unfavorable and just 11% favorable today.

FEBRUARY 18
IRAQ SITUATION

Interviewing Dates: 2/13–15/98
CNN/*USA Today*/Gallup Poll
Survey #GO 121392

> Asked in the United Kingdom:* If the British government decided to take military action against Iraq, would you personally approve or disapprove if British military forces were involved in air attacks on Iraq?

Approve	62%
Disapprove	32
No opinion	6

*Based on telephone interviews with a randomly selected national sample of adults in England, Scotland, and Wales conducted on February 11–16. For results based on a sample of this size, one can say with 95% confidence that the error attributable to sampling and other random effects could be ± 3 percentage points.

Asked in the United States: If the U.S. government decided to take military action against Iraq, would you personally approve or disapprove if U.S. military forces were involved in air attacks on Iraq?

Approve 76%
Disapprove 19
No opinion 5

	Approve	Dis-approve	No opinion
By Sex			
Male	81%	17%	2%
Female	72	21	7
By Ethnic Background			
White	78	17	5
Nonwhite	69	26	5
Black	68	27	5
By Education			
Postgraduate	72	25	3
College Graduate	82	15	3
College Incomplete	78	18	4
No College	75	19	6
By Region			
East	78	18	4
Midwest	72	20	8
South	79	15	6
West	75	23	2
By Age			
18–29 Years	73	26	1
30–49 Years	82	14	4
50–64 Years	80	16	4
65 Years and Over	63	24	13
By Household Income			
$75,000 and Over	84	15	1
$50,000 and Over	83	15	2
$30,000–$49,999	77	19	4
$20,000–$29,999	76	18	6
Under $20,000	73	20	7
By Politics			
Republicans	76	21	3
Democrats	80	14	6
Independents	74	21	5
By Political Ideology			
Conservative	77	19	4
Moderate	79	16	5
Liberal	70	26	4

Do you approve or disapprove of the way Bill Clinton is handling the situation in Iraq?

Approve 65%
Disapprove 27
No opinion 8

	Approve	Dis-approve	No opinion
By Sex			
Male	63%	32%	5%
Female	67	22	11
By Ethnic Background			
White	66	26	8
Nonwhite	65	28	7
Black	66	28	6
By Education			
Postgraduate	70	25	5
College Graduate	67	26	7
College Incomplete	66	28	6
No College	63	26	11
By Region			
East	71	22	7
Midwest	61	29	10
South	67	25	8
West	62	32	6
By Age			
18–29 Years	63	31	6
30–49 Years	67	26	7
50–64 Years	70	24	6
65 Years and Over	58	27	15
By Household Income			
$75,000 and Over	67	28	5
$50,000 and Over	69	27	4
$30,000–$49,999	65	27	8
$20,000–$29,999	68	24	8
Under $20,000	62	26	12

By Politics

Republicans	55	37	8
Democrats	76	17	7
Independents	64	27	9

By Political Ideology

Conservative	59	32	9
Moderate	70	25	5
Liberal	71	21	8

Selected National Trend

	Approve	Dis-approve	No opinion
1998			
January 24–25	48%	40%	12%
January 23–24	46	42	12
1997			
November 21–23	59	30	11
1996			
September 17–19	55	25	20
September 16–18	55	25	20
September 15–17	56	25	19
September 14–16	53	26	21
September 13–15	56	24	20
September 9–11	57	22	21

Asked of half sample: Which would you prefer that the United States do right now to resolve the current situation—continue to use diplomacy and sanctions to pressure Iraq into compliance with the United Nations inspections; or take military action, along with other countries, to force Iraq into complying?

Continue diplomacy	54%
Take military action	41
Neither; other (volunteered)	3
No opinion	2

Selected National Trend

	Continue diplomacy	Take military action	Neither; other; no opinion
1998			
January 30– February 1	46%	50%	4%
January 16–18	47	46	7

Asked of half sample: Regardless of how you feel about military action against Iraq, what do you think the goal of the United States should be if it does attack—to substantially reduce Iraq's capacity to develop weapons of mass destruction and threaten neighboring countries, or to immediately remove Saddam Hussein from power?

Remove Saddam from power	64%
Reduce weapons capacity	31
Neither; other (volunteered)	3
No opinion	2

	Remove Saddam from power	Reduce weapons capacity	Neither; other; no opinion
By Sex			
Male	59%	37%	4%
Female	69	25	6
By Ethnic Background			
White	63	32	5
Nonwhite	71	27	2
Black	72	25	3
By Education			
Postgraduate	40	55	5
College Graduate	47	47	6
College Incomplete	62	33	5
No College	76	20	4
By Region			
East	62	33	5
Midwest	66	28	6
South	68	27	5
West	59	39	2
By Age			
18–29 Years	61	36	3
30–49 Years	63	34	3
50–64 Years	63	27	10
65 Years and Over	71	24	5
By Household Income			
$75,000 and Over	46	45	9
$50,000 and Over	52	42	6
$30,000–$49,999	71	27	2
$20,000–$29,999	64	32	4
Under $20,000	73	21	6

By Politics

Republicans 56   41   3
Democrats.................... 70   26   4
Independents.............. 66   27   7

By Political Ideology

Conservative 63   32   5
Moderate..................... 68   30   2
Liberal 58   38   4

Asked of half sample: Would you favor or oppose U.S. forces taking military action against Iraq in order to substantially reduce Iraq's ability to produce weapons of mass destruction:

If it would result in substantial U.S. military casualties?

Favor... 38%
Oppose.. 56
No opinion... 6

If it would result in substantial casualties among Iraqi civilians?

Favor... 47%
Oppose.. 45
No opinion... 8

If it would turn many countries in the Middle East, such as Jordan and Saudi Arabia, against the United States?

Favor... 44%
Oppose.. 47
No opinion... 9

Note: By a margin of 54% to 41%, Americans prefer that at least for now the United States continues with diplomatic efforts to avoid war with Iraq. However, if we should actually take military action, 76% say that they would support it, and only 19% would not.

These results are from the latest Gallup Poll, which also shows that support for any military action is conditional: if Americans believed that there would be substantial U.S. military casualties, they would oppose the effort by 56% to 38%. If substantial Iraqi civilian casualties were projected, they would be about evenly divided over war with Iraq, or if some Arab countries such as Jordan and Saudi Arabia indicated that they would turn against the United States as a result.

Whatever the reservations, public support for Bill Clinton's policy on Iraq has jumped from 48% to 65% over the past two weeks. And even before the president's speech on Tuesday [February 10], in which he outlined the reasons for possible military action, a majority believed that he had already explained why such efforts might be necessary.

Americans seem willing to live with Saddam Hussein in power if he complies with United Nations resolutions. By a 2-to-1 margin, they reply that UN sanctions should continue against Iraq only until he complies with all UN resolutions, and not necessarily until he leaves office. However, if Saddam refused to comply, thus bringing the United States into war, Americans then say, by a 2-to-1 majority, that we should try to remove him from power immediately, rather than just reduce his war-making potential.

Despite their desire for the United States to oust Saddam from power in case of war, Americans are about evenly divided over whether such an effort would succeed, with 47% saying that it would, and 50% saying that it would not. On the other hand, most respondents believe that military action would be successful in getting Iraq to allow UN inspectors to do their job of investigating that country's weapons capacity.

As for partisan differences, President Clinton receives higher marks from Democrats than Republicans on his handling of the Iraq situation, but even Republicans give him majority approval of 55%, compared with 64% among independents and 76% among Democrats. On the issue of going to war, however, there are only slight differences by party. Republicans would support military action by a margin of 76% to 21%, compared with a margin of 80% to 14% among Democrats. And members of both parties support continued diplomatic efforts for now, by 53% to 46% among Republicans and 56% to 38% among Democrats. Opposition to military action in the event of substantial U.S. military casualties is also about the same among the partisan groups. The lack of partisanship on this issue may reflect the fact that the first effort against Saddam in 1991 was led by George Bush, a Republican president.

As shown in the gender gap in previous Gallup Polls, men are more supportive of military

action against Iraq than are women. However, a strong majority of women as well as men would approve if the United States actually took military action. And a majority of men as well as women would oppose such efforts if there were substantial U.S. casualties. In both cases, women express less support for war by about 10 percentage points.

The gender gap is most significant on what actions the United States should take now. Men are about evenly divided over continuing with diplomatic efforts or launching air strikes (49% to 48%, respectively), while women are clearly in favor of continued diplomacy, by 59% to 34%.

FEBRUARY 27
IRAQ SITUATION

Interviewing Date: 2/24/98*
CNN/*USA Today*/Gallup Poll
Survey #GO 121733

As you may know, UN Secretary General Kofi Annan has recently worked out an agreement with Iraq over UN weapons inspections in that country. From what you have heard or read, do you favor or oppose that agreement?

Favor... 56%
Oppose... 18
No opinion... 26

	Favor	Oppose	No opinion
By Sex			
Male	57%	20%	23%
Female	55	16	29
By Age			
18–29 Years	50	17	33
30–49 Years	59	18	23
50 Years and Over	58	18	24
By Politics			
Republicans	62	15	23
Democrats	62	15	23
Independents	47	22	31

*Polls conducted entirely in one day are subject to additional error or bias not found in polls conducted over several days.

What do you think President Clinton's response should be to that agreement—accept the agreement and start reducing U.S. military forces in the Persian Gulf; conditionally accept the agreement but maintain U.S. military strength in the Persian Gulf; or reject the agreement and go forward with a military attack on Iraq?

Accept.. 12%
Conditionally accept................................ 68
Reject... 14
Other (volunteered) 1
No opinion... 5

	Accept	Conditionally accept	Reject	Other; no opinion
By Sex				
Male	11%	68%	16%	5%
Female	13	67	12	8
By Age				
18–29 Years	12	65	20	3
30–49 Years	13	70	12	5
50 Years and Over	10	65	14	11
By Politics				
Republicans	10	67	17	6
Democrats	10	71	14	5
Independents	15	66	12	7

Which of the following statements better describes your personal reaction to how the crisis with Iraq has been resolved—you are relieved because military action was avoided and you think the peace process deserved a chance, or you are worried because you think the agreement will just give Saddam Hussein more time to build weapons of mass destruction?

Relieved... 43%
Worried.. 49
Other (volunteered) 5
No opinion... 3

	Relieved	Worried	Other; no opinion
By Sex			
Male	40%	52%	8%
Female	45	46	9

By Age

18–29 Years	36	59	5
30–49 Years	45	46	9
50 Years and Over	43	48	9

By Politics

Republicans	42	53	5
Democrats	44	50	6
Independents	42	46	12

How would you rate the leadership Bill Clinton has shown in the recent confrontation with Iraq—would you say it has been very strong, moderately strong, moderately weak, or very weak?

Very strong	28%
Moderately strong	47
Moderately weak	17
Very weak	5
No opinion	3

	Very strong	Moderately strong	Moderately weak	Very weak*
By Sex				
Male	28%	44%	19%	7%
Female	27	49	16	3
By Age				
18–29 Years	15	47	28	8
30–49 Years	27	51	17	4
50 Years and Over	38	40	11	5
By Politics				
Republicans	18	42	28	11
Democrats	44	44	8	2
Independents	22	52	17	3

*"No opinion"—at 6% or less—is omitted.

Note: Americans are not quite breathing a sigh of relief over the peaceful solution to the latest Iraq crisis, but they clearly go along with Bill Clinton's decision, announced Tuesday morning [February 24], to conditionally accept the terms of a United Nations agreement with Iraq over weapons inspections. A nationwide Gallup survey, conducted Tuesday evening, found 56% in favor of the settlement worked out by UN Secretary General Kofi Annan and already signed by Saddam Hussein. Only 18% oppose the agreement, while 26% have no opinion.

An even larger number (68%) supports President Clinton's cautious approach to the agreement, which includes the maintenance of U.S. military strength in the Persian Gulf. A small minority (just 14%) would prefer that Clinton reject the agreement and go forward with an attack. A similar number (12%) takes the opposite tack, saying that he should not only accept the agreement but also begin reducing U.S. forces in the Gulf.

Despite the public consensus in favor of the settlement, only 43% are relieved that the standoff was resolved without military force. About one-half (49%) are more worried than relieved because of the opportunity they believe it gives Saddam to build more weapons. This unease is reflected to an even greater extent in Americans' generally pessimistic outlook for peace with Iraq. Four out of five expect Saddam to violate the terms of the new agreement, similar to a Gallup Poll finding after the crisis with Iraq in November 1997. Perhaps as a result, 68% think that the United States is likely to take military action against Iraq within the next year. Also, support for using military force to remove Saddam from power is nearly as high today as it was before the latest peace agreement, with 61% in favor of such a mission.

Gallup finds no perceived clear winner emerging from this conflict. In one sense, Americans think that the agreement was a true compromise, with Clinton and Saddam each getting what he wanted. When pressed to say which man benefited more or who backed down more, respondents are generally split, with 42% indicating Clinton as the winner and 49% saying Saddam. In any case, Clinton clearly benefited in domestic political terms, winning praise from the public for his handling of the Iraq crisis. Three-quarters of the public, according to the new poll, think that Clinton's leadership in the confrontation with Iraq has been strong; only 22% consider it weak. And by a 2-to-1 margin (57% to 26%), they think that as a result of the confrontation the United States looks stronger, rather than weaker, to the rest of the world.

MARCH 5
PRESIDENTIAL EXTRAMARITAL AFFAIRS

Interviewing Dates: 1/30–2/1/98
CNN/*USA Today*/Gallup Poll
Survey #GO 121271

Do you think most presidents have or have not had extramarital affairs while they were president?

Have.. 59%
Have not 33
No opinion....................................... 8

	Have	Have not	No opinion
By Sex			
Male............................	55%	38%	7%
Female	63	28	9
By Ethnic Background			
White	57	35	8
Nonwhite	73	17	10
Black...........................	74	14	12
By Education			
Postgraduate	48	41	11
College Graduate........	49	43	8
College Incomplete.....	62	32	6
No College..................	64	27	9
By Region			
East	62	29	9
Midwest......................	51	42	7
South...........................	61	30	9
West............................	63	31	6
By Age			
18–29 Years................	68	30	2
30–49 Years................	55	37	8
50–64 Years................	58	33	9
65 Years and Over......	60	23	17
By Household Income			
$75,000 and Over	48	43	9
$50,000 and Over	51	41	8
$30,000–$49,999........	67	31	2
$20,000–$29,999........	64	26	10
Under $20,000............	62	28	10

By Politics			
Republicans	50	47	3
Democrats...................	65	23	12
Independents..............	60	33	7
By Political Ideology			
Conservative..............	50	43	7
Moderate....................	60	32	8
Liberal	74	19	7

Would you describe Bill Clinton's faults as worse than most other presidents, or as no worse than most other presidents?

Worse... 24%
No worse.. 75
No opinion....................................... 1

	Worse	No worse	No opinion
By Sex			
Male............................	28%	70%	2%
Female	20	79	1
By Ethnic Background			
White	27	71	2
Nonwhite	5	95	*
Black...........................	2	98	*
By Education			
Postgraduate	27	72	1
College Graduate........	31	67	2
College Incomplete.....	29	70	1
No College..................	17	81	2
By Region			
East	21	79	*
Midwest......................	22	77	1
South...........................	31	67	2
West............................	19	80	1
By Age			
18–29 Years................	19	78	3
30–49 Years................	25	74	1
50–64 Years................	25	74	1
65 Years and Over......	25	73	2
By Household Income			
$75,000 and Over	37	63	*
$50,000 and Over	35	64	1

$30,000–$49,999	24	75	1
$20,000–$29,999	13	85	2
Under $20,000	14	85	1

By Politics

Republicans	50	49	1
Democrats	6	94	*
Independents	22	75	3

By Political Ideology

Conservative	40	59	1
Moderate	18	81	1
Liberal	9	90	1

*Less than 1%

From what you have heard or read, do you believe that John F. Kennedy did or did not have extramarital affairs while he was president?

Yes, did	85%
Did not	10
No opinion	5

Finally, I'm going to read some issues a person might have in their life. For each one, please say if that is the kind of thing the American public would need to know about a presidential candidate in order to evaluate him or her, or whether it would not be necessary for the public to know about that issue. Please keep in mind that these are not meant to describe any particular candidates, but are just hypothetical issues. How about:

If the person has a pattern of not paying his or her debts?

Yes, need to know	83%
Not necessary	16
No opinion	1

	Yes, need to know	Not necessary	No opinion
By Sex			
Male	81%	18%	1%
Female	84	15	1
By Ethnic Background			
White	84	15	1

Nonwhite	71	28	1
Black	76	23	1

By Education

Postgraduate	81	18	1
College Graduate	90	10	*
College Incomplete	82	16	2
No College	81	18	1

By Region

East	76	23	1
Midwest	83	17	*
South	86	12	2
West	85	15	*

By Age

18–29 Years	76	23	1
30–49 Years	82	17	1
50–64 Years	86	13	1
65 Years and Over	89	11	*

By Household Income

$75,000 and Over	85	15	*
$50,000 and Over	82	18	*
$30,000–$49,999	85	14	1
$20,000–$29,999	81	17	2
Under $20,000	82	17	1

By Politics

Republicans	88	12	*
Democrats	81	18	1
Independents	80	19	1

By Political Ideology

Conservative	88	12	*
Moderate	85	15	*
Liberal	72	26	2

*Less than 1%

If the person were an alcoholic?

Yes, need to know	83%
Not necessary	16
No opinion	1

	Yes, need to know	Not necessary	No opinion
By Sex			
Male	81%	18%	1%
Female	85	14	1

By Ethnic Background			
White	83	16	1
Nonwhite	83	16	1
Black	87	12	1
By Education			
Postgraduate	84	14	2
College Graduate	83	17	*
College Incomplete	80	18	2
No College	85	14	1
By Region			
East	79	21	*
Midwest	84	15	1
South	84	14	2
West	85	14	1
By Age			
18–29 Years	77	23	*
30–49 Years	84	15	1
50–64 Years	83	15	2
65 Years and Over	88	12	*
By Household Income			
$75,000 and Over	82	17	1
$50,000 and Over	81	18	1
$30,000–$49,999	85	14	1
$20,000–$29,999	84	14	2
Under $20,000	82	17	1
By Politics			
Republicans	90	9	1
Democrats	81	18	1
Independents	80	19	1
By Political Ideology			
Conservative	89	11	*
Moderate	84	16	*
Liberal	71	27	2

*Less than 1%

If the person has a gambling problem?

Yes, need to know	80%
Not necessary	19
No opinion	1

	Yes, need to know	*Not necessary*	*No opinion*
By Sex			
Male	79%	20%	1%
Female	81	19	*

By Ethnic Background			
White	79	20	1
Nonwhite	82	18	*
Black	86	14	*
By Education			
Postgraduate	81	18	1
College Graduate	84	16	*
College Incomplete	80	20	*
No College	79	20	1
By Region			
East	79	21	*
Midwest	76	24	*
South	80	18	2
West	86	13	1
By Age			
18–29 Years	72	27	1
30–49 Years	83	16	1
50–64 Years	79	20	1
65 Years and Over	84	15	1
By Household Income			
$75,000 and Over	80	20	*
$50,000 and Over	79	21	*
$30,000–$49,999	87	13	*
$20,000–$29,999	74	24	2
Under $20,000	78	21	1
By Politics			
Republicans	88	12	*
Democrats	79	21	*
Independents	75	23	2
By Political Ideology			
Conservative	87	13	*
Moderate	81	19	*
Liberal	67	32	1

*Less than 1%

If the person had used drugs in the past?

Yes, need to know	56%
Not necessary	42
No opinion	2

	Yes, need to know	*Not necessary*	*No opinion*
By Sex			
Male	57%	40%	3%
Female	55	44	1

By Ethnic Background			
White	56	42	2
Nonwhite	55	43	2
Black	61	36	3
By Education			
Postgraduate	52	48	*
College Graduate	52	46	2
College Incomplete	54	44	2
No College	59	39	2
By Region			
East	53	46	1
Midwest	56	43	1
South	57	39	4
West	55	43	2
By Age			
18–29 Years	46	53	1
30–49 Years	54	44	2
50–64 Years	64	33	3
65 Years and Over	62	37	1
By Household Income			
$75,000 and Over	52	46	2
$50,000 and Over	54	45	1
$30,000–$49,999	61	39	*
$20,000–$29,999	41	53	6
Under $20,000	63	36	1
By Politics			
Republicans	70	29	1
Democrats	47	49	4
Independents	53	45	2
By Political Ideology			
Conservative	71	27	2
Moderate	52	47	1
Liberal	37	61	2

*Less than 1%

If the person were a homosexual?

Yes, need to know	44%
Not necessary	54
No opinion	2

	Yes, need to know	Not necessary	No opinion
By Sex			
Male	46%	52%	2%
Female	42	57	1

By Ethnic Background			
White	44	54	2
Nonwhite	44	56	*
Black	44	56	*
By Education			
Postgraduate	29	70	1
College Graduate	42	57	1
College Incomplete	42	56	2
No College	50	49	1
By Region			
East	36	62	2
Midwest	41	57	2
South	50	48	2
West	48	51	1
By Age			
18–29 Years	31	68	1
30–49 Years	41	58	1
50–64 Years	56	43	1
65 Years and Over	54	39	7
By Household Income			
$75,000 and Over	42	57	1
$50,000 and Over	41	58	1
$30,000–$49,999	52	48	*
$20,000–$29,999	35	64	1
Under $20,000	47	48	5
By Politics			
Republicans	61	37	2
Democrats	36	63	1
Independents	40	58	2
By Political Ideology			
Conservative	60	39	1
Moderate	40	59	1
Liberal	25	72	3

*Less than 1%

If the person has had extramarital affairs?

Yes, need to know	33%
Not necessary	65
No opinion	2

	Yes, need to know	Not necessary	No opinion
By Sex			
Male	33%	66%	1%
Female	34	64	2

By Ethnic Background			
White	35	63	2
Nonwhite	24	76	*
Black	23	77	*

By Education			
Postgraduate	25	75	*
College Graduate	33	67	*
College Incomplete	33	65	2
No College	36	62	2

By Region			
East	23	76	1
Midwest	35	64	1
South	40	57	3
West	34	66	*

By Age			
18–29 Years	30	69	1
30–49 Years	32	67	1
50–64 Years	37	61	2
65 Years and Over	38	59	3

By Household Income			
$75,000 and Over	32	67	1
$50,000 and Over	32	67	1
$30,000–$49,999	36	64	*
$20,000–$29,999	26	71	3
Under $20,000	38	61	1

By Politics			
Republicans	55	43	2
Democrats	16	83	1
Independents	33	65	2

By Political Ideology			
Conservative	48	51	1
Moderate	29	70	1
Liberal	16	82	2

*Less than 1%

By Ethnic Background			
White	26	72	2
Nonwhite	26	73	1
Black	25	75	*

By Education			
Postgraduate	19	80	1
College Graduate	25	73	2
College Incomplete	23	76	1
No College	31	67	2

By Region			
East	23	75	2
Midwest	22	77	1
South	31	67	2
West	28	71	1

By Age			
18–29 Years	21	78	1
30–49 Years	24	75	1
50–64 Years	34	64	2
65 Years and Over	30	67	3

By Household Income			
$75,000 and Over	26	71	3
$50,000 and Over	26	73	1
$30,000–$49,999	27	73	*
$20,000–$29,999	20	78	2
Under $20,000	32	66	2

By Politics			
Republicans	40	58	2
Democrats	19	79	2
Independents	24	75	1

By Political Ideology			
Conservative	38	60	2
Moderate	23	76	1
Liberal	15	83	2

*Less than 1%

If the person had a child out of wedlock?

Yes, need to know	26%
Not necessary	72
No opinion	2

	Yes, need to know	Not necessary	No opinion
By Sex			
Male	29%	69%	2%
Female	24	75	1

Note: In the wake of the allegations that President Bill Clinton had sexual relations with former White House intern Monica Lewinsky, pundits have noted with surprise that his job approval rating has not suffered. Furthermore, the public seems unconcerned about what Clinton does in his personal life so long as he does a good job in leading the country.

A recent Gallup Poll suggests that perhaps one reason the public has not reacted more negatively to

the allegations is that most Americans think Clinton's personal behavior in this area is not much different from that of other presidents: 59% reply that other presidents have had extramarital affairs, while 75% think that Clinton's personal faults are no worse than those of most of his predecessors.

Such findings do not mean, however, that the public is not concerned about the moral values of their presidents. Americans do look for strong moral leadership, but they take a largely pragmatic view. While 61% think that a president must have strong moral values to be effective, only about one-half that number (31%) say that it is critical for him to have high moral values in his personal life. Another 55% find it important but not critical. When asked which characteristic is most important in rating how a president is handling his job, 55% say that it is how he manages the government, 22% cite his position on the issues, and just 16% say that it is moral values.

When respondents are asked what they need to know to evaluate a presidential candidate, 65% say that they do not need to know whether the candidate has had extramarital affairs, and 72% whether the candidate has had a child out of wedlock. They are more divided on whether they need to know if the candidate is a homosexual or not, but a slight majority (54%) says that information is not pertinent. Still, eight in ten do want to know whether a presidential candidate is an alcoholic or has a gambling problem or has a pattern of not paying debts, and 56% want to know if he has used drugs.

In recent years, President John F. Kennedy's sexual exploits have become almost common knowledge, but with little effect on his high standing among the general public. In 1990, 84% approved of his performance in office, while today 77% approve. Most people (85%) believe that Kennedy did have extramarital affairs while in office; but among this group, his approval rating is still 75%.

MARCH 13
PUERTO RICO

Interviewing Dates: 3/6–9/98
CNN/*USA Today*/Gallup Poll
Survey #GO 121850

As you may know, the people of Puerto Rico may have an opportunity later this year to vote on the status of Puerto Rico. Do you personally think Puerto Rico should become a completely independent nation, should remain a territory of the United States, or should be admitted to the United States as the fifty-first state?

Become independent	28%
Remain U.S. territory	26
Admitted as state	30
None; other (volunteered)	5
No opinion	11

	Become inde-pendent	Remain U.S. territory	Admitted as state	None; other; no opinion
By Sex				
Male	27%	24%	35%	14%
Female	28	27	26	19
By Ethnic Background				
White	27	27	30	16
Nonwhite	32	22	35	11
Black	31	21	38	10
By Education				
Postgraduate	21	23	41	15
College Graduate	24	27	34	15
College Incomplete	27	27	33	13
No College	32	25	25	18
By Region				
East	32	23	29	16
Midwest	30	23	31	16
South	26	26	33	15
West	25	29	27	19
By Age				
18–29 Years	31	30	28	11
30–49 Years	24	26	37	13
50–64 Years	34	24	22	20
65 Years and Over	29	23	27	21
By Household Income				
$75,000 and Over	28	26	35	11

$50,000 and Over...... 28	29	29	14
$30,000– $49,999 24	27	35	14
$20,000– $29,999 31	23	34	12
Under $20,000 31	24	25	20

By Politics

Republicans..... 29	30	27	14
Democrats 27	26	32	15
Independents ... 28	21	31	20

By Political Ideology

Conservative ... 31	28	28	13
Moderate 29	27	31	13
Liberal............. 25	23	35	17

Note: As the issue heats up in Congress, public opinion in the United States splits three ways on the political future of Puerto Rico. According to a new Gallup Poll, 28% would like to see the Caribbean island become an independent nation, 30% prefer to admit it as the fifty-first state, and 26% prefer to maintain it as a U.S. commonwealth. The people of Puerto Rico may have an opportunity to choose among these three paths later this year, if a bill providing for a national referendum on the island passes the U.S. Congress.

The current distribution of public opinion about Puerto Rico's status is similar to what Gallup found in 1977, when it asked a similar question. At that time, 20% favored Puerto Rican independence, 24% favored U.S. statehood, and 33% favored continuing its status as a commonwealth. Support for admitting Puerto Rico as a state is related to respondents' level of education. Those with higher levels are most likely to favor making it the fifty-first state, although even among the most highly educated group, opinion is basically mixed.

There is little difference in opinion about Puerto Rico among Americans according to party affiliation, with 27% of Republicans and 32% of Democrats favoring statehood. Only minor differences are seen across various age groups or among those living in different regions of the country.

Despite the lack of a clear consensus for statehood versus independence, previous Gallup Polls have found that either decision would be acceptable. In a 1991 survey, two-thirds of Americans would support granting full independence to Puerto Rico if a majority of Puerto Ricans voted for it in a national referendum. At the same time, 60% would favor U.S. statehood if Puerto Ricans chose that route. The Puerto Rico Political Status Act passed the U.S. House by a 209-to-208 vote on March 4, 1998, and calls for a national plebiscite in Puerto Rico by the end of 1998. The bill is expected to be taken up by the Senate later this year.

MARCH 20
PRESIDENT CLINTON/ KATHLEEN WILLEY

Interviewing Date: 3/16/98*
CNN/*USA Today*/Gallup Poll
Survey #GO 122072

As you may know, a woman named Kathleen Willey was interviewed on the CBS program "60 Minutes" this Sunday [March 15] describing an incident in which she said President Clinton make an unwanted sexual advance toward her in the White House. Did you happen to see the actual interview with Kathleen Willey when it was shown on "60 Minutes" last night? [Those who replied "no" were asked: Did you see parts of the interview rebroadcast later on the news; did you not see any of the interview but you heard or read about it; or do you not know anything about the interview?]

Yes, saw actual interview...............................	26%
No, but saw rebroadcast	24
No, but heard or read about it........................	27
Do not know about interview	22
No opinion..	1

Asked of entire sample: Kathleen Willey has said that Bill Clinton made a sexual advance toward her in the White House, and Clinton says he did not. Whom do you tend to believe more—Kathleen Willey, or Bill Clinton?

*Polls conducted entirely in one evening are subject to additional error or bias not found in polls conducted over several days.

Willey 43%
Clinton 40
No opinion 17

	Willey	Clinton	No opinion
By Sex			
Male	46%	43%	11%
Female	39	38	23
By Age			
18–29 Years	41	41	18
30–49 Years	47	36	17
50 Years and Over	39	45	16
By Politics			
Republicans	73	17	10
Democrats	19	62	19
Independents	42	38	20
By "60 Minutes" Interview			
Saw Interview	46	41	13
Saw Rebroadcast	40	48	12
Heard About It	48	35	17
Do Not Know	36	37	27

How would you compare Kathleen Willey's charges against Bill Clinton to the charges made against him by other women—do you think Willey's charges are more serious than the others, or not?

Yes, more serious 22%
No 61
No opinion 17

	Yes, more serious	No	No opinion
By Sex			
Male	24%	61%	15%
Female	20	62	18
By Age			
18–29 Years	15	72	13
30–49 Years	25	57	18
50 Years and Over	22	60	18
By Politics			
Republicans	35	54	11
Democrats	14	70	16
Independents	19	59	22

By "60 Minutes" Interview			
Saw Interview	27	64	9
Saw Rebroadcast	25	67	8
Heard About It	20	61	19
Do Not Know	13	54	33

Do you think there is or is not enough cause right now for Congress to begin hearings into whether or not President Clinton should be impeached?

Yes, enough cause 24%
Not enough 71
No opinion 5

	Yes, enough cause	Not enough	No opinion
By Sex			
Male	24%	71%	5%
Female	24	71	5
By Age			
18–29 Years	27	69	4
30–49 Years	28	67	5
50 Years and Over	17	78	5
By Politics			
Republicans	51	44	5
Democrats	4	94	2
Independents	22	71	7
By "60 Minutes" Interview			
Saw Interview	27	71	2
Saw Rebroadcast	21	76	3
Heard About it	19	73	8
Do Not Know	28	66	6

Thinking about the sexual charges against President Clinton and all the related legal issues, which of the following statements do you agree with more—these are important matters that the press should continue to cover and investigate, or these matters are no big deal and the press should stop pursuing this story?

Continue to cover 44%
Stop pursuing 49

Other (volunteered) 4

No opinion 3

	Continue to cover	Stop pursuing	Other; no opinion
By Sex			
Male	45%	48%	7%
Female	43	52	5
By Age			
18–29 Years	41	54	5
30–49 Years	47	45	8
50 Years and Over	43	51	6
By Politics			
Republicans	70	21	9
Democrats	24	71	5
Independents	44	50	6
By "60 Minutes" Interview			
Saw Interview	47	49	4
Saw Rebroadcast	42	50	8
Heard About it	48	45	7
Do Not Know	37	55	8

Note: The public appears to be reacting no differently to Kathleen Willey's charges of sexual improprieties committed by Clinton than to previous allegations involving Paula Jones and Monica Lewinsky. Although respondents are divided between Clinton and Willey over the issue of who is telling the truth, approval of the president's job performance and personal feelings about him remain high and are essentially unchanged by Sunday night's "60 Minutes" interview [March 15] and the subsequent publicity.

One-fourth of those interviewed in a Gallup Poll conducted on Monday watched Willey on "60 Minutes." Many of the rest either saw parts of it rebroadcast later or heard or read about it. Despite this unusually widespread exposure, only 22% say that Willey's charges against Clinton are more serious than those made by other women. The rest say that they are the same in seriousness or else have no opinion. There is little difference in views between those who actually saw the broadcast live and those who did not.

The public's more-of-the-same reaction to Willey's charges may explain why Clinton's job approval rating—at 67% Monday night—was not immediately affected by the interview and remains

roughly in line with measurements taken in past weeks. The number of respondents who have a favorable opinion of Clinton (60%) is also within the same range as has been measured on five occasions since the middle of January. His favorability rating, in fact, is well over twice as high as the comparable ratings of the other major participants in the developments of the last eight weeks, including Willey, Lewinsky, Jones, and Special Prosecutor Kenneth Starr. (The percentage of those who are familiar enough with Willey to be able to give an opinion about her, however, is much lower than for the others.)

Willey's charges, as reported in depositions published last week as well as on her "60 Minutes" appearance, have set up a classic he-said, she-said scenario. Clinton has denied the assertions, and the public is divided over whom to believe. Forty-three percent believe Willey's account, while 40% believe Clinton's. There is little difference in these views between those who saw the live broadcast and those who did not. Furthermore, both genders are about evenly divided as to whether Clinton or Willey is telling the truth. This split is almost the same as the one between those who believe Clinton rather than Paula Jones. Simultaneously, the public is nearly evenly divided in response to a question that asks who would be believed if Monica Lewinsky at some point declares publicly that she had an affair with Clinton.

About one in four says that the accumulated evidence against Clinton is enough for Congress to begin hearings now into whether or not he should be impeached. This group includes about one-half of the Republicans interviewed in the sample. Meanwhile, the media continue to give the sexual allegations against the president high priority and extraordinary visibility. The public, however, is divided on the appropriateness of this type of coverage. Just under one-half (49%) says that the charges are "no big deal" and the press should stop pursuing the story, while 44% think that the press should continue to cover it.

MARCH 28
ECONOMIC CONDITIONS/PERSONAL FINANCES/BUSINESS CONDITIONS

Interviewing Dates: 3/20–22/98
CNN/*USA Today*/Gallup Poll
Survey #GO 122065

How would you rate economic conditions in this country today—excellent, good, only fair, or poor?

Excellent 20%
Good 46
Fair.. 27
Poor 7
No opinion.. *

*Less than 1%

	Excellent	Good	Fair	Poor*
By Sex				
Male	29%	44%	22%	5%
Female.............	12	48	31	9
By Ethnic Background				
White...............	21	47	25	7
Nonwhite.........	14	38	37	11
Black	14	38	35	13
By Education				
Postgraduate....	33	49	15	3
College				
Graduate......	25	54	17	4
College				
Incomplete ..	21	47	26	6
No College	15	42	33	10
By Region				
East..................	16	45	28	11
Midwest	27	50	20	3
South	18	46	29	7
West	19	43	29	9
By Age				
18–29 Years	10	39	38	13
30–49 Years	20	50	25	5
50–64 Years	25	47	23	5
65 Years				
and Over......	29	45	19	7
By Household Income				
$75,000				
and Over......	40	46	11	3
$50,000				
and Over......	33	51	13	3
$30,000–				
$49,999	16	53	28	3
$20,000–				
$29,999	23	37	33	7
Under				
$20,000	9	40	36	15
By Politics				
Republicans.....	21	46	28	5
Democrats	23	46	24	7
Independents ...	16	47	27	10
By Political Ideology				
Conservative ...	23	42	26	9
Moderate	19	50	25	6
Liberal.............	17	44	32	7

*"No opinion"—at less than 1%—is omitted.

Selected National Trend

	Excellent	Good	Fair	Poor*
1997				
Dec. 18–21	7%	41%	38%	12%
Nov. 6–9..........	10	48	33	9
Aug. 22–25**..	8	41	38	13
May 6–7	7	39	38	15
Jan. 31–				
Feb. 2	4	38	43	15
1996				
Oct. 26–29.......	5	42	39	13
Aug. 30–				
Sept. 1†	3	34	46	16
July 18–21.......	5	38	43	14
May 9–12........	3	27	50	19
April 9–10.......	1	26	52	20
March 15–17...	2	31	48	18
Jan. 5–7	1	28	47	23
1995				
Nov. 6–8..........	2	28	47	22
May 11–14	2	27	50	20
1994				
Dec. 16–18.......	2	25	52	21
Nov. 2–6..........	2	28	49	20
Oct. 22–25.......	1	25	52	21
July 15–17.......	1	26	52	21
April 22–24.....	1	23	49	26
Jan. 15–17.......	‡	22	54	24
1993				
Dec. 4–6..........	1	20	57	21
Nov. 2–4..........	1	16	50	33

Aug. 8–10........ ‡ 10 49 40
June 29–30...... 1 14 52 32
Feb. 12–14 ...... ‡ 14 46 39
1992
Dec. 18–20...... 2 16 34 47
Dec. 4–6 .... 1 14 41 43
Oct. 23–25....... ‡ 11 45 43
Sept. 11–15 ..... 1 10 37 51
Aug. 31–
   Sept. 2† 1 9 37 53
June 12–14† 1 11 47 41
April 9–12† 1 11 40 48
Jan. 3–6 .... ‡ 12 46 41

*"No opinion"—at 2% or less—is omitted.
**Asked of half sample
†Registered voters
‡Less than 1%

Right now, do you think that economic conditions in the country as a whole are getting better or getting worse?

Better	69%
Worse	21
Same (volunteered)	8
No opinion	2

	Better	Worse	Same	No opinion
By Sex				
Male	73%	17%	8%	2%
Female	64	24	9	3
By Ethnic Background				
White	69	21	8	2
Nonwhite	67	23	8	2
Black	67	26	5	2
By Education				
Postgraduate	70	13	14	3
College Graduate	74	22	4	*
College Incomplete	73	18	7	2
No College	63	25	9	3
By Region				
East	63	25	8	4
Midwest	73	17	9	1
South	71	19	8	2
West	67	23	7	3
By Age				
18–29 Years	72	22	5	1
30–49 Years	67	23	8	2
50–64 Years	71	19	8	2
65 Years and Over	66	17	14	3
By Household Income				
$75,000 and Over	77	12	9	2
$50,000 and Over	78	13	8	1
$30,000–$49,999	70	19	7	4
$20,000–$29,999	73	16	11	*
Under $20,000	57	33	8	2
By Politics				
Republicans	64	24	10	2
Democrats	74	16	6	4
Independents	67	22	9	2
By Political Ideology				
Conservative	63	24	10	3
Moderate	71	19	8	2
Liberal	74	19	5	2

*Less than 1%

Selected National Trend

	Better	Worse	Same	No opinion
1997				
Dec. 18–21	49%	39%	8%	4%
Nov. 6–9	51	37	9	3
May 6–7	50	40	7	3
Jan. 31–Feb. 2	46	39	12	3
1996				
Oct. 26–29	50	38	7	5
Aug. 30–Sept. 1*	52	37	8	3
July 18–21	43	46	9	2
May 9–12	39	49	9	3

1992

Aug. 31–			
Sept. 2* 29	59	10	2
Aug. 10–12*.... 24	65	10	1
June 12–14* 28	61	9	2
April 20–22* ... 40	45	13	2
March 20–22* .. 37	51	11	1
Jan. 31–			
Feb. 1* 22	70	7	1
Jan. 3–6 22	71	6	1
1991			
Dec. 5–8 19	69	9	3

*Registered voters

Economic Outlook
(Based on Combination of Previous Two Questions)

Rated Positive	59%
Rated Negative	18
Rated Mixed	21
Undesignated	2

Selected National Trend

	Positive	Negative	Mixed	Unde-signated
1997				
Dec. 18–21 ...... 36%	31%	28%	5%
Nov. 6–9.......... 46	28	23	3
May 6–7 38	36	23	3
Jan. 31–			
Feb. 2 33	40	24	3
1996			
Oct. 26–29....... 37	33	25	5
Aug. 30–			
Sept. 1 31	36	29	4
July 18–21....... 32	40	25	3
May 9–12 22	47	28	3
1992			
Aug. 31–			
Sept. 2 7	66	25	2
June 12–14 8	65	25	2

We are interested in how people's financial situation may have changed. Would you say that you are financially better off now than you were a year ago, or are you financially worse off now?

Better off...	55%
Worse off..	20
Same (volunteered)..	24
No opinion..	1

	Better off	Worse off	Same	No opinion
By Sex				
Male 58%	23%	19*	*
Female............. 52	25	22	1
By Ethnic Background				
White............... 53	26	20	1
Nonwhite......... 64	16	20	*
Black 70	10	20	*
By Education				
Postgraduate.... 60	27	12	1
College Graduate...... 67	22	11	*
College Incomplete .. 56	19	23	2
No College 49	28	23	*
By Region				
East................. 53	29	17	1
Midwest 58	22	20	*
South 54	23	22	1
West 55	23	21	1
By Age				
18–29 Years 68	11	19	2
30–49 Years 61	19	20	*
50–64 Years 48	24	27	1
65 Years and Over...... 29	54	16	1
By Household Income				
$75,000 and Over...... 69	20	11	*
$50,000 and Over...... 66	21	13	*
$30,000– $49,999 59	20	21	*
$20,000– $29,999 56	27	17	*
Under $20,000 44	26	28	2

By Politics

	Better off	Worse off	Same	No opinion
Republicans..... 54	26	18	2	
Democrats....... 57	24	18	1	
Independents ... 53	22	24	1	

By Political Ideology

Conservative ... 54	25	20	1	
Moderate 55	26	18	1	
Liberal............. 59	18	22	1	

*Less than 1%

Selected National Trend

	Better off	Worse off	Same	No opinion
1997				
June 26–29	44%	26%	29%	1%
May 6–7	45	38	25	2
1996				
March 8–10	49	29	21	1
1994				
Dec. 16–18	40	31	29	*
May 20–22	40	26	33	1
March 7–8	34	34	31	1
1993				
Dec. 4–6	36	31	33	*

*Less than 1%

Now, looking ahead, do you expect that at this time next year you will be financially better off than now, or worse off than now?

Better off..	71%
Worse off..	9
Same (volunteered).......................................	14
No opinion..	6

	Better off	Worse off	Same	No opinion
By Sex				
Male 74%	8%	12%	6%	
Female............. 67	10	17	6	

By Ethnic Background

White............... 69	9	16	6	
Nonwhite......... 83	5	8	4	
Black 85	2	9	4	

By Education

Postgraduate.... 71	9	15	5	
College Graduate...... 80	6	12	2	
College Incomplete .. 77	7	10	6	
No College 63	11	19	7	

By Region

East................. 69	9	17	5	
Midwest 67	11	17	5	
South 75	5	13	7	
West 70	12	11	7	

By Age

18–29 Years 88	6	4	2	
30–49 Years 81	6	10	3	
50–64 Years 61	13	18	8	
65 Years and Over...... 31	16	39	14	

By Household Income

$75,000 and Over...... 81	7	10	2	
$50,000 and Over...... 81	7	10	2	
$30,000–$49,999 76	6	13	5	
$20,000–$29,999 69	7	19	5	
Under $20,000 64	12	17	7	

By Politics

Republicans..... 67	10	18	5	
Democrats 70	7	16	7	
Independents ... 74	9	11	6	

By Political Ideology

Conservative ... 68	11	15	6	
Moderate 73	7	15	5	
Liberal............. 75	9	12	4	

Selected National Trend

	Better off	Worse off	Same	No opinion
1997				
June 26–29	59%	20%	17%	4%

May 6–7 60	20	17	3
1996			
March 8–10 66	11	16	7
1994			
Dec. 16–18 63	17	17	3
May 20–22 59	16	21	4
March 7–8 53	19	22	6
1993			
Dec. 4–6 56	18	22	4

How would you describe business conditions in your community—would you say they are very good, good, not too good, or bad?

Very good..	23%
Good..	54
Not too good..	16
Bad...	6
No opinion...	1

Selected National Trend

	Very good	Good	Not too good	Bad*
1997				
Aug. 22–25......	15%	50%	25%	9%
1996				
March 8–10	13	58	21	6
1991				
July 11–14.......	5	43	37	12
May 16–19	6	44	37	12
March 21–24 ...	5	39	37	18
1990				
July 19–22.......	10	47	30	11
1975				
Jan. 10–15	4	37	39	17
1971				
Feb. 19–22	5	39	37	12
1970				
July 31–				
Aug. 2..........	9	44	30	9
1964				
Nov. 20–25......	17	55	20	5
June 25–30	13	44	28	9
Feb. 28–				
March 5	11	44	31	9
1963				
April 4–9	10	45	31	10
1962				
Dec. 13–18	12	52	26	6
Oct. 19–24.......	10	45	30	8
Aug. 23–28......	10	47	30	7
July 26–31.......	8	45	32	8
June 28–				
July 3...........	14	47	28	6
1961				
Oct. 19–24.......	9	45	33	9

*"No opinion"—at 8% or less—is omitted.

Note: A new poll finds that Americans now hold a rosier view of the economy than at any point in Gallup surveys spanning the past four decades. The latest increases in public confidence about the economy represent a continuation of the gradual improvements that Gallup has recorded since Bill Clinton became president, but even in this context the latest jump in the measure of economic confidence is extraordinary.

Among the indicators updated in the new poll is a question about business conditions that was first asked before man walked on the moon or Bill Clinton graduated from high school. Other questions have trends dating back to the Carter presidency. All of the measures now pick up levels of public optimism that are the highest ever recorded on each question.

According to the new Gallup survey, two-thirds of respondents now rate the nation's economy in positive terms, as either excellent or good, while just 34% consider it only fair or poor. In terms of personal finances, seven in ten feel optimistic about their earnings next year, and an even higher number (75%) say that business conditions in their own communities are in good or very good shape.

At 66%, the number rating the economy as excellent or good is at a record high and is up significantly from even the most recent measure in December 1997. At that time, fewer than one-half (48%) used positive terms to describe the economy, while 50% gave it the lower marks. This economic measure has been asked consistently since 1992 and has shown a high degree of change in public perceptions. In President George Bush's last year in office, there was nearly universal agreement that the economy was in trouble. Positive ratings dropped to an all-time low of 10% in August 1992, while the negative ratings hit 90%. Opinion

has grown increasingly positive since Bush left office, but through most of 1997 the more negative assessments outweighed the positive. The current balance of opinion about the economy is nearly 2-to-1 positive. Public opinion about the direction taken by the economy is also exceptionally bright with 69% saying that it is getting better and only 21% saying worse. The positive outlook figure is up from 49% in December 1997, and from 19% in December 1991.

Respondents' judgments about their personal finances have also improved in the past year. More than one-half (55%) say that they are better off financially now than they were a year ago. Looking ahead, 71% expect to be better off next year than they are today. Both figures are about 10 points higher than Gallup recorded in June of last year and represent record high scores on a trend that dates back to 1976.

During the darkest economic days of the Carter administration, such as those in March 1980, only 30% felt that they were better off financially than the previous year, and only 36% were optimistic about the coming year. By the end of Ronald Reagan's second term, those figures had risen to 47% and 63%, respectively. Today, these same indicators are highly positive, at 55% and 71%.

According to Gallup's survey, 54% think that business conditions in their community are good and another 23% say very good. Just 16% rate their local economy as not too good and only 6% as bad. This measure was asked continuously from 1961 to 1975, and it was re-asked from 1990 through today. Throughout both time periods, those rating business conditions in their community as very good never exceeded 17%, and the highest figure ever viewing them as good or very good combined was 72%.

APRIL 3
PAULA JONES

Interviewing Date: 4/1/98*
CNN/*USA Today*/Gallup Poll
Survey #GO 122382

*Polls conducted entirely in one day are subject to additional error or bias not found in polls conducted over several days.

As you may know, a federal judge today dismissed Paula Jones's sexual harassment lawsuit against Bill Clinton, which means that there will be no trial in this case. Do you think the judge made the right decision or the wrong decision?

Right decision.. 63%
Wrong decision... 25
No opinion... 12

	Right decision	Wrong decision	No opinion
By Sex			
Male............................	63%	25%	12%
Female	63	26	11
By Age			
18–29 Years.................	58	30	12
30–49 Years.................	61	26	13
50 Years and Over........	67	23	10
By Politics			
Republicans	42	42	16
Democrats....................	84	9	7
Independents................	59	28	13

Still thinking about the Paula Jones case, do you think the decision to dismiss it was fair or unfair to Paula Jones?

Fair... 47%
Unfair... 37
Other (volunteered) 5
No opinion... 11

	Fair	Unfair	Other	No opinion
By Sex				
Male	44%	39%	6%	11%
Female.............	50	36	4	10
By Age				
18–29 Years	37	49	6	8
30–49 Years	47	39	5	9
50 Years and Over......	51	31	5	13

By Politics

Republicans..... 31	53	5	11
Democrats....... 66	19	5	10
Independents ... 41	43	5	11

Next, do you think the decision to dismiss the case was good for the country or bad for the country?

Good	63%
Bad	24
Other (volunteered)	8
No opinion	5

	Good	Bad	Other	No opinion
By Sex				
Male	63%	25%	10%	2%
Female.............	63	23	7	7
By Age				
18–29 Years	59	31	5	5
30–49 Years	61	25	10	4
50 Years and Over......	67	21	8	4
By Politics				
Republicans.....	48	37	11	4
Democrats.......	78	9	8	5
Independents ...	61	28	7	4

As you know, Paula Jones has claimed that Bill Clinton, while governor of Arkansas, made sexual advances toward her in a hotel room, which she declined. Do you think that some incident between Bill Clinton and Paula Jones probably did occur while he was governor of Arkansas, or probably did not occur?

Did occur	58%
Did not occur	23
No opinion	19

	Did occur	Did not occur	No opinion
By Sex			
Male............................	61%	22%	17%
Female	56	24	20

	Did occur	Did not occur	No opinion
By Age			
18–29 Years...............	60	24	16
30–49 Years...............	66	17	17
50 Years and Over......	50	28	22
By Politics			
Republicans	82	10	8
Democrats..................	40	34	26
Independents..............	58	21	21

Selected National Trend

	Did occur	Did not occur	No opinion
1998			
February 13–15...........	62%	29%	9%
January 16–18.............	58	29	13
1997			
May 30– June 1......................	72	19	9
1994			
May 20–22..................	53	38	9

Asked of those who replied that something probably did occur: Based on what you think probably happened, do you think the incident should be considered sexual harassment, or should not be considered sexual harassment?

Should	50%
Should not	43
No opinion	7

Selected National Trend

	Should	Should not	No opinion
1998			
February 13–15...........	49%	45%	6%
January 16–18.............	50	41	9
1997			
May 30– June 1......................	46	43	11
1994			
May 20–22..................	39	50	11

In your view, should the investigations into the sexual allegations involving Bill Clinton continue, or should they stop now?

Continue	31%
Stop now	67
No opinion	2

	Continue	*Stop now*	*No opinion*
By Sex			
Male............................ 34%	64%	2%
Female 28	70	2
By Age			
18–29 Years................ 36	64	*
30–49 Years................ 34	65	1
50 Years and Over...... 25	71	4
By Politics			
Republicans 53	42	5
Democrats................... 11	89	*
Independents............... 33	65	2

*Less than 1%

Note: Most Americans applaud the decision by U.S. District Judge Susan Webber Wright to dismiss the Jones sexual harassment lawsuit against President Bill Clinton, indicating their agreement by a margin of 63% to 25%. Also, two in three (67%) say that the investigations into sexual allegations against Clinton should stop, up from 61% a week and a half ago. These findings come from a special Gallup Poll conducted on Wednesday evening [April 1], after the judge's decision was announced earlier in the day.

The poll also shows that despite their support for ending the lawsuit, respondents are not strongly convinced that the decision was fair to Paula Jones, with 47% saying it was and 37% saying it was not. Still, 63% find the decision good for the country, while only 24% find it bad.

The public continues to believe that some incident between Clinton and Jones probably occurred, but only about three in ten think that sexual harassment was involved—about the same number who have expressed that view for the past year. When the lawsuit was first filed in 1994, 21% thought that an incident involving sexual harassment probably occurred.

Although the Jones case involved allegations of sexual harassment, an issue that normally concerns women more than men, that is not the case here. An identical percentage of men and women approves of the judge's decision and thinks that it was good for the country. And women are 6 percentage points more likely than men to think that the decision was fair to Jones and to want to stop the investigations into sexual allegations involving Clinton—the opposite pattern of what might be expected.

This slightly greater support by women for Clinton's side of the issue is not so much a gender as a partisan difference, however. Women are 14 points more likely than men to be Democrats, while men are about 8 points more likely than women to be Republicans. And it is the partisan orientation that most strongly relates to people's response to the Jones lawsuit. Thus, Democrats agree most with the judge's decision, by 84% to 9%; independents also agree, but by a smaller margin of 59% to 28%; and Republicans show the least agreement, with 42% saying that it was the right decision but an equal number saying that it was wrong.

This partisan response to the judge's decision is found throughout the poll. Most Republicans say the decision was unfair to Jones, while most Democrats take the opposite point of view, and independents are about evenly divided. All three groups agree that the decision was good for the country, but Republicans are the least convinced (48% good, 37% bad). Independents say yes by a 2-to-1 margin, Democrats by a 9-to-1 margin. Of the three groups, only the Republicans express a moderate willingness to continue with the investigations, with 53% in favor and 42% opposed. However, both Democrats and independents say that the investigations should be stopped: Democrats by 89% to 11%, and independents by 65% to 33%.

APRIL 10
MICROSOFT CORPORATION

Interviewing Dates: 3/6–9/98
CNN/*USA Today*/Gallup Poll
Survey #GO 121850

As you may know, the Justice Department and Congress are conducting investigations into the business practices used by Microsoft to market and distribute its software. How

closely have you been following the news about these investigations—very closely, somewhat closely, not too closely, or not at all?

Very closely	8%
Somewhat closely	30
Not too closely	35
Not at all	25
No opinion	2

	Very closely	Somewhat closely	Not too closely	Not at all*
By Income				
$75,000 and Over	18%	46%	25%	11%
$50,000 and Over	13	42	33	12
$30,000– $49,999	7	31	42	20
$20,000– $29,999	5	30	32	32
Under $20,000	5	16	33	43

*"No opinion"—at 3% or less—is omitted.

Do you favor or oppose the Justice Department's efforts to force Microsoft to change the way it packages its Internet browser software?

Favor	33%
Oppose	39
No opinion	28

	Favor	Oppose	No opinion
By Income			
$75,000 and Over	41%	47%	12%
$50,000 and Over	38	42	20
$30,000–$49,999	36	42	22
$20,000–$29,999	32	39	29
Under $20,000	26	37	37

Thinking about Microsoft, the computer software company that produces Windows 95 and other products—do you have a favorable or unfavorable opinion of the Microsoft Corporation?

Favorable	58%
Unfavorable	13
Neutral; neither (volunteered)	15
Mixed (volunteered)	1
No opinion	11
Never heard of	2

	Favorable	Unfavor- able	Neutral; neither; mixed	No opinion
By Income				
$75,000 and Over	76%	12%	11%	1%
$50,00 and Over	70	14	13	3
$30,000– $49,999	63	15	14	8
$20,000– $29,999	58	9	22	11
Under $20,000	37	17	27	19

Which of the following statements do you agree with more—Microsoft uses illegal sales and business tactics to force people to buy its products and keep other products from being used, or Microsoft uses legally acceptable business tactics to sell and distribute its products?

Illegal tactics	16%
Legal tactics	57
Neither (volunteered)	7
No opinion	20

	Illegal tactics	Legal tactics	Neither	No opinion
By Income				
$75,000 and Over	16%	75%	2%	7%
$50,000 and Over	16	70	5	9
$30,000– $49,999	16	57	10	17
$20,000– $29,999	13	58	6	23
Under $20,000	19	42	7	32

Now thinking about Bill Gates, the founder and CEO of Microsoft—do you have a favorable or unfavorable opinion of Bill Gates?

Favorable 55%
Unfavorable 16
Neutral; neither (volunteered) 16
Mixed (volunteered) 1
No opinion 3
Never heard of 3

	Favorable	Unfavor- able	Neutral; neither; mixed	No opinion
By Income				
$75,000 and Over	70%	14%	15%	1%
$50,000 and Over	65	14	18	3
$30,000– $49,999	55	14	23	8
$20,000– $29,999	54	19	18	9
Under $20,000	41	20	23	16

Note: Americans have mixed reactions to the Justice Department's probe of charges that computer software giant Microsoft improperly forces buyers of its software products to use its Internet browser. While they do not think that Microsoft's actions are illegal, there is as much support for the Department's investigations as there is opposition, and no strong sentiment to drop the investigations. Overall, the public has very positive views of both Microsoft and its chairman, Bill Gates, and thinks that the company has had a net positive impact on the computer industry—views held by both the general public and by those who are computer and Internet users.

On balance, the public's opinion of Microsoft is very positive. Fifty-eight percent of those interviewed in a March Gallup Poll have a favorable view, while only 13% express an unfavorable one. The rest either have a neutral opinion or do not know enough about the company to rate it.

The survey indicates that 64% use a personal computer either at work or at home. These PC users, who are highly likely to be using Microsoft operating systems or software, have an even more positive opinion of Microsoft than that of the general population: 71% favorable to 15% unfavorable. A smaller segment, about 38%, reports regularly using the Internet either at home or at work. Among these Internet users, opinions about Microsoft are 75% favorable and 15% unfavorable.

Among respondents overall, opinions about Gates, the billionaire founder and CEO of Microsoft, mirror the attitudes toward his company, with 55% feeling favorably about him and 16% unfavorably. Among PC users and Internet users, Gates's image is even more positive, with about two-thirds expressing favorable views.

In testimony before Congress last month, critics of Microsoft often referred to the company as a monopoly. However, this sentiment does not pervade public attitudes, as only 43% agree that the term "monopoly" applies to Microsoft; 41% say that it does not. Internet users are somewhat more likely than the general public to say that Microsoft is a monopoly, by a margin of 55% to 41%. PC users, on the other hand, are about as divided as the public as a whole, saying that it is a monopoly by just 49% to 44%.

That Microsoft is viewed so positively despite the fact that a substantial portion of the U.S. population perceives it to be a monopoly suggests that the company's dominant position within the computer software industry may be seen as a plus by many people. In fact, 75% agree that Microsoft's impact on the computer industry has been more positive than negative, compared to only 8% who say more negative. Among both PC and Internet users, there is even more unanimity, with almost nine in ten members of both groups agreeing that the company's impact has been positive.

Survey respondents were asked about the Justice Department's efforts to force Microsoft to change the way it packages its Internet browser software. The reaction is mixed: 33% favor such actions, 39% oppose them, and 28% have no opinion. The reactions among PC and Internet users generally reflect this same division of opinion.

When assessing the specific allegations made by the Justice Department, the public tends to side with the software company. Only 16% believe that Microsoft has used illegal tactics to force people to buy its products and to keep other products

from being used, while 57% say that it has not. PC users and Internet users are even less likely to believe the allegations.

Few respondents are aware of the details in the dispute between Microsoft and the Justice Department: only 8% have been following news accounts of the probe very closely, with another 30% following somewhat closely. These groups, who presumably are most knowledgeable about the issues, are slightly more negative toward the Department's actions than those who know less about it. Only 39% of those who have been following the investigation very closely favor such government actions, while 57% oppose them. Those following the case somewhat closely have similar reactions, with a favor-to-oppose ratio of 39% to 52%. Still, despite these generally pro-Microsoft attitudes, the public is apparently in no hurry to see the Department's inquiry shut down, as it favors a continuation of the probe by 48% to 37%. Among those following the story closely, attitudes are somewhat more evenly divided.

APRIL 18
CONFIDENCE IN PRESIDENT CLINTON OR REPUBLICANS IN CONGRESS

Interviewing Dates: 3/20–22/98
CNN/*USA Today*/Gallup Poll
Survey #GO 122065

Whom do you have more confidence in— President Clinton or the Republicans in Congress—when it comes to handling the following issues:

Taxes?

Clinton	50%
Republicans	38
Both (volunteered)	2
Neither (volunteered)	4
No opinion	6

	Clinton	Repub- licans	Both; neither	No opinion
By Sex				
Male	48%	42%	6%	4%
Female	52	35	6	7

By Ethnic Background				
White	47	41	6	6
Nonwhite	71	24	2	3
Black	79	15	2	4
By Education				
Postgraduate	43	51	3	3
College Graduate	44	48	7	1
College Incomplete	45	44	7	4
No College	58	28	6	8
By Region				
East	54	34	7	5
Midwest	44	43	7	6
South	52	37	6	5
West	50	40	4	6
By Age				
18–29 Years	57	31	7	5
30–49 Years	46	43	5	6
50–64 Years	48	44	5	3
65 Years and Over	56	31	6	7
By Household Income				
$75,000 and Over	34	62	4	*
$50,000 and Over	43	52	3	2
$30,000– $49,999	46	42	6	6
$20,000– $29,999	54	32	10	4
Under $20,000	64	23	5	8
By Politics				
Republicans	20	71	5	4
Democrats	75	15	4	6
Independents	54	32	8	6
By Political Ideology				
Conservative	32	56	6	6
Moderate	53	35	6	6
Liberal	77	16	5	2

*Less than 1%

Selected National Trend

	Clinton	Republicans	Both; neither	No opinion
1997				
June 26–29	43%	40%	10%	7%
Jan. 31–				
Feb. 2	44	46	6	4
1996				
Nov. 21–24	42	44	9	5
April 9–10	44	41	9	6
March 15–17	43	45	8	4
1995				
Aug. 28–30	39	45	9	7
May 11–14	42	45	9	4
March 27–29	38	48	9	5
Feb. 24–26	37	50	8	5
1994				
Dec. 16–18	36	52	8	4
Dec. 2–5	33	55	8	4

Medicare?

Clinton	54%
Republicans	33
Both (volunteered)	2
Neither (volunteered)	4
No opinion	7

	Clinton	Republicans	Both; neither	No opinion
By Sex				
Male	52%	35%	6%	7%
Female	56	31	5	8
By Ethnic Background				
White	51	36	6	7
Nonwhite	75	15	5	5
Black	84	8	2	6
By Education				
Postgraduate	51	42	6	1
College Graduate	46	44	5	5
College Incomplete	51	35	6	8
No College	61	26	4	9
By Region				
East	60	27	4	9
Midwest	49	40	6	5
South	55	31	6	8
West	53	35	5	7
By Age				
18–29 Years	59	30	2	9
30–49 Years	52	35	7	6
50–64 Years	52	38	4	6
65 Years and Over	60	27	6	7
By Household Income				
$75,000 and Over	41	49	8	2
$50,000 and Over	46	44	7	3
$30,000–$49,999	53	35	5	7
$20,000–$29,999	56	31	5	8
Under $20,000	66	19	5	10
By Politics				
Republicans	24	67	5	4
Democrats	83	8	3	6
Independents	54	27	8	11
By Political Ideology				
Conservative	35	56	3	6
Moderate	63	24	6	7
Liberal	70	14	7	9

Selected National Trend

	Clinton	Republicans	Both; neither	No opinion
1997				
June 26–29	49%	35%	9%	7%
Jan. 31–				
Feb. 2	54	37	6	3
1996				
Nov. 21–24	53	34	8	5
1995				
Aug. 28–30	45	38	9	8
May 11–14	49	36	8	7

The federal budget?

Clinton	53%
Republicans	38

Both (volunteered).. 1
Neither (volunteered) 4
No opinion... 4

	Clinton	Repub- licans	Both; neither	No opinion
By Sex				
Male	50%	43%	4%	3%
Female.............	56	33	6	5
By Ethnic Background				
White...............	49	41	5	5
Nonwhite.........	75	19	3	3
Black	85	14	1	*
By Education				
Postgraduate....	44	44	10	2
College Graduate......	45	51	3	1
College Incomplete...	50	42	6	2
No College	60	29	4	7
By Region				
East..................	55	34	6	5
Midwest	50	41	6	3
South	55	35	5	5
West	50	42	4	4
By Age				
18–29 Years	59	32	2	7
30–49 Years	48	41	8	3
50–64 Years	54	43	2	1
65 Years and Over......	57	32	4	7
By Household Income				
$75,000 and Over......	38	52	10	*
$50,000 and Over......	43	49	7	1
$30,000– $49,999	51	39	6	4
$20,000– $29,999	57	34	4	5
Under $20,000	66	24	4	6

By Politics

	Clinton	Repub-	Both;	No op.
Republicans.....	19	75	2	4
Democrats	81	11	5	3
Independents ...	56	31	8	5

By Political Ideology

	Clinton			
Conservative ...	32	59	4	5
Moderate	59	31	6	4
Liberal.............	76	16	5	3

*Less than 1%

Selected National Trend
(Federal Budget Deficit)

	Clinton	Repub- licans	Both; neither	No opinion
1997				
June 26–29	40%	39%	14%	7%
Jan. 31– Feb. 2	41	47	9	3
1996				
Nov. 21–24......	42	42	11	5
April 9–10.......	42	2	10	6
March 15–17 ...	40	43	11	6
1995				
Aug. 28–30......	35	44	13	8
May 11–14	39	42	12	7
March 27–29 ...	37	49	10	4
Feb. 24–26	32	52	10	6
1994				
Dec. 16–18......	37	47	12	4
Dec. 2–5..........	34	50	10	6
1993				
Aug. 8–10........	48	36	11	5

Education?

Clinton.. 59%
Republicans 31
Both (volunteered)... 2
Neither (volunteered) 4
No opinion.. 4

	Clinton	Repub- licans	Both; neither	No opinion
By Sex				
Male	56%	34%	6%	4%
Female.............	62	28	6	4

By Ethnic Background

White............... 56	33	6	5
Nonwhite......... 79	17	3	1
Black 88	11	1	*

By Education

Postgraduate.... 53	37	9	1
College			
Graduate..... 53	39	5	3
College			
Incomplete... 58	32	7	3
No College 64	25	5	6

By Region

East................. 63	26	4	7
Midwest 58	32	7	3
South 60	31	6	3
West 55	34	6	5

By Age

18–29 Years 69	24	2	5
30–49 Years 56	32	9	3
50–64 Years 54	40	3	3
65 Years			
and Over...... 59	27	6	8

By Household Income

$75,000			
and Over...... 47	45	8	*
$50,000			
and Over...... 52	39	8	1
$30,000–			
$49,999 58	32	5	5
$20,000–			
$29,999 63	26	7	4
Under			
$20,000 68	22	5	5

By Politics

Republicans..... 29	61	7	3
Democrats 82	8	4	6
Independents ... 64	25	7	4

By Political Ideology

Conservative ... 38	53	5	4
Moderate 68	22	6	4
Liberal............. 79	12	6	3

*Less than 1%

Selected National Trend

	Clinton	Repub- licans	Both; neither	No opinion
1997				
Jan. 31–				
Feb. 2 .... 57%		35	6%	2%
1996				
April 9–10....... 56		32	6	6

Note: After Bill Clinton announced in his State of the Union address last January that the federal budget would be balanced, the public mood became more positive, with higher approval ratings for both the president and Congress. But according to the latest Gallup Poll, in situations where he and the Republicans in Congress may disagree with each other over the budget, the public has become decidedly more likely to place its confidence in Clinton rather than in Congress.

Last June, respondents were evenly divided over which party could do a better job of dealing with the budget: 40% had more confidence in the president, while 39% had more confidence in the Republicans. But today, the public expresses more confidence in the president by a margin of 53% to 38%, a net swing of 13 percentage points.

This increase in support for Clinton suggests that people give him more credit for achieving a balanced budget than they give Congress. Some evidence for this idea is provided by a Gallup Poll conducted in early January, before the State of the Union speech, when 63% said that Clinton deserved substantial credit for having cut the deficit and 54% named Congress. Although some people think that both the president and Congress deserve credit, more cite Clinton than Congress.

The public's increased confidence in Clinton on the budget issue comes disproportionately from young citizens and from those who consider themselves politically independent. Last June, by a margin of 43% to 39%, people under age 30 expressed more confidence in the Republicans in Congress than in the president, while today they express more confidence in Clinton by 59% to 32%, a net swing of 31 points. The other age groups show net swings of just 11 to 15 points. Among self-declared partisan groups, independents show the largest swing in support for Clinton. Last June, they expressed more confidence in the Republicans by 41% to 32%, but

now they express more confidence in Clinton by 56% to 31%, a net swing of 34 points. Republicans show a net swing toward Clinton of just 5 points, and Democrats of 12 points.

There has also been an increase in support for Clinton on taxes, an issue that typically has favored Republicans. When the GOP first won majority control of the House in 1994, respondents expressed more confidence in the ability of congressional Republicans to handle this issue than the president, by a margin of 55% to 33%. During the 1996 election campaign, however, they were about evenly divided; and last June they tilted slightly toward Clinton by 43% to 40%. In the latest poll, they express more confidence in Clinton than in Congress by a margin of 50% to 38%. On two other issues, Medicare and education, there has been little change in the public's relative level of confidence. The public has typically expressed more confidence in Clinton than in Congress on these issues, and the latest poll reaffirms that advantage.

APRIL 25
CONGRESSIONAL ELECTIONS

Interviewing Dates: 4/17–19/98
CNN/*USA Today*/Gallup Poll
Survey #GO 122406

If the elections for Congress were being held today, which party's candidate would you vote for in your congressional district—the Democratic party's candidate, or the Republican party's candidate? [Those who were undecided were asked: As of today, do you lean more toward the Democratic party's candidate, or toward the Republican party's candidate?]

	Total	Registered voters
Democratic candidate	46%	46%
Republican candidate	44	45
Other (volunteered); no opinion	10	9

Based on Total Sample

	Democratic candidate	Republican candidate	Other; no opinion
By Sex			
Male	44%	47%	9%
Female	47	41	12

By Ethnic Background

	Democratic candidate	Republican candidate	Other; no opinion
White	40	49	11
Nonwhite	76	13	11
Black	80	11	9

By Education

Postgraduate	46	48	6
College Graduate	45	48	7
College Incomplete	46	46	8
No College	45	41	14

By Region

East	51	40	9
Midwest	38	51	11
South	41	47	12
West	55	33	12

By Age

18–29 Years	48	42	10
30–49 Years	47	44	9
50–64 Years	43	44	13
65 Years and Over	42	45	13

By Household Income

$75,000 and Over	32	62	6
$50,000 and Over	41	50	9
$30,000–$49,999	50	41	9
$20,000–$29,999	45	50	5
Under $20,000	52	34	14

By Politics

Republicans	10	90	*
Democrats	90	6	4
Independents	38	36	26

By Political Ideology

Conservative	25	69	6
Moderate	49	36	5
Liberal	75	16	9

*Less than 1%

Selected National Trend

	Democratic candidate	Republican candidate	Other; no opinion
1998			
January 16–18*	51%	40%	9%
1997			
November 6–9*	49	42	9

October 27–29* 46	46	8
August 22–25* 51	41	8
July 25–27* 48	43	9
1996		
November 3–4** 47	48	5
November 3–4* 49	44	7
August 30–		
September 1* 51	41	8
June 18–19* 50	43	7
January 5–7* 44	48	8
1995		
November 2–6* 46	46	8

*Registered voters
**Likely voters

Note: A new Gallup survey provides good news for the Republican party with respect to this year's congressional races, finding Republican candidates leading the Democrats for the first time since last fall. If the current numbers were to be sustained until Election Day, Republicans would easily retain control of the House of Representatives.

When asked which party's candidate they support in their congressional district this year, regular midterm election voters—people who say that they are currently registered and who voted in 1994—favor the Republicans over the Democrats by a margin of 46% to 45%. This Republican electoral advantage is even greater when looking at the race among a smaller group of survey respondents who appear most likely to go to the polls in November. Among this likely voter group, Republicans lead by 7 points (50% to 43%).

While the current test election numbers are promising for the Republicans, it should be noted that the GOP does not enjoy the solid public preference on issues that it did when it won an upset victory at the polls four years ago. In 1994 the Republicans won a majority of seats in Congress at a time when there was considerable voter dissatisfaction with President Bill Clinton and the Democratic party. At the same time, Republicans seemed successfully to present themselves as better in dealing with economic matters. This year the Republicans' strength appears to be rooted in a different dynamic: the public's general satisfaction with incumbent officeholders regardless of party. Because Republicans now outnumber Democrats in

Congress, they are poised to benefit most from the voters' satisfaction with the status quo.

The year is clearly emerging as a good one for incumbents. Gallup Polls in recent months have recorded high levels of public confidence in the economy as well as strong optimism about personal finances. Overall, well over one-half now say that they are satisfied with the way things are going. Furthermore, respondents seem happy with both parties, giving record high ratings to President Clinton and Congress since the beginning of 1998. According to the latest Gallup survey, 63% approve of the job that Clinton is doing. At the same time, 58% believe that Congress under Republican leadership since 1994 has been a success. And for the first time in two decades, more Americans approve, rather than disapprove, of the job that Congress is doing.

An even more direct measure of public satisfaction can be found in the high percentage (64%) of those who say that the U.S. representative in their district deserves to be reelected. A majority (56%) also says that most members of Congress deserve another term—something that has not happened previously on this trend, which dates back to 1991. These results are in sharp contrast to 1994, when Clinton's popularity was in the low 40s and incumbency was viewed by voters with suspicion. At that time, when the Democrats had majority control of Congress, barely one-half (53%) said that their member of Congress deserved to be reelected, and only 39% said that most members deserved another term.

Historically, Gallup Polls show that midterm voters are much more Republican than is the public at large. This slant can occur because voter turnout in midterms is relatively low, as in 1994, when fewer than 40% of eligible voters showed up at the polls. Therefore, as the election draws closer, it becomes increasingly useful to isolate the core group of respondents most reflective of the voters likely to turn out in midterm elections.

One subgroup that Gallup looks at is regular midterm voters—those who are registered to vote and who participated in the 1994 election. Among this group, 48% now say that they would vote for the Republican candidate in their district, while 45% would vote for the Democratic candidate. This result is in contrast to the race among all national

adults surveyed, among whom the Democrats lead narrowly by 46% to 44%. However, when restricting the test congressional election results even further to those respondents who currently appear highly likely to vote, the Republican advantage expands from a 3-point lead over the Democrats to a 7-point lead (50% to 43%).

With over six months to go before the election, and with many political controversies in Washington unresolved, current predictions about the outcome of the congressional elections are highly subject to change. However, a statistical model based on test election data that allowed Gallup to predict actual House seat changes in 1994 and 1996 suggests that if the election were truly being held today, Republicans would win 235 seats to the Democrats' 200, representing a slight increase in the number of seats held by Republicans.

MAY 1
MOST IMPORTANT PROBLEM

Interviewing Dates: 4/17–19/98
CNN/*USA Today*/Gallup Poll
Survey #GO 122406

What do you think is the most important problem facing this country today? *

Economic problems

Economy in general	6%
Taxes	6
Federal budget deficit	5
Unemployment; jobs	5
Trade relations; trade deficit	1
High cost of living; inflation	1
Recession	**
Other	3

Noneconomic problems

Crime; violence	20
Ethics; moral decline; family decline	16
Education	13
Drugs; drug abuse	12
Poverty; homelessness	10
Welfare	8
Dissatisfaction with government, Clinton, Republicans	8

Medicare; Social Security	8
Health care	6
Youth; teen pregnancy	6
International issues; foreign affairs	4
Racism; race relations	2
Immigration; illegal aliens	2
Environment	2
Foreign aid; focus overseas	2
AIDS	1
Abortion	1
Guns; gun control	1
Military downsizing	1
Media; television	1
Other	9

*Total adds to more than 100% due to multiple replies. Respondents may name up to three problems.
**Less than 1%

Selected National Trend

	Dec. 18–21, 1997	Aug. 22–25, 1997	Jan. 10–13, 1997
Economic problems			
Economy in general	8%	6%	9%
Taxes	6	4	4
Federal budget deficit	5	5	8
Unemployment; jobs	8	12	12
Trade relations; trade deficit	2	*	1
High cost of living; inflation	1	1	2
Recession	*	–	*
Other	4	6	4
Noneconomic problems			
Crime; violence	16	20	23
Ethics; moral decline; family decline	11	13	9
Education	12	11	10
Drugs; drug abuse	12	15	17
Poverty; homelessness	14	8	10
Welfare	6	8	8
Dissatisfaction with government, Clinton, Republicans	6	9	7

Medicare;			
Social Security........	4	4	6
Health care..................	7	6	7
Youth; teen			
pregnancy	2	4	–
International issues;			
foreign affairs	10	2	3
Racism; race			
relations	5	3	4
Immigration;			
illegal aliens............	4	3	2
Environment	3	2	1
Foreign aid;			
focus overseas.........	3	1	1
AIDS...........................	1	1	1
Abortion......................	–	1	1
Guns; gun control	–	1	–
Military downsizing ...	–	–	–
Media; television	–	–	–
Other...........................	12	11	14

*Less than 1%

Note: Americans today continue to have no over-arching, shared national concern that dominates their thinking, unlike the situation at other points in time since the end of World War II. A new Gallup Poll asking the public to name the most important problem facing this country finds that respondents' answers are scattered across a variety of social and economic issues, without much concentration on any specific one. There is relatively little concern about economic issues, and virtually no mention of issues relating to the threat of war. Additionally, despite the extensive publicity given to the crises besetting the White House over the past three months, very few name these issues as our nation's most pressing concerns. All of these findings are consistent with recent Gallup Poll results that show respondents in a particularly positive frame of mind about the direction that the country is taking across economic and political dimensions.

The most frequent response to Gallup's most-important-problem question is crime and violence, mentioned by 20%. (Each respondent was allowed to name up to three problems.) Even though this is the top vote getter in the current poll, the number who mention crime is low compared to other recent surveys. In 1994, for example, about one-half men-tioned crime and violence as the most important problem facing the country. The next four men-tioned are: ethics, morality, and a decline in family values (16%), education (13%), drugs and drug abuse (12%), and poverty and homelessness (10%). Grouped behind at 8% are welfare, dissatisfaction with the government and/or President Bill Clinton, and Medicare and Social Security concerns.

All together, about 25% mention some form of economic issue as the nation's top problem, in-cluding such loosely related issues as trade rela-tions, taxes, the federal budget deficit, and more direct concerns with the economy in general and unemployment. Here again, the historical record shows a low number. As recently as 1991 through 1993, two-thirds or more of the public named some type of economic concern, including 27% who in 1992 specifically mentioned unemploy-ment. And during most of the 1970s, inflation was consistently cited as the nation's number-one problem, at some points mentioned by 70% to 80% of the public.

Worry about foreign policy, international rela-tions, or war is almost totally missing from the forefront of concerns today—in sharp contrast to many other periods since World War II when for-eign policy issues dominated the public's responses to this question. In the early 1950s the Korean War was the nation's top problem. The threat of war, nuclear proliferation, and communism dominated in the mid- to late 1950s and into the 1960s. The Vietnam War moved ahead in 1965 and remained a dominant problem well into the early 1970s. War and peace issues also were highly likely to be top-of-mind through the mid-Reagan years of the 1980s and again in 1990 and 1991, at the time of the Gulf War tensions. Today, in an environment in which communism as a threat has essentially evaporated, only 4% mention international issues or foreign af-fairs as the most important problem.

MAY 9
"SEINFELD"

Interviewing Dates: 4/17–19/98
CNN/*USA Today*/Gallup Poll
Survey #GO 122406

What do you think is the funniest show on television today?

"Seinfeld" 20%
"Home Improvement" 7
"Frasier" 5
"The Cosby Show" 4
"Friends" 4
"America's Funniest Home Videos" 3
"The Drew Carey Show" 3
"South Park" 3
"Ally McBeal" 2
"The Simpsons" 2
"3rd Rock From the Sun" 1
"Kids Say the Darndest Things" 1
"Mad About You" 1
"Family Matters" 1
"King of the Hill" 1
Other 20
None 4
No opinion 18

By Age

	18–29 years	30–49 years	50–64 years	65 years and over
"Seinfeld"	30%	23%	15%	9%
"Home Improvement"	5	8	7	4
"Frasier"	2	7	7	2
"The Cosby Show"	1	1	5	12
"Friends"	7	4	2	–
"America's Funniest Home Videos"	1	4	4	2
"The Drew Carey Show"	2	5	2	1
"South Park"	8	2	–	–
"Ally McBeal"	1	3	3	–
"The Simpsons"	5	3	1	–
"3rd Rock From the Sun"	3	2	–	1
"Kids Say the Darndest Things"	1	–	2	4
"Mad About You"	1	1	1	1
"Family Matters"	1	1	1	–
"King of the Hill"	–	1	–	–
Other	22	20	19	18
None	1	3	7	9
No opinion	9	12	24	37

Do you plan to watch the last episode of "Seinfeld" when it airs on Thursday, May 14?

Yes 44%
No 50
No opinion 6

By Age

	Yes	No	No opinion
18–29 Years	63%	34%	3%
30–49 Years	48	47	5
50–64 Years	31	62	7
65 Years and Over	25	67	8

Which of the following phrases best describes you—you are a big "Seinfeld" fan; you are somewhat of a "Seinfeld" fan; or you are not a "Seinfeld" fan?

Big fan 15%
Somewhat of a fan 34
Not a fan 49
No opinion 2

By Age

	Big fan	Somewhat of a fan	Not a fan	No opinion
18–29 Years	24%	40%	35%	1%
30–49 Years	16	43	41	*
50–64 Years	11	23	62	4
65 Years and Over	6	15	72	7

*Less than 1%

Asked of "Seinfeld" fans: Which one of the main characters on "Seinfeld" would you say is your favorite—Jerry, George, Kramer, or Elaine?

Kramer	58%
Elaine	15
Jerry	12
George	12
Other (volunteered)	1
No opinion	2

	Kramer	Elaine	Jerry	George*
By Age				
18–29 Years	64%	15%	8%	10%
30–49 Years	58	15	14	10
50–64 Years	48	18	13	17
65 Years and Over	50	11	15	15

*"Other" and "no opinion"—at 9% or less—are omitted.

Also asked of "Seinfeld" fans: For the next question, assume that the "Seinfeld" characters were real people. Aside from how funny you think they are, would you generally consider them to be likeable people or annoying people?

Likeable	54%
Annoying	39
Both; mixed (volunteered)	6
Neither; other (volunteered)	*
No opinion	1

*Less than 1%

	Likeable	annoying	Both; mixed; neither; other	No opinion
By Age				
18–29 Years	53%	43%	4%	–
30–49 Years	53	39	7	1
50–64 Years	55	38	6	1
65 Years and Over	66	20	5	9

Also asked of "Seinfeld" fans: Which one of the following TV shows would you most like to see replace "Seinfeld" in its time slot on Thursday nights—"Frasier," "Just Shoot Me," "Mad About You," or "3rd Rock From the Sun"?

"Frasier"	35%
"Mad About You"	29
"3rd Rock From the Sun"	16
"Just Shoot Me"	10
None (volunteered)	4
Other (volunteered)	2
No opinion	4

	"Frasier"	"Mad About You"	"3rd Rock"	"Just Shoot Me"*
By Age				
18–29 Years	29%	33%	14%	16%
30–49 Years	3	30	17	9
50–64 Years	38	27	21	3
65 Years and Over	49	19	10	8

*"None," "other," and "no opinion"—at 14% or less—are omitted.

Note: With the final episode of "Seinfeld" less than a week away, the highly rated situation comedy is poised to go out with the proverbial bang. According to the latest Gallup Poll, 44% expect to watch that episode next week, with another 6% who are not sure. The survey also shows that about one-half of respondents think of themselves as "Seinfeld" fans.

Long rated one of television's most watched shows, the comedy easily wins the public's rating as the funniest show on television today. Almost three times as many people mention "Seinfeld" as any other comedy currently on television.

Cosmo Kramer emerges as the undisputed favorite among the four leading characters. More than one-half of the show's fans (58%) cite the klutzy eccentric as their favorite, compared with 15% who choose Elaine, and 12% each who choose Jerry and George. Although the real-life Jerry Seinfeld described the four characters to *TV Guide* by saying "there's nothing really likeable about them except that they remind you of yourself," fans apparently disagree. When asked to assume that the characters were real and then to indicate whether they were mostly likeable or annoying, fans select the "likeable" characterization by 54% to 39%.

Men and women are equally attracted to "Seinfeld," but among the show's fans these two

groups express distinctly different preferences for the characters. As the one female among the major players, Elaine appeals much more strongly to women than to men: three times more women than men choose her as their favorite. George, on the other hand, appeals more to men than to women, with twice as many men as women choosing him as their favorite character. While Kramer is the favorite of both sexes, his popularity is clearly stronger among men than women. Jerry, on the other hand, is the sole character to find greater appeal among fans of the sex opposite to his own.

The fans of "Seinfeld" tend to come disproportionately from younger rather than from older people. Among people under 30, almost two in three are fans, compared to 59% in the 30-to-49 age group, 34% among the 50-to-64 age group, and only 21% among those 65 or older. Although Kramer is the most popular character among all age groups, fans under 50 are somewhat more likely to name him than those who are older. Six in ten younger fans choose him as their favorite, compared with one-half of the older viewers.

Given a choice of four NBC shows as possible replacements for "Seinfeld" in the 9 P.M. Thursday time slot, the top preference of "Seinfeld" fans is "Frasier," chosen by 35%. "Mad About You" comes in second with 29% of the vote, followed by "3rd Rock From The Sun" (16%) and "Just Shoot Me" (10%).

MAY 15
PRESIDENTIAL NOMINEES
FOR THE YEAR 2000

Interviewing Dates: 5/8–10/98
CNN/USA Today/Gallup Poll
Survey #GO 122847

Asked of Republicans and those leaning Republican: I'm going to read a list of people who may be running in the Republican primary for president in the next election. As I read each name, please tell me if you have a favorable or unfavorable opinion of this person or if you have never heard of him or her:

Former Tennessee Governor Lamar Alexander?

Favorable	23%
Unfavorable	19
No opinion	23
Never heard of	35

Missouri Senator John Ashcroft?

Favorable	16%
Unfavorable	7
No opinion	24
Never heard of	53

Family Research Council Chairman Gary Bauer?

Favorable	13%
Unfavorable	5
No opinion	20
Never heard of	62

Political commentator Pat Buchanan?

Favorable	33%
Unfavorable	47
No opinion	17
Never heard of	3

Texas Governor George W. Bush?

Favorable	75%
Unfavorable	10
No opinion	11
Never heard of	4

Red Cross Chairwoman Elizabeth Dole?

Favorable	68%
Unfavorable	15
No opinion	7
Never heard of	10

Businessman Steve Forbes?

Favorable	49%
Unfavorable	23
No opinion	17
Never heard of	11

House Speaker Newt Gingrich?

Favorable	47%
Unfavorable	43
No opinion	7
Never heard of	3

Ohio Congressman John Kasich?

Favorable	17%
Unfavorable	6
No opinion	17
Never heard of	60

Former Congressman Jack Kemp?

Favorable	56%
Unfavorable	22
No opinion	13
Never heard of	9

Arizona Senator John McCain?

Favorable	29%
Unfavorable	12
No opinion	16
Never heard of	43

Former Vice President Dan Quayle?

Favorable	50%
Unfavorable	42
No opinion	8
Never heard of	*

*Less than 1%

Also asked of Republicans and those leaning Republican: Now suppose that each of the people whose names I just mentioned were running for the Republican nomination for president in the year 2000. Which of those candidates would you be most likely to support? Who would be your second choice? And who would be your third choice?

	First mention	Total mentions
Lamar Alexander	2%	5%
John Ashcroft	*	3
Gary Bauer	1	2
Pat Buchanan	3	12
George W. Bush	30	53
Elizabeth Dole	14	38
Steve Forbes	7	22
Newt Gingrich	6	18
John Kasich	1	5
Jack Kemp	9	25

John McCain	4	9
Dan Quayle	9	23
None; wouldn't vote (volunteered)	2	2
Other (volunteered)	2	4
No opinion	10	10

*Less than 1%

Asked of Democrats and those leaning Democratic: I'm going to read a list of people who may be running in the Democratic primary for president in the next election. As I read each name, please tell me if you have a favorable or unfavorable opinion of this person, or if you have never heard of him:

Former New Jersey Senator Bill Bradley?

Favorable	36%
Unfavorable	12
No opinion	24
Never heard of	28

House Democratic leader Dick Gephardt?

Favorable	40%
Unfavorable	17
No opinion	20
Never heard of	23

Vice President Al Gore?

Favorable	73%
Unfavorable	20
No opinion	7
Never heard of	*

*Less than 1%

The Reverend Jesse Jackson?

Favorable	47%
Unfavorable	42
No opinion	10
Never heard of	1

Nebraska Senator Bob Kerrey?

Favorable	27%
Unfavorable	12
No opinion	19
Never heard of	42

Massachusetts Senator John Kerry?

Favorable 28%
Unfavorable 10
No opinion 23
Never heard of 39

Minnesota Senator Paul Wellstone?

Favorable 11%
Unfavorable 8
No opinion 15
Never heard of 66

Also asked of Democrats and those leaning Democratic: Now suppose that each of the people whose names I just mentioned were running for the Democratic nomination for president in the year 2000. Which of those candidates would you be most likely to support? And who would be your second choice?

	First mention	Total mentions
Bill Bradley	8%	16%
Dick Gephardt	7	17
Al Gore	51	65
Jesse Jackson	12	24
Bob Kerrey	3	12
John Kerry	2	9
Paul Wellstone	1	3
None; wouldn't vote (volunteered)	3	3
Other (volunteered)	1	1
No opinion	12	12

Note: Vice President Al Gore and Texas Governor George W. Bush continue to be the early favorites for the Democratic and Republican nominations for the year 2000 presidential election, even though history shows that the shape of the race can change radically before the primary season begins in earnest more than one and one-half years from now. A new Gallup Poll also shows that Gore and Bush would be running neck and neck if the general election were held today.

Gore and the Reverend Jesse Jackson are the only two Democrats tested in the May 8–10 survey who have near-universal name recognition among Democrats. Gore's image is strongly positive, with 73% of Democrats saying that they have a favorable opinion of the vice president. The more controversial Jackson has an image that splits roughly one-half favorable and one-half unfavorable. The other five potential Democratic candidates in the poll—former New Jersey Senator Bill Bradley, House Democratic leader Dick Gephardt, and Senators Bob Kerry, John Kerrey, and Paul Wellstone—all have much weaker name recognition, with 40% or more of Democrats having never heard of them or not knowing enough about them to have an opinion.

This name identification disparity helps explain why Gore wins so overwhelmingly when Democrats are asked to indicate their first choice for the Democratic nomination in 2000. He gets 51% of the votes of Democrats, compared to 12% for Jackson. Bradley and Gephardt receive 8% and 7%, respectively.

There are a number of well-known Republicans who are potential candidates in 2000, although several have strongly negative images. About eight in ten Republicans know enough about six GOP contenders to have an opinion of them: Governor Bush, former Vice President Dan Quayle, House Speaker Newt Gingrich, Elizabeth Dole, Pat Buchanan, and former vice presidential nominee Jack Kemp. Of these, three—Bush, Dole, and Kemp—have generally positive images, particularly Bush and Dole. The other three—Quayle, Gingrich, and Buchanan—have much more negative ones, particularly former presidential candidate and current political commentator Pat Buchanan, who is viewed unfavorably by 47% of Republicans, compared to just 33% who have a favorable opinion. Speaker Gingrich has a 47% favorable, 43% unfavorable image among Republicans, while Quayle's image is similarly split at 50% favorable, 42% unfavorable.

The other potential Republican candidates tested in the poll are less well known. Magazine publisher and 1996 candidate Steve Forbes is known by about 70% of Republicans (his image tilts favorable), but five other potential candidates—former Tennessee Governor Lamar Alexander, Missouri Senator John Ashcroft, Chairman of the Family Research Council Gary Bauer, Ohio Congressman John Kasich, and Arizona Senator John McCain—are known by less than one-half of the Republicans in the poll.

Alexander's low name recognition comes despite the fact that he was a well-publicized candidate in the 1996 campaign, and McCain's despite the fact that the Vietnam veteran has been one of the more visible senators in Washington over the last several years. Out of all of these possible candidates, Bush wins the Republican trial heat, with 30% of the vote, followed by Red Cross President Elizabeth Dole with 14%. Kemp and Quayle are next, with 9% each. Elizabeth Dole, however, essentially ties Bush among Republican women, a perhaps important finding given the degree to which Bill Clinton utilized his favorable standing among women to win the 1992 and 1996 elections. In a head-to-head match between Gore and Bush, Bush wins by a 50%-to-46% margin. If Gingrich were the Republican nominee, however, Gore would win overwhelmingly by a 62%-to-32% margin.

Handicapping the presidential field this far before an election often has little relationship to what eventually happens. In some years the front-runners are well established this far out, while in others the eventual winners of the nominations are not even sufficiently well known to be included in these types of trial heats. In 1994, two years before the 1996 election, Bob Dole had already become the front-runner for the Republican nomination in Gallup polling. In March 1990, on the other hand, Democrats had a hard time coming up with a favorite for the 1992 election. In an open-ended question, Clinton essentially did not show up at all; and when a list of possible candidates was prepared by Gallup, Clinton was not well-enough known to be included on the list. (Mario Cuomo, 1988 nominee Michael Dukakis, and Jesse Jackson were the top vote-getters at that point, but none of them was seriously in the race for the nomination by the time 1992 came around.)

Similarly, in 1986 the eventual 1988 Democratic nominee, Dukakis, was also not well enough known to be included in a Democratic trial heat. Gary Hart was the runaway leader at that time, followed by Cuomo, businessman Lee Iacocca, and Jackson. On the Republican side, however, then-Vice President George Bush was already established as the front-runner for his party's nomination.

In early 1982, Massachusetts Senator Edward Kennedy was leading former Vice President Walter Mondale and Ohio Senator John Glenn as the favorite among Democrats for the 1984 nomination. By late 1982, however, Mondale, the eventual nominee, had become the front-runner.

MAY 22
VIAGRA

Interviewing Dates: 5/8–10/98
CNN/*USA Today*/Gallup Poll
Survey #GO 122847

As you may know, Viagra is a new prescription drug which helps solve the problem experienced by men who are sexually impotent. In general, do you think that Viagra will prove to be a good thing or a bad thing for society as a whole?

Good thing	59%
Bad thing	23
Other (volunteered)	3
No opinion	15

	Good thing	Bad thing	Other	No opinion
By Sex				
Male	64%	20%	2%	14%
Female	54	25	4	17
By Age				
18–29 Years	59	28	3	10
30–49 Years	66	19	3	12
50–64 Years	57	21	3	19
65 Years and Over	42	28	4	26

Asked of men: Would you, personally, like to try Viagra at some point in the next year or so, or is that something you would not like to do?

Yes, would	13%
Would not	79
Already tried it (volunteered)	1
No opinion	7

	Would	Would not	Already tried it	No opinion
By Age				
18–29 Years....	5%	92%	1%	2%
30–49 Years....	9	86	*	5
50–64 Years....	20	73	*	7
65 Years and Over......	30	49	3	18

*Less than 1%

Asked of married women: Would you, personally, like your husband to try Viagra in the next year or so, or is that something you would not like him to do?

Yes, would.. 15%
Would not... 72
No opinion.. 13

	Would	Would not	No opinion
By Age			
18–29 Years................	–	90%	10%
30–49 Years................	14	76	10
50–64 Years................	28	55	17
65 Years and Over......	10	76	14

Asked of half sample: In your view, should the costs of Viagra be covered by health insurance plans, or should men who use Viagra have to pay for it on their own?

Covered by insurance 42%
Men have to pay 50
Other (volunteered) 4
No opinion.. 4

	Covered by insurance	Men have to pay	Other	No opinion
By Sex				
Male	64%	20%	2%	14%
Female.............	54	25	4	17
By Age				
18–29 Years....	59%	28%	3%	10%
30–49 Years....	66	19	3	12
50–64 Years....	57	21	3	19

65 Years and Over......	42	28	4	26

Asked of half sample: In your view, should the costs of Viagra be covered by Medicare, or should Medicare recipients who use Viagra have to pay for it on their own?

Covered by Medicare 36%
Recipients have to pay.................................... 55
It depends (volunteered)................................. 2
No opinion... 7

	Covered by medicare	Recipients have to pay	It depends	No opinion
By Sex				
Male	35%	58%	1%	6%
Female............	37	53	3	7
By Age				
18–29 Years....	31	62	1	6
30–49 Years....	39	54	1	6
50–64 Years....	35	57	3	5
65 Years and Over......	36	50	2	12

Note: Seemingly out of the blue, Viagra hit the headlines and drugstore shelves this month with a level of intensity rarely seen for prescription drugs. By the first week of May, two-thirds of Americans knew what the new impotency medication was all about. According to a recent Gallup Poll, 64% are familiar with the new drug. And more impressive, 13% of men (roughly one in every eight) already express an interest in taking Viagra sometime within the next year.

Viagra is not without potential risk and limitations. These include medical side effects for men and repercussions for women involved with men who take the prescription. Still, the majority (59%) thinks that Viagra will prove to be a good thing for society, presumably on the assumption that it will promote healthy sexual relationships for some couples. One in four thinks that its overall effect will be bad, while the rest are not sure.

From a medical point of view, the market for Viagra is clearly greatest among older men. The Gallup Poll confirms this in the latest public opin-

ion survey, finding 25% of all men ages 50 and older saying that they would like to try Viagra sometime in the next year or so. Interest drops sharply to a mere 8% among men under 50.

This generational pattern for the impotency pill is reflected among married women as well. Asked whether they would like their husbands to try Viagra in the next year, 21% of women ages 50 and older say that they would, compared to only 12% of those ages 18 to 49.

The Gallup Poll suggests that respondents think of Viagra more as a nonessential elective drug rather than as a medically necessary one. When asked who should pay for the prescription costs, reported to be about $10 per dose, only 42% say that a Viagra prescription should be covered by private health insurance. One-half say that men who use it should have to pay for it themselves.

Although older men are most likely to need the drug, there is even less public support for Medicare coverage of Viagra. Only 36% think that Medicare should cover the prescription costs of Viagra, while 55% say that Medicare recipients should have to pay for it on their own.

MAY 29
RACE RELATIONS

Interviewing Dates: 4/17–19/98
CNN/*USA Today*/Gallup Poll
Survey #GO 122406

How would you rate the state of race relations in the United States these days—very good, somewhat good, neither good nor bad, somewhat bad, or very bad?

Very good	4%
Somewhat good	33
Neither good nor bad	22
Somewhat bad	30
Very bad	9
No opinion	2

	Very, some- what good	Neither good nor bad	Some- what, very bad	No opinion
By Sex				
Male	38%	23%	36%	3%
Female	35	21	42	2
By Ethnic Background				
White	39	22	37	2
Nonwhite	27	19	52	2
Black	26	17	55	2
By Education				
Postgraduate	34	22	44	*
College Graduate	34	19	45	2
College Incomplete	34	26	39	1
No College	40	19	37	4
By Region				
East	38	21	38	3
Midwest	40	20	37	3
South	36	20	43	1
West	34	27	37	2
By Age				
18–29 Years	32	30	38	*
30–49 Years	33	21	45	1
50–64 Years	42	16	40	2
65 Years and Over	46	20	29	5
By Household Income				
$75,000 and Over	37	26	37	*
$50,000 and Over	36	24	40	*
$30,000– $49,999	35	18	45	2
$20,000– $29,999	34	22	43	1
Under $20,000	42	23	32	3
By Politics				
Republicans	44	23	31	2
Democrats	34	22	42	2
Independents	33	21	44	2
By Political Ideology				
Conservative	42	23	34	1
Moderate	36	22	40	2
Liberal	32	20	47	1

*Less than 1%

Do you think a major new race initiative is needed to improve race relations in this country, or not?

Yes 46%
No 51
No opinion 3

	Yes	No	No opinion
By Sex			
Male	42%	55%	3%
Female	49	47	4
By Ethnic Background			
White	43	54	3
Nonwhite	59	35	6
Black	68	27	5
By Education			
Postgraduate	41	58	1
College Graduate	42	57	1
College Incomplete	43	54	3
No College	50	45	5
By Region			
East	54	44	2
Midwest	43	53	4
South	49	47	4
West	33	62	5
By Age			
18–29 Years	52	47	1
30–49 Years	44	54	2
50–64 Years	43	54	3
65 Years and Over	45	46	9
By Household Income			
$75,000 and Over	35	64	1
$50,000 and Over	40	59	1
$30,000–$49,999	45	54	1
$20,000–$29,999	61	35	4
Under $20,000	48	47	5
By Politics			
Republicans	38	58	4
Democrats	55	41	4
Independents	43	54	3

By Political Ideology

Conservative	39	58	3
Moderate	46	50	4
Liberal	57	41	2

Note: When Bill Clinton launched what he termed a national dialogue on race relations in June of last year, he argued that a new initiative was needed to lessen racial tensions. An Advisory Board appointed by him has been spending the last eleven months holding town meetings as part of its effort to further that goal. But according to a recent Gallup Poll, the idea of the initiative itself divides the country along racial lines. By a margin of 54% to 43%, whites are inclined to say that such an initiative is not needed, while nonwhites say that it is, by a margin of 59% to 35%.

A major factor in whites' views about the race initiative is their assessment of the current state of race relations in the country. Whites are about evenly divided on this issue: 39% find race relations good, while 37% say that they are bad. Another 22% take a middle position, with race relations as neither good nor bad. Whites who take the most optimistic view oppose a new race initiative by 65% to 32%, while whites who say that race relations are bad support the initiative by 58% to 40%. Those who hold the middle view oppose it by 60% to 37%.

Feelings about the state of race relations in the country among nonwhites, however, have little impact on their views about a new race initiative. Their overall rating is more pessimistic, with 52% saying that the state of race relations is bad, and just 27% saying good. But even those with the most optimistic view express majority support for a new race initiative.

JUNE 6
BILINGUAL EDUCATION

Interviewing Dates: 5/8–10/98
CNN/*USA Today*/Gallup Poll
Survey #GO 122847

When there are a large number of non-English-speaking students in a public school, these students are usually taught using one of the

following two methods. Please tell me which one you prefer—immersion, which means teaching these students all of their subjects in English, while giving them intensive training in how to read and speak English; or bilingual education, which means teaching these students their core subjects such as math and history in their native language, while providing them gradual training in how to read and speak English?

Immersion... 63%
Bilingual education.. 33
Both; it depends (volunteered) 1
Neither; other (volunteered) 1
No opinion.. 2

	Immer-sion	Bilingual educa-tion	Both; it depends; neither; other	No opinion
By Sex				
Male	63%	33%	2%	2%
Female.............	60	36	2	2
By Ethnic Background				
White...............	63	33	2	2
Nonwhite.........	65	34	1	*
Black	63	36	1	*
By Education				
Postgraduate....	64	30	6	*
College Graduate......	70	28	1	1
College Incomplete	67	32	1	*
No College	58	37	2	3
By Region				
East.................	69	26	3	2
Midwest	65	33	1	1
South	58	39	1	2
West	61	34	3	2
By Age				
18–29 Years	53	43	3	1
30–49 Years	61	37	1	1
50–64 Years	68	26	3	3
65 Years and Over......	74	22	*	4
By Household Income				
$75,000 and Over......	65	31	3	1
$50,000 and Over......	65	32	2	1
$30,000–$49,999	67	33	*	*
$20,000–$29,999	63	34	2	1
Under $20,000	58	35	2	5
By Politics				
Republicans.....	68	32	*	*
Democrats	60	35	2	3
Independents ...	62	34	3	1
By Political Ideology				
Conservative ...	70	29	*	1
Moderate	61	34	2	3
Liberal.............	56	40	3	1

*Less than 1%

Note: Support for bilingual education has been weak in Gallup surveys conducted for the past twenty years for Phi Delta Kappa, the national education society. In 1980 an overwhelming 82% of the public approved requiring children who cannot speak English to "learn English in special classes before they are enrolled in public schools." In 1988 a similar question—"Would you favor or oppose the local public schools providing instruction in a student's native language, whatever it is, in order to help him or her become a more successful learner?"—received only 42% approval, with a plurality of 49% disapproving.

A poll in 1993 offered three choices for dealing with students who did not speak English. Only 27% supported an alternative of providing instruction in the students' native languages while they learn English. The rest preferred requiring students to learn English in special classes before receiving instruction in any other subjects (46%) or the more Draconian solution of requiring them to learn English in classes paid for at their parents' expense before being allowed to enroll in public schools (25%).

Today the public strongly supports the idea of the "immersion" of non-English-speaking public school students in regular classes, by a 63%-to-33% margin. These national poll results closely

mirror the results of a ballot initiative approved by California voters earlier this week that called for the elimination of bilingual education in that state.

Proposition 227, approved by a 61%-to-39% margin, mostly outlaws bilingual education in California in favor of programs that provide a year of intensive English instruction followed by transition into regular classrooms. A good deal of speculation since Tuesday's election has focused on the implications of the initiative on bilingual programs elsewhere across the country.

Results from a May survey show that respondents are generally in agreement with California voters in their opposition to bilingual education. The Gallup questions offered two options: bilingual education, which provides for teaching students in their native language with gradual transition to English; or immersion, which means teaching students in English while providing intensive training in how to read and speak English. As noted above, the public chooses the immersion option by a 63%-to-33% margin, quite similar to the result in California.

Exit polls in California showed that white voters support the initiative at a significantly higher level than others. Across the United States, however, there is little difference in support for immersion versus bilingual education between whites and nonwhites. The biggest differences are in terms of age, with young people (particularly those 18 to 29) significantly more in favor of bilingual education than are older Americans. Liberals are also stronger in their support than conservatives, although the immersion method wins along all ideological groups.

JUNE 13
PRESIDENT CLINTON/STARR
INVESTIGATION/CHINA CONTROVERSY

Interviewing Dates: 6/5–7/98
CNN/*USA Today*/Gallup Poll
Survey #GO 123254

Do you approve or disapprove of the way Bill Clinton is handling his job as president?

Approve	60%
Disapprove	34
No opinion	6

	Approve	Dis-approve	No opinion
By Sex			
Male	59%	36%	5%
Female	61	32	7
By Ethnic Background			
White	57	37	6
Nonwhite	79	13	8
Black	79	9	12
By Education			
Postgraduate	57	41	2
College Graduate	56	34	10
College Incomplete	60	35	5
No College	64	30	6
By Region			
East	72	23	5
Midwest	57	34	9
South	58	36	6
West	54	42	4
By Age			
18–29 Years	59	34	7
30–49 Years	64	31	5
50–64 Years	58	39	3
65 Years and Over	56	36	8
By Household Income			
$75,000 and Over	52	43	5
$50,000 and Over	55	40	5
$30,000–$49,999	60	35	5
$20,000–$29,999	63	33	4
Under $20,000	66	27	7
By Politics			
Republicans	32	63	5
Democrats	88	9	3
Independents	58	33	9
By Political Ideology			
Conservative	41	54	5
Moderate	70	25	5
Liberal	78	17	5

Selected National Trend

	Approve	Dis-approve	No opinion
1998			
May 8–10	64%	31%	5%
April 17–19	63	31	6

March 20–22	66	28	6
March 16*	67	29	4
March 6–9	63	31	6
February 20–22	66	29	5
February 13–15	66	30	4
January 30–February 1	69	28	3
January 28*	67	28	5
January 25–26	59	37	4
January 24–25	60	35	5
January 23–24	58	36	6
January 16–18	60	30	10
January 6–7	59	32	9

*Based on one-night poll

Do you approve or disapprove of the way Bill Clinton is handling the economy?*

Approve	71%
Disapprove	22
No opinion	7

*Asked in random order with foreign affairs and race relations

	Approve	Dis-approve	No opinion
By Sex			
Male	70%	23%	7%
Female	73	21	6
By Ethnic Background			
White	70	23	7
Nonwhite	78	16	6
Black	78	17	5
By Education			
Postgraduate	75	19	6
College Graduate	79	18	3
College Incomplete	70	22	8
No College	70	24	6
By Region			
East	79	16	5
Midwest	70	25	5
South	68	24	8
West	68	23	9

By Age			
18–29 Years	66	28	6
30–49 Years	77	18	5
50–64 Years	67	27	6
65 Years and Over	69	21	10
By Household Income			
$75,000 and Over	71	21	8
$50,000 and Over	70	23	7
$30,000–$49,999	73	24	3
$20,000–$29,999	73	22	5
Under $20,000	73	22	5
By Politics			
Republicans	50	41	9
Democrats	93	5	2
Independents	69	23	8
By Political Ideology			
Conservative	57	35	8
Moderate	79	16	5
Liberal	83	13	4

Selected National Trend

	Approve	Dis-approve	No opinion
1998			
April 17–19	73%	20%	7%
January 25–26	69	25	6
January 24–25	70	25	5
January 23–24	73	22	5

Annual Averages

	Approve	Dis-approve	No opinion
1997	59%	33%	8%
1996	51	43	6
1995	45	48	7
1994	44	50	6
1993	41	50	9

Regardless of your opinion of Ken Starr or the Lewinsky controversy, do you think it is appropriate or inappropriate that Secret Service personnel who worked directly with President Clinton have been called as witnesses to testify about matters related to the president?

Appropriate 45%
Inappropriate 54
No opinion 1

	Appropriate	Inappro-priate	No opinion
By Sex			
Male	47%	51%	2%
Female	44	55	1
By Ethnic Background			
White	48	51	1
Nonwhite	32	67	1
Black..........................	30	68	2
By Education			
Postgraduate	47	52	1
College Graduate........	49	51	*
College Incomplete.....	44	55	1
No College.................	44	54	2
By Region			
East	37	60	3
Midwest......................	48	50	2
South..........................	50	50	*
West...........................	44	56	*
By Age			
18–29 Years...............	51	47	2
30–49 Years...............	41	59	*
50–64 Years...............	51	48	1
65 Years and Over......	41	57	2
By Household Income			
$75,000 and Over	47	52	1
$50,000 and Over	47	53	*
$30,000–$49,999........	46	53	1
$20,000–$29,999........	47	51	2
Under $20,000............	43	56	1
By Politics			
Republicans	65	34	1
Democrats...................	47	51	2
Independents...............	26	73	1
By Political Ideology			
Conservative..............	63	36	1
Moderate.....................	36	63	1
Liberal	35	65	*

*Less than 1%

Regardless of your opinion of Ken Starr or the Lewinsky controversy, do you think it is appropriate or inappropriate for White House lawyers paid by the government who work directly with President Clinton to be called as witnesses to testify about matters related to the president?

Appropriate 43%
Inappropriate 54
No opinion 3

	Appropriate	Inappro-priate	No opinion
By Sex			
Male	46%	51%	3%
Female	40	57	3
By Ethnic Background			
White	45	52	3
Nonwhite	31	64	5
Black..........................	30	66	4
By Education			
Postgraduate	54	44	2
College Graduate........	48	50	2
College Incomplete.....	46	52	2
No College.................	37	59	4
By Region			
East	37	60	3
Midwest......................	44	52	4
South..........................	45	52	3
West...........................	46	53	1
By Age			
18–29 Years...............	47	52	1
30–49 Years...............	45	53	2
50–64 Years...............	44	53	3
65 Years and Over......	33	59	8
By Household Income			
$75,000 and Over	52	46	2
$50,000 and Over	50	49	1
$30,000–$49,999........	43	56	1
$20,000–$29,999........	40	57	3
Under $20,000............	38	59	3
By Politics			
Republicans	63	34	3
Democrats...................	26	72	2
Independents...............	43	54	3

By Political Ideology

Conservative	55	42	3
Moderate	37	62	1
Liberal	37	61	2

As you may know, President Clinton is scheduled to make an official visit to China later this month. Do you approve or disapprove of Clinton's decision to visit China at this time?

Approve	54%
Disapprove	34
No opinion	12

	Approve	Dis- approve	No opinion
By Politics			
Republicans	43%	48%	9%
Democrats	72	19	9
Independents	49	35	16
By Political Ideology			
Conservative	45	46	9
Moderate	59	31	10
Liberal	66	19	15

Some people have charged that the Clinton administration allowed China to get sensitive missile technology because of large contributions to the Democratic party in 1996. How closely have you followed recent news reports on this issue—very closely, somewhat closely, not too closely, or not at all?

Very closely	15%
Somewhat closely	30
Not too closely	33
Not at all	21
No opinion	1

	Very closely	Somewhat closely	Not too closely	Not at all*
By Politics				
Republicans	24%	34%	26%	14%
Democrats	10	26	42	21
Independents	14	29	30	27
By Political Ideology				
Conservative	20	32	31	17
Moderate	14	30	35	21
Liberal	11	26	34	28

*"No opinion"—at 2% or less—is omitted.

Do you think these allegations concerning the Clinton administration and China are definitely true, probably true, probably not true, or definitely not true?

Definitely true	9%
Probably true	43
Probably not true	31
Definitely not true	4
No opinion	13

	Definitely true	Prob- ably true	Prob- ably not true	De- finitely not true*
By Politics				
Republicans	18%	58%	14%	1%
Democrats	2	32	45	5
Independents	7	42	31	5
By Political Ideology				
Conservative	17	49	21	2
Moderate	4	43	33	5
Liberal	4	40	40	3

*"No opinion"—at 16% or less—is omitted.

Asked of half sample: Which of the following statements best describes your view of Bill Clinton's involvement in this matter—Bill Clinton did something illegal; he did something unethical but not illegal; or he did not do anything seriously wrong?

Illegal	15%
Unethical but not illegal	41
Nothing seriously wrong	32
No opinion	12

	Illegal	Unethical but not illegal	Nothing seriously wrong	No opinion
By Politics				
Republicans	35%	42%	12%	11%
Democrats	3	28	58	11
Independents	11	50	26	13
By Political Ideology				
Conservative	25	44	20	11
Moderate	8	45	36	11
Liberal	6	29	54	11

Still thinking about the controversy involving the Clinton administration and China, do you think the Justice Department is doing enough to investigate this matter, or should a special committee of Congress also be investigating it?

Justice doing enough 33%
Congress also should investigate................... 49
Justice doing too much (volunteered) 14
No opinion... 4

	Justice doing enough	Congress also should investigate	Justice doing too much	No opinion
By Politics				
Republicans.....	18%	69%	12%	1%
Democrats	45	34	16	5
Independents ...	35	47	13	5
By Political Ideology				
Conservative ...	25	61	11	3
Moderate	39	44	12	5
Liberal.............	40	39	16	5

Note: President Bill Clinton continues to coast through 1998 with relatively high public approval of his job performance and thus far has avoided any large-scale public condemnation over the troublesome controversies swirling around him. Neither Kenneth Starr's investigations nor the China satellite and fundraising charges have, to date, generated public alarm or dampened the overall ratings of the president.

Clinton's job approval rating today is 60%, down slightly from recent months when approval was in the mid to high 60s. Still, this 60% level is comparable to public support for Clinton after his reelection in 1996 and all through 1997, long before anyone had heard of Monica Lewinsky.

Approval of the president's handling of the economy has been extraordinarily high all year. During his entire first term, Clinton averaged only 45% approval on the economy. His average approval score rose to 51% in 1997 and is 71% in 1998 so far. These ratings are consistent with improved public assessments of the nation's economy over the same time period and may be partly responsible for Clinton's current resiliency.

Just as Clinton is maintaining high marks on the economy, the new poll finds that he is holding his ground in Gallup surveys about the investigations being conducted by Starr. The Independent Counsel recently seemed to be gaining momentum, winning a series of court decisions in his efforts to investigate the president. Starr also received some media praise for his handling of the investigation. Nevertheless, the American people are as negative as ever toward Starr, with only 29% expressing a favorable view of him and 50% an unfavorable view.

Moreover, respondents are even more likely today than they were in January to believe that Starr's investigation into the relationship between Clinton and Lewinsky is politically motivated rather than a legitimate search for the truth. A little over one-third believe that Starr is mostly trying to uncover the facts, but 57% say that he is mostly trying to damage Clinton politically. In January less than one-half of the public thought that Starr's primary motive was political.

This public cynicism about the Starr investigation may explain why Americans tolerate what they consider to be Clinton's uncooperative stance. More than one-half say that Clinton is trying to obstruct and delay the investigation, while only 35% think that he is trying to cooperate. However, when it comes to at least two specific areas where the president could be accused of obstruction—the subpoena of Secret Service personnel and of White House lawyers to testify—a majority agrees with Clinton that it is inappropriate to require these employees to testify about matters related to the president. If Starr's investigation eventually results in proof of serious crimes, the consequence could be House proceedings to impeach the president. As of today, however, very few respondents (just 19%) think that this course is warranted.

In addition to the Starr investigation, President Clinton recently found himself caught up in controversy over his policies toward China and the possibility of improper influence-peddling by China within the Democratic party. About one-half of Americans tend to think that the charges concerning the Clinton administration and China are true. Only 15%, however, believe that Clinton did anything illegal in the matter. Another 41% think that he may have done something unethical,

while 32% believe that he did nothing seriously wrong.

These perceptions of wrongdoing with regard to China are not particularly widespread. In comparison, twice as many Americans believe that Clinton may have done something illegal in regard to the Whitewater affair. Furthermore, they are paying relatively little attention to the Clinton-China controversy compared to other events in the news. Only 15% are following it very closely, while one-half are not following it closely.

The public generally thinks that in addition to the investigations being conducted by the Justice Department, an investigation by Congress into the China allegations would be advisable. In the meantime, by a 54%-to-34% margin, a majority supports Clinton's decision to proceed with his scheduled visit to China later this month.

JUNE 19
NUCLEAR WEAPONS

Interviewing Dates: 6/5–7/98
CNN/*USA Today*/Gallup Poll
Survey #GO 123254

Do you think it was a good thing or a bad thing that the atomic bomb was developed?

Good thing.. 36%
Bad thing 61
No opinion... 3

Selected National Trend

	Good thing	Bad thing	No opinion
1990	37%	56%	7%
1949	59	29	12
1947	55	38	7
1945	69	17	14

Asked of half sample: Thinking about the countries of the world that currently have nuclear capabilities, do you feel the national security of the United States is seriously threatened right now, or not?

Yes, threatened 41%
No 58
No opinion 1

	Yes, threatened	No	No opinion
By Sex			
Male	35%	65%	*
Female	46	52	2
By Ethnic Background			
White	41	57	2
Nonwhite	37	62	1
Black	37	62	1
By Education			
Postgraduate	35	65	*
College Graduate	42	57	1
College Incomplete	41	58	1
No College	42	56	2
By Region			
East	42	58	*
Midwest	39	60	1
South	38	59	3
West	46	53	1
By Age			
18–29 Years	27	72	1
30–49 Years	45	55	*
50–64 Years	44	55	1
65 Years and Over	43	50	7
By Household Income			
$75,000 and Over	31	69	*
$50,000 and Over	35	65	*
$30,000–$49,999	40	60	*
$20,000–$29,999	41	56	3
Under $20,000	47	52	1
By Politics			
Republicans	58	41	1
Democrats	29	69	2
Independents	38	61	1
By Political Ideology			
Conservative	47	52	1
Moderate	40	60	*
Liberal	29	68	3

*Less than 1%

Asked of half sample: Thinking about the countries of the world that currently have nuclear capabilities, do you feel the chances for world peace are seriously threatened right now, or not?

Yes, threatened 66%
No 32
No opinion 2

	Yes, threatened	No	No opinion
By Sex			
Male	66%	32%	2%
Female	60	38	2
By Ethnic Background			
White	66	33	1
Nonwhite	64	26	10
Black...........................	71	20	9
By Education			
Postgraduate	60	39	1
College Graduate........	58	38	4
College Incomplete.....	65	34	1
No College..................	70	26	4
By Region			
East	64	35	1
Midwest......................	62	33	5
South...........................	70	27	3
West............................	64	35	1
By Age			
18–29 Years................	74	25	1
30–49 Years................	67	33	*
50–64 Years................	62	36	2
65 Years and Over......	57	34	9
By Household Income			
$75,000 and Over	53	47	*
$50,000 and Over	61	39	*
$30,000–$49,999........	64	36	*
$20,000–$29,999........	79	19	2
Under $20,000............	67	31	2
By Politics			
Republicans	65	33	2
Democrats...................	65	33	2
Independents...............	67	30	3
By Political Ideology			
Conservative...............	69	30	1
Moderate.....................	61	37	2
Liberal	71	27	2

*Less than 1%

Asked of half sample: Next, I'm going to read a list of countries, some of which have and some of which do not have nuclear weapons. As I read each one, please tell me whether you think possession of nuclear weapons by that country would pose a serious threat to world peace, or not:

Iraq?

Yes, threat.. 89%
No 9
No opinion 2

Iran?

Yes, threat.. 83%
No 12
No opinion 5

Pakistan?

Yes, threat.. 66%
No 30
No opinion 4

China?

Yes, threat.. 61%
No 34
No opinion 5

Russia?

Yes, threat.. 48%
No 48
No opinion 4

India?

Yes, threat.. 47%
No 47
No opinion 6

Israel?

Yes, threat... 43%
No 53
No opinion... 4

Brazil?

Yes, threat... 17%
No 73
No opinion... 10

Great Britain?

Yes, threat... 13%
No 83
No opinion... 4

For each of the following possibilities, please tell me whether you think it is very likely, fairly likely, fairly unlikely, or very unlikely to happen:

That we will get into a nuclear war within the next ten years?

Very likely... 19%
Fairly likely 18
Fairly unlikely 30
Very unlikely... 31
No opinion... 2

Selected National Trend

	Very likely	Fairly likely	Fairly unlikely	Very unlikely*
1991	11%	17%	35%	34%
1990	8	13	33	42
1983	16	24	28	25
1982	19	29	24	21
1981	19	28	26	23

*"No opinion"—at 7% or less—is omitted.

That the United States will be attacked by another country using nuclear weapons within the next ten years?

Very likely... 19%
Fairly likely 17

Fairly unlikely 28
Very unlikely... 34
No opinion... 2

That terrorists will explode a nuclear bomb in the United States within the next ten years?

Very likely... 23%
Fairly likely 27
Fairly unlikely 24
Very unlikely... 23
No opinion... 3

That other countries will use nuclear weapons against each other within the next ten years?

Very likely... 37%
Fairly likely 34
Fairly unlikely 16
Very unlikely... 11
No opinion... 2

Note: In the wake of nuclear tests by India and Pakistan, a new Gallup Poll shows little change in the past decade either in Americans' evaluation of the atomic bomb or in their feelings about whether the United States might become involved in a nuclear war. Most people today think that the development of the atomic bomb was a bad thing, that the chances of world peace are seriously threatened as a consequence of several countries having a nuclear capability, and that within the next ten years it is likely that some countries—not including the United States—will use nuclear weapons against another. On the other hand, most respondents believe that our security is not threatened and that it is unlikely the United States will be involved in a nuclear war within the next decade.

According to the current Gallup survey, 61% believe that the development of the atomic bomb was a bad thing, while just 36% say that it was a good thing. In 1990, Americans expressed a similar view, by a margin of 56% to 37%. These replies represent a reversal of the positive views held by the public right after Japan's surrender in August 1945, shortly after atomic bombs had been dropped on the two Japanese cities of Hiroshima

and Nagasaki. Since the surrender was widely attributed to the bombs, it is not surprising that most Americans at the time thought that the development of the atomic bomb was a good thing, by a margin of 69% to 17%. By 1949, after the Soviets had tested their own atomic bomb and the Cold War had begun, the margin in favor of the bomb was smaller, at 59% to 29%.

Despite their negative views about the atomic bomb, Americans remain sanguine about the possibility of the United States becoming involved in a nuclear war: by a margin of 61% to 37%, they think that it is unlikely to happen within the next ten years. These results mark a slightly less optimistic attitude than in 1991, however, when 69% thought it unlikely that the United States would become involved in a nuclear war within the next decade, and 28% thought it likely. Still, both of the 1990 polls show considerably more optimism than those in the early 1980s, when respondents were about evenly divided on whether the country would become involved in a nuclear war. In April 1982, for example, 48% thought it likely to happen within a decade, while 45% thought it unlikely.

Today, two in three Americans say that the chances for world peace are seriously threatened by the nuclear capabilities of other countries. However, they are much less worried about U.S. security, with a majority saying that the nation is not threatened by the nuclear capabilities of other countries. When asked to evaluate the threat to world peace espoused by specific nations who either now have or could have nuclear weapons, 66% say that Pakistan would pose a serious threat, compared with 47% who name India. Iran and Iraq are seen as the most threatening among the countries mentioned; more than eight in ten Americans believe that these two Middle Eastern countries would pose a serious threat if they had nuclear weapons.

JUNE 27
PRESIDENT CLINTON'S TRIP TO CHINA

Interviewing Dates: 6/22–23/98
CNN/*USA Today*/Gallup Poll
Survey #GO 123479

Asked of half sample: What is your overall opinion of China—very favorable, mostly favorable, mostly unfavorable, or very unfavorable?

Very favorable	5%
Mostly favorable	34
Mostly unfavorable	42
Very unfavorable	9
No opinion	10

	Very favor- able	Mostly favor- able	Mostly unfavor- able	Very unfa- vorable*
By Sex				
Male	7%	32%	42%	9%
Female	4	36	40	9
By Ethnic Background				
White	6	34	43	8
Nonwhite	4	41	33	12
Black	4	38	34	13
By Education				
Postgraduate	3	25	55	11
College Graduate	11	24	48	10
College Incomplete	4	39	39	7
No College	6	35	37	10
By Region				
East	6	31	35	13
Midwest	6	40	40	3
South	5	36	45	12
West	4	29	46	6
By Age				
18–29 Years	6	44	36	6
30–49 Years	6	36	44	7
50–64 Years	1	34	39	17
65 Years and Over	6	18	45	8
By Household Income				
$75,000 and Over	3	33	45	14
$50,000 and Over	3	35	47	11

$30,000–$49,999	5	34	46	6
$20,000–$29,999	7	39	38	8
Under $20,000	9	36	37	6

By Politics

Republicans	3	28	51	12
Democrats	5	40	35	7
Independents	7	34	40	8

By Political Ideology

Conservative	4	27	50	10
Moderate	3	37	40	11
Liberal	9	40	36	5

*"No opinion"—at 23% or less—is omitted.

Selected National Trend

	Very favorable	Mostly favorable	Mostly unfavorable	Very unfavorable*
1997	5%	28%	36%	14%
1996	6	33	35	16
1994	4	36	38	15
1993	10	43	24	15
1989 Aug.	5	29	32	22
1989 Feb.	12	60	10	3
1987	8	57	23	5
1983	6	37	31	21
1980	6	36	30	24
1979	5	25	31	33
1976	3	17	29	45
1967	**	5	16	75

*"No opinion"—at 17% or less—is omitted.
** Less than 1%

Do you approve or disapprove of Clinton's decision to visit China at this time?

Approve 58%
Disapprove 32
No opinion 10

	Approve	Disapprove	No opinion
By Sex			
Male	58%	35%	7%
Female	58	29	13

By Ethnic Background

White	56	34	10
Nonwhite	68	20	12
Black	71	16	13

By Education

Postgraduate	67	30	3
College Graduate	60	32	8
College Incomplete	60	30	10
No College	53	34	13

By Region

East	67	24	9
Midwest	58	27	15
South	54	37	9
West	54	38	8

By Age

18–29 Years	65	28	7
30–49 Years	58	31	11
50–64 Years	53	39	8
65 Years and Over	55	33	12

By Household Income

$75,000 and Over	59	35	6
$50,000 and Over	57	36	7
$30,000–$49,999	55	34	11
$20,000–$29,999	58	35	7
Under $20,000	62	24	14

By Politics

Republicans	43	49	8
Democrats	69	19	12
Independents	60	29	11

By Political Ideology

Conservative	47	44	9
Moderate	61	27	12
Liberal	69	23	8

While Clinton is actually in China, do you think he should or should not publicly criticize China for its human rights policies?

Should 43%
Should not 51
Not familiar with policies (volunteered) 2
No opinion 4

	Should	Should not	Not familiar with policies	No opinion
By Sex				
Male	48%	49%	1%	2%
Female.............	39	53	4	4
By Ethnic Background				
White...............	45	50	2	3
Nonwhite.........	36	60	3	1
Black	36	59	3	2
By Education				
Postgraduate....	49	48	*	3
College Graduate......	53	44	1	2
College Incomplete...	45	48	2	5
No College	37	57	3	3
By Region				
East.................	48	50	1	1
Midwest	39	55	3	3
South	42	50	3	5
West	44	51	1	4
By Age				
18–29 Years	42	54	3	1
30–49 Years	45	50	2	3
50–64 Years	50	47	1	2
65 Years and Over......	35	55	3	7
By Household Income				
$75,000 and Over......	53	46	*	1
$50,000 and Over......	52	46	*	2
$30,000–$49,999	43	52	3	2
$20,000–$29,999	43	53	1	3
Under $20,000	36	54	4	6
By Politics				
Republicans.....	46	48	1	5
Democrats	39	54	4	3
Independents ...	45	51	2	2

By Political Ideology				
Conservative ...	45	50	1	4
Moderate	45	50	2	3
Liberal.............	41	55	2	2

*Less than 1%

Do you think Clinton's visit will or will not significantly improve China's treatment of its citizens?

Will	20%
Will not	70
No opinion	10

	Will	Will not	No opinion
By Sex			
Male............................	18%	76%	6%
Female	21	66	13
By Ethnic Background			
White	18	73	9
Nonwhite	30	57	13
Black...........................	28	57	15
By Education			
Postgraduate	15	80	5
College Graduate........	12	84	4
College Incomplete.....	18	72	10
No College..................	24	63	13
By Region			
East	19	67	14
Midwest	20	68	12
South...........................	20	73	7
West............................	21	72	7
By Age			
18–29 Years................	18	75	7
30–49 Years................	19	73	8
50–64 Years................	20	71	9
65 Years and Over......	23	59	18
By Household Income			
$75,000 and Over	13	83	4
$50,000 and Over	14	79	7
$30,000–$49,999........	16	77	7
$20,000–$29,999........	23	71	6

Under $20,000	30	53	17

By Politics

Republicans	14	79	7
Democrats	27	61	12
Independents	17	73	10

By Political Ideology

Conservative	15	77	8
Moderate	21	70	9
Liberal	24	65	11

Which of the following statements comes closer to your view—the United States should link human rights issues in China with U.S.-China trade policy, even if doing so hurts U.S. economic interests; or the United States should not link human rights issues in China with U.S.-China trade policy because doing so might hurt U.S. economic interests?

Should link rights, trade	47%
Should not link rights, trade	45
No opinion	8

	Should link rights, trade	Should not link rights, trade	No opinion
By Sex			
Male	50%	46%	4%
Female	45	44	11
By Ethnic Background			
White	49	44	7
Nonwhite	35	55	10
Black	35	54	11
By Education			
Postgraduate	65	31	4
College Graduate	56	41	3
College Incomplete	51	43	6
No College	36	53	11
By Region			
East	50	42	8
Midwest	43	51	6
South	44	47	9
West	53	40	7

By Age

18–29 Years	39	56	5
30–49 Years	54	41	5
50–64 Years	55	37	8
65 Years and Over	32	51	17

By Household Income

$75,000 and Over	62	35	3
$50,000 and Over	60	37	3
$30,000–$49,999	51	43	6
$20,000–$29,999	41	53	6
Under $20,000	33	55	12

By Politics

Republicans	51	41	8
Democrats	46	45	9
Independents	45	49	6

By Political Ideology

Conservative	43	48	9
Moderate	50	44	6
Liberal	51	43	6

Asked of half sample: Which of the following best describes your view of the relationship between China and the United States—would you say China is an ally, friendly but not an ally, unfriendly but not an enemy, an enemy of the United States, or haven't you heard enough about that yet to say?

An ally	3%
Friendly	28
Unfriendly	25
An enemy	8
Haven't heard enough; no opinion	36

Selected National Trend

	An ally	Friendly	Un-friendly	An enemy*
1997	4%	21%	27%	9%
1983**	5	47	18	3

*"Haven't heard enough" and "no opinion"—at 39% or less—are omitted.
**Los Angeles Times* survey

Note: A solid majority of Americans approves of Bill Clinton's decision to visit China this week,

despite some controversy over the message that may be sent regarding human rights. Not only do respondents think that the president should make this state visit to China but, on balance, they also agree with him that U.S. criticism of Beijing's human rights policies should not be made publicly on his trip.

A Gallup Poll taken this past weekend finds 58% approving of Clinton's visit to China and only 32% opposed. Despite this support, the survey reveals a high degree of wariness toward the world's most populous country. Public opinion of China tilts negative, with 51% saying that they have an unfavorable view of the country and only 39% holding a favorable view. Americans are split into three groups in their assessment of U.S.-China relations: one-third view China as an ally or at least friendly, another third consider it an enemy or at least unfriendly, while the remainder are unsure about its stance toward the United States.

Attitudes toward China are less positive than they were in the 1980s, before the Tiananmen Square incident in Beijing, but are still much more positive than they were thirty years ago. In 1967, Americans had an almost universally negative attitude about what was then commonly known as Red China.

Today, one-half of respondents say that President Clinton should not criticize China publicly for its human rights policies during his visit, while only 43% say that he should. This division is relatively uniform throughout society, including among self-identified Republicans and Democrats, and liberals and conservatives. The same poll finds that only 47%—down from 55% last year—support linking U.S.-China trade policy with human rights issues if that linkage would hurt our nation's economic interests.

The public is about evenly split over whether the Clinton visit will or will not significantly improve U.S. relations with China. Close to one-half of Americans (48%) are doubtful that the trip will have a major positive impact on relations, while 42% say that it will. To the extent that the president's visit reflects an effort to produce some indirect positive influence on human rights policies there, Americans are skeptical. Only about two in ten (20%) say that the visit will significantly improve China's treatment of its own citizens.

The most troublesome finding for Clinton in the new poll might be the public's approval rating for his handling of relations with China. Unlike Clinton's overall job rating, where those approving clearly outnumber his detractors by 60% to 34%, the president's ratings on China are evenly split. Only 40% approve of his handling of relations with China, while 37% disapprove; the rest (23%) have no opinion.

Clinton's approval rating on China is substantially lower than the 53% approval rating he receives for his handling of foreign affairs overall. The low China rating could reflect the specific controversy over the transfer of missile technology to that country in addition to the general controversy about the proposed trip.

JULY 3
Y2K COMPUTER BUG

Interviewing Dates: 6/5–7/98
CNN/*USA Today*/Gallup Poll
Survey #GO 123254

As you may know, most computer systems around the world have to be reprogrammed so that they can accurately recognize the date once we reach the year 2000. Do you think that computer mistakes due to the year 2000 issue will cause major problems or only minor problems?

Major problems	48%
Minor problems	47
No problems (volunteered)	1
No opinion	4

	Major problems	Minor problems	No problems	No opinion
By Sex				
Male	44%	51%	1%	4%
Female	52	44	*	4
By Ethnic Background				
White	48	48	*	4
Nonwhite	51	44	*	5
Black	54	41	*	5

By Education

Postgraduate.... 41	55	1	3
College Graduate...... 46	52	*	2
College Incomplete... 49	49	*	2
No College...... 50	43	1	6

By Region

East.................. 48	47	1	4
Midwest 48	49	*	3
South 50	45	1	4
West 47	49	*	4

By Age

18–29 Years 52	45	1	2
30–49 Years 50	48	*	2
50–64 Years 43	52	1	4
65 Years and Over...... 45	42	2	11

By Household Income

$75,000 and Over...... 44	56	*	*
$50,000 and Over...... 44	54	*	2
$30,000–$49,999 46	49	1	4
$20,000–$29,999 55	41	1	3
Under $20,000 52	43	1	4

By Politics

Republicans..... 53	43	1	3
Democrats 47	48	1	4
Independents ... 45	50	1	4

By Political Ideology

Conservative ... 53	44	*	3
Moderate 44	51	1	4
Liberal............. 49	49	*	2

*Less than 1%

Do you think that computer mistakes due to the year 2000 issue will cause major problems or only minor problems for you personally?

Major problems 20%
Minor problems 73
No problems (volunteered)............................ 4
No opinion... 3

	Major problems	Minor problems	No problems	No opinion
By Sex				
Male 16%	78%	4%	2%
Female............. 24	68	4	4
By Ethnic Background				
White.............. 19	74	4	3
Nonwhite......... 28	66	1	5
Black 30	65	*	5
By Education				
Postgraduate.... 16	79	3	2
College Graduate...... 20	77	2	1
College Incomplete... 17	76	5	2
No College 24	68	3	5
By Region				
East................. 19	73	4	4
Midwest 22	71	4	3
South 22	73	3	2
West 18	75	4	3
By Age				
18–29 Years 21	76	3	*
30–49 Years 22	73	4	1
50–64 Years 22	71	4	3
65 Years and Over...... 13	71	5	11
By Household Income				
$75,000 and Over...... 18	77	4	1
$50,000 and Over...... 15	81	4	*
$30,000–$49,999 19	77	3	1
$20,000–$29,999 14	78	4	4
Under $20,000 31	60	4	5

By Politics

Republicans..... 23	73	2	2
Democrats 21	71	4	4
Independents ... 18	75	4	3

By Political Ideology

Conservative ... 22	74	2	2
Moderate 19	74	4	3
Liberal 20	72	6	2

*Less than 1%

Note: A Gallup Poll asking Americans about the so-called Y2K computer bug finds that they are not alarmed—at least not yet—about the possibility that computer systems will wreak havoc with their lives at the dawn of the new millennium. Only one in five thinks that computer mistakes due to problems recognizing the year 2000 will cause major problems in their own lives, while 73% foresee only minor problems at worst.

Computers still programmed with a two-digit rather than a four-digit date field will interpret the year 2000 as "1900," which may lead to system-wide errors in programs that rely on dates. Some alarmed citizens are reportedly responding to the problem by building bunkers, storing food, and arming themselves in anticipation that these errors will trigger Doomsday.

Although most respondents are not concerned about the impact that Y2K will have on them personally, they show somewhat more concern about the effect it may have on others. Forty-eight percent think that Y2K will cause major problems around the world, while another 48% anticipate only minor problems or none at all.

Some analysts have predicted Y2K snafus as critical as air traffic control breaking down and Social Security checks going out incorrectly. Concern, or lack thereof, about such possibilities appears to be uniform across various societal groups. Men and women, college graduates and those with less formal education, and upper- and lower-income Americans all express about equal levels of concern that Y2K might cause significant problems for themselves or the world. Gallup will continue to ask Americans about the millennium computer glitch between now and the year 2000 to track the extent to which publicity about business and government preparedness affects them.

JULY 11
PRESIDENT CLINTON'S TRIP TO CHINA

Interviewing Dates: 7/7–8/98
CNN/*USA Today*/Gallup Poll
Survey #GO 123690

Do you approve or disapprove of Clinton's decision to visit China at this time?

	July 7–8, 1998	June 22–23, 1998
Approve 64%	58%
Disapprove.................................... 27	32
No opinion 9	10

Do you think Clinton's visit did or did not significantly improve U.S. relations with China?

	July 7–8, 1998	June 22–23, 1998*
Did 49%	42%
Did not 38	48
No opinion 13	10

*Question wording: *Do you think Clinton's visit will or will not significantly improve U.S. relations with China?*

Do you think Clinton's visit did or did not significantly improve China's treatment of its citizens?

	July 7–8, 1998	June 22–23, 1998*
Did 22%	20%
Did not 61	70
No opinion 17	10

*Question wording: *Do you think Clinton's visit will or will not significantly improve China's treatment of its citizens?*

As you may know, the United States grants a trade status to most nations it trades with known as Most Favored Nation status. In your opinion, should the United States grant this same status to China, or not?

	July 7–8, 1998	May 30– June 1, 1997
Should	35%	35%
Should not	55	53
No opinion	10	12

Note: Americans approve of President Bill Clinton's trip to China earlier this month by 64% to 27%, according to the latest Gallup Poll, and by a smaller margin they believe that his visit significantly improved U.S. relations with that country. But the public remains unconvinced that the trip will lead to a significant improvement in China's treatment of its own citizens, despite Clinton's public discussion of human rights during his visit. The poll also shows little improvement in China's image among Americans and continued public opposition to most-favored-nation status for China in its trade relations with the United States.

Before Clinton left for China, 58% of respondents approved of the planned visit; in the current poll conducted after his return, 64% express approval. The increase comes mostly from an 11-point jump among Democrats, although approval among Republicans and independents has moved up by 3 to 4 points as well.

Public assessment of the trip's potential effectiveness is also higher after the visit than before, with a plurality (49%) now saying that the trip significantly improved relations between China and the United States. In late June, Americans expressed more skepticism, with only 42% saying that the visit would improve relations and 48% saying that it would not. Higher ratings after the visit are found among both Republicans and Democrats.

Whatever positive goals that Clinton's visit might have achieved in U.S. relations with China, the public—by a margin of 61% to 22%—does not believe that the trip will lead to better treatment by China of its own citizens. These views are little changed from before the visit, when 70% said that it would not help, and just 20% said that it would. These negative perceptions may help to

explain why respondents also remain opposed to granting most-favored-nation trade status to China. Only 35% say that it should be granted, while 55% say that it should not. Typically, Americans do not pay much attention to trade issues, so their views on this question should be seen mostly as reflections of their general skepticism about the Beijing government.

The poll also shows that following Clinton's visit, respondents express slightly more favorable views of China than before, with 44% now feeling favorably toward the country, and 47% unfavorably. Last month, the ratio was 39% favorable to 51% unfavorable. The increase is mostly partisan, however, coming almost exclusively from a 10-point jump in positive ratings among Democrats.

JULY 18
NORTHERN IRELAND

Interviewing Dates: 7/13–14/98
CNN/*USA Today*/Gallup Poll
Survey #GO 123792

In the situation in Northern Ireland, are your sympathies more with the Irish Catholics, or more with the Irish Protestants?

Irish Catholics	30%
Irish Protestants	16
Both (volunteered)	8
Neither (volunteered)	22
No opinion	24

	Irish Catholics	Irish Protestants	Both	Neither*
By Sex				
Male	32%	16%	6%	26%
Female	27	17	9	18
By Ethnic Background				
White	31	18	7	21
Nonwhite	21	11	11	25
Black	19	9	14	28
By Education				
College Graduate	33	18	4	24

College
Incomplete... 31	15	8	26
No College 25	19	7	17

By Region
East.................. 38	11	9	19
Midwest 27	17	7	21
South 25	18	8	24
West 30	19	8	23

By Age
18–29 Years 40	15	6	17
30–49 Years 31	18	6	17
50–64 Years 26	16	9	30
65 Years and Over...... 18	16	13	28

By Household Income
$50,000 and Over...... 29	19	7	25
$20,000–$49,999 34	15	11	19
Under $20,000 25	17	3	20

By Politics
Republicans..... 23	26	9	19
Democrats 36	13	7	21
Independents ... 29	12	7	25

By Political Ideology
Conservative ... 25	23	8	24
Moderate 33	14	8	21
Liberal............. 34	13	8	18

*"No opinion"—at 35% or less—is omitted.

What would you, personally, prefer to see happen in Northern Ireland—for it to remain part of the United Kingdom, or for it to become united with the Republic of Ireland?

Remain part of United Kingdom	17%
Unite with Republic...	50
None; other (volunteered)	4
It doesn't matter; don't care (volunteered).....	14
No opinion..	15

	Remain part of United Kingdom	Unite with Republic	None; other	It doesn't matter; don't care*
By Sex				
Male 16%		53%	5%	14%
Female............. 18		47	2	14
By Ethnic Background				
White............... 17		52	3	14
Nonwhite......... 14		40	6	16
Black 15		39	8	17
By Education				
College Graduate...... 18		56	5	14
College Incomplete... 16		53	4	12
No College 19		42	4	17
By Region				
East.................. 22		51	4	16
Midwest 15		52	4	15
South 13		48	5	15
West 19		50	2	12
By Age				
18–29 Years 32		42	1	13
30–49 Years 17		51	3	14
50–64 Years 9		58	6	16
65 Years and Over...... 10		44	5	15
By Household Income				
$50,000 and Over...... 16		54	4	12
$20,000–$49,999 20		50	5	11
Under $20,000 13		43	1	24
By Politics				
Republicans..... 14		54	2	12
Democrats 15		52	5	11
Independents ... 21		44	5	19
By Political Ideology				
Conservative ... 16		53	3	14
Moderate 19		48	3	12
Liberal............. 13		52	5	17

*"No opinion"—at 26% or less—is omitted.

As you may know, the leaders of the two opposing sides in Northern Ireland have reached a new compromise agreement concerning the governance of Northern Ireland. Are you generally optimistic or pessimistic that this agreement will lead to lasting peace in Northern Ireland?

Optimistic 37%
Pessimistic 49
No opinion 14

	Optimistic	Pessimistic	No opinion
By Sex			
Male	43%	45%	12%
Female	32	51	17
By Ethnic Background			
White	38	51	11
Nonwhite	30	40	30
Black	33	37	30
By Education			
College Graduate	35	61	4
College Incomplete	31	61	8
No College	40	36	24
By Region			
East	36	50	14
Midwest	34	56	10
South	37	41	22
West	42	51	7
By Age			
18–29 Years	44	45	11
30–49 Years	36	50	14
50–64 Years	34	53	13
65 Years and Over	33	45	22
By Household Income			
$50,000 and Over	38	54	8
$20,000–$49,999	40	49	11
Under $20,000	31	40	29
By Politics			
Republicans	36	52	12
Democrats	36	51	13
Independents	39	44	17
By Political Ideology			
Conservative	38	50	12
Moderate	38	49	13
Liberal	37	47	16

Note: In spite of the recent political agreement that keeps Northern Ireland in the United Kingdom, fewer than one in five Americans favors this solution to the Irish question. According to a recent Gallup Poll, respondents would prefer to see Northern Ireland become part of the Republic of Ireland than remain with the United Kingdom by a wide 50%-to-17% margin.

When asked to say where their personal sympathies lie in the centuries-old dispute in Northern Ireland, support for the Catholics is less widespread. A majority of Americans (54%) are neutral or have no opinion about the two sides in the conflict. (Perhaps expressing neutrality seems, to some respondents, to be the responsible stance.) Among those who do take sides, however, 30% say that their sympathies lie with the Catholics and 16% with the Protestants.

The new poll was conducted in the wake of news about a firebomb that killed three young Catholic brothers in Belfast, the latest victims of the Troubles in Northern Ireland that have resurfaced as the plebiscite on the recent peace agreement draws near. When asked about their outlook for the agreement recently worked out between England and the conflicting sides in Northern Ireland, Americans are generally doubtful that the new terms of governance will lead to lasting peace in the area. Only 37% are optimistic that it will succeed, while about one-half (49%) are pessimistic.

JULY 25
HOMOSEXUALITY

Interviewing Dates: 6/22–23/98
CNN/*USA Today*/Gallup Poll
Survey #GO 123479

Do you personally believe homosexual behavior is morally wrong or is not morally wrong?

Yes, morally wrong 59%
No, not morally wrong 35
No opinion 6

	Yes, morally wrong	No, not morally wrong	No opinion
By Sex			
Male	62%	32%	6%
Female	56	39	5
By Ethnic Background			
White	57	37	6
Nonwhite	68	25	7
Black	73	20	7
By Education			
Postgraduate	39	55	6
College Graduate	52	41	7
College Incomplete	53	39	8
No College	70	26	4
By Region			
East	52	43	5
Midwest	58	37	5
South	66	26	8
West	56	39	5
By Age			
18–29 Years	50	48	2
30–49 Years	55	38	7
50–64 Years	65	30	5
65 Years and Over	70	21	9
By Household Income			
$75,000 and Over	51	45	4
$50,000 and Over	54	42	4
$30,000–$49,999	60	34	6
$20,000–$29,999	60	32	8
Under $20,000	62	31	7
By Politics			
Republicans	70	24	6
Democrats	55	40	5
Independents	53	40	7
By Political Ideology			
Conservative	80	14	6
Moderate	55	38	7
Liberal	36	62	2

Asked of half sample: In your view, is homosexuality something a person is born with, or is homosexuality due to other factors such as upbringing or environment?

Born with	31%
Other factors	47
Both (volunteered)	6
Neither (volunteered)	3
No opinion	13

	Born with	Other factors	Both; neither	No opinion
By Sex				
Male	26%	53%	9%	12%
Female	35	42	10	13
By Ethnic Background				
White	32	48	8	12
Nonwhite	27	47	14	12
Black	23	49	14	14
By Education				
Postgraduate	37	34	20	9
College Graduate	32	51	13	4
College Incomplete	31	48	6	15
No College	30	50	7	13
By Region				
East	38	44	9	9
Midwest	33	48	10	9
South	23	51	11	15
West	35	44	4	17
By Age				
18–29 Years	24	60	9	7
30–49 Years	32	46	11	11
50–64 Years	33	48	8	11
65 Years and Over	35	37	7	21
By Household Income				
$75,000 and Over	42	38	11	9
$50,000 and Over	37	43	12	8
$30,000–$49,999	31	51	4	14

$20,000–			
$29,999 19	57	11	13
Under			
$20,000 38	41	6	15

By Politics

Republicans..... 28	54	9	9
Democrats 35	41	8	16
Independents ... 31	48	10	11

By Political Ideology

Conservative ... 22	57	9	12
Moderate 36	46	7	11
Liberal............ 41	37	14	8

Selected National Trend

	Born with	Other factors	Both; neither	No opinion
1996	31%	40%	16%	13%
1989	19	48	14	19
1982	17	52	15	16
1977	12	56	17	15

Note: Is homosexuality a biological trait that people are born with, or is it grounded in their environment and upbringing? A recent Gallup Poll finds that Americans lean toward the "nurture" rather than the "nature" explanation for sexual orientation by a 47%-to-31% margin.

This point of contention is once again in the news as conservative religious groups launch a new advertising campaign suggesting to gays that they can change their sexual orientation and be "cured" if they so desire. Senate Majority Leader Trent Lott and professional football player Reggie White have also recently denounced homosexuality as a sin, and Lott has even publicly compared homosexuality to alcoholism and kleptomania. In contrast, gay rights leaders argue that homosexual orientation is a genetic condition like skin color or gender.

While a plurality still believes that upbringing is a more important determinant of sexual orientation than genetics, the margin in favor of that position has become less pronounced over the last decade. Gallup first asked Americans in 1977 whether homosexuality is something a person is born with or due to other factors, such as upbringing or environment. At that time, only 12% chose the "nature" side of the argument, while 56% said that it was upbringing or environment. These attitudes did not change substantially between 1977 and the late 1980s.

However, by 1996 there was a significant change in public attitudes when the number of those choosing "nature" had increased to 31%, compared to 40% who said environment. The most recent Gallup Poll shows that the 31% "nature" response has held constant, but that a slightly higher number (47%) now chooses the environmental position.

It appears, however, that these attitudes are not necessarily firmly held. A Gallup question asks if the cause of homosexuality is "always due to the way a person is born, always due to factors such as upbringing or environment," or if it "depends on the person." In response, 63% say that it depends on the individual, with less than 20% choosing either of the more absolute notions.

Whatever the public's views about the roots of homosexual orientation, there remains a clear majority who believes that homosexual behavior is immoral. Fifty-nine percent say that homosexual behavior is morally wrong, about one-third say that it is not morally wrong, while the rest have no opinion.

There is a strong relationship between age and this morality measure: 70% of those age 65 and older say that it is morally wrong, compared to 50% of those age 18 to 29. Belief that homosexual behavior is morally wrong is also higher in the South than elsewhere in the country, higher among those with lower levels of education, slightly higher among men than among women, and higher among Republicans and conservatives than among Democrats and liberals.

AUGUST 1
PRESIDENT CLINTON/STARR INVESTIGATION

Interviewing Date: 7/29/98*
CNN/*USA Today*/Gallup Poll
Survey #GO 123693

Do you approve or disapprove of the way Bill Clinton is handling his job as president?

*Based on one-night poll

Approve 65%
Disapprove 31
No opinion 4

	Approve	Dis-approve	No opinion
By Sex			
Male 66%		32%	2%
Female 65		30	5
By Age			
18–29 Years 61		33	6
30–49 Years 67		30	3
50 Years and Over 65		31	4
By Politics			
Republicans 36		61	3
Democrats 89		11	*
Independents 66		26	8
By Lewinsky Affair Allegations			
Total True 54		42	4
Total Not True 84		12	4

*Less than 1%

I'm going to describe some of the allegations being made. As I read each one, please say whether you think it is definitely true, probably true, probably not true, or definitely not true:

The allegation that Bill Clinton had sexual relations of any kind with Monica Lewinsky?

Definitely true 19%
Probably true 47
Probably not true 17
Definitely not true 8
No opinion 9

	Definitely true	Prob-ably true	Prob-ably not true	De-finitely not true*
By Sex				
Male 25%	46%	11%	10%
Female 14	48	22	5

	Definitely true	Prob-ably true	Prob-ably not true	De-finitely not true*
By Age				
18–29 Years 26	50	13	9
30–49 Years 18	52	12	5
50 Years and Over 16	40	24	10
By Politics				
Republicans 32	50	10	6
Democrats 5	43	29	12
Independents ... 21	48	12	6
By Lewinsky Affair Allegations				
Total True 29	71	–	–
Total Not True .... –	–	68	32
By Clinton Approval				
Approve 8	47	21	11
Disapprove 43	46	8	2

*"No opinion"—at 13% or less—is omitted.

Selected National Trend

	Definitely true	Prob-ably true	Prob-ably not true	De-finitely not true*
1998				
April 17–19 ..... 17%	47%	17%	9%
Feb. 20–22 14	45	22	9
Feb. 13–15 22	45	18	9
Jan. 30–Feb. 1 11	44	27	12
Jan. 28** 8	44	26	11
Jan. 25–26** ... 17	44	23	9
Jan. 23–24** ... 12	48	24	9
Jan. 21** 7	47	27	10

*"No opinion"—at 11% or less—is omitted.
**Question wording: *The allegation that Bill Clinton had an extramarital affair with Monica Lewinsky?*

The allegation that Bill Clinton lied under oath while president?

Definitely true 16%
Probably true 40
Probably not true 27
Definitely not true 10
No opinion 7

	Definitely true	Probably true	Probably not true	Definitely not true*
By Sex				
Male	22%	38%	26%	11%
Female	11	42	29	8
By Age				
18–29 Years	23	50	19	6
30–49 Years	16	42	26	7
50 Years and Over	12	32	35	15
By Politics				
Republicans	30	46	17	4
Democrats	3	29	47	17
Independents	17	45	19	8
By Lewinsky Affair Allegations				
Total True	24	53	18	2
Total Not True	**	14	57	27
By Clinton Approval				
Approve	4	36	36	15
Disapprove	40	47	11	**

*"No opinion"—at 11% or less—is omitted.
**Less than 1%

The allegation that Bill Clinton participated in an effort to obstruct justice while president?

Definitely true.. 12%
Probably true 31
Probably not true 31
Definitely not true 16
No opinion.. 10

	Definitely true	Probably true	Probably not true	Definitely not true*
By Sex				
Male	18%	31%	27%	20%
Female	8	32	34	12
By Age				
18–29 Years	17	38	19	20
30–49 Years	11	32	35	9
50 Years and Over	12	26	34	19
By Politics				
Republicans	22	48	19	7
Democrats	3	16	45	28
Independents	13	31	28	12
By Lewinsky Affair Allegations				
Total True	18	42	25	8
Total Not True	2	14	51	31
By Clinton Approval				
Approve	4	23	42	22
Disapprove	31	49	9	3

*"No opinion"—at 16% or less—is omitted.

Next, we'd like to know what your reaction would be if Monica Lewinsky tells the grand jury that she and Bill Clinton did have sex and also that, without asking her to lie, Clinton discussed ways to hide their alleged sexual relationship from investigators. Would you feel this is a serious enough matter that Congress should consider impeachment; it is very serious, but not enough for impeachment; it is not very serious; or it is not serious at all?

Congress should consider impeachment 24%
Not serious enough for impeachment............. 41
Not very serious... 13
Not serious at all... 21
None; other (volunteered) .... *
No opinion.. 1

*Less than 1%

	Congress should consider impeachment	Not serious enough for impeachment	Not very serious	Not serious at all*
By Sex				
Male	27%	37%	13%	22%
Female	21	44	13	20
By Age				
18–29 Years	30	33	20	17

30–49 Years 22	51	8	18
50 Years and Over...... 22	35	14	27

By Politics

Republicans..... 42	46	4	8
Democrats 9	35	18	36
Independents ... 23	41	15	19

By Lewinsky Affair Allegations

Total True 34	42	12	12
Total Not True............. 5	35	19	40

By Clinton Approval

Approve 11	41	18	28
Disapprove...... 52	40	1	7

*"None," "other," and "no opinion"—at 2% or less—are omitted.

As you may know, Monica Lewinsky and Independent Counsel Ken Starr have just reached an immunity agreement—that is, Lewinsky has agreed to testify before the grand jury in exchange for a promise that Starr will not charge her with any crime. Do you favor or oppose this immunity agreement between Starr and Lewinsky?

Favor...	40%
Oppose..	54
No opinion......................................	6

	Favor	Oppose	No opinion
By Sex			
Male............................ 49%		47%	4%
Female 32		60	8
By Age			
18–29 Years............... 47		51	2
30–49 Years............... 44		50	6
50 Years and Over...... 33		60	7
By Politics			
Republicans 53		41	6
Democrats.................. 27		65	8
Independents.............. 43		53	4

By Lewinsky Affair Allegations

Total True.................. 51	44	5	
Total Not True........... 20	77	3	

By Clinton Approval

Approve..................... 31	63	6	
Disapprove................. 60	35	5	

As you may know, President Clinton agreed today to testify on August 17 in Ken Starr's investigation. Do you favor or oppose Clinton's decision?

Favor..	85%
Oppose..	12
No opinion......................................	3

	Favor	Oppose	No opinion
By Sex			
Male............................ 86%	10%	4%
Female 82	15	3
By Age			
18–29 Years............... 90	9	1
30–49 Years............... 90	7	3
50 Years and Over...... 76	20	4
By Politics			
Republicans 86	10	4
Democrats.................. 78	19	3
Independents.............. 89	9	2

By Lewinsky Affair Allegations

Total True.................. 88	10	2
Total Not True........... 77	20	3

By Clinton Approval

Approve..................... 85	12	3
Disapprove................. 84	13	3

As you may know, grand jury witnesses almost always appear in person at the courthouse without their lawyers present, but Clinton's testimony will be videotaped at the White House with his lawyer present during questioning. Do you favor or oppose Clinton being allowed to testify in this manner?

Favor.. 59%
Oppose.. 39
No opinion... 2

	Favor	Oppose	No opinion
By Sex			
Male............................	59%	40%	1%
Female	59	39	2
By Age			
18–29 Years................	51	48	1
30–49 Years................	64	34	2
50 Years and Over......	60	40	*
By Politics			
Republicans	38	61	1
Democrats...................	73	25	2
Independents..............	63	36	1
By Lewinsky Affair Allegations			
Total True	49	50	1
Total Not True	78	20	2
By Clinton Approval			
Approve......................	76	22	2
Disapprove..................	23	76	1

*Less than 1%

Which comes closer to your opinion concerning the investigation being conducted by Independent Counsel Ken Starr—Clinton is trying to obstruct and delay the investigation, or Clinton is trying to cooperate with the investigation?

Obstruct and delay... 51%
Cooperate... 44
No opinion.. 5

	Obstruct and delay	Cooperate	No opinion
By Sex			
Male............................	57%	40%	3%
Female	47	47	6
By Age			
18–29 Years................	52	47	1
30–49 Years................	52	42	6
50 Years and Over......	51	43	6

By Politics			
Republicans	75	21	4
Democrats...................	29	67	4
Independents..............	52	41	7
By Lewinsky Affair Allegations			
Total True	68	28	4
Total Not True	14	82	4
By Clinton Approval			
Approve......................	34	60	6
Disapprove..................	86	12	2

Note: Despite being the first president in history to agree to testify before a grand jury investigation to answer questions about whether he engaged in criminal behavior, Bill Clinton does not seem to have suffered in the eyes of the American public. According to the latest Gallup Poll, 65% approve of the job he is doing as president, a few points higher than three weeks ago and about average for his ratings this year, which have been the highest of his presidency. Respondents also show little change in their assessment of whether he engaged in an extramarital sexual relationship or lied under oath while president, and they remain divided on whether he or Monica Lewinsky is more credible in accounts of what happened between them.

The poll also shows that Americans oppose the immunity agreement between Lewinsky and Independent Counsel Kenneth Starr by a margin of 54% to 40%. This agreement allows the former White House intern to testify before the grand jury without fear that she will be prosecuted for any statements she might make that would contradict former sworn testimony. On the other hand, 85% support Clinton's decision to testify. Also, by a margin of 59% to 39%, they favor the special conditions granted to the president, which allow him to have his attorneys present when being questioned and to be videotaped rather than appear personally before the grand jury.

With respect to the testimony that Lewinsky might give before a grand jury, the public does not seem especially inclined to think that it should lead to Clinton's impeachment. If Lewinsky says that she and the president had sex and that—without asking her to lie—he discussed ways to hide their alleged sexual relationship from investigators,

about one-quarter thinks that would be serious enough to warrant impeachment proceedings by Congress; but three-quarters disagree. One-third (34%) thinks that the charges would not be very serious, while another 41% think the matter very serious but not sufficient for impeachment. Even among the 66% who already believe that there probably was a sexual relationship between Clinton and Lewinsky, just 34% would favor impeachment proceedings if Lewinsky testified as just described.

Two-thirds are inclined to believe that Clinton had sexual relations with Lewinsky, and 56% are inclined to think that he lied about it under oath—numbers that have changed very little over the past five months. However, since an April poll, respondents have become somewhat less likely to believe that Clinton tried to obstruct justice. In the current poll, they say that he has not done so by a margin of 47% to 43%, while last April they thought he had, by a margin of 50% to 42%. This improvement could be a reflection of recent news reports which suggest that Lewinsky may testify that Clinton never asked her to lie about their alleged sexual relationship.

By a small margin (51% to 44%), the public also continues to believe that Clinton is trying to delay the investigation rather than cooperate, but these numbers represent a slight improvement since early June. At that time, 57% thought that Clinton was trying to obstruct and delay the investigation, while only 35% believed that he was trying to cooperate.

If Clinton's testimony should differ from Lewinsky's, respondents are mostly divided on which they would be more likely to believe. If Lewinsky says that she and the president had sexual relations while he continues to deny it, the public is slightly more inclined to believe her, by a margin of 48% to 44%. On the other hand, if Lewinsky says that Clinton advised her to lie under oath, the public is more inclined to believe Clinton's denial, by a margin of 49% to 44%.

AUGUST 8
TRUST IN THE NEWS MEDIA

Interviewing Dates: 7/13–14/98
CNN/*USA Today*/Gallup Poll
Survey #GO 123792

Apart from how frequently you use them as sources of news, we'd like to know whether or not you can trust the accuracy of the news and information you get from each of the following news sources. Do you feel you can trust the accuracy of the news and information you get from:

Local newspapers in your area?

	July 13–14, 1998	March 6–9, 1998
Yes, can trust	65%	61%
No, cannot trust	18	22
Mixed (volunteered)	15	14
No opinion	2	3

National newspapers such as the New York Times, *the* Wall Street Journal, *and* USA Today?

	July 13–14, 1998	March 6–9, 1998
Yes, can trust	52%	49%
No, cannot trust	20	20
Mixed (volunteered)	13	11
No opinion	15	20

Nightly network news programs on ABC, CBS, or NBC?

	July 13–14, 1998	March 6–9, 1998
Yes, can trust	66%	61%
No, cannot trust	16	20
Mixed (volunteered)	16	16
No opinion	2	3

Morning news and interview programs on the national television networks?

	July 13–14, 1998	March 6–9, 1998
Yes, can trust	51%	48%
No, cannot trust	22	22
Mixed (volunteered)	11	13
No opinion	16	17

CNN News or CNN Headline News?

	July 13–14, 1998	March 6–9, 1998
Yes, can trust	66%	64%
No, cannot trust	13	13
Mixed (volunteered)	10	9
No opinion	11	14

Cable news programs other than CNN such as CNBC, MSNBC, or the Fox News Channel?

	July 13–14, 1998	March 6–9, 1998
Yes, can trust	52%	46%
No, cannot trust	18	19
Mixed (volunteered)	9	12
No opinion	21	23

C-SPAN?

	July 13–14, 1998	March 6–9, 1998
Yes, can trust	43%	39%
No, cannot trust	18	17
Mixed (volunteered)	6	6
No opinion	33	38

Public television news?

	July 13–14, 1998	March 6–9, 1998
Yes, can trust	57%	60%
No, cannot trust	15	14
Mixed (volunteered)	10	10
No opinion	18	16

Local television news from television stations in your area?

	July 13–14, 1998	March 6–9, 1998
Yes, can trust	73%	67%
No, cannot trust	12	14
Mixed (volunteered)	11	15
No opinion	4	4

National Public Radio?

	July 13–14, 1998	March 6–9, 1998
Yes, can trust	51%	47%
No, cannot trust	20	18
Mixed (volunteered)	7	8
No opinion	22	27

Local radio news from radio stations in your area?

	July 13–14, 1998	March 6–9, 1998
Yes, can trust	63%	57%
No, cannot trust	16	18
Mixed (volunteered)	10	12
No opinion	11	13

National network news on radio other than National Public Radio?

	July 13–14, 1998	March 6–9, 1998
Yes, can trust	47%	42%
No, cannot trust	23	21
Mixed (volunteered)	8	12
No opinion	22	25

Radio talk shows?

	July 13–14, 1998	March 6–9, 1998
Yes, can trust	23%	22%
No, cannot trust	48	41
Mixed (volunteered)	10	13
No opinion	19	24

Television talk shows?

	July 13–14, 1998	March 6–9, 1998
Yes, can trust	18%	20%
No, cannot trust	61	53
Mixed (volunteered)	13	15
No opinion	8	12

Discussions with your friends or family?

	July 13–14, 1998	March 6–9, 1998
Yes, can trust	66%	60%
No, cannot trust	16	17
Mixed (volunteered)	15	17
No opinion	3	6

Half-hour television entertainment news programs such as "Hard Copy," "Entertainment Tonight," and others?

	July 13–14, 1998	March 6–9, 1998
Yes, can trust	25%	28%
No, cannot trust	53	47
Mixed (volunteered)	12	14
No opinion	10	11

News on the computer using the Internet or an on-line computer service?

	July 13–14, 1998	March 6–9, 1998
Yes, can trust	26%	24%
No, cannot trust	29	27
Mixed (volunteered)	8	8
No opinion	37	41

Weekly news magazines?

	July 13–14, 1998	March 6–9, 1998
Yes, can trust	46%	43%
No, cannot trust	26	23
Mixed (volunteered)	10	12
No opinion	18	22

Television news programs on Sunday morning?

	July 13–14, 1998	March 6–9, 1998
Yes, can trust	49%	47%
No, cannot trust	20	18
Mixed (volunteered)	9	9
No opinion	22	26

Television newsmagazine shows during the evening such as "60 Minutes," "20/20," "Prime Time Live," or "Dateline NBC," and others?

	July 13–14, 1998	March 6–9, 1998
Yes, can trust	66%	64%
No, cannot trust	17	15
Mixed (volunteered)	13	16
No opinion	4	5

Trust Index
(Percent "Can Trust" Minus Percent "Cannot Trust")

	July 1998	March 1998	Point change
Local television news	+64	+54	+10
CNN News, CNN Headline News	+59	+59	0
Local radio news	+53	+44	+9
Public television news	+51	+54	–3
Television news-magazine shows	+51	+51	0
Discussions with friends	+51	+46	+5
Nightly network news	+51	+43	+8
Local newspapers	+48	+40	+8
Cable news other than CNN	+44	+35	+9
National Public Radio	+39	+40	–1
National newspapers	+39	+37	+2
Sunday morning news	+37	+40	–3
C-SPAN	+36	+36	0
Morning news, interviews	+34	+31	+3
National network radio news	+30	+27	+3
Weekly news magazines	+24	+27	–3
Internet	–5	–5	0
Television half-hour entertainment news	–31	–22	–9
Radio talk shows	–31	–24	–7
Television talk shows	–46	–38	–8

In general, do you think news organizations get the facts straight, or do you think that their stories and reports are often inaccurate?

Get facts straight... 50%
Often inaccurate 45
No opinion.. 5

Selected National Trend

	Get facts straight	Often inaccurate	No opinion
1989			
August 9–28*	54%	44%	2%
1988			
August 24	40	50	10
May 13........................	48	43	9
January 8–17*.............	44	48	8
1985			
August 17	50	38	12
June 22........................	55	34	11

*Special telephone survey

Note: Several recent instances of journalistic inaccuracy and news source falsification have sent shock waves through America's news organizations, including those involving CNN, *Time* magazine, the *Boston Globe*, and the *Cincinnati Enquirer*. Contrary to the emerging conventional wisdom, however, new Gallup Poll data provide no evidence that the media's reputation or credibility among the American public has taken any immediate hits.

The most prominent media controversy this year has involved the "Tailwind" investigative news story broadcast by CNN and published in *Time* magazine. That story alleged, among other things, that the United States had used nerve gas against U.S. defectors during the Vietnam War. The Defense Department denounced the charges as false, and a CNN review conducted in response to the ensuing furor concluded that there had not been enough evidence to substantiate the charges. This sobering conclusion led to a highly publicized retraction of the story by both news organizations involved.

A mid-July Gallup Poll found that most respondents (71%) had heard or read about the CNN and *Time* nerve-gas story controversy. Among this group, however, only 42% knew that the two news organizations had publicly retracted the story. Another 6% believed (incorrectly) that the organiza-

tions were standing behind the story, while the remaining one-half (52%) were not sure how CNN and *Time* had handled the controversy. Taken together, these findings suggest that barely one-third (30%) are fully aware of the facts surrounding the incident.

Other results from the poll suggest that the media self-scrutiny resulting from the controversies may have overestimated the impact of recent scandals on the public. While respondents have at least an imperfect understanding of the facts in the "Tailwind" controversy, most are totally unaware of three other media situations. First, only 35% have heard or read about *Boston Globe* columnist Patricia Smith, who was forced to quit her job after admitting to fabricating quotes in her columns. Second, only 27% are familiar with the sanctions taken against the *Cincinnati Enquirer* for illegally obtaining information about the Chiquita Banana company. And third, only 26% are aware that *New Republic* reporter Stephen Glass was fired for fabricating all or part of twenty-seven magazine articles.

Whatever the degree of awareness of specific scandals, the mid-July Gallup Poll finds public opinion of overall accuracy in media to be no better or worse today than it was a decade ago. According to the survey, just 50% think that news organizations get the facts straight, while almost as many (45%) think that they are often inaccurate. Although not very positive, these results are essentially unchanged from 1989, when the question was last asked. At that time 54% thought that the media mostly got the facts right, while 44% thought that they were often inaccurate.

Public skepticism about the accuracy of the news media in general stands in sharp contrast to the much higher trust ratings that specific news organizations receive when respondents are asked about them by name. In July the Gallup Poll updated a measure of the public's trust in each of twenty sources of news. This measure was first conducted in March of this year before many of the major scandals became known. The list includes some generic news outlets such as local newspapers and weekly magazines as well as specific news organizations such as CNN, National Public Radio, and C-Span. In the March 1998 survey, many of these news outlets and organizations scored extremely well on the issue of trust. Public trust was particularly high in the electronic news

media such as CNN, public television news, and local television news.

Gallup updated this rating of specific news sources in July; and despite the CNN-*Time* episode and other incidents of journalistic malfeasance, the poll records little change in public perceptions compared to March. The few changes that were observed are mostly in the direction of increased, rather than decreased, public confidence in many of the traditional news media, including local television news, local radio news, the nightly network news, local newspapers, and cable news other than CNN.

Public trust in CNN, the news outlet perhaps most closely associated with a journalistic scandal this year, has undergone no change between March and July. The pioneer cable network—with a 66% "can trust" level among the entire public—has essentially the same ratings today as it did in March, when 64% said that they could trust the accuracy of its news and information. In terms of a "net trust" measure (which looks only at those who have an opinion and subtracts the percentage of those who say that they cannot trust the news outlet from the percentage of those who say that they can), CNN has remained exactly the same, at 59% "net trust."

The media category of weekly news magazines (which includes *Time* magazine, although it was not mentioned to respondents by name) saw a slight, though not statistically significant, decline in "net trust." Among the public as a whole, the "can trust" figure for news magazines was 43% in March and is 46% today. However, the "net trust" figure among respondents who have an opinion declined from 27% in March to 24% today.

Most of the other news sources tested in the Gallup media monitor saw slight improvements in public trust or remained statistically the same. The exceptions are radio talk shows, television talk shows, and half-hour "infotainment" television shows, whose "net trust" levels all fell by significant amounts between March and July.

AUGUST 15
PRESIDENT CLINTON/STARR INVESTIGATION

Interviewing Dates: 8/10–12/98
CNN/*USA Today*/Gallup Poll
Survey #GO 123694

How strongly would you say you approve or disapprove of the way Bill Clinton is handling his job as president—would you say very strongly, or not so strongly?

Very strongly approve 43%
Not so strongly approve 22
Not so strongly disapprove............................ 8
Very strongly disapprove 22
No opinion... 5

	Very strongly approve	Not so strongly approve	Not so strongly disapprove	Very strongly disapprove*
By Sex				
Male	39%	22%	8%	27%
Female.............	45	22	8	18
By Ethnic Background				
White...............	38	23	9	25
Nonwhite.........	65	17	4	8
Black	75	16	2	3
By Education				
Postgraduate....	38	21	9	27
College Graduate......	45	20	11	20
College Incomplete...	42	24	7	25
No College	43	22	7	20
By Region				
East.................	53	19	6	18
Midwest	41	20	13	22
South	41	24	7	24
West	35	25	5	25
By Age				
18–29 Years	39	30	9	16
30–49 Years	41	24	8	21
50–64 Years	51	14	6	25
65 Years and Over......	42	15	8	31
By Household Income				
$75,000 and Over......	45	20	9	25
$50,000 and Over......	43	21	9	25

$30,000–$49,999 40	25	7	22
$20,000–$29,999 42	21	8	24
Under $20,000 53	24	4	12

By Politics

Republicans..... 20	25	10	41
Democrats 68	17	6	6
Independents ... 37	25	8	21

By Political Ideology

Conservative ... 29	18	10	37
Moderate 45	25	9	16
Liberal 63	22	3	9

*"No opinion"—at 10% or less—is omitted.

Selected National Trend

	Very strongly approve	Not so strongly approve	Not so strongly dis-approve	Very strongly dis-approve*
1998				
Jan. 30–Feb. 1 .... 51%	18%	7%	21%
1997				
Jan. 30–Feb. 2 34	26	9	22
1996				
Jan. 12–15 26	20	17	30
1995				
Jan. 16–18 21	26	17	28
1994				
July 15–17....... 19	23	15	34
June 3–6 26	20	15	32

*"No opinion"—at 9% or less—is omitted.

As you may know, President Clinton is scheduled to testify before the grand jury in Ken Starr's investigation on [Monday] August 17. I'm going to read some ways Bill Clinton might handle this situation. For each one, please tell me whether that action by Clinton would or would not cause you to lose confidence in him as president:

If he were to testify under oath before the grand jury that he did have sex with Monica Lewinsky?

Would lose confidence	26%
Would not	71
No opinion..	3

	Would lose confidence	Would not	No opinion
By Sex			
Male........................... 28%	69%	3%
Female 24	72	4
By Ethnic Background			
White 27	69	4
Nonwhite 22	78	*
Black........................... 19	81	*
By Education			
Postgraduate 24	73	3
College Graduate........ 26	73	1
College Incomplete..... 28	69	3
No College.................. 25	72	3
By Region			
East 21	76	3
Midwest...................... 26	70	4
South........................... 31	66	3
West............................ 23	73	4
By Age			
18–29 Years................ 31	66	3
30–49 Years................ 24	75	1
50–64 Years................ 25	72	3
65 Years and Over...... 25	66	9
By Household Income			
$75,000 and Over 24	74	2
$50,000 and Over 28	71	1
$30,000–$49,999........ 25	73	2
$20,000–$29,999........ 28	68	4
Under $20,000............ 20	75	5
By Politics			
Republicans 37	60	3
Democrats................... 20	78	2
Independents.............. 23	73	4
By Political Ideology			
Conservative............... 34	62	4

Moderate	25	72	3
Liberal	14	83	3

By Lewinsky Affair Allegations

Total True	27	70	3
Total Not True	27	71	2

By Clinton Approval

Approve	19	79	2
Disapprove	42	53	5

*Less than 1%

If he were to testify under oath before the grand jury that he did not have sex with Monica Lewinsky?

Would lose confidence	33%
Would not	60
No opinion	7

	Would lose confidence	Would not	No opinion
By Sex			
Male	34%	59%	7%
Female	31	62	7
By Ethnic Background			
White	35	57	8
Nonwhite	17	80	3
Black	11	87	2
By Education			
Postgraduate	35	59	6
College Graduate	37	59	4
College Incomplete	36	57	7
No College	29	63	8
By Region			
East	30	63	7
Midwest	32	60	8
South	32	61	7
West	36	57	7
By Age			
18–29 Years	29	65	6
30–49 Years	34	60	6
50–64 Years	34	62	4
65 Years and Over	34	53	13

By Household Income

$75,000 and Over	35	58	7
$50,000 and Over	37	57	6
$30,000–$49,999	38	57	5
$20,000–$29,999	27	63	10
Under $20,000	22	74	4

By Politics

Republicans	51	41	8
Democrats	15	79	6
Independents	34	59	7

By Political Ideology

Conservative	43	50	7
Moderate	31	62	7
Liberal	20	75	5

By Lewinsky Affair Allegations

Total True	43	50	7
Total Not True	3	93	4

By Clinton Approval

Approve	19	75	6
Disapprove	62	29	9

If he were to appear before the grand jury but refuse to answer questions about his relationship with Monica Lewinsky?

Would lose confidence	53%
Would not	44
No opinion	3

	Would lose confidence	Would not	No opinion
By Sex			
Male	55%	43%	2%
Female	51	45	4
By Ethnic Background			
White	56	41	3
Nonwhite	37	61	2
Black	26	72	2
By Education			
Postgraduate	53	45	2
College Graduate	56	41	3
College Incomplete	56	41	3
No College	51	46	3

By Region			
East	44	53	3
Midwest	55	41	4
South	54	43	3
West	60	38	2
By Age			
18–29 Years	62	37	1
30–49 Years	52	46	2
50–64 Years	50	48	2
65 Years and Over	51	42	7
By Household Income			
$75,000 and Over	55	43	2
$50,000 and Over	56	42	2
$30,000–$49,999	56	42	2
$20,000–$29,999	55	42	3
Under $20,000	44	53	3
By Politics			
Republicans	74	23	3
Democrats	34	62	4
Independents	54	44	2
By Political Ideology			
Conservative	64	32	4
Moderate	53	45	2
Liberal	38	59	3
By Lewinsky Affair Allegations			
Total True	62	36	2
Total Not True	30	67	3
By Clinton Approval			
Approve	38	60	2
Disapprove	86	11	3

If he were to cancel his upcoming appearance before the grand jury and refuse to testify?

Would lose confidence	60%
Would not	37
No opinion	3

	Would lose confidence	*Would not*	*No opinion*
By Sex			
Male	62%	36%	2%
Female	59	38	3
By Ethnic Background			
White	63	34	3
Nonwhite	47	51	2
Black	37	62	1
By Education			
Postgraduate	62	37	1
College Graduate	67	31	2
College Incomplete	65	32	3
No College	55	42	3
By Region			
East	56	41	3
Midwest	62	33	5
South	60	38	2
West	65	33	2
By Age			
18–29 Years	71	28	1
30–49 Years	59	39	2
50–64 Years	58	39	3
65 Years and Over	52	40	8
By Household Income			
$75,000 and Over	65	32	3
$50,000 and Over	64	34	2
$30,000–$49,999	65	34	1
$20,000–$29,999	60	38	2
Under $20,000	51	44	5
By Politics			
Republicans	80	19	1
Democrats	43	52	5
Independents	62	37	1
By Political Ideology			
Conservative	70	27	3
Moderate	61	37	2
Liberal	45	52	3
By Lewinsky Affair Allegations			
Total True	69	29	2
Total Not True	35	61	4
By Clinton Approval			
Approve	47	50	3
Disapprove	89	9	2

Asked of half sample: Next, I'm going to read some things that may or may not be true about President Clinton. For each one, please

say whether, if true, you would consider it serious enough to consider removing President Clinton from office:

If he had sex with a former White House intern in the Oval Office?

Yes, serious enough.. 31%
No 67
No opinion 2

	Yes, serious enough	No	No opinion
By Sex			
Male.............................	28%	71%	1%
Female	33	64	3
By Ethnic Background			
White	33	65	2
Nonwhite	17	79	4
Black............................	17	78	5
By Education			
Postgraduate	17	83	*
College Graduate........	34	66	*
College Incomplete.....	30	69	1
No College..................	33	63	4
By Region			
East	24	74	2
Midwest......................	34	66	*
South...........................	34	64	2
West............................	28	67	5
By Age			
18–29 Years................	39	60	1
30–49 Years................	26	71	3
50–64 Years................	28	72	*
65 Years and Over......	36	61	3
By Household Income			
$75,000 and Over	23	77	*
$50,000 and Over	28	71	1
$30,000–$49,999........	33	67	*
$20,000–$29,999........	33	64	3
Under $20,000............	26	71	3
By Politics			
Republicans	49	49	2
Democrats...................	18	82	*
Independents...............	29	67	4
By Political Ideology			
Conservative...............	42	55	3
Moderate.....................	28	71	1
Liberal	17	83	*
By Lewinsky Affair Allegations			
Total True	35	64	1
Total Not True	19	77	4
By Clinton Approval			
Approve.......................	17	82	1
Disapprove..................	62	36	2

*Less than 1%

If he lied to the American people about his relationship with Monica Lewinsky?

Yes, serious enough.. 46%
No 52
No opinion 2

	Yes, serious enough	No	No opinion
By Sex			
Male.............................	47%	52%	1%
Female	46	52	2
By Ethnic Background			
White	49	49	2
Nonwhite	31	66	3
Black............................	29	68	3
By Education			
Postgraduate	35	64	1
College Graduate........	43	55	2
College Incomplete.....	46	54	*
No College..................	50	47	3
By Region			
East	36	62	2
Midwest......................	48	50	2
South...........................	51	46	3
West............................	48	52	*
By Age			
18–29 Years................	55	45	*

30–49 Years	44	55	1
50–64 Years	41	56	3
65 Years and Over	50	48	2

By Household Income

$75,000 and Over	43	57	*
$50,000 and Over	43	55	2
$30,000–$49,999	49	51	*
$20,000–$29,999	55	42	3
Under $20,000	37	62	1

By Politics

Republicans	66	33	1
Democrats	29	71	*
Independents	48	48	4

By Political Ideology

Conservative	57	41	2
Moderate	42	56	2
Liberal	36	63	1

By Lewinsky Affair Allegations

Total True	53	46	1
Total Not True	28	70	2

By Clinton Approval

Approve	33	66	1
Disapprove	78	20	2

*Less than 1%

If he tried to influence Lewinsky to lie under oath about their relationship?

Yes, serious enough	59%
No	40
No opinion	1

	Yes, serious enough	No	No opinion
By Sex			
Male	65%	34%	1%
Female	53	45	2
By Ethnic Background			
White	62	37	1
Nonwhite	45	53	2
Black	46	52	2

By Education

Postgraduate	62	38	*
College Graduate	62	38	*
College Incomplete	59	40	1
No College	57	42	1

By Region

East	50	50	*
Midwest	63	36	1
South	59	39	2
West	63	36	1

By Age

18–29 Years	64	35	1
30–49 Years	56	43	1
50–64 Years	62	36	2
65 Years and Over	54	46	*

By Household Income

$75,000 and Over	60	40	*
$50,000 and Over	63	37	*
$30,000–$49,999	59	40	1
$20,000–$29,999	63	35	2
Under $20,000	43	56	1

By Politics

Republicans	78	20	2
Democrats	46	53	1
Independents	57	42	1

By Political Ideology

Conservative	65	33	2
Moderate	58	41	1
Liberal	48	52	*

By Lewinsky Affair Allegations

Total True	66	33	1
Total Not True	38	61	1

By Clinton Approval

Approve	46	53	1
Disapprove	92	7	1

*Less than 1%

If he was engaged in improper financial dealings while governor of Arkansas?

Yes, serious enough	59%
No	37
No opinion	4

	Yes, serious enough	No	No opinion
By Sex			
Male	60%	37%	3%
Female	58	37	5
By Ethnic Background			
White	62	34	4
Nonwhite	48	46	6
Black	45	50	5
By Education			
Postgraduate	56	42	2
College Graduate	61	35	4
College Incomplete	61	35	4
No College	59	37	4
By Region			
East	57	38	5
Midwest	60	36	4
South	57	38	5
West	63	35	2
By Age			
18–29 Years	68	30	2
30–49 Years	58	38	4
50–64 Years	65	32	3
65 Years and Over	44	49	7
By Household Income			
$75,000 and Over	64	33	3
$50,000 and Over	62	36	2
$30,000–$49,999	63	35	2
$20,000–$29,999	60	36	4
Under $20,000	49	40	11
By Politics			
Republicans	65	31	4
Democrats	49	47	4
Independents	65	31	4
By Political Ideology			
Conservative	64	32	4
Moderate	59	37	4
Liberal	55	42	3
By Lewinsky Affair Allegations			
Total True	67	31	2
Total Not True	36	58	6

By Clinton Approval			
Approve	49	46	5
Disapprove	84	15	1

If he lied under oath as a witness in the Paula Jones case?

Yes, serious enough	56%
No	40
No opinion	4

	Yes, serious enough	No	No opinion
By Sex			
Male	57%	38%	5%
Female	55	42	3
By Ethnic Background			
White	60	36	4
Nonwhite	36	61	3
Black	36	61	3
By Education			
Postgraduate	52	47	1
College Graduate	59	34	7
College Incomplete	59	39	2
No College	53	42	5
By Region			
East	51	45	4
Midwest	59	38	3
South	58	39	3
West	55	40	5
By Age			
18–29 Years	68	29	3
30–49 Years	55	41	4
50–64 Years	52	47	1
65 Years and Over	47	46	7
By Household Income			
$75,000 and Over	51	48	1
$50,000 and Over	57	41	2
$30,000–$49,999	60	36	4
$20,000–$29,999	61	37	2
Under $20,000	43	51	6
By Politics			
Republicans	69	26	5

Democrats	43	53	4
Independents	58	40	2

By Political Ideology
Conservative	60	36	4
Moderate	57	39	4
Liberal	49	49	2

By Lewinsky Affair Allegations
Total True	63	34	3
Total Not True	35	60	5

By Clinton Approval
Approve	42	54	4
Disapprove	90	8	2

If he lies under oath before the grand jury in the investigation being conducted by Ken Starr?

Yes, serious enough	60%
No	37
No opinion	3

	Yes, serious enough	No	No opinion
By Sex			
Male	65%	32%	3%
Female	56	41	3
By Ethnic Background			
White	64	34	2
Nonwhite	40	55	5
Black	40	57	3
By Education			
Postgraduate	59	39	2
College Graduate	66	31	3
College Incomplete	64	33	3
No College	56	41	3
By Region			
East	53	44	3
Midwest	63	35	2
South	60	36	4
West	65	34	1
By Age			
18–29 Years	73	26	1
30–49 Years	61	36	3
50–64 Years	54	44	2
65 Years and Over	50	46	4

By Household Income
$75,000 and Over	58	40	2
$50,000 and Over	62	36	2
$30,000–$49,999	66	31	3
$20,000–$29,999	63	35	2
Under $20,000	44	53	3

By Politics
Republicans	78	21	1
Democrats	45	52	3
Independents	61	36	3

By Political Ideology
Conservative	68	30	2
Moderate	59	37	4
Liberal	50	49	1

By Lewinsky Affair Allegations
Total True	68	30	2
Total Not True	37	59	4

By Clinton Approval
Approve	47	50	3
Disapprove	94	6	*

*Less than 1%

Note: A new Gallup Poll, taken days before he is scheduled to testify in Kenneth Starr's investigation, finds Bill Clinton still enjoying solid approval ratings for the job that he is doing as president and Americans still resistant to holding him publicly accountable for possible sexual misdeeds. Despite widespread belief that Clinton probably had sexual relations with Monica Lewinsky and that he possibly lied about it under oath, only 20% of Americans currently think that Clinton should be impeached and removed from office.

Perhaps most important for Clinton prior to his testimony on Monday [August 17], he continues to receive job approval ratings that are among the highest of his presidency. Sixty-five percent now approve of the job that he is doing as president, including 43% who strongly approve. Also, 60% have a favorable impression of him personally.

Clinton has vehemently denied having sexual relations with Lewinsky. Three-quarters of respondents, however, now tend to believe that he and Lewinsky probably had sexual relations of some kind, a number up slightly from last month.

Additionally, 64% tend to think that he lied under oath as president, presumably in his Paula Jones deposition. Nevertheless, most people say that their confidence in Clinton as president will remain regardless of whether he admits to or denies a sexual relationship with Lewinsky in his grand jury testimony next week.

There are indications, however, that clear-cut evidence that Clinton lied under oath could spell trouble for him. Fifty-six percent say that if it turns out to be true that he lied under oath in the Jones case, such an offense would be serious enough to consider impeaching him and removing him from office. Similarly, 60% say that lying now before the Starr grand jury might warrant impeachment.

Among the list of options available to Clinton, two strategies deemed not advisable from a public relations standpoint are either canceling his appearance before the grand jury, or appearing but refusing to answer questions. More than one-half of respondents say that they would lose confidence in Clinton as president if he were to follow such an obstructionist route.

Despite the impact that perjury could have on public opinion about impeachment issues, there is ample evidence in Gallup Poll data that Clinton's chances of politically surviving his upcoming testimony before the grand jury in Starr's investigation are relatively good. One strong advantage for the president is that his political stock with the public far exceeds that of his adversaries in this controversy. In addition to his overall job rating of 65%, another 75% approve of the way that he is managing the government, and 70% approve of his positions on major issues.

By contrast, both Lewinsky and Starr have extremely low personal ratings, which continue to decline. When she first appeared on the scene in January, 30% had a favorable view of Lewinsky and 50% an unfavorable one. Today, only 13% feel favorably toward the former intern, and 72% unfavorably. Throughout the year roughly one-quarter of respondents has had a favorable view of Starr, but his unfavorable ratings have grown from 24% in January to 54% today. Similarly, a majority now disapproves of the way that Republicans in Congress are handling the controversy, and only 33% approve—down from 44% who approved in January.

A second factor working in Clinton's favor is that most people say that his private sexual matters are not relevant to their evaluation of the job he is doing in office. Indeed, only 26% would lose confidence in Clinton as president if he were to testify under oath that he had sex with Lewinsky. Less than one-half (47%) think that having sex with a former White House intern in the Oval Office is relevant to how Clinton should be judged as president.

Third, while large majorities tend to believe that Clinton had sex with Lewinsky and that he has lied about it under oath, only 21% and 19%, respectively, currently say that these allegations are definitely true; the rest say that they are probably true. This number has remained low despite recent reports of Lewinsky's grand jury testimony describing these alleged relations and seems to suggest a public reluctant to fully accept that the charges are true, so long as Clinton denies them. Whether people would find DNA evidence linking Clinton to Lewinsky persuasive is an open question, but it seems clear that without solid evidence, they would rather give Clinton the benefit of the doubt.

This is not to say, however, that respondents have respect for Clinton's character. He receives exceptionally low marks on personal morality, with barely one-third of the public approving of the moral example he sets for the country and two-thirds disapproving. They are also closely split over whether they respect Clinton or not, with 53% saying yes and 44% saying no. And in a Gallup Poll conducted last week, only 34% said that the term "honest and trustworthy" applied to the president.

AUGUST 22
PRESIDENT CLINTON/HILLARY RODHAM CLINTON

Interviewing Dates: 8/10–12, 17,* 18,* 20*/98
CNN/USA Today/Gallup Poll
Surveys #GO 123694, 124075, 124094, 124115

*Based on interviews with 633, 884, and 628 national adults, 18 years and older, respectively. For results based on samples of these sizes, one can say with 95% confidence that the error attributable to sampling and other random effects could be ±4 percentage points. Polls conducted entirely in one evening are subject to additional error or bias not found in polls conducted over several days.

Do you approve or disapprove of the way Bill Clinton is handling his job as president?

	Aug. 20, 1998	Aug. 18, 1998	Aug. 17, 1998
Approve	61%	66%	62%
Disapprove	34	29	32
No opinion	5	5	6

	Aug. 20, 1998	Aug. 18, 1998	Aug. 17, 1998
By Sex			
Male			
Approve	56%	64%	56%
Disapprove	39	32	38
No Opinion	5	4	6
Female			
Approve	64	68	67
Disapprove	30	27	27
No Opinion	6	5	6
By Age			
18–29 Years			
Approve	56	62	58
Disapprove	38	33	38
No Opinion	6	5	4
30–49 Years			
Approve	56	69	60
Disapprove	38	28	33
No Opinion	6	3	7
50 Years and Over			
Approve	67	64	67
Disapprove	28	29	28
No Opinion	5	7	5
By Politics			
Republicans			
Approve	41	42	30
Disapprove	53	54	69
No Opinion	6	4	1
Democrats			
Approve	83	85	85
Disapprove	14	12	11
No Opinion	3	3	4
Independents			
Approve	56	63	60
Disapprove	37	30	30
No Opinion	7	7	10

By Those Who Heard "Monica Speech"

Yes, Heard			
Approve	N.A.	N.A.	64
Disapprove	N.A.	N.A.	32
No Opinion	N.A.	N.A.	4
Did Not Hear			
Approve	N.A.	N.A.	59
Disapprove	N.A.	N.A.	32
No Opinion	N.A.	N.A.	9

By Those Who Think Clinton Should Be Impeached

Should Be			
Approve	N.A.	20	N.A.
Disapprove	N.A.	76	N.A.
No Opinion	N.A.	4	N.A.
Should Not Be			
Approve	N.A.	84	N.A.
Disapprove	N.A.	11	N.A.
No Opinion	N.A.	5	N.A.

By Military Attack Against Terrorist Facilities

Support Decision			
Approve	64	N.A.	N.A.
Disapprove	31	N.A.	N.A.
No Opinion	5	N.A.	N.A.
Do Not Support			
Approve	47	N.A.	N.A.
Disapprove	49	N.A.	N.A.
No Opinion	4	N.A.	N.A.

Selected National Trend

	Approve	Dis-approve	No opinion
1998			
August 20*	61%	34%	5%
August 18*	66	29	5
August 17*	62	32	6
August 10–12	65	30	5
August 7–8	64	32	4
July 29*	65	31	4
July 7–8	61	34	5
June 22–23	60	34	6
June 5–7	60	34	6
May 8–10	64	31	5
April 17–19	63	31	6
March 20–22	66	28	6
March 16*	67	29	4

March 6–9	63	31	6
February 20–22	66	29	5
February 13–15	66	30	4
January 30–February 1	69	28	3
January 28*	67	28	5
January 25–26	59	37	4
January 24–25	60	35	5
January 23–24	58	36	6
January 16–18	60	30	10
January 6–7	59	32	9

*Based on one-night poll

Next, I'd like to get your overall opinion of some people in the news. As I read each name, please say if you have a favorable or unfavorable opinion of this person, or if you have never heard of him or her:

Bill Clinton?

	Aug. 20, 1998	Aug. 18, 1998	Aug. 10–12, 1998
Favorable	53%	55%	60%
Unfavorable	43	42	38
No opinion	4	3	2

	Aug. 20, 1998	Aug. 18, 1998	Aug. 10–12, 1998
By Sex			
Male			
Favorable	52%	52%	56%
Unfavorable	43	47	43
No Opinion	5	1	1
Female			
Favorable	54	57	64
Unfavorable	42	38	34
No Opinion	4	5	2
By Age			
18–29 Years			
Favorable	53	57	63
Unfavorable	42	43	36
No Opinion	5	*	1
30–49 Years			
Favorable	45	54	60
Unfavorable	48	44	38
No Opinion	7	2	2
50 Years and Over			
Favorable	61	55	59
Unfavorable	37	41	40
No Opinion	2	4	1
By Politics			
Republicans			
Favorable	31	27	36
Unfavorable	67	69	63
No Opinion	2	4	1
Democrats			
Favorable	78	81	85
Unfavorable	19	11	14
No Opinion	3	8	1
Independents			
Favorable	48	65	56
Unfavorable	43	28	41
No Opinion	9	7	3

*Less than 1%

Selected National Trend

	Favorable	Un-favorable	No opinion
1998			
August 7–8	58%	40%	2%
June 5–7	61	36	3
March 20–22	60	35	5
March 16*	60	37	3
February 20–22	64	34	2
February 13–15	58	39	3
January 30–February 1	65	34	1
January 28*	63	32	5
January 25–26	53	43	4
January 24–25	58	39	3
January 23–24	57	40	3

*Based on one-night poll

Hillary Rodham Clinton?

	Aug. 20, 1998	Aug. 18, 1998	Aug. 10–12, 1998
Favorable	60%	64%	60%
Unfavorable	30	29	36
No opinion	10	7	4

	Aug. 20, 1998	Aug. 18, 1998	Aug. 10–12, 1998
By Sex			
Male			
Favorable	52%	58%`	53%
Unfavorable	35	35	43
No Opinion	13	7	4
Female			
Favorable	68	70	67
Unfavorable	26	24	29
No Opinion	6	6	4
By Age			
18–29 Years			
Favorable	55	67	63
Unfavorable	32	27	34
No Opinion	13	6	3
30–49 Years			
Favorable	58	65	60
Unfavorable	32	31	34
No Opinion	10	4	6
50 Years and Over			
Favorable	67	60	59
Unfavorable	27	29	38
No Opinion	6	11	3
By Politics			
Republicans			
Favorable	44	40	36
Unfavorable	50	55	59
No Opinion	6	5	5
Democrats			
Favorable	80	81	85
Unfavorable	10	11	14
No Opinion	10	8	1
Independents			
Favorable	57	65	56
Unfavorable	32	28	37
No Opinion	11	7	7

Selected National Trend

	Favorable	Un-favorable	No opinion
1998			
August 20*	60%	30%	10%
August 18*	64	29	7
August 10–12	60	36	4
August 7–8	60	35	5
February 13–15	60	36	4
January 30–February 1	64	34	2
January 28*	61	34	5
January 24–25	61	33	6
January 23–24	60	35	5

*Based on one-night poll

Note: The American public continued to give Bill Clinton high marks for the job he is doing as president throughout one of the most tumultuous weeks in recent history. In a poll conducted immediately after his "Monica speech" to the nation late Monday evening [August 17], Clinton's job approval rating was at 62%, essentially unchanged from recent readings. In a Tuesday night poll [August 18], the president's job approval was 66%, one of the highest marks of his entire administration.

By Thursday evening [August 20], after the dramatic announcement of the U.S. strikes against terrorist facilities in Afghanistan and the Sudan, Clinton's job approval rating was down slightly to 61%. In the broadest sense, these data from three separate polls indicate a general maintenance of the president's job approval in the 60%-to-65% range, about where it has been during the entire period of time since the Monica Lewinsky scandal broke in mid-January of this year.

Presidential job approval ratings have often gone up after an international event such as occurred on Thursday. Clinton's did not, at least in the first snapshot poll conducted by Gallup on Thursday night. Given the complexity of the events swirling around the president this week, it is difficult to predict what longer-term impact either his Lewinsky confession or the terrorist attack will have on respondents' assessment of his performance in office.

Since January, the public has tended to believe that Clinton engaged in sexual relations with Lewinsky and that his denials were therefore untruthful. The president's announcement in his speech on Monday evening that he indeed had had an "inappropriate" relationship with Lewinsky thus came as no surprise to the majority of the public. This could be one reason why his job approval ratings did not suffer, as ordinarily might

be expected after such a dramatic confession of infidelity and untruthfulness.

Americans, however, were not satisfied that Clinton had unburdened himself with the truth in his brief speech. When given a choice, about six in ten of those polled by Gallup on Tuesday evening agreed that the president "told the truth on some matters, but tried to mislead the public on other matters," as opposed to the 29% who agreed that he was "completely open and honest about the Monica Lewinsky matter." Additionally, about one-half of those interviewed on Monday did not believe Clinton when he told the nation that he had done nothing illegal, and only one-third thought that Clinton had answered the questions put to him by the grand jury with the "whole truth and nothing but the truth."

At the same time—by a 63%-to-37% margin—the public agrees with Clinton's assertion in his speech that the Lewinsky matter is a private concern "that is nobody's business but his and his family's." And, despite criticism of the speech, particularly from lawmakers, the public in the Tuesday night poll thought that the speech did more good than harm, by a 45%-to-32% margin, while the rest said that it had no effect or they had no opinion.

For most of the five years of the president's term in office, his favorability rating has been the same as or higher than his job approval rating. Throughout most of 1998, however, Clinton's job approval has been higher than his favorability rating. The figures suggest that the public is now in a position where it doubts Clinton's personal qualities while still appreciating his leadership qualities.

In polls taken on Tuesday and Thursday nights, 55% and 53% of the public said that they had a favorable opinion of Clinton. In the same polls, 66% and 61% approved of the job that he is doing as president. These numbers underscore this "good job but less than stellar person" image that Clinton has created. The favorability numbers also represent a drop from previous weeks, when his job approval rating generally stayed the same. In addition, a bare majority (52%) continues to think that Clinton is honest and trustworthy enough to be president, a figure close to that obtained in previous polls conducted as far back as 1996.

There is no apparent groundswell of opinion demanding Clinton's resignation or impeachment.

About one-quarter agrees that Clinton should be "impeached and removed from office." In response to another question, only 23% say that it would be better if Clinton were to resign and turn the presidency over to Al Gore.

Respondents in this week's poll were also presented with various "what if" scenarios. If they were "convinced that Clinton lied under oath in testimony before the grand jury in Ken Starr's investigation on Monday," 49% of those interviewed said that Clinton should be impeached and removed from office. If they were convinced that Clinton obstructed justice, then 48% said that he should be impeached and removed from office. These findings suggest that the potential exists for public opinion to swing more in favor of impeachment if it becomes absolutely clear that these circumstances are true.

There is no sign that the scandal is having any immediate impact on this fall's congressional elections. Seventy-one percent say that the events will have no effect on their November vote for members of Congress, with the rest splitting evenly between saying that the events will make them more likely to vote Republican or more likely to vote Democratic.

AUGUST 29
CONGRESSIONAL ELECTIONS

Interviewing Dates: 8/21–23/98
CNN/*USA Today*/Gallup Poll
Survey #GO 124116

If the elections for Congress were being held today, which party's candidate would you vote for in your congressional district—the Democratic party's candidate, or the Republican party's candidate? [Those who were undecided were asked: As of today, do you lean more toward the Democratic party's candidate, or toward the Republican party's candidate?]

	Total	Registered voters	Likely voters*
Democratic candidate...	48%	47%	44%
Republican candidate...	42	43	48
Other (volunteered); undecided................	10	10	8

*"Likely voter" estimate assumes a 39% turnout among the voting age population (equivalent to the 1994 midterm election turnout).

	Total	Likely voters*
By Sex		
Male		
Democratic	45%	39%
Republican	44	53
Undecided	11	8
Female		
Democratic	50	49
Republican	40	43
Undecided	10	8
By Ethnic Background		
White		
Democratic	43	38
Republican	47	53
Undecided	10	9
Nonwhite		
Democratic	73	78
Republican	16	17
Undecided	11	5
Black		
Democratic	82	86
Republican	10	11
Undecided	8	3
By Education		
Postgraduate		
Democratic	45	44
Republican	50	54
Undecided	5	2
College Graduate		
Democratic	42	46
Republican	48	49
Undecided	10	5
College Incomplete		
Democratic	48	41
Republican	43	48
Undecided	9	11
No College		
Democratic	50	46
Republican	38	45
Undecided	12	9

By Region		
East		
Democratic	55	56
Republican	32	36
Undecided	13	8
Midwest		
Democratic	44	40
Republican	46	52
Undecided	10	8
South		
Democratic	47	45
Republican	45	49
Undecided	8	6
West		
Democratic	44	37
Republican	45	53
Undecided	11	10
By Age		
18–24 Years		
Democratic	46	29
Republican	44	60
Undecided	10	11
30–49 Years		
Democratic	46	45
Republican	43	48
Undecided	11	7
50–64 Years		
Democratic	53	50
Republican	38	42
Undecided	9	8
65 Years and Over		
Democratic	50	42
Republican	41	50
Undecided	9	8
By Household Income		
$75,000 and Over		
Democratic	42	41
Republican	53	54
Undecided	5	5
$50,000 and Over		
Democratic	42	40
Republican	51	55
Undecided	7	5
$30,000–$49,999		
Democratic	45	45
Republican	44	48
Undecided	11	7

$20,000–$29,999

Democratic	45	43
Republican	45	44
Undecided	10	13

Under $20,000

Democratic	64	61
Republican	25	30
Undecided	11	9

By Politics

Republicans

Democratic	5	7
Republican	91	89
Undecided	4	4

Democrats

Democratic	94	90
Republican	4	7
Undecided	2	3

Independents

Democratic	38	40
Republican	39	41
Undecided	23	19

By Political Ideology

Conservative

Democratic	31	25
Republican	60	68
Undecided	9	7

Moderate

Democratic	53	54
Republican	37	38
Undecided	10	8

Liberal

Democratic	74	83
Republican	15	9
Undecided	11	8

*The 39% turnout group

Selected National Trend

	Demo- cratic candidate	Repub- lican candidate	Other; un- decided
Total			
1998			
July 7–8	46%	40%	14%
May 8–10	49	41	10
April 17–19	46	44	10
January 16–18	50	39	11

Registered Voters
1998

July 7–8	46%	42%	12%
May 8–10	48	43	9
April 17–19	46	45	9
January 16–18	51	40	9

*Likely Voters**
1998

July 7–8	46%	46%	8%
April 17–19	44	50	6

*The 39% turnout group

In addition to other factors you may consider in your vote, suppose Ken Starr sends a report to Congress and the Republican leadership in Congress begins hearings to consider impeachment of President Clinton. Under those circumstances, which party's candidate would you vote for in your congressional district this November—the Democratic party's candidate, or the Republican party's candidate? [Those who were undecided were asked: As of today, do you lean more toward the Democratic party's candidate, or the Republican party's candidate?]

	Total	Registered voters	Likely voters*
Democratic candidate	48%	48%	44%
Republican candidate	42	43	48
No opinion	10	9	8

*The 39% turnout group

Now suppose that any impeachment hearings that might happen are concluded this fall and most Republicans vote for impeachment of Clinton and most Democrats vote against impeachment. Under those circumstances, which party's candidate would you vote for in your congressional district this November—the Democratic party's candidate, or the Republican party's candidate? [Those who were undecided were asked: As of today, do you lean more toward the Democratic party's candidate, or the Republican party's candidate?]

	Total	Registered voters	Likely voters*
Democratic candidate	52%	51%	47%

| Republican candidate... | 41 | 42 | 46 |
| No opinion.................. | 7 | 7 | 7 |

*The 39% turnout group

Note: Republicans currently enjoy a slight 4-point advantage over Democrats in the campaign for seats in the US. House of Representatives, with 48% of "likely voters" saying that they expect to vote for a Republican candidate in the fall election, and 44% expecting to vote for a Democrat. Last April, Republicans enjoyed a 6-point advantage among likely voters, but in July the two parties were tied at 46% each.

Among all "registered voters," Democrats fare much better, with Republicans currently trailing the Democrats by 47% to 43%. However, in midterm elections, when the turnout is typically below the 40% mark, Republicans are more likely to vote than Democrats, thus gaining an electoral advantage. In the current poll, the "turnout advantage" for the Republicans is 8 points: instead of trailing the Democrats by 4 points (among all registered voters), Republicans lead their opponents by 4 points (among likely voters), for a net swing of 8 points.

These results from the Gallup Poll are based on the overall percentage of voters who choose either Republican or Democratic candidates in the 435 congressional districts across the country. Because of the size of the national poll sample—1,317 respondents nationwide—the results in each district cannot be reported separately. Actual results, of course, will be based on the outcome in each of those separate congressional districts, so the poll results are only an approximation of the national vote.

A Gallup electoral model, however, converts the aggregate poll results into a prediction of how many House seats are likely to be won by each party. If the current results prevail in the November election, with Republicans winning by a 4-point margin, the Gallup model suggests that Republicans would be likely to retain control of the House, but with a reduced majority. The model predicts that the Republicans would win 220 seats, representing a loss of 8 seats. In the 1994 election, the model predicted that the Republicans would win 227 seats, and they actually won 231 seats,

four more than predicted. For midterm elections since 1950, the model has an average error of 6.5 seats, with the largest error of 12 seats.

In the current poll, respondents were asked how they would vote if the report from Independent Counsel Kenneth Starr prompted the Republicans to begin hearings to consider the impeachment of President Bill Clinton. The results were identical to the original vote question, with Republicans leading Democrats by 48% to 44% among likely voters. But when asked how they would vote if most Republicans in the House voted for impeachment and most Democrats in the House voted against impeachment (in the event that an impeachment vote actually took place), these same voters gave the Democrats a slight lead of 47% to 46%.

This small backlash could be enough for the Republicans to lose majority control of the House. Measured in the number of seats, the model predicts that the Republicans would win only 203 seats if they voted to impeach Clinton, giving majority control to the Democrats, compared with 220 seats (and majority control to the GOP) if Republicans only held hearings with no vote on impeachment. In fact, there is little likelihood that any impeachment vote could be presented to Congress before the election. Nevertheless, this hypothetical question illustrates the potential volatility of voter preferences in the wake of the Starr report and the response of Congress to its recommendations.

The major reason for the GOP turnout advantage is that Republicans vote at a higher rate than Democrats. Among registered voters in the current poll, Democrats enjoy a lead of 5 points in party identification, with 35% saying that they are Democrats and 30% saying Republicans. However, among likely voters, it is the GOP that enjoys a 5-point advantage in party identification by 39% to 34%, a net swing of 10 points in favor of Republicans.

SEPTEMBER 5
ECONOMIC CONDITIONS/STOCK MARKET

Interviewing Date: 9/1/98*
CNN/*USA Today*/Gallup Poll
Survey #GO 124208

*Polls such as this one, conducted entirely in one day, are subject to additional error or bias not found in polls conducted over several days.

How would you rate economic conditions in this country today—excellent, good, only fair, or poor?

Excellent... 11%
Good 54
Fair.. 25
Poor 9
No opinion... 1

	Excellent	Good	Fair	Poor*
By Sex				
Male	13%	54%	24%	9%
Female.............	10	53	27	9
By Age				
18–29 Years....	6	47	28	19
30–49 Years....	15	55	24	5
50 Years				
and Over......	11	54	26	8
By Income				
$50,000				
and Over......	18	61	16	5
$20,000–				
$49,999	8	57	26	8
Under				
$20,000	9	39	34	16
By Stock Ownership				
Own.................	15	58	20	7
Do Not Own....	6	47	33	13

*"No opinion"—at 2% or less—is omitted.

Selected National Trend

	Excellent	Good	Fair	Poor*
1998				
March 20–22 ...	20%	46%	27%	7%
1997				
Dec. 18–21	7	41	38	12
Nov. 6–9..........	10	48	33	9
Aug. 22–25**...	8	41	38	13
May 6–7	7	39	38	15
Jan. 31–				
Feb. 2	4	38	43	15
1996				
Oct. 26–29.......	5	42	39	13
Aug. 30–				
Sept. 1†	3	34	46	16
July 18–21.......	5	38	43	14
May 9–12	3	27	50	19
April 9–10.......	1	26	52	20
March 15–17 ...	2	31	48	18
Jan. 5–7	1	28	47	23
1995				
Nov. 6–8..........	2	28	47	22
May 11–14	2	27	50	20
1994				
Dec. 16–18	2	25	52	21
Nov. 2–6..........	2	28	49	20
Oct. 22–25.......	1	25	52	21
July 15–17.......	1	26	52	21
April 22–24.....	1	23	49	26
Jan. 15–17	‡	22	54	24
1993				
Dec. 4–6	1	20	57	21
Nov. 2–4..........	1	16	50	33
Aug. 8–10........	‡	10	49	40
June 29–30	1	14	52	32
Feb. 12–14	‡	14	46	39
1992				
Dec. 18–20	2	16	34	47
Dec. 4–6	1	14	41	43
Oct. 23–25.......	‡	11	45	43
Sept. 11–15	1	10	37	51
Aug. 31–				
Sept. 2†	1	9	37	53
June 12–14†	1	11	47	41
April 9–12†	1	11	40	48
Jan. 3–6	‡	12	46	41

*"No opinion"—at 2% or less—is omitted.
**Based on half sample
†Registered voters
‡Less than 1%

Next, please tell me whether the recent changes in the stock market have, or have not:

Made you feel less confident about the nation's economy?

Have.. 37%
Have not 59
Doesn't apply (volunteered); no opinion........ 4

	Have	Have not	Doesn't apply; no opinion
By Sex			
Male	35%	62%	3%
Female	39	56	5
By Age			
18–29 Years	32	64	4
30–49 Years	39	59	2
50 Years and Over	38	56	6
By Income			
$50,000 and Over	33	65	2
$20,000–$49,999	43	55	2
Under $20,000	32	62	6
By Stock Ownership			
Own	38	61	1
Do Not Own	36	57	7

Made you feel less confident about your own personal financial situation?

Have... 27%
Have not 69
Doesn't apply (volunteered); no opinion........ 4

	Have	Have not	Doesn't apply; no opinion
By Sex			
Male	25%	72%	3%
Female	28	67	5
By Age			
18–29 Years	24	72	4
30–49 Years	25	75	*
50 Years and Over	32	60	8
By Income			
$50,000 and Over	22	76	2
$20,000–$49,999	27	69	4
Under $20,000	41	56	3
By Stock Ownership			
Own	27	72	1
Do Not Own	22	76	2

*Less than 1%

Made you seriously consider canceling or postponing a big purchase, vacation, or other expenditure?

Have... 14%
Have not 82
Doesn't apply (volunteered); no opinion........ 4

	Have	Have not	Doesn't apply; no opinion
By Sex			
Male	15%	82%	3%
Female	14	82	4
By Age			
18–29 Years	13	82	5
30–49 Years	14	84	2
50 Years and Over	16	79	5
By Income			
$50,000 and Over	12	88	*
$20,000–$49,999	14	84	2
Under $20,000	22	71	7
By Stock Ownership			
Own	15	84	1
Do Not Own	13	78	9

*Less than 1%

Made you seriously consider shifting some of your own money out of the stock market?

Have... 15%
Have not 62
Doesn't apply (volunteered).......................... 21
No opinion... 2

	Have	Have not	Doesn't apply	No opinion
By Sex				
Male	20%	58%	20%	2%
Female	12	65	21	2
By Age				
18–29 Years	15	63	21	1
30–49 Years	18	65	17	*
50 Years and Over	14	57	25	4

By Income

$50,000 and Over......	21	73	6	*
$20,000–$49,999	16	60	21	3
Under $20,000	10	47	41	2

By Stock Ownership

Own.................	22	71	5	2
Do Not Own....	6	49	43	2

*Less than 1%

Thinking back to a month ago, how much more concerned about the stock market are you today than you were a month ago—are you a lot more concerned, a little more concerned, or not more concerned at all compared to a month ago?

A lot more..	20%
A little more..	36
Not more at all..	41
Less concerned (volunteered)........................	1
No opinion..	2

	A lot more	A little more	Not more at all	Less concerned; no opinion
By Sex				
Male	19%	38%	40%	3%
Female.............	21	35	42	2
By Age				
18–29 Years	13	36	47	4
30–49 Years	18	38	42	2
50 Years and Over......	26	36	35	3
By Income				
$50,000 and Over......	20	46	32	2
$20,000–$49,999	21	36	42	1
Under $20,000	18	25	55	2

By Stock Ownership

Own.................	25	39	35	1
Do Not Own....	12	34	50	4

Now, thinking about the next four months, what do you think is most likely to happen to the stock market by the end of this year—do you think the market will crash; drop, but not crash; stabilize about where it is now; or go up?

Crash..	4%
Drop but not crash	20
Stabilize	48
Go up	24
No opinion...	4

	Crash	Drop but not crash	Stabilize	Go up*
By Sex				
Male	4%	22%	45%	25%
Female.............	4	19	51	22
By Age				
18–29 Years	8	20	47	22
30–49 Years	3	18	52	25
50 Years and Over......	3	24	45	21
By Income				
$50,000 and Over......	2	16	48	32
$20,000–$49,999	7	24	47	19
Under $20,000	2	21	49	23
By Stock Ownership				
Own.................	3	18	50	26
Do Not Own....	5	24	45	20

*"No opinion"—at 7% or less—is omitted.

Note: A new Gallup Poll finds public confidence in the economy generally holding strong in spite of giant swings in the New York stock market on Monday and Tuesday [August 31 and September 1], following several weeks of declining stock prices. Americans are now less optimistic than they were

earlier this year that the economy will continue to improve, but overall they show considerable confidence in the soundness of both the economy and the stock market itself.

After falling by 513 points on Monday, the Dow Jones Industrial Average rose 288 points on Tuesday. The poll taken on Tuesday evening found respondents doubtful that the market will fully recover by the end of this year. At the same time, most indicated that the market's behavior this week has not shaken their confidence in the economy or in their own financial situation.

The most positive sign of economic confidence in the new poll is the continued high rating of the economy, changed relatively little since it was last measured in March. Two-thirds of respondents still describe current economic conditions as either excellent or good, another quarter says that conditions are only fair, while just 9% consider them poor.

The current 65% excellent/good rating represents a high point on this basic economic measure that Gallup first asked in January 1992. At that time, during the Bush administration, only 12% rated the economy in positive terms, while close to nine in ten thought that it was only fair or poor. Since Bill Clinton's election in November 1992, public confidence in the economy has slowly but steadily increased to its current high level.

Perhaps as a result of the stock market plunge on Monday—or because of the steady drop in the market since it peaked in mid-July—Americans are now less certain than they were earlier this year that economic conditions in the country are improving. However, the current outlook is still roughly comparable to what it was last year. Today, 45% think that economic conditions are getting better, down from 69% in March; 41% now say that they are getting worse, up from 21%. By comparison, in December 1997, 49% saw things getting better and 39% getting worse.

Asked how the recent changes in the market have affected them personally, only a few more than one-third (37%) say that the market has made them feel less confident about the nation's economy. Even fewer (27%) say that it has shaken their confidence in their own financial situation. Looking at the subset of stockholders interviewed in the poll, just 22% of this group have considered

shifting money out of the market as a result of recent events.

In the wake of the recent turbulent activity on Wall Street, respondents seem to be concerned rather than alarmed about the stock market. Only 20% of the total and 25% of self-reported stockholders are now a lot more concerned than they were a month ago about the direction that the stock market may take in the next year. The rest are either a little more concerned or not concerned at all.

Asked to predict what is most likely to happen by the end of 1998, about half the public (48%) thinks that the stock market will stabilize at its current level. An additional one-quarter (24%) thinks that the market will either crash or drop significantly by the year's end, while an equal number thinks that it will go up.

This ambivalence about the market's short-term future is reflected in the public's sense of whether investing one thousand dollars in stocks would be a good or bad idea right now. Forty-six percent say that it would be a good idea, and 48% a bad one. However, among the subset of those who already own stock, confidence in the market is much higher, with 60% saying that now would be a good time to buy.

SEPTEMBER 12
THE STARR REPORT

Interviewing Date: 9/10/98*
CNN/*USA Today*/Gallup Poll
Survey #GO 124288

As you may know, yesterday the office of Independent Counsel Kenneth Starr sent its report on the investigation of Bill Clinton to Congress. Do you think that Congress should release the report immediately, release it but wait until after Clinton's attorneys have reviewed it and prepared a response, or never release the report?

*Polls such as this one, conducted entirely in one day, are subject to additional error or bias not found in polls conducted over several days.

Release it immediately 34%
Release it but wait 42
Never release it.. 21
No opinion.. 3

	Release it immediately	Release it but wait	Never release it	No opinion
By Sex				
Male	38%	41%	18%	3%
Female.............	30	44	24	2
By Age				
18–29 Years	32	51	16	1
30–49 Years	35	45	18	2
50 Years and Over......	33	35	28	4
By Politics				
Republicans.....	48	32	16	4
Democrats	23	51	24	2
Independents ...	32	43	23	2
By Clinton Approval				
Approve	20	50	28	2
Disapprove......	55	31	10	4
By Those Who Think Clinton Should Be Impeached				
Should Be........	55	28	13	4
Should Not Be	22	51	26	1

How interested are you, personally, in reading or learning about the findings contained in the Starr report—very interested, somewhat interested, not too interested, or not interested at all?

Very interested 20%
Somewhat interested....................................... 29
Not too interested 23
Not interested at all 27
No opinion.. 1

	Very interested	Somewhat interested	Not too interested	Not interested at all*
By Sex				
Male	23%	30%	22%	25%
Female.............	19	29	23	28

By Age				
18–29 Years	12	29	36	23
30–49 Years	23	31	20	26
50 Years and Over......	23	30	18	28
By Politics				
Republicans.....	29	37	20	12
Democrats	19	25	26	30
Independents ...	17	28	21	33
By Clinton Approval				
Approve	15	24	25	36
Disapprove......	31	40	17	10
By Those Who Think Clinton Should Be Impeached				
Should Be........	33	39	16	11
Should Not Be	14	25	26	35

*"No opinion"—at 2% or less—is omitted.

What do you think Congress should do with Ken Starr's report—hold hearings to investigate the charges contained in the report, or take no action on the report and end the investigation into these matters immediately?

Hold hearings 56%
End investigation.. 38
Other (volunteered) 2
No opinion.. 4

	Hold hearings	End investigation	Other	No opinion
By Sex				
Male	59%	36%	3%	2%
Female.............	52	41	1	6
By Age				
18–29 Years	55	42	*	3
30–49 Years	61	35	1	3
50 Years and Over......	52	39	4	5
By Politics				
Republicans.....	65	30	1	4
Democrats	48	46	3	3
Independents ...	55	38	2	5

By Clinton Approval

Approve 40	53	2	5
Disapprove 83	14	1	2

By Those Who Think Clinton Should Be Impeached

Should Be........ 88	9	1	2
Should Not Be 39	54	2	5

*Less than 1%

Just your impression—do you think the Starr report is a fair and accurate account of Clinton's actions, or an unfair and distorted account of Clinton's actions?

Fair and accurate	47%
Unfair and distorted..	33
Other (volunteered)	2
No opinion..	18

	Fair and accurate	Unfair and distorted	Other	No opinion
By Sex				
Male 52%	31%	1%	16%
Female............. 43	34	2	21
By Age				
18–29 Years 51	31	*	18
30–49 Years 52	29	2	17
50 Years and Over...... 41	37	2	20
By Politics				
Republicans..... 74	11	1	14
Democrats 31	48	2	19
Independents ... 42	35	2	21
By Clinton Approval				
Approve 30	49	2	19
Disapprove 76	6	2	16
By Those Who Think Clinton Should Be Impeached				
Should Be........ 80	2	2	16
Should Not Be 31	50	1	18

*Less than 1%

Note: A Thursday night [September 10] Gallup Poll, conducted after the Starr report had been released to Congress but before its contents were made public, shows mixed reactions. Bill Clinton still rates positively on three key indicators of the health of his presidency—job approval, whether he should be impeached and removed from office, and whether he should resign—but a majority of respondents believes that Congress should go ahead with its proposed hearings to investigate the charges contained in the report, and a plurality believes the Starr report to be fair and accurate.

The announcement of the release of the report in and of itself did not substantially change Americans' opinions about Clinton's basic performance as president, or their desire to see him remain in office. Six in ten approve of the job that he is doing, and about the same percentage think that the president should not resign and that he should not be impeached and removed from office. This majority support for his job performance and majority belief that he should remain in office are down slightly but are generally consistent with the types of reactions recorded in previous polling on these questions. At the same time, almost six in ten would support a congressional vote to censure Clinton with a formal resolution expressing disapproval of his actions.

Over three quarters of respondents agree with Congress that the report's contents should be made public, although a majority of these people say that Congress should have allowed Clinton's attorneys to review it in order to prepare a response. Only 21% reply that the report should never have been released. The public is, however, sensitive to its possibly salacious contents. Seven in ten of those polled say that the details of sexual encounters should not be released along with the rest of the report. At the same time, interest in reading it or learning about its findings is less widespread than might be expected: 50% of those interviewed on Thursday night are not too or not at all interested in what it contains.

Previous survey research has suggested that a majority of Americans thinks that the entire Starr investigation into the Clinton-Lewinsky matter should be halted. Now, on the eve of the Starr report's release, a smaller number (38%) says that Congress should take no action on the report and

end the investigation. Fifty-six percent support the idea of Congress holding hearings on the report's contents. Additionally, by a 47%-to-33% margin, the public thinks that the report will contain a fair and accurate account of Clinton's actions, as opposed to the unfair and distorted account that some of the president's supporters have asserted.

The public is split down the middle on its feelings about whether or not members of the two parties in Congress will be able to conduct the investigation of the issues addressed in the Starr report in a fair and bipartisan way. Additionally, a majority thinks that it is somewhat or very important that the final decision of Congress on this matter be reached before the November election—an occurrence unlikely to happen.

SEPTEMBER 19
PRESIDENT CLINTON/STARR
INVESTIGATION

Interviewing Dates: 9/14–15/98
CNN/*USA Today*/Gallup Poll
Survey #GO 124310

If the investigations into the Clinton-Lewinsky matter continue, what position would you prefer the U.S. representative from your congressional district to take—should he or she favor impeaching and removing Clinton from office; favor a formal reprimand or censure of Clinton, but not removing him from office; or favor taking no formal action against Clinton?

Impeachment	27%
Reprimand or censure	45
No formal action	24
No opinion	4

	Impeachment	Reprimand or censure	No formal action	No opinion
By Sex				
Male	32%	40%	25%	3%
Female	23	50	23	4
By Ethnic Background				
White	30	45	21	4
Nonwhite	14	46	37	3
Black	11	46	41	2
By Education				
Postgraduate	35	49	15	1
College Graduate	30	52	13	5
College Incomplete	30	48	19	3
No College	23	41	32	4
By Region				
East	21	48	27	4
Midwest	27	46	23	4
South	31	43	23	3
West	32	43	21	4
By Age				
18–29 Years	25	45	28	2
30–49 Years	28	48	23	1
50–64 Years	27	44	25	4
65 Years and Over	28	40	21	11
By Household Income				
$75,000 and Over	37	44	18	1
$50,000 and Over	33	50	15	3
$30,000–$49,999	28	49	21	2
$20,000–$29,999	24	46	28	2
Under $20,000	21	37	36	6
By Politics				
Republicans	51	35	10	4
Democrats	7	56	33	4
Independents	27	43	26	4
By Political Ideology				
Conservative	42	38	17	3
Moderate	21	52	24	3
Liberal	13	51	33	3
By Clinton Approval				
Approve	7	56	35	2
Disapprove	66	27	4	3
By Voter Status				
Registered Voters	29	45	23	3

	Support	Oppose	No difference	No opinion
Regular Midterm Voters	31	45	21	3
Likely Voters*	38	41	19	2

*Estimated at 35% to 39% of total sample

Thinking about the elections in November, if your member of Congress favors impeaching Clinton, would that make you more likely to support or to oppose your member of Congress in the November election, or would that make no difference to your vote?

Support	24%
Oppose	33
No difference	41
No opinion	2

	Support	Oppose	No difference	No opinion
By Sex				
Male	29%	29%	40%	2%
Female	20	36	42	2
By Ethnic Background				
White	26	31	41	2
Nonwhite	17	40	38	5
Black	16	45	34	5
By Education				
Postgraduate	30	34	35	1
College Graduate	30	35	32	3
College Incomplete	25	33	40	2
No College	21	31	45	3
By Region				
East	21	36	41	2
Midwest	20	33	43	4
South	27	30	41	2
West	30	30	37	3
By Age				
18–29 Years	19	31	50	*
30–49 Years	25	32	41	2
50–64 Years	28	37	31	4
65 Years and Over	24	31	41	4
By Household Income				
$75,000 and Over	29	28	41	2
$50,000 and Over	30	31	38	1
$30,000–$49,999	21	38	40	1
$20,000–$29,999	23	29	47	1
Under $20,000	22	30	44	4
By Politics				
Republicans	44	16	39	1
Democrats	8	46	42	4
Independents	22	35	41	2
By Political Ideology				
Conservative	39	22	38	1
Moderate	16	38	45	1
Liberal	13	47	35	5
By Clinton Approval				
Approve	10	47	40	3
Disapprove	52	6	41	1
By Voter Status				
Registered Voters	25	33	41	1
Regular Midterm Voters	28	31	40	1
Likely Voters**	34	31	34	1

*Less than 1%
**Estimated at 35% to 39% of total sample

What do you think Congress should do with Ken Starr's report—hold hearings to investigate the charges contained in the report, or take no action on the report and end the investigation into these matters immediately?

Hold hearings	50%
End investigation	44
Other (volunteered)	2
No opinion	4

	Hold hearings	End investi-gation	Other	No opinion
South	57	39		4
West	53	45		2

By Likely Voters*

	Hold hearings	End investi-gation	Other	No opinion
Republicans	73%	24%	1%	2%
Democrats	34	60	3	3
Independents	45	46	3	6

*Estimated at 35% to 39% of total sample

By Age

18–29 Years	66	33	1
30–49 Years	57	40	3
50–64 Years	56	40	4
65 Years and Over	58	38	4

Selected National Trend

	Hold hearings	End investi-gation	Other	No opinion
1998				
Sept. 13	46%	52%	*	2%
Sept. 11–12	52	44	2	2
Sept. 10	56	38	2	4

*Less than 1%

By Household Income

$75,000 and Over	39	59	2
$50,000 and Over	46	52	2
$30,000–$49,999	60	37	3
$20,000–$29,999	59	39	2
Under $20,000	75	20	5

By Politics

Republicans	35	63	2
Democrats	79	18	3
Independents	58	38	4

As of now, do you think Bill Clinton can be an effective president during his remaining two years in office, or not?

Yes, effective	58%
No	39
No opinion	3

By Political Ideology

Conservative	44	53	3
Moderate	63	34	3
Liberal	76	21	3

By Clinton Approval

Approve	82	16	2
Disapprove	17	80	3

	Yes, effective	No	No opinion
By Sex			
Male	52%	45%	3%
Female	64	33	3

By Voter Status

Registered Voters	55	42	3
Regular			
Midterm Voters	53	44	3
Likely Voters*	48	50	2

*Estimated at 35% to 39% of total sample

By Ethnic Background

White	55	42	3
Nonwhite	79	18	3
Black	86	12	2

By Education

Postgraduate	45	53	2
College Graduate	47	49	4
College Incomplete	55	41	4
No College	68	30	2

Overall, what kind of moral leadership do you think Bill Clinton provides as president— very strong, somewhat strong, somewhat weak, or very weak?

Very strong	10%
Somewhat strong	20
Somewhat weak	23
Very weak	45
No opinion	2

By Region

East	64	34	2
Midwest	59	37	4

Selected National Trend

	Very strong	Some- what strong	Some- what weak	Very weak*
1997				
Sept. 27–29**...	14%	39%	23%	21%
1996				
May 9–12	11	42	27	18

*"No opinion"—at 3% or less—is omitted.
**Likely voters

Note: After an extraordinary weekend of media coverage and intense scrutiny of the newly released Starr report, Gallup Polls show remarkably little change in the basic attitudes of the American public about the Clinton-Lewinsky situation. A majority continues to say that Bill Clinton should stay in office and not be impeached and removed, and to still believe that he can be an effective president over the remaining two years of his term. Additionally, while maintaining a negative opinion of Clinton as a person, and according him very low marks for his moral leadership, respondents remain steadfast in their approval of the job that he is doing in office.

Gallup polling conducted on Thursday through Sunday evenings [September 9–13] asked the public whether or not Clinton should be impeached, resign, or receive an official censure or reprimand from Congress. The numbers did not change significantly over that four-day period: 30% to 31% said that Clinton should be impeached and removed from office, 35% to 36% said that he should resign, and 58% to 60% said that he should be censured. If Clinton does remain in office, can he serve out his term as an effective president? About six in ten (58%) say yes; four in ten (39%) say no.

On Monday and Tuesday nights [September 14 and 15], Americans were asked what they would like their own representative in Congress to do in regard to the Clinton-Lewinsky matter. The results are essentially the same: 27% say that their representative should vote to impeach and remove Clinton from office, 45% say that he or she should vote to censure but not to remove him, and 24% think that no formal action should be taken. When asked what their reaction would be if a candidate for Congress in the fall elections favored impeach-

ment, more respondents say that this position would make them oppose that candidate's election than say that it would make them favor it, by a 33%-to-24% margin. The rest reply that a candidate's position on this issue would make no difference to them.

At the same time, there is a more mixed reaction to the idea of shutting down congressional hearings on the Starr report. Exactly one-half (50%) says that Congress should hold such hearings, while a slightly lower number (44%) says that Congress should take no action on the report and should end the investigation immediately.

Reactions to a series of different Gallup Poll questions reveal the disparate nature of public views of Clinton. Sixty-three percent approve of the job that he is doing as president, and 59% even say that they are "glad" he is president. At the same time, only 30% think that Clinton provides strong moral leadership for the country. That this perception does not figure more strongly in the overall equation of the public's desire for Clinton's impeachment or resignation is a paradox, given that a very high 72% says that a president's providing moral leadership is very important for the nation.

The divergent perceptions of Clinton are also evident when contrasted with results of other poll questions. When respondents are asked if they have a favorable or unfavorable opinion of Clinton without specifying which characteristics of the man are being evaluated, the results show a 51% favorable-to-47% unfavorable split. This number, while perhaps more positive than might be predicted, is low by historical standards and represents a 10-point drop from his favorability ratings in early June.

However, when they are asked about the president in a slightly modified way—"Thinking about Bill Clinton as a person, do you have a positive or negative opinion of him?"—the number with a positive opinion drops to 37%, with 56% saying that they have a negative opinion. Respect for Clinton is also down significantly, from 53% who respected him early in August to 43% who feel that way now.

What is America's best guess as to the future of Clinton's presidency? Sixty percent say that he will serve out the rest of his term, 33% say that he will be forced to leave, while the rest have no opinion.

SEPTEMBER 26
PRESIDENT CLINTON

Interviewing Dates: 9/23–24/98
CNN/*USA Today*/Gallup Poll
Survey #GO 124403

Do you approve or disapprove of the way Bill Clinton is handling his job as president?

Approve 66%
Disapprove... 31
No opinion 3

Selected National Trend

	Approve	Dis-approve	No opinion
1998			
September 21	66%	31%	3%
September 20..............	60	34	6
September 14–15........	63	35	2
September 11–12........	63	34	3
September 10..............	60	37	3
September 1	62	33	5
August 21–23	62	35	3
August 20*	61	34	5
August 18*	66	29	5
August 17*	62	32	6
August 10–12	65	30	5
August 7–8	64	32	4

*Based on one-night poll

Based on what you know at this point, do you think that Bill Clinton should or should not be impeached and removed from office?

Yes, should 29%
Should not 68
No opinion.. 3

Selected National Trend

	Yes, should	Should not	No opinion
1998			
September 21	32%	66%	2%
September 20..............	35	60	5
September 13..............	31	66	3
September 11–12........	30	64	6

September 10..............	31	63	6
August 21–23	29	67	4
August 18	26	70	4
August 17	25	69	6
August 10–12	20	76	4
August 7–8	23	75	2
June 5–7......................	19	77	4

Do you think Bill Clinton should or should not resign now and turn the presidency over to Al Gore?

Yes, should 33%
Should not 64
No opinion.. 3

Selected National Trend

	Yes, should	Should not	No opinion
1998			
September 21	39%	59%	2%
September 20..............	40	56	4
September 13..............	36	62	2
September 11–12........	35	61	4
September 10..............	35	61	4

Asked of half sample: Rather than removing President Clinton from office, do you think Congress should or should not resolve this matter by voting to censure Clinton—that is, pass a formal resolution expressing disapproval of his actions?

Yes, should 56%
Should not 39
No opinion.. 5

	Yes, should	Should not	No opinion
By Politics			
Republicans	51%	47%	2%
Democrats...................	55	37	8
Independents..............	59	36	5
By Political Ideology			
Conservative..............	47	48	5
Moderate.....................	61	33	6
Liberal	60	37	3

Asked of half sample: Rather than removing President Clinton from office, do you think Congress should or should not resolve this matter by voting to censure Clinton—that is, pass a formal resolution expressing disapproval of his actions as well as require him to admit to perjury and pay a heavy fine for the costs of the investigation?

Yes, should 47%
Should not 42
Censure, but not pay fine (volunteered) 4
No opinion 7

	Yes, should	Should not	Censure, but no fine	No opinion
By Politics				
Republicans.....	58%	40%	1%	1%
Democrats	44	41	5	10
Independents ...	40	46	4	10
By Political Ideology				
Conservative ...	44	44	4	8
Moderate	55	38	2	5
Liberal.............	38	49	6	7

In determining what course of action to take in the Clinton investigation, Congress may face three major choices in the near future. As I read those choices please tell me which you would prefer it take—Congress should continue to hold hearings on whether to impeach Clinton; Congress should vote to censure Clinton and allow him to serve out his remaining two years in office, and stop holding hearings; or Congress should not hold hearings or censure Clinton, and should drop the matter altogether?

	Total	Likely voters*
Continue hearings	27%	35%
Censure Clinton	37	32
Drop matter..................................	35	33
None; other (volunteered).............	**	**
No opinion	1	**

*Estimated at 39% of total sample
**Less than 1%

Note: Public support for Bill Clinton remains strong despite the release on Monday [September 21] of 2,800 pages of documents related to the investigation by Independent Counsel Kenneth Starr, along with videotapes of the president's testimony before the grand jury. According to the latest Gallup Poll, conducted on Wednesday and Thursday of this week [September 23 and 24], 66% approve of the way that Clinton is handling his job, the same percentage who approved on Monday night but 6 points higher than his ratings on the day before the taped testimony and documents were made available to the public.

In fact, it appears as though the release of those items may have caused a slight rallying around the president. Not only did his approval rating improve, but public support for Clinton's impeachment and resignation also fell during the week. Currently, 29% say that Clinton should be impeached and removed from office, down from 35% last Sunday [September 20]. And 33% say that he should resign, down from 40% last Sunday.

While support for Clinton increased in the wake of Congress's release of the documents and taped testimony, public perceptions of the Republicans in Congress became decidedly more negative. The poll shows that respondents disapprove of the way that congressional Republicans have handled the controversy, by a margin of 59% to 32%. In the days immediately following delivery of Starr's report to Congress, they were far less negative, disapproving of the way that congressional Republicans were handling the controversy by just 48% to 43%.

Consistent with their high ratings of Clinton, most people do not want to see the president impeached, but they do support some kind of censure. By a margin of 56% to 39%, they favor a proposed congressional resolution that would condemn Clinton for his actions while allowing him to remain in office. However, if such a resolution would also require Clinton to admit perjury and pay a heavy fine for the costs of the investigation, support drops to a margin of 47% to 42%.

While Republican leaders in Congress have indicated that they intend to continue hearings on whether to impeach Clinton, most Americans indicate that the hearings should stop now. Just 27%

say that Congress should continue to hold impeachment hearings, 37% say that it should vote to censure Clinton and stop the hearings, while another 35% want Congress to drop the matter now without holding more hearings or censuring the president.

Most opinions about this controversy are highly partisan, with Republicans much more critical of Clinton than either independents or Democrats. Only 35% of Republicans want him to remain in office, for example, compared with 63% of independents and 87% of Democrats. Similar divisions are found on presidential approval and on the way that Republicans in Congress are handling the controversy.

There is much greater agreement on one of the proposals for censure, however. If Congress were to pass a resolution disapproving of Clinton's actions but allow the president to finish his second term, that action would be supported by 51% of Republicans, 59% of independents, and 55% of Democrats. If the resolution also required Clinton to admit perjury and fined him heavily, only Republicans would give majority support to that proposal, by 58% to 40%. Independents would lean against it, with 40% in favor and 46% opposed, while Democrats would be almost evenly divided, by 44% and 41%.

While Clinton enjoys high ratings for his job performance and continued support for remaining in office, the public disapproves of the way that he has handled the situation involving Monica Lewinsky, by a margin of 66% to 30%. By a similar margin, it disagrees with the president when he asserted that he did not perjure himself before the grand jury, with 66% saying that he did commit perjury and just 25% saying that he did not. And if people were forced to choose between Clinton's and Starr's versions of what happened, more would believe Starr (47%) than Clinton (37%). Finally, only 38% have a positive opinion of Clinton "as a person," while 55% have a negative opinion.

Still, when asked to rate Clinton on a scale of minus 5 to plus 5, from "very unfavorable" to "very favorable," 63% give him a positive score and 36% a negative one. These scores are considerably better than those he received four years ago, just before the 1994 midterm elections, when only 51% rated him positively and 48% negatively. These ratings seem to reflect people's views of Clinton as president rather than their views of him personally. The low scores he received in 1994 were given at a time when only 44% approved of the way that Clinton was handling his job as president, 22 points lower than those he receives today.

OCTOBER 3
CONGRESSIONAL ELECTIONS

Interviewing Dates: 9/23–24/98
CNN/*USA Today*/Gallup Poll
Survey #GO 124403

Asked of likely voters*: If the elections for Congress were being held today, which party's candidate would you vote for in your congressional district—the Democratic party's candidate, or the Republican party's candidate? [Those who were undecided were asked: As of today, do you lean more toward the Democratic party's candidate, or toward the Republican party's candidate?]

Democratic candidate 51%
Republican candidate 45
Other (volunteered); undecided 4

*"Likely voter" estimate assumes a 39% turnout among the voting age population (equivalent to the 1994 midterm election turnout).

	Democratic candidate	Republican candidate	Other; undecided
By Politics			
Republicans	8%	91%	1%
Democrats....................	96	3	1
Independents...............	47	41	12

Selected National Trend*

	Democratic candidate	Republican candidate	Other; undecided
1998			
September 14–15*......	48%	47%	5%
September 11–12*......	47	46	7

August 21–23*	 44	48	8
July 7–8*	 46	46	8
April 17–19*	 44	50	6

*Likely voters

Note: With only five weeks to go before the 1998 elections, increasing attention is being paid to the views of that key group of Americans known as "likely voters." The voters in this group, rather than the entire electorate, will determine whether the Republican party will lose its slim majority in Congress, maintain its margin, or pick up new seats. As a result of their electoral influence, likely voters' views about Bill Clinton may also have more weight than those of others regarding the investigation of the president in Congress and any possible impeachment process.

In polling terms, likely voters are a subset of survey respondents in a nationally representative sample of adult Americans. Using their answers to questions about past voting behavior and current voting intent, the Gallup Poll classifies respondents in terms of their probability of voting. It is on the basis of this methodology that Gallup has predicted the winning candidate or party in nearly every presidential and congressional election since 1936.

Voter turnout must be taken into account in any pre-election poll, but it is particularly important in midterm elections because of their relatively low turnout. Historical turnout rates show that in every midterm election for Congress since 1974, just 35% to 40% of eligible U.S. voters have gone to the polls. By contrast, upwards of 50% generally turn out to vote in the presidential elections.

The importance of accurately defining likely voters is evidenced by the 1994 midterm elections. In that year, Gallup found that a majority said that they preferred the Democratic candidate in the race for Congress in their district. But among likely voters—defined as the 41% most likely to vote—Gallup found a 6-point advantage for Republican candidates, a result that proved to be identical with the outcome of the national two-party vote for Congress.

In 1998 the Gallup Poll continues to find that likely voters tend to be more Republican than the public at large, a pattern seen throughout most pre-election polling in Gallup's history. Although

there has been much speculation about the effect that the investigation of President Clinton may be having on partisan motivation to vote or not to vote, Gallup finds nothing extraordinary or unique thus far in the predicted turnout patterns for the November election.

In Gallup's latest survey, conducted on September 23–24, Democrats have the advantage in party identification among all national adults, with 36% identifying themselves as Democrats, 29% as Republicans, and 35% as independents. However, among likely voters in the same survey, Republicans and Democrats are evenly split at 37%.

This shift toward Republicans as one moves from national adults to likely voters is mirrored in the voter choice for Congress. Among all national adults surveyed in late September, the Democrats currently lead the Republicans by 11 points (50% to 39%), with 11% undecided. Among likely voters, that gap shrinks to 6 points, with 51% favoring the Democrats, 45% the Republicans, and only 4% undecided. These likely voter figures assume a turnout rate of 39%, similar to voter turnout in the last midterm election. However, if the predicted turnout drops even lower, any Democratic advantage would shrink even more. Nevertheless, one of the factors working in the Democrats' favor is that Democratic voters are currently slightly more loyal to their ticket's candidates in their local races (with 96% of Democrats favoring the candidate of their own party) than Republicans are to GOP candidates (with a 91% voting-Republican rate).

Because likely voters tend to be more Republican, their views about Clinton tend to be more critical than those of the public at large. The recent poll found the president's job approval rating at 66% among all national adults surveyed, but just 60% among likely voters. A less pronounced difference is found on the critical questions of whether Clinton should or should not be impeached and removed from office. Exactly one-third of likely voters, compared to 29% of all national adults, thinks that he should be impeached and removed. When combined with those who say that Clinton should not be impeached but should resign, a total of 41% of likely voters, compared to 37% of all national adults, would like to see Clinton leave office one way or the other at this time.

If members of the U.S. House and Senate are listening closely to their own constituents or to voters of their own political party, as might be expected, it is possible that Republican members of Congress are being pressed to pursue impeachment. More than one-half of all Republicans in the electorate (56%) favor impeachment and removing Clinton from office. A total of two-thirds of Republicans think that he should leave office either through impeachment or resignation. By contrast, only 6% of Democrats in the latest poll say that Clinton should be impeached and, adding in those who think that he should resign, only 15% want to see him leave office by one of these two routes.

A group critical to the survival of Clinton's presidency as well as to the outcome of the November elections is political independents. In Gallup's last several surveys, including the most recent one taken in late September, independents expressed political views more in line with Democrats than with Republicans. For instance, only 29% of independents think that President Clinton should be impeached and removed from office; and a total of 37%, still well under half, think that he should leave office through impeachment or resignation.

Independent likely voters also favor the Democratic candidate over the Republican one in their congressional races by a 47%-to-41% margin. This preference is a reversal of the 1994 vote, when independents favored Republicans by a 4-point margin. While these data reveal the mood of the electorate as of late September, much can still change between now and November 3. The latest poll finds that only 36% of respondents currently have given much thought to the midterm elections, well below the level of attention that Gallup normally finds as Election Day draws near.

OCTOBER 10
PRESIDENT CLINTON/CONGRESSIONAL IMPEACHMENT HEARINGS

Interviewing Dates: 10/6–7/98
CNN/*USA Today*/Gallup Poll
Survey #GO 124563

As you may know, Congress is currently considering whether to hold hearings into the charges against Bill Clinton, in order to determine whether or not he should be impeached. Would you favor or oppose Congress holding those hearings?

Favor.. 44%
Oppose.. 53
No opinion.. 3

	Favor	Oppose	No opinion
By Sex			
Male..............................	51%	47%	2%
Female	38	59	3
By Education			
College Graduate........	55	44	1
College Incomplete.....	43	57	*
No College..................	39	56	5
By Age			
18–29 Years................	42	56	2
30–49 Years................	48	51	1
50 Years and Over......	41	54	5
By Politics			
Republicans	69	30	1
Democrats...................	25	71	4
Independents..............	44	53	3
By Clinton Approval			
Approve	24	74	2
Disapprove..................	80	17	3
By Those Who Think Clinton Should Be Impeached			
Should Be	90	9	1
Should Not Be	21	76	3

*Less than 1%

Based on what you know at this point, do you think that Bill Clinton should or should not be impeached and removed from office?

Yes, should 32%
Should not 65
No opinion.. 3

	Yes, should	Should not	No opinion
By Sex			
Male	39%	58%	3%
Female	25	71	4
By Education			
College Graduate	38	60	2
College Incomplete	31	65	4
No College	29	67	4
By Age			
18–29 Years	29	68	3
30–49 Years	33	65	2
50 Years and Over	32	63	5
By Politics			
Republicans	58	38	4
Democrats	15	82	3
Independents	29	67	4
By Clinton Approval			
Approve	11	86	3
Disapprove	72	25	3

Selected National Trend

	Yes, should	Should not	No opinion
1998			
September 23–24	29%	68%	3%
September 21	32	66	2
September 20	35	60	5
September 13	31	66	3
September 11–12	30	64	6
September 10	31	63	6
August 21–23	29	67	4
August 18	26	70	4
August 17	25	69	6
August 10–12	20	76	4
August 7–8	23	75	2
June 5–7	19	77	4

Do you think Bill Clinton should or should not resign now and turn the presidency over to Al Gore?

Yes, should	34%
Should not	64
No opinion	2

	Yes, should	Should not	No opinion
By Sex			
Male	38%	60%	2%
Female	30	68	2
By Education			
College Graduate	44	54	2
College Incomplete	33	65	2
No College	29	70	1
By Age			
18–29 Years	29	70	1
30–49 Years	38	60	2
50 Years and Over	32	65	3
By Politics			
Republicans	59	37	4
Democrats	18	81	1
Independents	32	66	2
By Clinton Approval			
Approve	14	85	1
Disapprove	72	25	3
By Those Who Think Clinton Should Be Impeached			
Should Be	83	15	2
Should Not Be	10	89	1

Selected National Trend

	Yes, should	Should not	No opinion
1998			
September 23–24	33%	64%	3%
September 21	39	59	2
September 20	40	56	4
September 13	36	62	2
September 11–12	35	61	4
September 10	35	61	4

Finally, we would like to ask you one overall question about what you would prefer to see happen with President Clinton—would you prefer to see him stay in office for the remaining two years of his term; or would you prefer to see him leave office before the end of his term, either through impeachment or resignation?

Stay in office 65%
Leave office.. 34
No opinion.. 1

	Stay in office	Leave office	No opinion
By Sex			
Male............................	59%	41%	*
Female	71	28	1
By Education			
College Graduate........	54	45	1
College Incomplete.....	65	35	*
No College..................	71	28	1
By Age			
18–29 Years................	72	27	1
30–49 Years................	61	38	1
50 Years and Over......	65	34	1
By Politics			
Republicans	37	62	1
Democrats...................	84	15	1
Independents...............	66	33	1
By Clinton Approval			
Approve	90	10	*
Disapprove..................	20	79	1

*Less than 1%

Net Who Want Clinton to Leave Office
(Either Through Impeachment or Resignation)

	Leave Office	Stay in Office; No Opinion
1998		
October 6–7	39%	61%
September 23–24	37	63
September 21	42	58
September 20	45	55
September 13	40	60
September 11–12	39	61

Do you approve or disapprove of the way Congress is handling its job?

Approve 44%
Disapprove... 48
No opinion... 8

	Approve	Dis-approve	No opinion
By Sex			
Male............................	48%	47%	5%
Female	41	48	11
By Education			
College Graduate........	53	42	5
College Incomplete.....	47	49	4
No College..................	38	50	12
By Age			
18–29 Years................	47	44	9
30–49 Years................	47	47	6
50 Years and Over......	40	50	10
By Politics			
Republicans	63	31	6
Democrats...................	34	58	8
Independents...............	41	50	9
By Clinton Approval			
Approve	32	60	8
Disapprove..................	66	26	8

Selected National Trend

	Approve	Dis-approve	No opinion
1998			
September 11–12........	55%	36%	9%
May 8–10....................	44	48	8
April 17–19................	49	40	11
February 13–15...........	57	33	10
January 30– February 1................	56	35	9
January 16–18.............	42	47	11
1997			
December 18–21.........	39	52	9
October 27–29	36	53	11
August 22–25	41	48	11
July 25–27	34	57	9
May 6–7......................	32	58	10
April 18–20................	30	59	11
February 24–26...........	37	48	15
January 31– February 2...............	36	51	13
January 10–13.............	41	49	10

1996

October 26–29 34	51	15
August 5–7 39	49	12
May 9–12.................... 30	65	5
April 9–10.................. 35	57	8

Note: According to a Gallup Poll conducted on Tuesday and Wednesday of this week [October 6 and 7], the public has mixed feelings about the House vote on Thursday [October 8] to initiate hearings on the possible impeachment of President Bill Clinton. Respondents oppose the hearings by a small margin, but on the other hand they show a slight preference for an unlimited scope to the inquiry rather than one limited to charges related solely to Clinton's relationship with Monica Lewinsky. The public also strongly prefers a time limit on the hearings and, as has been the case for the past several months, strongly opposes removing Clinton from office.

The poll shows that the public opposes the hearings by a margin of 53% to 44%. On the other hand, when asked how wide the scope of the hearings should be if Congress decides to proceed with them, one-half say that they support the investigation of any charges that are brought to the Judiciary Committee, 30% think that the investigation should be limited to the Lewinsky matter, while another 15% say that no charges should be investigated at all.

Although Republican leaders have promised no unnecessary delays in conducting the hearings, Congress has not set any specific time limits on how long the process may take. By contrast, a large majority of the public (69%) would prefer Congress to impose a deadline for the hearings, while just 24% agree with an open-ended schedule.

On the prospect of Clinton's leaving office, views have not changed much over the past several months: by 65% to 32% the public opposes impeachment of the president and his removal from office. By a similar margin (64% to 34%), Clinton should not resign. And, when asked overall whether he should stay in office for the remainder of his term or leave either through impeachment or resignation, respondents again support Clinton's continuation in office by nearly 2 to 1 (65% to 34%). A majority believes that Congress should resolve the matter by censuring

Clinton—passing a formal resolution disapproving his actions. This proposal is supported by a 53%-to-38% margin, similar to poll results two weeks ago.

The impeachment controversy seems to have hurt the Republicans among the general public, with approval of the Republican-controlled Congress dropping from 55% less than a month ago to just 44% today. A related question shows by a 58%-to-34% margin that people disapprove of the way that the Republicans are handling the investigation. Their view about the Democrats, on the other hand, is evenly divided: 44% approve of the way that they are handling the investigation, while 45% disapprove.

While some commentators have suggested a parallel between the Watergate impeachment hearings of Richard Nixon and the current hearings about Bill Clinton, the public sees these two events very differently, at least with respect to the seriousness of the charges against each president. By an overwhelming margin of 64% to 10%, respondents say that the charges against Nixon were more serious than those against Clinton, while 23% say that the charges are equally serious.

OCTOBER 17
CONGRESSIONAL ELECTIONS

Interviewing Dates: 10/9–12/98
CNN/*USA Today*/Gallup Poll
Survey #GO 124591

Asked of likely voters*: If the elections for Congress were being held today, which party's candidate would you vote for in your congressional district—the Democratic party's candidate, or the Republican party's candidate? [Those who were undecided were asked: As of today, do you lean more toward the Democratic party's candidate, or toward the Republican party's candidate?]

Democratic candidate 47%
Republican candidate 46
Other (volunteered); undecided..................... 7

*"Likely voters" estimate assumes a 39% turnout among the voting age population (equivalent to the 1994 midterm election turnout).

	Demo-cratic candidate	Repub-lican candidate	Other; undecided
By Sex			
Male	44%	50%	6%
Female	49	43	8
By Ethnic Background			
White	42	52	6
Nonwhite	78	11	11
Black	86	2	12
By Education			
Postgraduate	48	47	5
College Graduate	40	58	2
College Incomplete	48	47	5
No College	46	42	12
By Region			
East	46	45	9
Midwest	48	43	9
South	46	48	6
West	48	47	5
By Age			
18–29 Years	45	39	16
30–49 Years	47	50	3
50–64 Years	53	41	6
65 Years and Over	42	46	12
By Household Income			
$75,000 and Over	42	56	2
$50,000 and Over	47	50	3
$30,000–$49,999	40	53	7
$20,000–$29,999	53	41	6
Under $20,000	57	26	17
By Politics			
Republicans	5	93	2
Democrats	88	6	6
Independents	38	46	16
By Political Ideology			
Conservative	29	66	5
Moderate	55	35	10
Liberal	82	13	5

Selected National Trend

	Demo-cratic candidate	Repub-lican candidate	Other; undecided
1998			
September 23–24*	51%	45%	4%
September 14–15*	48	47	5
September 11–12*	47	46	7
August 21–23*	44	48	8
July 7–8*	46	46	8
April 17–19*	44	50	6

*Likely voters

Asked of the entire sample: Please tell me whether or not you think each of the following political officeholders deserves to be reelected:

The U.S. representative in your congressional district?

Yes	68%
No	16
No opinion	16

	Yes	No	No opinion
By Sex			
Male	69%	19%	12%
Female	66	14	20
By Ethnic Background			
White	69	15	16
Nonwhite	61	22	17
Black	59	22	19
By Education			
Postgraduate	72	16	12
College Graduate	67	19	14
College Incomplete	68	13	19
No College	67	17	16
By Region			
East	70	16	14
Midwest	68	16	16
South	67	17	16
West	65	17	18
By Age			
18–29 Years	68	15	17

	Yes	No	No opinion
30–49 Years	70	17	13
50–64 Years	64	19	17
65 Years and Over	67	14	19

By Household Income

	Yes	No	No opinion
$75,000 and Over	73	20	7
$50,000 and Over	72	17	11
$30,000–$49,999	65	17	18
$20,000–$29,999	71	16	13
Under $20,000	65	15	20

By Politics

	Yes	No	No opinion
Republicans	78	9	13
Democrats	62	18	20
Independents	64	21	15

By Political Ideology

	Yes	No	No opinion
Conservative	75	14	11
Moderate	68	15	17
Liberal	53	28	19

Selected National Trend

	Yes	No	No opinion
1998			
April 17–19	64%	19%	17%
1997			
October 27–29	62	18	20
August 22–25	63	21	16
1996			
October 27–28*	62	19	19
May 9–12	65	22	13
January 12–15	62	21	17
1994			
November 2–6	53	29	18
October 22–25	54	30	16
October 18–19	57	29	14
October 7–9	54	29	17
July 15–17	60	27	13
March 25–27	60	23	17
February 26–28	59	28	13

*Likely voters

Most members of the U.S. House of Representatives?

Yes	58%
No	26
No opinion	16

	Yes	No	No opinion
By Sex			
Male	59%	29%	12%
Female	57	23	20
By Ethnic Background			
White	60	24	16
Nonwhite	46	38	16
Black	46	38	16
By Education			
Postgraduate	57	25	18
College Graduate	59	26	15
College Incomplete	58	28	14
No College	58	25	17
By Region			
East	58	29	13
Midwest	57	27	16
South	59	23	18
West	58	26	16
By Age			
18–29 Years	62	26	12
30–49 Years	60	27	13
50–64 Years	53	28	19
65 Years and Over	52	22	26
By Household Income			
$75,000 and Over	62	28	10
$50,000 and Over	63	26	11
$30,000–$49,999	59	26	15
$20,000–$29,999	59	25	16
Under $20,000	53	27	20
By Politics			
Republicans	77	10	13
Democrats	49	35	16
Independents	50	32	18
By Political Ideology			
Conservative	66	20	14
Moderate	58	25	17
Liberal	45	43	12

Selected National Trend

	Yes	No	No opinion
1998			
April 17–19.................. 56%		28%	16%
1997			
October 27–29 50		29	21
August 22–25 56		27	17
1996			
October 27–28* 55		26	19
May 9–12.................... 50		35	15
January 12–15............. 47		38	15
1994			
November 2–6 39		45	16
October 22–25 43		44	13
October 18–19 44		42	14
October 7–9 37		48	15
July 15–17 41		43	16
March 25–27............... 46		38	16
February 26–28........... 42		44	14

*Likely voters

Note: This year's closely watched midterm elections for Congress are now less than three weeks away, and there is not yet a clear picture of what the results likely will be. In most off-year elections, the president's party loses seats, which would suggest that this year history is on the side of the Republicans. In addition, Bill Clinton's yearlong crisis in the White House initially led many observers to assume that the Republicans would do even better this year against the party of a wounded president. Recent Gallup polling, however, gives mixed signals on the election; and, with the late-breaking time frame for this year's serious campaigning, it is likely that much can change between now and November 3.

In terms of the straightforward ballot question that asks respondents whom they are going to vote for in their congressional district, the latest Gallup Poll shows the two parties essentially tied among those who are most likely to vote on Election Day. This is an increase for Republicans compared to Gallup's preceding survey conducted in late September, but it is similar to earlier polls last month.

If this 50-50 split were to hold through Election Day, it would represent a positive scenario for Democrats. Gallup analysis suggests that Republicans need to take a majority of the national two-party vote to maintain or expand their number of seats in the House.

Turnout is the key to midyear elections and, in low-interest contests, Republicans are usually disproportionately represented at the polls. Thus, if turnout is low this year, the Republicans would have the advantage. But if Democrats generate a high level of interest and vote in higher than usual numbers, it could spell a Democratic victory, or at the least a situation in which Republicans gain no seats.

A question designed to measure enthusiasm for voting this year suggests an apparent edge for Republicans. A higher percentage of Republicans indicate in Gallup's most recent poll that this year they are "more enthusiastic about the election" than "less enthusiastic." Democrats, on the other hand, show the opposite pattern. When this same question was asked in 1994, Republicans also indicated more enthusiasm than Democrats, although voters from both parties in that year were less likely to be enthusiastic. A relatively higher turnout among Republican voters in 1994 is often credited with helping them achieve the historic gains that produced their majority in the House.

Several other indicators in the data provide evidence of the possibility of a positive outcome for Republicans this November. The percentage of respondents who say that their U.S. Representative deserves reelection is at 68%, an all-time high for this measure and significantly higher than that measured before the 1994 elections. The results for the same question asked about most members of the House are also as high as they have ever been (at 58%), and this too is considerably higher than it was in 1994. These signs of contentment with Congress as it is now constituted may suggest that the Republican-controlled House has a good chance of maintaining the status quo.

On the other hand, Democrats hold the perceptual edge among respondents on many of the key issues that are most likely to drive this election. The top six issues, ranked by the public in terms of their priority, are education, the economy, crime, Social Security, taxes, and health-care policy. People were asked to indicate whether the Democrats or the Republicans could do a better

job of handling each one, and the Democrats have the edge on all but crime. Democrats do particularly well on education, Social Security, and health-care policy.

The only issues other than taxes on which Republicans are close to the Democrats are foreign affairs (a tie) and the impeachment proceedings, where Republicans hold a 3-point advantage. (This impeachment advantage exists despite the fact that on a different question, Republicans in Congress are given a slightly lower approval rating for their handling of the Clinton investigation than are their Democratic counterparts.) When asked whom they want to have more influence over the direction the nation takes in the next year, 53% of the public choose Bill Clinton, compared to 39% who choose the Republicans in Congress.

OCTOBER 24
PERSONAL SATISFACTION LEVELS

Interviewing Dates: 4/23–5/31/98
CNN/*USA Today*/Gallup Poll
Special survey

Please tell me whether you are generally satisfied or dissatisfied with each of the following:

Your family life?

Satisfied 91%
Dissatisfied 9
No opinion .... *

*Less than 1%

Your housing situation?

Satisfied 86%
Dissatisfied 14
No opinion .... *

*Less than 1%

Your health today?

Satisfied 86%
Dissatisfied 14
No opinion .... *

*Less than 1%

The availability of convenient transportation when you need it?

Satisfied 85%
Dissatisfied 14
No opinion 1

The opportunities you have to succeed in life?

Satisfied 84%
Dissatisfied 15
No opinion 1

Your standard of living?

Satisfied 78%
Dissatisfied 22
No opinion .... *

*Less than 1%

Your safety from physical harm?

Satisfied 78%
Dissatisfied 21
No opinion 1

The future facing your family?

Satisfied 76%
Dissatisfied 20
No opinion 4

Your job or the work you do?

Satisfied 75%
Dissatisfied 16
No opinion 9

Your level of education?

Satisfied 74%
Dissatisfied 26
No opinion .... *

*Less than 1%

Your family or household income?

Satisfied 70%
Dissatisfied 29
No opinion 1

The amount of leisure time you have?

Satisfied 64%
Dissatisfied 36
No opinion .... *

*Less than 1%

Your financial net worth or savings?

Satisfied 56%
Dissatisfied 43
No opinion 1

Note: A new Gallup Poll finds that Americans are generally satisfied and happy with their lives, and that in many instances these levels of well-being are as high as they have been in decades. The in-depth Gallup Poll Social Audit on Haves and Have-nots asked respondents to rate whether or not they are satisfied with thirteen specific aspects of their lives. Although a majority of the public is satisfied with each aspect measured, there is a wide range of variation, from 91% who express satisfaction with family life to 56% who claim satisfaction with their financial net worth or savings. In addition to family life, other high levels of satisfaction are recorded for people's housing situation, their health, the availability of transportation, and opportunities to succeed in life. At the bottom end of the spectrum, in addition to the lesser number satisfied with their net worth and savings, relatively lower numbers are satisfied with their amount of leisure time (64%) and their household income (70%).

Eight of these satisfaction dimensions have been tracked across time, and the current readings of most of these register toward the high end of their historical range. There are two exceptions, however, that show decreases in satisfaction over time: "your job or the work you do," which is 15 percentage points below its high point of 90% recorded in 1969; and "the amount of leisure time you have," which is currently 12 points below its 1963 level of 76%.

There are several interesting aspects of the ratings on the amount of leisure time. For one thing, satisfaction with the amount of leisure time available skyrockets at retirement. Only 55% of

employed adults express satisfaction with this dimension, compared with 95% of those who say that they are retired. The leisure time question is also notable for being the only one in the set that is negatively related to measures of socioeconomic status, both objective (income and education) and subjective (shape of personal finances). People with higher socioeconomic status and optimism about their personal finances are least satisfied with the amount of leisure time available.

In addition to the thirteen aspects measured, another satisfaction dimension included in the study is a relatively general one: "the way things are going in your personal life." Fully 85% express satisfaction in response to this question. Historically, this measure has been quite stable; taken forty-three times over the past two decades, it has never exceeded 87% nor dropped below the level of 73% recorded in July 1979.

Gallup asked two other questions intended to provide a broad assessment of personal well-being. The first is a simple question asking respondents whether they are very, fairly, or not too happy. Forty-five percent claim to be very happy, while another 50% are fairly happy. This combined total of over 90% claiming to be very or fairly happy is generally consistent with measurements recorded by Gallup stretching back to 1948.

The second assessment of general well-being is based on a set of three questions developed by survey pioneer Hadley Cantril and asked eight times by Gallup since the early 1960s. The questions ask respondents to imagine a ladder, with steps numbered from zero (the lowest) to ten (the highest). The bottom step represents "the worst possible life for you," and the top step "the best possible life for you." Respondents then are asked on which step "you feel you personally stand at the present time." Using the same scale, respondents next are asked on which step of the ladder they stood five years ago; and, finally, on which step they expect to stand five years into the future.

When asked on which step they stand at the present time, 44% place themselves on one of the top three steps, 80% above the middle step, another 13% directly on the middle one, and only 7% on steps zero to four. Respondents are even more positive when they assess their future, with 72% saying that they will stand on steps eight, nine, or ten in

five years' time. However, they are much less positive when they look back, with only 26% saying that they stood on one of the top three steps five years go.

Current ratings both of one's present position and of one's anticipated position five years into the future are well above any ratings previously recorded by Gallup at eight different points in time spanning thirty-four years. Ratings of one's position five years ago have been remarkably stable—and low—over the historical period beginning in 1964.

OCTOBER 31
CONGRESSIONAL ELECTIONS

Interviewing Dates: 10/23–25/98
CNN/*USA Today*/Gallup Poll
Survey #GO 124708

> *Asked of likely voters*: If the elections for Congress were being held today, which party's candidate would you vote for in your congressional district—the Democratic party's candidate, or the Republican party's candidate? [Those who were undecided were asked: As of today, do you lean more toward the Democratic party's candidate, or toward the Republican party's candidate?]*

Democratic candidate 47%
Republican candidate 49
Other (volunteered); undecided...................... 4

*Semi-final pre-election figures. "Likely voter" estimate assumes a 39% turnout among the voting age population (equivalent to the 1994 midterm election turnout).

Generic Congressional Ballot

1950–1994 Final Pre-Election Figures
(Based on Likely Voters)

	Democratic candidate	Republican candidate	Democratic advantage/ disadvantage
1994	46.5%	53.5%	-7
1990	54	46	+8
1986*	–	–	–

1982	55	45	+10
1978	55	45	+10
1974	60	40	+20
1970	53	47	+6
1966	52.5	47.5	+5
1962	55.5	45.5	+10
1958	57	43	+14
1954	51.5	48.5	+3
1950	51	49	+2

*No final pre-election measurement in 1986

Generic Congressional Ballot

1998 Semi-Final and 1950–1994 Final Pre-Election Figures
(Based on National Adults)

	Democratic candidate	Republican candidate	Democratic advantage/ disadvantage
1998 (semi-final)	52%	48%	+4
1994	52	48	+4
1990*	56	44	+12
1986**	–	–	–
1982*	59	41	+18
1978	62	38	+24
1974	68	32	+36
1970	59	41	+18
1966	51	49	+2
1962	60	40	+20
1958	58	42	+16
1954	63	37	+26
1950	51	50†	+1

*Registered voters
**No final pre-election measurement in 1986
†Figures were rounded

Note: The latest Gallup Poll, taken one week before the midterm congressional elections, finds the Republican and Democratic parties running neck and neck in the race for control of Congress. When asked which congressional candidate they plan to support in their local House district, 49% of "likely voters" across the country now say that they plan to vote Republican, while 47% say that they will vote Democratic. The Republican and Democratic parties have been close on this

important indicator of the congressional vote since July, with the lead switching back and forth between the two parties from survey to survey.

Other Gallup measures of the public's political mood suggest that incumbent officeholders will do well on Election Day. Two-thirds say that their own member of Congress deserves reelection, up substantially from 1994. And close to one-half of the public (47%) now says that it approves of the job Congress is doing, a positive evaluation compared with previous years.

Since Republicans are the majority party in Congress, it might seem logical that these perceptions bode well for them in the election. Still, given the closeness in the number of seats held by each party in Congress (228 Republicans versus 206 Democrats), and of current voter preferences on Gallup's "generic ballot," public satisfaction with the status quo does not necessarily mean that the Republicans will retain control of the U.S. House of Representatives.

With less than 40% of Americans expected to vote in the midterm elections next Tuesday [November 3], Gallup's latest results underscore the significance of voter turnout to the outcome. In order to hold on to their current majority, the GOP needs Republican voters to turn out in substantially greater numbers than Democratic voters, as they did in 1994. The potential for this type of turnout is not evident in the latest Gallup polling and thus, as of today, the Republicans' ability to maintain majority control of the House would appear to be in jeopardy.

Prior to the Republicans taking control of Congress in 1994, voter turnout was not usually an important factor in determining the control of Congress, as public support for Democratic candidates far exceeded support for Republicans. In fact, from 1954 through 1992, Democrats typically led Republicans by 10 to 20 points among all national adults in Gallup's "generic congressional ballot" poll measure; on occasion, such as in 1974, the Democrats held more than a 30-point advantage. Thus, given the Democrats' strong numerical superiority among the general public, even a large Republican voter turnout in those elections affected only the degree to which Democrats maintained control of the House, not the basic question of majority control.

The gap between public support for Republican and Democratic congressional candidates began to shrink in 1993, and by 1994 the two parties had become highly competitive. Among national adults surveyed by Gallup in 1994, for example, the Democrats' advantage over Republicans on the congressional preference question had dropped to single digits, and in Gallup's final pre-election survey in 1994 the Democratic advantage was only 4 percentage points. Among likely voters in that same survey, Republicans led Democrats by 7 points, which turned out to be the actual margin of the GOP victory in the national two-party vote. Thus, given the closeness of Republican and Democratic congressional preferences in 1994, voter turnout made the critical difference and allowed the Republicans to capture a majority of seats in Congress for the first time in fifty years.

In the four years since they took control of Congress, the Republicans have maintained their competitive positioning with the Democrats but have not managed to become the solid majority choice of voters, as was the case for the Democrats in years past. Hence, support for Republican candidates among all respondents—not just likely voters—is currently very similar to that of November 1994, just prior to the Republicans winning majority control of the House.

There is a difference between this year and 1994, however, in terms of the projected pool of likely voters. In 1994 final pre-election survey results among those determined to be most likely to vote showed a substantial 7-point Republican lead. This year, as already noted, the Republicans are ahead by only 2 points among this same likely voter group.

A Gallup analysis of eleven previous midterm elections suggests that to maintain a majority of seats in Congress, the Republicans will need to win more than 50% of all votes cast for Congress across the country. Whether their current 2-point lead over Democrats among likely voters is sufficient for the Republicans to retain their majority control is unclear at this point.

Between today and November 3, two factors will be important in determining the outcome of the congressional elections. First, there could be last-minute shifts in voters' preferences, including

the impact of undecided voters who must finally make up their minds. Second, turnout could skew more heavily to voters of one party or the other than is evident in the latest polling. None of this is lost on the two political parties, whose last-minute campaign tactics appear to be focused almost entirely on activating their hard-core supporters to turn out and vote in key congressional districts across the country. Major efforts are also under way by labor unions, Christian conservative groups, and others to mobilize their voters over this final weekend. In an election this close, these types of turnout efforts could make an important difference.

As of today, the Clinton impeachment issue does not appear to be a major factor affecting voter decisionmaking or turnout. While close to one-half of likely voters say that they will be sending a message about the Lewinsky matter with their ballot, these voters are evenly split between those who say that they will be sending a message in support of Clinton and those who say that they oppose him. Previous polling this month also shows that the forthcoming impeachment proceedings are the public's lowest priority among nine issues tested for their importance in deciding the congressional vote on November 3.

NOVEMBER 2
CONGRESSIONAL ELECTIONS—
FINAL POLL

Interviewing Dates: 10/29–11/1/98
CNN/*USA Today*/Gallup Poll
Survey #GO 124709

Asked of likely voters*: If the elections for Congress were being held today, which party's candidate would you vote for in your congressional district—the Democratic party's candidate, or the Republican party's candidate?

Democratic candidate	49%
Republican candidate	45
Other (volunteered); undecided	6

*"Likely voter" estimate assumes a 39% turnout among the voting age population (equivalent to the 1994 midterm election turnout).

Asked of likely voters*: In general, are you satisfied or dissatisfied with the way things are going in the United States at this time?

	Oct. 29–Nov. 1, 1998	Nov. 2–6, 1994
Satisfied	60%	30%
Dissatisfied	34	66
No opinion	6	4

Asked of likely voters*: How would you rate economic conditions in this country today—excellent, good, only fair, or poor?

	1998 pre-election survey	1994 pre-election survey
Excellent, good	66%	30%
Only fair, poor	33	69
No opinion	1	1

Note: Just one day before the election [on Tuesday, November 3], likely voters across the country favor Democratic over Republican congressional candidates by a margin of 49% to 45%, according to the latest Gallup Poll, conducted over the weekend. These results represent a slight shift in sentiment from a survey conducted a week ago, when Republicans had a 2-point advantage. (The undecided vote is allocated proportionally to the two parties; thus, in 1998, the 49%-to-45% Democratic lead over the Republican candidate gives a 51.8%-to-48.2% two-party vote.)

It is unclear exactly how the national vote will translate into actual seats won by the two parties in each of the 435 congressional districts. Currently, the Republicans enjoy majority control in the House with 228 seats, with 206 for the Democrats (and one independent seat). The president's political party usually loses seats in midterm elections, suggesting that if this were a typical year, Republicans could expect to gain seats. The current Democratic advantage on the House vote question, however, suggests that such Republican gains could be limited this year, and that Democrats could even win more

seats. A gain of 12 seats by the Democrats would allow them to recapture majority control, which they last held in 1992.

While many political experts have predicted a substantially lower voter turnout this year than in 1994, the poll gives mixed signals on whether this will actually happen. The number of Americans who are enthusiastic about the election this year is comparable to those in 1994, suggesting that turnout could be similar. However, just 50% this year say that they have paid much attention to the election, compared with 56% four years ago. This lower level of interest could indicate a lower turnout.

If the turnout is lower than 39%, the advantage that Democrats have over Republicans in the election would be smaller. The current estimate is based on an assumed turnout of 39% of eligible Americans, the same as in 1994. But if the turnout drops to 35%, for example, the poll suggests that the Democratic lead over the Republicans would shrink to just 2 points.

The latest poll shows that in the past week Republican enthusiasm for voting in Tuesday's election, relative to Democratic enthusiasm, has dropped slightly. The net result is that Republicans are now essentially no more or less enthusiastic about voting than are Democrats, in contrast to 1994, when Republicans were significantly more enthusiastic.

The mood of the public is substantially more positive this year than at the time of the 1994 midterm election. Twice as many people this year as in 1994 give the economy a high rating, and twice as many also express satisfaction in general with the way that things are going in the country. Respondents also presently give higher approval ratings to both the president and Congress. Today, 66% approve of the way that Bill Clinton is handling his job as president, up 20 points from 1994. And 44% approve of the job that Congress is doing, almost double the number in 1994.

It does not appear that the controversy over the relationship between Clinton and Monica Lewinsky, and the subsequent congressional vote to hold impeachment hearings, will hurt—or help—either party. Among likely voters, about one-quarter say that their vote will be a message against Clinton, while the same number say that their vote will be a message in support of the pres-

ident, with just over a majority saying that their vote will not be about him at all.

Likely voters remain opposed to the impeachment of Clinton by a better than 2-to-1 majority (66% to 29%), which is about the same as among the public overall. Forty percent of likely voters say that he should resign, compared with 36% of the public overall. The largest difference between the general public and voters relates to their attitudes toward censuring Clinton for his behavior. By a margin of 47% to 44%, voters say that he should be censured, but the general public opposes censure by 49% to 40%.

NOVEMBER 14
NEWT GINGRICH—AN ANALYSIS*

Newt Gingrich's announcement last week that he would step down as Speaker of the House of Representatives marked the culmination of the congressional career of a politician who has never been a popular figure among Americans. From the moment he became a well-known face on the political landscape, Gingrich has generated negative public reactions. He has consistently received more unfavorable than favorable ratings in terms of his personal image, has also been given generally low approval ratings for the job he has done as Speaker, and almost always has fared poorly when compared to his sometime nemesis, Bill Clinton. Still, perhaps ironically, Gingrich was enjoying what were for him relatively high ratings from the public this year, significantly up from his low-water marks in 1995 and 1996.

Gingrich's Negative Image Became Apparent in Late 1994

Newt Gingrich moved into the national consciousness as the leader of the successful Republican effort to gain control of the House of Representatives in 1994. Gallup's first measure of the public's impression of Gingrich came in October of that year, immediately before the historic November election. At that point, even

*This analysis was written by Frank Newport, editor in chief, The Gallup Organization.

though almost six in ten Americans had no opinion at all of the Georgia Congressman, his image was already slightly more negative than positive.

Immediately after the Republicans' election success—and for the only time in eighteen different measures of his image since that time—Gingrich's image tilted positive. In a November 1994 poll, 29% of the public had a favorable opinion of Gingrich, and 25% a negative opinion. By December of that same year, however, his image had moved back into negative territory. It has remained more negative than positive ever since.

The public appeared to turn particularly strongly against the Speaker after his budget confrontation with Bill Clinton and the resulting U.S. Government shutdown in late 1995. (Publicity at the time, including a famous front-page caricature in the *New York Daily News*, included the allegation that Gingrich had closed down the government because he was given a bad seat at the back of Air Force One when returning from the funeral of Yitzhak Rabin in Israel.) By January 1996, 57% of Americans said that their image of Gingrich was unfavorable, compared with 37% who had a favorable image. This 2-to-1 negative-to-positive image ratio persisted throughout most of 1996 and 1997.

Gingrich Fared Somewhat Better in 1998

Despite his ultimate downfall this month, Gingrich's image had actually become somewhat more positive in several polls conducted earlier this year. In February, for example, the number of Americans with an unfavorable image of Gingrich dropped below 50% for the first time since August 1995. (This was generally consistent with a more positive mood that Americans had about many aspects of government following Bill Clinton's January State of the Union Address.)

Although Gingrich's image dipped in a June Gallup Poll, by October—the last measure before the elections—he had a partially rehabilitated image, with 42% of the public giving him a favorable image rating, and 49% unfavorable. Thus, there was some evidence that Gingrich was on the way back up in the minds of the public, but these measures were taken before the outcome of the November 3rd election, the subsequent criticism

Gingrich and other Republican leaders took as a result, and his eventual resignation last week.

Job Ratings Parallel Evaluations of Gingrich's Image

From time to time, Gallup has also asked Americans to indicate their approval or disapproval of the job Gingrich was doing as Speaker of the House. Comparable to the public's rating of his image, Gingrich's job approval rating was quite low in 1995 and particularly in 1996—generally in the 30% range. Gingrich's job approval in two polls conducted in late January shot up into the positive range, and in April there was an essential tie between those who gave him positive and negative job performance ratings—the highest on this measure since he became Speaker.

Gingrich in Context: Comparisons to Clinton, Gephardt, and Wright

In many ways, the November election this year has been viewed as a showdown between Gingrich and Bill Clinton. If it was, Clinton clearly had the more positive public opinion base with which to operate. The president's image and job approval ratings have generally been more positive than those of Gingrich, even throughout the past eleven months when the Monica Lewinsky crisis dominated the news and threatened Clinton's entire presidency. In January of this year, for example, after the Lewinsky matter became headline news, Gingrich's job approval ratings of 46% and 48% were well below Clinton's own job approval ratings of 58% and 60%. In April, while Gingrich had a 45% approval rating, Clinton's was 63%. And, despite the Lewinsky revelations, Bill Clinton's favorable image ratings this year have consistently been more positive than Gingrich's. In February, June, and October of this year, Gingrich had 37%, 32%, and 42% favorable image ratings. At those same times, Clinton's favorable image ratings were much higher, at 58%, 61%, and 54%.

It is not possible to compare Gingrich's ratings with previous Speakers or House leaders, since most were not prominent enough to be measured in

Gallup Polls. In an early October poll, however, House Democratic Leader Dick Gephardt was included in an image rating list, and he had a favorable-to-unfavorable image of 48% to 20%, much more positive than Gingrich's 42% favorable and 49% unfavorable numbers in the same poll.

On the other hand, Democratic Speaker of the House Jim Wright was negatively evaluated in a May 1989 Gallup Poll, when he received a 41% unfavorable and only 19% favorable image rating. This poll was taken in the middle of Wright's own problems with ethics charges, a controversy which provoked his resignation (and which was the result in part of the efforts of Congressman Newt Gingrich of Georgia).

Gingrich for President?

There has been some discussion that Newt Gingrich might entertain the possibility of running for president in 2000 or 2004. The early signs for such a run are not encouraging for the Speaker. In a poll earlier this year, Gallup pitted Republicans against Al Gore in a hypothetical 2000 presidential ballot. Current Republican front-runner Texas Governor George W. Bush was essentially tied with the vice president at that time, while in the same poll Gingrich was soundly defeated by Gore, by a 62%-to-32% margin.

NOVEMBER 21
REPUBLICAN PARTY—AN ANALYSIS*

Although the Republican party maintained a majority of seats in the U.S. House and Senate in the November midterm elections, its public image is now far below its 1994 heyday. Only 57% of Americans have a favorable view of the Republican party today, compared with 70% after the November 1994 elections.

Not only has the percentage of Americans saying they have a favorable opinion of the Republicans dropped, but the party has lost its superiority over the Democrats on this basic image measure. In 1994, Republicans enjoyed a 15-point advantage in favorability over the Democrats,

*This analysis was written by Lydia Saad, managing editor, The Gallup Organization.

70% vs. 55%. Gallup polling conducted one week after this year's midterm elections finds the Republicans with an 11-point favorability compared to the Democrats, 57% vs. 68%.

Ratings of Parties

	Republican favorability	Democratic favorability	Republican advantage/ disadvantage
Nov. 13–15, 1998	57%	68%	−11
Oct. 26–29, 1996	63	70	−7
Jan. 8–14, 1996	61	62	−1
Nov. 28–29, 1994	70	55	+15
Dec. 17–19, 1993	73	68	+5
Dec. 4–6, 1992	62	73	−11

For most of the forty years that Gallup has measured party favorability, the Democratic party has been viewed more favorably than the Republican party. Two recent exceptions include 1991, when George Bush was a popular Republican president, as well as 1993 and 1994, when Bill Clinton was lagging in popularity. The current 11-point lead for the Democrats is the widest advantage since Clinton's election in 1992.

Public Lacks Confidence in GOP Direction

Republicans' lower favorability ratings are reflected in other measures of public support for their leadership. In late November 1994 a solid 55% majority of Americans felt that the policies being proposed by the Republican leaders in the U.S. House and Senate would move the country in the "right direction," compared to only 27% who felt it would move things in the "wrong direction."

That strong mandate for Republican leadership began to collapse in the fall of 1995 during the confrontation between Congress and the president over the budget, which resulted in a temporary government shutdown. While support for Republican leadership recovered somewhat during 1996 and through much of 1998, the postelection survey finds Americans now evenly divided on this matter. Today, only 43% believe the GOP would move the

country in the right direction, while nearly as many (40%) say the wrong direction.

Other Image Measures

A measure of the perceived political ideology of the two major parties shows that Americans are now less likely than in 1994 to believe the political views of the Republican party strike the right balance between liberalism and conservatism. Only 41% now say the views of the Republican party are "about right," compared to 54% in 1994. The percentage saying the Republicans' views are "too conservative" has increased from 31% to 39%, as has the percentage saying "too liberal," increasing from 11% to 15%.

While views of Republican party politics have become more polarized since 1994, the Democratic image has become more mainstream. In 1994, 50% of Americans thought the Democratic party was too liberal, compared to only 32% who said "about right." Today those figures are nearly reversed, with only 37% saying "too liberal" and 50% "about right."

In another measure, roughly two-thirds of Americans believe the Republican party generally favors the rich, while a mere 24% say the middle class and only 2% say the poor. There is less public consensus about class partiality in the Democratic party, with 43% saying the party favors the middle class, 28% the poor, and 20% the rich. These perceptions of the Democrats have remained generally constant between 1994 and today.

Republican Leadership Changes

With Newt Gingrich's surprise resignation from Congress earlier this month, the election of Republican leaders for the new Congress took on special importance. Some debate ensued about whether the GOP would be better off choosing leaders with more moderate, mainstream agendas or more well-honed and -articulated conservative agendas.

By a 55%-to-36% margin, Americans say they would prefer to see the Republican leaders in Congress promote policies that are "more moderate" rather than "more conservative," compared with the policies they now promote. It is not surprising that Democrats and even political independents say they would prefer to see Republican policies become more moderate; however, even among rank-and-file Republicans, only 50% say they would like their leaders in Congress to promote more conservative policies, while 44% say they should follow a more moderate agenda.

NOVEMBER 25
CRIME

Interviewing Dates: 10/23–25/98
CNN/*USA Today*/Gallup Poll
Survey #GO 124708

How often do you, yourself, worry about the following—very frequently, pretty frequently, pretty seldom, or very seldom:

Getting murdered?

	Oct. 23–25, 1998	Oct. 13–18, 1993
Very frequently	6%	8%
Pretty frequently	8	11
Pretty seldom	19	18
Very seldom	66	62
No opinion	1	1

Getting mugged?

	Oct. 23–25, 1998	Oct. 13–18, 1993
Very frequently	7%	11%
Pretty frequently	12	15
Pretty seldom	26	23
Very seldom	54	51
No opinion	1	*

*Less than 1%

Your home being burglarized when you're not there?

	Oct. 23–25, 1998	Oct. 13–18, 1993
Very frequently	12%	14%
Pretty frequently	19	21

Pretty seldom	26	22
Very seldom	42	42
No opinion	1	1

Yourself or someone in your family getting sexually assaulted or raped?

	Oct. 23–25, 1998	Oct. 13–18, 1993
Very frequently	12%	15%
Pretty frequently	16	23
Pretty seldom	25	22
Very seldom	46	39
No opinion	1	1

Being attacked while driving your car?

	Oct. 23–25, 1998	Oct. 13–18, 1993
Very frequently	7%	12%
Pretty frequently	11	16
Pretty seldom	25	22
Very seldom	54	47
No opinion	3	3

How much confidence do you have in the ability of the police to protect you from violent crime—a great deal, quite a lot, not very much, or none at all?

Great deal	19%
Quite a lot	36
Not very much	37
None at all	8
No opinion	*

*Less than 1%

Selected National Trend

	Great deal	Quite a lot	Not very much	None at all*
1995	20%	30%	39%	9%
1993	14	31	45	9
1990	17	35	46	**
1989	14	34	42	8
1985	15	37	39	6
1981	15	34	42	8

*"No opinion"—at 3% or less—is omitted.
**Less than 1%

Overall, do you feel more threatened or less threatened by crime today than you did five years ago?

More threatened	47%
Less threatened	41
Same (volunteered)	11
No opinion	1

Asked of those who replied "less threatened": Do you feel less threatened by crime because of changes you have made in your life to protect yourself from crime, or because you feel there is less crime?

Changes made	44%
Less crime	45
Other (volunteered)	7
No opinion	4

Note: According to a Gallup Poll conducted last month, Americans are slightly less fearful today than five years ago that they themselves will be victimized by major violent crimes. They also express more confidence in the ability of the police to protect the public. But while actual crime rates have fallen over the past several years—with the latest statistics released this week by the FBI—the poll shows that just as many people feel safer because of steps they have taken to protect themselves as those who feel safer because they believe that there actually is less crime. Indeed, although this is the sixth straight year that a decline has been announced, a majority of Americans is not even aware that the crime rate has actually fallen in the United States.

In the poll, respondents were asked how frequently they worry about five different types of crime happening to them personally. For all five types, the number who say they worry very or pretty frequently is smaller today than it was in 1993. A 10-point drop was found on two items: concern about being attacked while driving a car, and having someone in the family sexually assaulted or raped. Today, 28% worry frequently about possible sexual assault, compared with 38% five years ago. And 18% currently worry about

being attacked while driving a car, compared with 28% who said so in 1993.

Fear of being mugged is down by 7 points, from 26% who worried about it in 1993 to 19% today. There are also modest drops in the fear of being murdered (14% today, down 5 points from 1993) and in the fear of having one's home burglarized (31% today, down 4 points). At the same time that fear of specific crimes has declined, confidence in the police's ability to protect the public from violent crime has increased. Today, a majority of the public (55%) has a great deal or quite a lot of confidence in the police, compared with 45% five years ago.

Despite these more positive feelings, just 35% say that there is less crime in the United States than there was a year ago, while 52% think that there is more. However, when it comes to the area where they actually live, the figures are almost reversed: 48% say that there has been a decline in crime in the past year, compared with just 31% who say that there has been an increase. Thus, it would appear that respondents' more positive feelings reflect their perceptions of an improved climate in their own neighborhoods rather than in the country as a whole.

It is perhaps ironic that despite the lower levels of fear expressed in the current survey than in the 1993 one, people do not necessarily remember being more afraid of crime when they think back five years ago. Today, only 41% remember feeling more threatened by crime five years ago than they are today, while 47% remember feeling less threatened. These perceptions contradict the poll results from both 1993 and 1998, but it is often the case that people think of the past more positively than is warranted.

Those who say that they feel less threatened today are evenly divided on the reason for their more positive feelings: 45% say that it is because they feel there is actually less crime, while 44% say that it is because of changes they have made in their lives to protect themselves from being victimized. These perceptions are highly related to age, however, with those over 50 mostly saying that they feel safer because there has been an actual decline in crime, while those under 50 say that it is mostly because they have taken precautionary steps.

DECEMBER 5
U.S. SPACE PROGRAM

Interviewing Dates: 11/20–22/98
CNN/*USA Today*/Gallup Poll
Survey #GO 124977

How would you rate the job being done by NASA, the U.S. space agency—would you say it is doing an excellent, good, only fair, or poor job?

Excellent	26%
Good	50
Fair	17
Poor	4
No opinion	3

Selected National Trend

	Excellent	Good	Fair	Poor*
Jan. 30– Feb. 1, 1998	21%	46%	21%	4%
July 1994	14	43	29	6
Dec. 1993	18	43	30	7
Sept. 1993	7	36	35	11
May 1991	16	48	24	6
July 1990	10	36	34	15

*"No opinion"—at 11% or less—is omitted.

Some people feel that the U.S. space program should concentrate on unmanned missions like Voyager 2, *which sent back information from planets such as Neptune. Others say we should concentrate on maintaining a manned space program like the space shuttle and space station. Which comes closer to your view?*

Unmanned missions	32%
Manned programs	52
Neither; both (volunteered)	10
No opinion	6

Selected National Trend

	Unmanned missions	Manned programs	Neither; both	No opinion
May 1991	39%	49%	*	12%
July 1990	34	48	6	12
July 1989	40	43	9	8

*Less than 1%

It is now almost thirty years since the United States first landed men on the moon. Do you think the space program has brought enough benefits to this country to justify its costs, or don't you think so?

Yes, brought enough benefits.......................... 58%
No... 36
No opinion... 6

Selected National Trend

	Yes, brought enough benefits	No	No opinion
July 1994	47%	47%	6%
1979*	41	53	6

*NBC News/AP Poll

Note: The U.S. space agency, NASA—benefiting from the recent publicity surrounding the shuttle mission of Senator John Glenn—is receiving its most positive evaluations of the decade. Three in four Americans give the agency high marks for the way that it is doing its job, and almost six in ten think that the benefits of the space program justify its costs. As the United States and Russia begin the long process of building an Earth-orbiting space station, a majority of Americans also say that a manned space program is worth its additional costs and risks compared to a total reliance on unmanned missions.

A November Gallup Poll, conducted after the seventy-seven-year-old Glenn's successful shuttle flight, finds that 76% of Americans rate NASA as doing an excellent or good job. These are the most positive numbers on this basic NASA job evaluation since Gallup began asking the question in 1990. (NASA's lowest rating, at 43%, came in September 1993.) There is also continuing public sentiment that the space program is providing benefits that outweigh its costs. When asked directly if the space program has brought enough benefits to justify its costs, 58% say yes. Twenty years ago, in answer to the same question, the positive responses were significantly lower, with more Americans saying that the benefits were not worth the costs than saying that they were.

Over the years, the emphasis by NASA on a manned space program has generated controversy, with critics arguing that a reliance on unmanned missions and probes would provide a more cost-efficient scientific return on taxpayer dollars than does the more costly manned program. Despite these arguments, the American public agrees that the manned approach is worthwhile, by a 52%-to-32% margin—a significant change from nine years ago, in 1989, when almost as many of those interviewed were in favor of the unmanned program as the manned program.

Despite the overall positive public evaluations that NASA receives, it is clear that space has a much lower priority for most Americans than other programs on which federal tax dollars could be spent. Respondents were asked about their views on federal funding for four different programs: space, improving medical and health care, providing food for low-income families, and improving the quality of public education. They strongly support increased federal spending on education and health care: three-quarters say that funding for these programs should be increased. There is mixed sentiment about food programs, with about as many of those polled (42%) saying that spending should stay the same as saying that it should be increased (44%). The views on increased spending on the space program are relatively more negative. Only 21% want it increased, while 47% want it to stay the same and 26% want it reduced. These numbers are slightly more positive than in 1993, but roughly the same as those of earlier Gallup surveys conducted in the late 1980s and early 1990s.

DECEMBER 12
PRESIDENT CLINTON/CONGRESSIONAL IMPEACHMENT HEARINGS

Interviewing Dates: 12/8, 9, 10/98
CNN/*USA Today*/Gallup Poll
Surveys #GO 125378, 125379, 125380

How closely have you been following the congressional impeachment proceedings against Bill Clinton—very closely, somewhat closely, not too closely, or not at all?

	Dec. 10, 1998	Dec. 9, 1998	Dec. 8, 1998
Very closely	20%	16%	19%
Somewhat closely	36	38	36
Not too closely	31	29	28
Not at all	12	17	17
No opinion	1	*	*

*Less than 1%

	Dec. 10, 1998	Dec. 9, 1998	Dec. 8, 1998
By Sex			
Male			
Very Closely	22%	17%	17%
Somewhat Closely	35	41	38
Not Too Closely	30	25	29
Not At All*	12	16	16
Female			
Very Closely	17	15	20
Somewhat Closely	38	34	35
Not Too Closely	33	32	27
Not At All*	11	19	18
By Age			
18–29 Years			
Very Closely	9	6	6
Somewhat Closely	36	35	29
Not Too Closely	39	33	36
Not At All*	16	26	29
30–49 Years			
Very Closely	14	10	16
Somewhat Closely	40	41	35
Not Too Closely	31	33	32
Not At All*	14	16	17
50 Years and Over			
Very Closely	30	26	29
Somewhat Closely	34	36	41
Not Too Closely	27	24	19
Not At All*	8	13	10
By Politics			
Republicans			
Very Closely	28	19	21
Somewhat Closely	37	48	44
Not Too Closely	28	24	21
Not At All*	6	9	14
Democrats			
Very Closely	18	19	24
Somewhat Closely	39	39	34

	Dec. 10, 1998	Dec. 9, 1998	Dec. 8, 1998
Not Too Closely	30	27	29
Not At All*	13	15	13
Independents			
Very Closely	13	11	14
Somewhat Closely	34	30	34
Not Too Closely	36	34	31
Not At All*	16	24	21

*"No opinion"—at 1% or less—is omitted.

As you may know, the House Judiciary Committee is holding hearings on whether to recommend impeachment of Bill Clinton to the full House of Representatives. In your view, should the House Judiciary Committee vote for or against impeachment?

	Dec. 10, 1998	Dec. 9, 1998	Dec. 8, 1998
Vote for	34%	34%	34%
Vote against	63	61	59
No opinion	3	5	7

	Dec. 10, 1998	Dec. 9, 1998	Dec. 8, 1998
By Sex			
Male			
Vote For	36%	41%	40%
Vote Against	61	55	54
No Opinion	3	4	6
Female			
Vote For	32	28	29
Vote Against	64	66	63
No Opinion	4	6	8
By Age			
18–29 Years			
Vote For	41	29	28
Vote Against	55	61	58
No Opinion	4	10	14
30–49 Years			
Vote For	36	38	37
Vote Against	61	58	58
No Opinion	3	4	5
50 Years and Over			
Vote For	28	34	35
Vote Against	68	62	60
No Opinion	4	4	5

By Politics

Republicans

Vote For	68	67	63
Vote Against	29	28	35
No Opinion	3	5	2

Democrats

Vote For	5	12	17
Vote Against	94	84	79
No Opinion	1	4	4

Independents

Vote For	35	34	28
Vote Against	59	60	60
No Opinion	6	6	12

Note: The American public's attitudes about the historic impeachment process unfolding in Washington, DC, evaluated by a series of Gallup Polls conducted this past week, can be summarized succinctly: the president's guilty, but don't impeach him. Despite the wrangling in the House Judiciary Committee hearings on the issue of whether or not Bill Clinton's actions were or were not technically illegal, there is little doubt in the public's mind that they were. Americans believe—in some instances confirming what they have said in polls for many months—that Clinton committed perjury, engaged in illegal acts, and misused and abused his office.

As far back as April of this year, a clear majority of the public said that Clinton had lied under oath. In September, 66% said that he had committed perjury. In polling this week, well over one-half of those surveyed agree that the allegations contained in three of the four draft articles of impeachment circulated by the Judiciary Committee majority are true, and one-half believe that the fourth—obstruction of justice—is true. At the same time, it is clear that the majority does not think that these offenses rise to the level of being impeachable. This, too, has been a consistent finding over the past several months.

The public's basic attitudes about impeachment are stable and straightforward: about one-third of those interviewed have said in response to questions asked about impeachment that they favor it. About 60% or more have consistently opposed it. These opinions are obtained in response to general questions asking about "impeaching and removing Clinton from office" as well as to very specific questions that differentiate between the impeachment role of the House and the trial role of the Senate, and to questions about the actions that should be taken by the House Judiciary Committee.

Censure appears to be a preferred alternative. When asked this week directly about censuring the president, 55% favor it. In response to a different question, about 61% this past weekend said that they favor censure if an impeachment measure is not passed. However, the public does not think that Clinton will ultimately be impeached. As of Tuesday night [December 8], only 37% of those polled said that the House would vote to convict him and send the issue to the Senate for trial.

The impeachment proceedings thus far have generated only mid-range attention from the public. As of Thursday night of this week [December 10], 56% said that they were following the congressional impeachment proceedings very or somewhat closely. This percentage is significantly lower than the attention levels measured by Gallup for other major news events, such as the death of Princess Diana and the United Parcel Service strike.

DECEMBER 19
IRAQ SITUATION

Interviewing Date: 12/16/98
CNN/*USA Today*/Gallup Poll
Survey #GO 125479

As you may know, the United Nations chief weapons inspector has reported that Iraq has not complied with its agreement to allow UN inspections of possible weapons facilities. In response, the United States and Britain have launched an air attack against Iraq this evening. Do you approve or disapprove of this attack?

	Dec. 16, 1998	Aug. 20, 1998*
Approve	74%	66%
Disapprove	13	19
No opinion	13	15

*Question wording: *As you may know, earlier today the United States launched military attacks against terrorist facilities in the countries of Afghanistan and the Sudan. Do you approve or disapprove of those attacks?*

How much confidence do you have in President Clinton's ability to handle the situation in Iraq—a great deal, a moderate amount, only a little, or none at all?

	Dec. 16, 1998	Jan. 16–18, 1998
Great deal	52%	21%
Moderate amount	24	44
Only a little	10	20
None at all	12	13
No opinion	2	2

Why do you personally think Bill Clinton ordered today's military strike—solely because he felt it was in the best interests of the country, or in part to divert public attention away from the impeachment proceedings?

	Dec. 16, 1998	Aug. 20, 1998*
Best interests	62%	58%
Divert attention	30	36
Neither (volunteered)	4	2
No opinion	4	4

Question wording: Why do you personally think Bill Clinton ordered today's military strike [against terrorist facilities in the countries of Afghanistan and the Sudan]—solely because he felt it was in the best interests of the country, or in part to divert public attention away from the Monica Lewinsky controversy?

Do you think this attack will or will not achieve significant goals for the United States?

	Dec. 16, 1998	Nov. 13–15, 1998
Will	48%	48%
Will not	32	42
No opinion	20	10

Note: Americans support Wednesday's [December 16] air attack against Iraq by a margin of 74% to 13%, according to a Gallup Poll conducted from six to nine o'clock that same evening. They also express a high level of confidence in President Bill Clinton's ability to handle the situa-tion in Iraq, with 52% saying that they have a great deal of confidence and another 24% a moderate amount.

Despite the controversy over the timing of the attack—occurring as it did just one day before the House of Representatives was scheduled to vote on the impeachment of President Clinton—respondents accept, by a 2-to-1 margin (62% to 30%), the president's word that the attack was ordered solely in the best interests of the country. They seem unsure, however, whether or not the attack will make much difference. Despite their support, just under one-half (48%) expect it to achieve significant goals, while another 32% think that it will not and 20% are unsure.

As often occurs with military actions, men are much more supportive of the air strike than are women, although support is strong among both groups. Men approve by 81% to 10%, while women approve by the lesser margin of 69% to 16%. On the other hand, there is little partisan difference in support of the strike, with 79% of Republicans, 74% of independents, and 71% of Democrats indicating their approval.

Republicans are considerably more skeptical than are Democrats on the timing of the strike, however, with 47% of the GOP attributing patriotic motives to the president and 45% selfish motives. Democrats, on the other hand, express overwhelming confidence in Clinton's motives, with 80% saying that he acted in the best interests of the country, and just 16% to divert attention from the impeachment proceedings. Independents also express positive views by a 2-to-1 margin.

DECEMBER 24
PRESIDENT CLINTON

Interviewing Dates: 12/19–20/98
CNN/*USA Today*/Gallup Poll
Survey #GO 125526

Do you approve or disapprove of the way Bill Clinton is handling his job as president?

Approve	73%
Disapprove	25
No opinion	2

	Approve	Dis-approve	No opinion
By Sex			
Male	65%	32%	3%
Female	79	19	2
By Ethnic Background			
White	70	27	3
Nonwhite	86	12	2
Black	91	7	2
By Education			
Postgraduate	76	23	1
College Graduate	61	37	2
College Incomplete	72	26	2
No College	75	22	3
By Region			
East	78	21	1
Midwest	72	28	*
South	69	27	4
West	74	23	3
By Age			
18–29 Years	71	25	4
30–49 Years	71	26	3
50–64 Years	74	25	1
65 Years and Over	76	23	1
By Household Income			
$75,000 and Over	69	30	1
$50,000 and Over	71	29	*
$30,000–$49,999	74	22	4
$20,000–$29,999	68	26	6
Under $20,000	76	24	*
By Politics			
Republicans	41	58	1
Democrats	91	8	1
Independents	69	26	5
By Political Ideology			
Conservative	54	43	3
Moderate	76	22	2
Liberal	91	8	1

*Less than 1%

National Trend
(For the Year 1998)

	Approve	Dis-approve	No opinion
December 19–20	73%	25%	2%
December 15–16	63	33	4
December 12–13	64	34	2
December 4–6	66	30	4
November 20–22	66	30	4
November 13–15	66	31	3
October 29–November 1	66	30	4
October 23–25	65	32	3
October 9–12	65	32	3
October 6–7	63	34	3
September 23–24	66	31	3
September 21	66	31	3
September 20	60	34	6
September 14–15	63	35	2
September 11–12	63	34	3
September 10	60	37	3
September 1	62	33	5
August 21–23	62	35	3
August 20*	61	34	5
August 18*	66	29	5
August 17*	62	32	6
August 10–12	65	30	5
August 7–8	64	32	4
July 29	65	31	4
July 13–14	63	31	6
July 7–8	61	34	5
June 22–23	60	34	6
June 5–7	60	34	6
May 8–10	64	31	5
April 17–19	63	31	6
April 1	67	28	5
March 20–22	66	28	6
March 16*	67	29	4
March 6–9	63	31	6
February 20–22	66	29	5
February 13–15	66	30	4
January 30–February 1	69	28	3
January 28*	67	28	5
January 25–26	59	37	4
January 24–25	60	35	5
January 23–24	58	36	6
January 16–18	60	30	10
January 6–7	59	32	9

*Based on one-night poll

Note: Despite the fact that he is only the second president in U.S. history to be impeached by the

House of Representatives, Bill Clinton received a 73% job approval rating from the American public this past weekend, the highest of his administration and one of the higher ratings given any president since the mid-1960s. The 73% job approval, based on a Gallup Poll conducted on December 19–20, came at the end of one of the most eventful weeks in recent American history. Not only did the House convene to debate and then pass two of four articles of impeachment against the president, but the week also saw an intensive four-day U.S. and British air attack against Iraq and its leader, Saddam Hussein.

Both of these events most probably had an impact on the spike in Clinton's job evaluation. Even though his job approval ratings have been high all year, the weekend's 73% marked a 10-percentage point increase from a survey conducted on Tuesday and Wednesday of last week [December 15–16], which partially overlapped the beginning of the Iraq attack, and a 9-point increase from a poll conducted the previous weekend. The 73% figure is also about 7 to 8 points higher than the ratings that Clinton received in a number of polls taken throughout most of October and November.

It is clear that last week's air strikes against Iraq were overwhelmingly popular with the American people: 78% approved and only 18% disapproved. Additionally, the attacks appear to have been viewed as legitimate by most respondents. The criticism that they were ordered by Clinton in part to divert attention away from the impeachment proceedings was endorsed by only 25% of the public; rather, most thought that the air strikes were "in the best interests of the country."

Dramatic, sharply focused events that involve Americans placed in harm's way on foreign soil are part of a class of occurrences known as rally events, so named because they typically cause the public to "rally 'round the flag" and usually result in increased job approval ratings for the sitting president. In recent years, such events have included Operation Desert Storm and the invasion of Panama in the Bush administration, and air strikes against Libya and the invasion of Grenada in the Reagan administration. Given these past experiences, it might be expected that the Iraq strikes would boost President Clinton's job approval numbers.

At the same time, the House vote on Saturday [December 19] was an historic event of great significance and one that dominated television and news coverage. As has generally been the case for several months, public opinion about this impeachment action, though not as sharply defined as the reaction to the Iraq attacks, is strongly negative, with disapproval of the House vote running ahead of approval by a 63%-to-35% margin. Other measures included in Gallup's most recent poll underscore this negative reaction. There has been a significant drop in favorable opinions of the Republican party at the same time that 54% agree that the Republicans in Congress have abused their Constitutional authority.

This negative reaction to the congressional emphasis on impeachment, combined with the positive reaction to the Iraq strikes, may have resulted this past weekend in a renewed focus by the public on what it perceives Clinton to be doing right. A parallel phenomenon occurred last January, as the Lewinsky crisis first broke, when a successful State of the Union address by Clinton resulted in an increase rather than a decrease in his job approval.

Clinton's job approval rating has been at or above the 60% level in thirty-eight separate Gallup surveys conducted since late January. His previous high rating was 69%, registered in late January and early February after his State of the Union address. Since October he has averaged a 66% job approval number, in contrast to the much lower ratings that he received in the earlier years of his administration: 49% in 1993, 45% in 1994, and 47% in 1995. Even in 1996, a year in which Clinton was re-elected to his second term, his average job approval rating was 56% and averaged only 58% last year.

How does Clinton's most recent quarterly average of 66% stand up historically? Except for George Bush, it is the highest quarterly rating enjoyed by any president since Lyndon Johnson in 1965—higher than any average quarter for Ronald Reagan, Jimmy Carter, Gerald Ford, or Richard Nixon.

Bush was an exception to the recent trend of lower presidential approval ratings, fueled in large part by successful U.S. intervention on foreign shores during the first years of his administration.

His job approval rating was 66% in 1989, the first year of his administration. It edged up to 67% in 1990 and averaged 69.5% in 1991, the year which saw Bush receive the highest single job approval rating in Gallup history (89%), just after the country's victory in the Gulf War.

This weekend's 73% job approval for Clinton, the best in the six years of his administration, is also high compared with other recent presidents. Bush, as noted, exceeded that figure in a number of polls, conducted after the Gulf War and after the invasion of Panama in late 1989 and early 1990, but Reagan never achieved the 70% level in the eight years of his administration. Carter had a rating of 75% in March of his first year in office (the "honeymoon" period), but he did not return to those heights during the remainder of his term. Ford received a 71% job approval immediately after taking office, but his numbers quickly fell after his presidential pardon of Nixon, who himself never reached the 70% level, even in his relatively popular first term from 1969 to 1973. (Before Nixon, however, 70+% ratings were more common, occurring numerous times in the administrations of Johnson, John F. Kennedy, and Dwight Eisenhower.)

Clinton ends 1998 not only with the looming prospect of a trial in the U.S. Senate that could possibly result in his removal from office, but also with an exceptionally high vote of confidence from the public. It may not be surprising that respondents clearly favor a quick resolution to the impeachment process next year—without a Senate trial or a Clinton resignation. In response to a three-part choice, only 31% of those polled this past weekend say that the Senate should proceed with the trial. The rest either want a vote of censure without a trial (36%) or the matter dropped altogether (32%); only 30% want Clinton to resign. And, if there is a Senate trial, only 29% say that the Senate should vote to convict Clinton and remove him from office.

DECEMBER 31
MOST ADMIRED PERSON

Interviewing Dates: 12/28–29/98
CNN/*USA Today*/Gallup Poll
Survey #GO 125579

What man whom you have heard or read about, living today in any part of the world, do you admire most? And who is your second choice?

The following are listed in order of frequency of mention, with first and second choices combined.

Bill Clinton
Pope John Paul II
Billy Graham
Michael Jordan
John Glenn
Colin Powell
Ronald Reagan
George Bush
Nelson Mandela ⎫
Bill Gates   ⎭ tie

What woman whom you have heard or read about, living today in any part of the world, do you admire most? And who is your second choice?

The following are listed in order of frequency of mention, with first and second choices combined.

Hillary Rodham Clinton
Oprah Winfrey
Elizabeth Dole
Margaret Thatcher
Barbara Bush
Madeleine Albright
Maya Angelou
Queen Elizabeth
Janet Reno
Monica Lewinsky

Next, I'd like to get your overall opinion of some people who were in the news this year. As I read each name, please say if you have a favorable or unfavorable opinion of this person, or if you have never heard of him or her:

	Favorable	Unfavor-able	No opinion; never heard of
Mark McGwire	87%	3%	10%
Pope John Paul II	86	8	6

Sammy Sosa	83	2	15
John Glenn	83	7	10
Queen Elizabeth	68	21	11
Hillary Rodham Clinton	67	29	4
Bill Gates	66	16	18
Madeleine Albright	64	14	22
Jerry Seinfeld	63	23	14
Tony Blair	58	8	34
Alan Greenspan	57	9	34
Al Gore	57	28	15
Janet Reno	57	29	14
Bill Clinton	56	42	2
Prince Charles	54	35	11
Jesse Ventura	53	14	33
Boris Yeltsin	47	35	18
Benjamin Netanyahu	46	20	34
Dick Gephardt	46	22	32
Jack Kevorkian	40	47	13
Newt Gingrich	38	51	11
Yassar Arafat	35	45	20
Ken Starr	32	58	10
Henry Hyde	31	29	40
Trent Lott	29	25	46
Kathleen Willey	20	30	50
Paula Jones	16	72	12
Linda Tripp	11	75	14
Monica Lewinsky	11	82	7
Saddam Hussein	1	96	3

Note: A new Gallup Poll produces two different rankings of public figures in the news and around the world. One is based on Americans' top-of-mind choice for the man and woman whom they most admire, while the other is based on separate ratings of thirty prominent newsmakers of 1998.

Once again, Bill and Hillary Clinton are cited in Gallup's year-end poll as the most admired man and woman "living today in any part of the world." President Clinton has been the top choice for Most Admired Man for all six years of his presidency. Hillary Rodham Clinton has held the number-one position intermittently, running behind or even with Mother Teresa of Calcutta on a few occasions.

This year neither the president nor the First Lady has any strong competition for Americans' choice as the man and woman whom they most admire. The number citing Hillary Rodham Clinton in Gallup's Most Admired Woman poll doubled in the past year, from 14% last December to 28% today. She is trailed by Oprah Winfrey at 8%. Elizabeth Dole, Margaret Thatcher, and Barbara Bush complete the list of the five most admired women of 1998.

The percentage naming Bill Clinton as most admired (18%) is consistent with the percentage naming him in previous years. Pope John Paul II, in second place, is mentioned this year by 7%. The Reverend Billy Graham, basketball superstar Michael Jordan, and astronaut/senator John Glenn round out the top five men. This marks Graham's thirty-fifth consecutive appearance on Gallup's Most Admired Man list.

Historically speaking, Americans' choice of the president and First Lady is not unusual. In the six decades that Gallup has run the Most Admired survey, the sitting president is nearly always chosen as the top man, while the top woman is very often the First Lady. The few exceptions to this pattern occurred when the job approval rating of the sitting president fell below 50%. Some examples include Jimmy Carter in 1980, Richard Nixon in 1974, and Lyndon Johnson in 1967. Clinton's job approval rating has been above 60% for most of 1998 and reached 73% in a Gallup Poll taken earlier this month.

Gallup's Most Admired question is an open-ended measure based on the unprompted recall of survey respondents. However, Gallup also asked respondents to give their individual opinions of thirty prominent names and faces in the news this year. Based on this question, Bill and Hillary Clinton rank in the middle of the pack while two "Cardinals" receive the highest favorable ratings: St. Louis slugger Mark McGwire with 87% and Pope John Paul II with 86%. Two other newsmakers with almost as high appeal are John Glenn and baseball MVP Sammy Sosa; both men are viewed favorably by more than four in five Americans (83%).

The four least-liked news figures of 1998 include a foreign leader and three women linked to Bill Clinton. Iraqi president Saddam Hussein is viewed favorably by only 1% and unfavorably by 96%. The next least popular figure of 1998 is Monica Lewinsky, with 11% favorable and 82% unfavorable ratings, while Linda Tripp and Paula

Jones follow close behind. In addition to these four, newsmakers whose unfavorable score is higher than their favorable score include Ken Starr, Kathleen Willey, Newt Gingrich, Yassar Arafat, and Dr. Jack Kevorkian.

Following the eclectic quartet at the top of the list, a large group of 1998 newsmakers enjoys favorable ratings above 50%. This group includes several of the more prominent members of government—Bill Clinton, Al Gore, Janet Reno, Alan Greenspan, and Madeleine Albright as well as First Lady Hillary Rodham Clinton. Great Britain's political leaders, including Prime Minister Tony Blair, Prince Charles, and Queen Elizabeth, also fall into this positive category.

Others rated favorably by one-half to two-thirds of Americans are Microsoft Chairman Bill Gates, television actor Jerry Seinfeld, and the governor-elect of Minnesota, Jesse "The Body" Ventura. Dick Gephardt, Trent Lott, Henry Hyde, and Benjamin Netanyahu all have net favorable ratings, but, given either high unfavorable scores and/or high levels of "no opinion," none of them receives a favorable score above 50%.

APPENDIX

This appendix contains the national findings for additional questions reported in the CNN/*USA Today*/Gallup Poll from January 6–7, 1998, through December 28–29, 1998. The questions, arranged here by topic without editorial commentary, have been indexed. Contributing to these polls were William Schneider and Keating Holland of CNN and Jim Norman of *USA Today*.

◆ ◆ ◆

Interviewing Dates: 1/6–7/98
CNN/*USA Today*/Gallup Poll
Survey #GO 120910

When it comes to dealing with the tough choices involved both in cutting programs to reduce the budget deficit and still maintaining needed federal programs, whose approach do you prefer—the Republicans in Congress or President Clinton's?

Republicans 39%
President Clinton's 43
Neither (volunteered) 6
Both (volunteered) 2
No opinion 10

In your opinion, is the current federal budget deficit a very serious problem for the country, a fairly serious problem, not a serious problem, or is this something you haven't thought much about?

Very serious 40%
Fairly serious 34
Not serious 7
No opinion 19

~

Do you approve or disapprove of the presence of U.S. troops in Bosnia?

Approve 53%
Disapprove 42
No opinion 5

~

Some people say that abortion is an act of murder, while other people disagree with this. What is your view—do you think abortion is an act of murder, or don't you feel this way?

Yes, murder 48%
No, not murder 45
No opinion 7

If you could vote on this issue directly, would you vote for or against the following—a law which would make it illegal to perform a specific abortion procedure conducted in the last six months of pregnancy known as a "partial birth" abortion, except in cases necessary to save the life of the mother?

For (make illegal) 61%
Against (keep legal) 36
No opinion 3

~

Do you think the current economic problems in Asia are most likely to have a very negative impact, a somewhat negative impact, no impact, a somewhat positive impact, or a very positive impact on the U.S. economy?

Very negative 8%
Somewhat negative 44
No impact 8
Somewhat positive 25
Very positive 8
No opinion 7

In your view, should the United States contribute funds to the international effort to help solve the financial crisis in several Asian countries, or should the United States not contribute financially to this effort?

Should contribute 36%
Should not contribute 59
No opinion 5

~

Asked of half sample: What do you think should be the penalty for murder committed by a man—the death penalty, or life imprisonment with absolutely no possibility of parole?

Death penalty 54%
Life imprisonment 36
Other; neither (volunteered) 5
No opinion 5

Asked of half sample: What do you think should be the penalty for murder committed by a woman—the death penalty, or life imprisonment with absolutely no possibility of parole?

Death penalty 50%
Life imprisonment 38
Other; neither (volunteered) 7
No opinion 5

~

Would you like to lose weight, put on weight, or stay at your present weight?

Lose weight 58%
Put on weight 6
Stay at present weight 36
No opinion .... *

*Less than 1%

At this time, are you seriously trying to lose weight?

Yes 28%
No 72

~

As you may know, NASA, the U.S. space agency, recently announced plans to send John Glenn, the 76-year-old senator and former astronaut, on a ten-day space mission. Do you think NASA made the right decision, or the wrong decision, to allow John Glenn to go back into space?

Right decision 73%
Wrong decision 23
No opinion 4

◆   ◆   ◆

Interviewing Dates: 1/16–18/98
CNN/*USA Today*/Gallup Poll
Survey #GO 121034

In general, do you think the political views of each of the following are too conservative, too liberal, or about right:

Bill Clinton?

Too conservative 12%
Too liberal 32
About right 52
No opinion 4

The Republican leaders in Congress?

Too conservative 36%
Too liberal 18
About right 39
No opinion 7

The Democratic leaders in Congress?

Too conservative 13%
Too liberal 35
About right 46
No opinion 6

Do you think Al Gore is qualified to serve as president, or not?

Yes, qualified... 35%
No 56
No opinion 9

I'm going to read a list of some of the issues that may be discussed in the election campaigns for Congress this year. Some of these issues may be very important to you in determining how you will vote this fall and some may not be at all important. Please indicate how important each issue is to you in determining how you will vote by mentioning a number between one and five. The higher the number, the more important you feel the issue is; the lower the number, the less important. Using any number from one to five, how would you rate the importance of each of the following in determining how you will vote:

Taxes?

Five.. 49%
Four 25
Three.. 19
Two.. 4
One 3
No opinion .... *

*Less than 1%

The federal budget deficit?

Five.. 34%
Four 29
Three.. 26
Two.. 6
One 4
No opinion 1

Medicare?

Five.. 50%
Four 21
Three.. 17
Two.. 8
One 4
No opinion .... *

*Less than 1%

The economy?

Five.. 51%
Four 26
Three.. 18
Two.. 2
One 2
No opinion 1

Crime?

Five.. 56%
Four 21
Three.. 15
Two.. 4
One 3
No opinion 1

~

Do you think abortions should be legal under any circumstances, legal only under certain circumstances, or illegal in all circumstances?

Legal, any circumstances 23%
Legal, certain circumstances 59
Illegal, all circumstances 17
No opinion 1

With respect to the abortion issue, would you consider yourself to be pro-choice or pro-life?

Pro-choice.. 48%
Pro-life.. 45
Don't know what terms mean (volunteered)... 2
Mixed; both; neither (volunteered)................ 3
No opinion 2

◆   ◆   ◆

Interviewing Dates: 1/23–26/98
CNN/*USA Today*/Gallup Poll
Survey #GO 121132

Since the start of 1993, when Bill Clinton became president, in general would you say his presidency has been a success, or a failure?

	Jan. 24–25, 1998	Jan. 23–24, 1998
Success..	70%	71%
Failure..	26	25
No opinion	4	4

Whom do you want to have more influence over the direction the nation takes in the next year—Bill Clinton, or the Republicans in Congress?

	Jan. 24–25, 1998	Jan. 23–24, 1998
Clinton	49%	46%
Republicans	40	41
Both equally; neither (volunteered)	6	7
No opinion	5	6

How do you think President Clinton will go down in history—as an outstanding, above average, average, below average, or poor president?

	Jan. 24–25, 1998	Jan. 23–24, 1998
Outstanding	8%	7%
Above average	23	23
Average	37	41
Below average	16	14
Poor	14	14
No opinion	2	1

Overall, what kind of a moral example do you think Bill Clinton sets as president—very good, good, poor, or very poor?

	Jan. 25–26, 1998	Jan. 24–25, 1998	Jan. 23–24, 1998
Very good	8%	8%	9%
Good	31	33	33
Poor	29	27	25
Very poor	29	28	29
No opinion	3	4	4

Next, I'm gong to read off some personal characteristics and qualities. As I read each one, please tell me whether you think it applies or does not apply to Bill Clinton:

Has a clear plan for solving the country's problems?

	Jan. 25–26, 1998	Jan. 24–25, 1998	Jan. 23–24, 1998
Applies	49%	48%	47%
Does not apply	45	45	46
No opinion	6	7	7

Can bring about the changes this country needs?

	Jan. 25–26, 1998	Jan. 24–25, 1998	Jan. 23–24, 1998
Applies	53%	55%	54%
Does not apply	42	41	42
No opinion	5	4	4

Keeps his promises?

	Jan. 25–26, 1998	Jan. 24–25, 1998	Jan. 23–24, 1998
Applies	45%	45%	45%
Does not apply	50	49	50
No opinion	5	6	5

Based on what you know and have seen in the news, how do you feel toward each of the following—very sympathetic, somewhat sympathetic, somewhat unsympathetic, or very unsympathetic:

Bill Clinton?

	Jan. 24–25, 1998	Jan. 23–24, 1998
Very sympathetic	17%	18%
Somewhat sympathetic	32	31
Somewhat unsympathetic	16	18
Very unsympathetic	32	30
No opinion	3	3

Hillary Rodham Clinton?

	Jan. 24–25, 1998	Jan. 23–24, 1998
Very sympathetic	36%	39%
Somewhat sympathetic	34	32
Somewhat unsympathetic	10	12
Very unsympathetic	17	15
No opinion	3	2

Monica Lewinsky?

	Jan. 24–25, 1998	Jan. 23–24, 1998
Very sympathetic	9%	8%
Somewhat sympathetic	30	31
Somewhat unsympathetic	26	25

	Jan. 24–25, 1998	Jan. 23–24, 1998
Very unsympathetic	27	29
No opinion	8	7

Do you believe Bill Clinton is engaged in a coverup of any matters concerning Monica Lewinsky, or not?

	Jan. 24–25, 1998	Jan. 23–24, 1998
Yes	51%	51%
No	39	39
No opinion	10	10

Do you think Bill Clinton should or should not address the allegations related to Monica Lewinsky in a formal speech or press conference to the nation sometime in the very near future?

	Jan. 24–25, 1998	Jan. 23–24, 1998
Should	65%	62%
Should not	31	34
No opinion	4	4

Do you think it would be appropriate or inappropriate for Bill Clinton to address these matters during his State of the Union speech on Tuesday evening [January 27]?

	Jan. 24–25, 1998	Jan. 23–24, 1998
Appropriate	22%	21%
Inappropriate	75	75
No opinion	3	4

Just your best guess, what effect do you think the controversy over Bill Clinton and Monica Lewinsky will have on President Clinton's ability to serve in office—it will not harm Clinton; it will harm Clinton, but only temporarily; it will permanently harm Clinton, but he will remain in office; or Clinton will eventually resign or be removed from office?

	Jan. 25–26, 1998	Jan. 24–25, 1998	Jan. 23–24, 1998
Not harm Clinton	11%	11%	12%
Harm temporarily	42	42	41
Permanently harm	29	28	31
Clinton will resign or be removed	15	16	13
No opinion	3	3	3

◆　◆　◆

Interviewing Date: 1/27/98
CNN/*USA Today*/Gallup Poll
Survey #GO 121201

How confident are you in Bill Clinton's abilities to carry out his duties as president—very confident, somewhat confident, not too confident, or not at all confident?

	Speech Watchers Pre-speech*	Post-speech*
Very confident	33%	48%
Somewhat confident	33	30
Not too confident	16	14
Not at all confident	18	8
No opinion	**	**

*Clinton's State of the Union on January 27
**Less than 1%

Overall, what kind of a moral example do you think Bill Clinton sets as president—very good, good, poor, or very poor?

	Speech Watchers Pre-speech*	Post-speech*
Very good	9%	16%
Good	26	33
Poor	26	24
Very poor	35	23
No opinion	4	4

*Clinton's State of the Union on January 27

What was your overall reaction to President Clinton's speech tonight—very positive, somewhat positive, somewhat negative, or very negative?

	Post-speech*
Very positive	52%
Somewhat positive	32
Somewhat negative	11

Very negative 5
Both; mixed (volunteered)............................. **
No opinion... **

*Clinton's State of the Union on January 27
**Less than 1%

Next, thinking about the federal budget which Congress and President Clinton will work on during the coming year, do you expect that the budget will be balanced, meaning the government will spend the same amount of money as it takes in; or the budget will not be balanced, meaning the government will spend more money than it takes in?

	Post-speech*
Will be balanced	52%
Will not be balanced	45
No opinion	3

*Clinton's State of the Union on January 27

Which of the following statements comes closer to how you feel about the new programs that President Clinton proposed tonight—they would cost too much money or give the government too much power, or they would help solve important problems without costing too much money or giving the government too much power?

	Post-speech*
Too much money or power	38%
Help solve problems	58
Neither; other (volunteered)	1
No opinion	3

*Clinton's State of the Union on January 27

Thinking about the reasons why you watched President Clinton's speech this evening, would you say you only watched in order to hear what Clinton had to say about the state of the nation and his proposals for the coming year, or you watched in part to see what would happen and how Clinton handled the situation in light of the recent controversy?

	Post-speech*
To hear state of the nation	67%

To see Clinton handle situation	25
Both equally (volunteered)	7
Neither; other (volunteered)	1
No opinion	–

*Clinton's State of the Union on January 27

~

If the goal of a balanced budget in 1999 is reached, would you consider this to be one of the most significant achievements of the last twenty-five years, a major achievement but not one of the most significant, a minor achievement, or no achievement at all?

Most significant	27%
Major	52
Minor	14
No achievement	3
No opinion	4

If you had to choose, who would you say deserves more of the credit for reducing the deficit—President Clinton, or the Republicans in Congress?

Clinton	42%
Republicans	39
Both equally (volunteered)	9
Neither (volunteered)	5
No opinion	5

Now we have some more specific questions about what the government should do with a budget surplus. As I read a list of various proposals, please say whether you think each one should be a top priority for using the surplus, a high priority, a low priority, or not a priority at all:

Reducing the national debt?

Top priority	31%
High priority	48
Low priority	15
Not a priority	3
No opinion	3

Cutting federal income taxes for most Americans?

Top priority	22%
High priority	42

Low priority.. 28
Not a priority 6
No opinion... 2

Strengthening Social Security for the long term?

Top priority.. 32%
High priority... 53
Low priority.. 11
Not a priority 2
No opinion... 2

Strengthening Medicare for the long term?

Top priority.. 28%
High priority... 55
Low priority.. 12
Not a priority 3
No opinion... 2

Increasing federal funds for repairing and building public schools?

Top priority.. 25%
High priority... 50
Low priority.. 20
Not a priority 3
No opinion... 2

Providing tax credits to parents for child care?

Top priority.. 20%
High priority... 43
Low priority.. 30
Not a priority 5
No opinion... 2

Providing tax credits to reduce pollution?

Top priority.. 15%
High priority... 41
Low priority.. 35
Not a priority 7
No opinion... 2

Increasing spending on highway construction?

Top priority.. 11%

High priority.. 29
Low priority... 51
Not a priority 7
No opinion.. 2

◆　◆　◆

Interviewing Dates: 1/30–2/1/98
CNN/*USA Today*/Gallup Poll
Survey #GO 121271

Do you think that the increased attention being given to the private lives of public officials and candidates is a good thing or a bad thing for politics and government in this country?

Good thing.. 26%
Bad thing 72
No opinion... 2

Which one of the following characteristics is the most important one to you in rating how a president is handling his job—his moral values, his positions on issues, or his ability to manage the government?

Moral values... 16%
Positions on issues.. 22
Managing government................................... 55
No opinion... 7

Next, we have some questions about the allegations being reported in the news that President Clinton had an extramarital affair with a White House intern named Monica Lewinsky. As I read each one, please say whether you think it is definitely true, probably true, probably not true, or definitely not true:

The allegation that Bill Clinton had sexual relations of any kind with Monica Lewinsky?

Definitely true.. 11%
Probably true 44
Probably not true 27
Definitely not true 12
No opinion... 6

The allegation that Bill Clinton lied under oath about having an affair with Monica Lewinsky?

Definitely true.. 11%
Probably true 41
Probably not true 27
Definitely not true 14
No opinion.. 7

The allegation that Bill Clinton participated in an effort to obstruct justice by getting Monica Lewinsky to lie under oath about the affair?

Definitely true.. 9%
Probably true 35
Probably not true 32
Definitely not true 18
No opinion.. 6

The allegation that Bill Clinton had sexual relations of any kind with any other woman besides his wife or Monica Lewinsky since he became president?

Definitely true.. 16%
Probably true 46
Probably not true 22
Definitely not true 9
No opinion.. 7

Based on what you know at this point, do you think the House of Representatives should or should not begin proceedings to impeach Bill Clinton and remove him from office?

Should begin proceedings 13%
Should not 85
No opinion.. 2

Next, I am going to read some statements concerning the controversy over Bill Clinton and Monica Lewinsky and would like to know how you feel about each one:

Do you strongly agree, somewhat agree, somewhat disagree, or strongly disagree with the following statement—at a time like this, it is important to support the president until the facts of the matter become better known?

Strongly agree... 66%
Somewhat agree 22
Somewhat disagree... 6
Strongly disagree.. 5
No opinion.. 1

Do you think Monica Lewinsky is or is not part of a right-wing conspiracy to damage Bill Clinton's presidency?

Is part of conspiracy 35%
Is not.. 57
No opinion.. 8

From what you've heard or read, do you think it was Bill Clinton or Monica Lewinsky who took the first steps to establish a relationship between them, or do you think no significant relationship existed?

Clinton first... 19%
Lewinsky first.. 32
No significant relationship existed................. 35
No opinion.. 14

Next, as I read some statements concerning Hillary Clinton, please say whether each one describes or does not describe your views of Hillary Clinton in terms of the controversy over Monica Lewinsky:

You feel sorry for her?

Describes views... 42%
Does not describe 57
No opinion.. 1

You admire her for the way she has handled the controversy?

Describes views... 72%
Does not describe 25
No opinion.. 3

You are disappointed in her for the way she has handled the controversy?

Describes views... 19%
Does not describe 77
No opinion.. 4

In your view, does Hillary Clinton believe or not believe that her husband had sexual relations with Monica Lewinsky?

Believes 46%
Does not believe 43
She is unsure (volunteered) 2
No opinion.. 9

Have you either talked to people or wondered to yourself about what Hillary Clinton should do if the allegations concerning Bill Clinton and Monica Lewinsky having an affair are true?

Yes, talked or wondered 46%
No 51
No opinion 3

Next, we have some general questions about the importance of moral values in a president. Do you feel that a person must have strong moral values in order to be an effective president, or can someone be an effective president regardless of his moral values?

Strong moral values 61%
Effective regardless 37
No opinion 2

How important is it to you that a president have high moral values in his personal life—critical, important but not critical, or is it not important to you?

Critical 31%
Important but not critical 55
Not important 13
No opinion 1

When it comes to the moral standards of our presidents, do you think American presidents are held to a higher standard or a lower standard now than they were in the past?

Higher standard 63%
Lower standard 29
Same standard; no change (volunteered) 5
No opinion 3

Asked of those with an opinion: And do you consider that a good thing or a bad thing?

	Total	Higher standard	Lower standard
Good thing	45%	62%	6%
Bad thing	49	32	91
Neither (volunteered)...	4	4	3
No opinion	2	2	*

*Less than 1%

◆ ◆ ◆

Interviewing Dates: 2/13–15/98
CNN/*USA Today*/Gallup Poll
Survey #GO 121392

How important do you think it is for the president to provide moral leadership for the country—very important, somewhat important, only slightly important, or not at all important?

Very important 65%
Somewhat important.. 22
Slightly important.. 8
Not at all important... 4
No opinion 1

If you had to choose, would you rather have someone as president who does set a good moral example for the country, but whose political views you do not generally agree with; or who does not set a good moral example for the country, but whose views you generally do agree with?

Good example, do not agree with views 48%
Not good example, agree with views 41
No opinion 11

~

Asked of half sample: If you had to choose, how would you rather see the current situation in Iraq resolved—through diplomatic pressure and economic sanctions, or through military air strikes launched by the United States and other countries?

	United States	United Kingdom*
Diplomatic pressure, sanctions.....	69%	79%
Military air strikes	25	16
Neither; other (volunteered)	3	1
No opinion	3	4

*Gallup/United Kingdom Poll: interviews in England, Scotland, and Wales, 2/11–16/98

Do you think Iraq, under Saddam Hussein, does or does not represent a threat to world peace?

	United States	United Kingdom*
Yes, does	89%	84%
Does not	10	12
No opinion	1	4

*Gallup/United Kingdom Poll: 2/11–16/98

In general, do you personally regard the present crisis in the Middle East involving Iraq as very serious, fairly serious, not very serious, or not at all serious?

	United States	United Kingdom*
Very serious	59%	61%
Fairly serious	34	34
Not very serious	4	2
Not at all serious	2	2
No opinion	1	1

*Gallup/United Kingdom Poll: 2/11–16/98

As you may know, there are currently international economic sanctions on Iraq which limit Iraq's trade with other nations. Do you feel that the United Nations should continue these sanctions until Saddam Hussein complies with all UN resolutions; or the United Nations should continue these sanctions as long as Saddam Hussein is in power, regardless of whether he complies with all UN resolutions?

	United States	United Kingdom*
Until Saddam complies	64%	62%
As long as Saddam is in power	30	29
UN should lift sanctions now (volunteered)	2	3
Other (volunteered)	**	1
No opinion	4	5

*Gallup/United Kingdom Poll: 2/11–16/98
**Less than 1%

From what you know, do you think it is or is not possible to destroy Iraq's weapons of mass destruction by using air strikes?

	United States	United Kingdom*
Yes, possible	48%	33%
Not possible	41	51
No opinion	11	16

*Gallup/United Kingdom Poll: 2/11–16/98

Do you think that if the Americans and the British launch air strikes against Iraq, there is or is not a risk of dangerous chemicals and bacteria leaking into the atmosphere?

	United States	United Kingdom*
Yes, risk	85%	88%
Not a risk	10	7
No opinion	5	5

*Gallup/United Kingdom Poll: 2/11–16/98

If Saddam Hussein places Iraqi civilians at sites which he thinks the United States might attack, do you think the United States should attack those sites anyway, or should the United States refrain from attacking those sites?

	United States	United Kingdom*
Attack	50%	65%
Refrain from attacking	41	29
No opinion	9	6

*Question wording: *Some people say that another crucial part of crippling Saddam Hussein's military capability is direct attacks on military targets, although this does carry the risk of civilian casualties. Do you think that American and British air forces should or should not make attacks on military targets?* Gallup/United Kingdom Poll: 2/11–16/98

Asked of half sample: Do you believe that one of the objectives of British and American military action in the [Persian] Gulf should or should not be the removal of Saddam Hussein from power?

	United States	United Kingdom*
Yes, should	87%	87%
Should not	10	8
No opinion	3	5

*Gallup/United Kingdom Poll: 2/11–16/98

~

Much of the information in the news about the Monica Lewinsky controversy is based on information that has been leaked to the media by sources close to the situation. Where do you think most of the leaks are coming from— the White House, Ken Starr or others in the

Independent Counsel's office, or from other sources?

White House	17%
Starr or Independent Counsel's office	26
Other sources	46
No opinion	11

Do you think Ken Starr is or is not involved in a systematic campaign to leak information about the investigation in order to harm Bill Clinton politically?

Yes, is	50%
Is not	37
No opinion	13

Next, I'd like to ask you some questions about the way Ken Starr is conducting his investigation into the Lewinsky matter. Regardless of your opinion of Ken Starr or the Lewinsky controversy, do you think it is appropriate or inappropriate that Monica Lewinsky's mother was called as a witness to testify about matters relating to her daughter?

Appropriate	31%
Inappropriate	64
No opinion	5

Regardless of your opinion of Ken Starr or the Lewinsky controversy, do you think it is appropriate or inappropriate that Secret Service agents who worked directly with President Clinton have been called as witnesses to testify about matters related to the president?

Appropriate	43%
Inappropriate	53
No opinion	4

Do you think that what Bill Clinton has said in public about the Monica Lewinsky matter has been completely true, mostly true, mostly false, or completely false?

	Feb. 13–15, 1998	Jan. 30– Feb. 1, 1998
Completely true	8%	11%
Mostly true	37	37
Mostly false	36	34
Completely false	14	12
No opinion	5	6

In your view, is Bill Clinton hiding something concerning his role in these matters, or don't you think so?

	Feb. 13–15, 1998	Jan. 30– Feb. 1, 1998
Yes, hiding something	67%	62%
Don't think so	27	33
No opinion	6	5

~

Asked of half sample: Which of the following statements best describes your view of Bill Clinton's fund-raising activities—Clinton did something illegal; Clinton did something unethical but not illegal; or Clinton did not do anything seriously wrong?

Illegal	19%
Unethical but not illegal	41
Nothing seriously wrong	33
No opinion	7

Asked of half sample: Which of the following statements best describes your view of Al Gore's fund-raising activities—Gore did something illegal; Gore did something unethical but not illegal; or Gore did not do anything seriously wrong?

Illegal	15%
Unethical but not illegal	40
Nothing seriously wrong	30
No opinion	15

From what you have heard or read, do you think that Chinese government officials did or did not attempt to influence the outcome of the U.S. elections last year by donating money to the Democratic party?

Yes, did attempt	61%
Did not	24
No opinion	15

~

Do you think Bill Clinton has or has not adequately explained to the American people

why military action may need to be taken against Iraq?

Has...54%
Has not...39
No opinion...7

Next, we'd like to know your opinion about the chances that military air strikes against Iraq would succeed in accomplishing each of the following goals. Do you think military air strikes would definitely succeed, probably succeed, probably not succeed, or definitely not succeed at:

Getting Iraq to allow United Nations inspectors to investigate that country's weapons-producing capacity?

Definitely succeed..21%
Probably succeed..46
Probably not succeed.......................................24
Definitely not succeed.....................................5
No opinion...4

Substantially reducing Iraq's capacity to develop weapons of mass destruction?

Definitely succeed..23%
Probably succeed..46
Probably not succeed.......................................23
Definitely not succeed.....................................3
No opinion...5

Removing Saddam Hussein from power?

Definitely succeed..16%
Probably succeed..31
Probably not succeed.......................................39
Definitely not succeed.....................................11
No opinion...3

Compared to President Bush, how much confidence do you have in President Clinton to handle any crises involving Iraq—more confidence in Clinton than in Bush, about the same amount of confidence in Clinton and Bush, or less confidence in Clinton than in Bush?

More in Clinton than Bush.............................26%
About the same...35
Less in Clinton than Bush...............................38
No opinion...1

Do you think the Monica Lewinsky controversy is seriously distracting President Clinton from attending to the Iraq crisis, or not?

Yes...45%
No 52
No opinion...3

◆　　◆　　◆

Interviewing Dates: 2/20–22/98
CNN/*USA Today*/Gallup Poll
Survey #GO 121706

Asked of half sample: Do you think Bill Clinton has or has not adequately explained to the American people why military action may need to be taken against Iraq?

Has...52%
Has not...42
No opinion...6

Asked of half sample: Do you feel you have a clear idea of what the U.S. military involvement in the Iraq situation is all about—that is, why the United States may attack Iraq?

Yes...75%
No 23
No opinion...2

In general, if the United States government decided to launch an air attack on Iraq, would you support or oppose that attack?

Support 70%
Oppose..25
No opinion...5

As you may know, United Nations inspectors have been in Iraq to investigate that country's weapons-producing capacity. Iraq has announced that it would not allow these in-

vestigations to continue at certain sites. Which would you prefer that the United States do right now to resolve the current situation involving Iraq—continue to use diplomacy and sanctions to pressure Iraq into complying with the United Nations inspections; or take military action, along with other countries, to force Iraq into complying with United Nations inspections?

	Feb. 20–22, 1998	Feb. 13–15, 1998
Continue diplomacy, sanctions	48%	54%
Take military action	45	41
Neither; other (volunteered)	4	3
No opinion	3	2

Asked of half sample: In the event that all serious diplomatic efforts break down and Iraq has not complied with the United Nations inspections, do you think the United States should or should not take military action against Iraq?

Should	68%
Should not	27
No opinion	5

Would you support or oppose an attack on Iraq if the goal of that attack is to reduce Iraq's weapons capacity, but not to remove Saddam Hussein from power?

Support	46%
Oppose	46
No opinion	8

Still thinking about the situation in Iraq, how confident are you—very confident, somewhat confident, not too confident, or not at all confident—that each of the following will happen:

The United States will be able to accomplish its goals with very few or no American casualties?

Very confident	22%
Somewhat confident	31
Not too confident	27

Not at all confident	17
No opinion	3

The U.S. effort to reduce Iraq's capacity to develop weapons of mass destruction will succeed?

Very confident	23%
Somewhat confident	39
Not too confident	24
Not at all confident	10
No opinion	4

The United States can launch military attacks on Iraq without provoking an increase in terrorism against the United States?

Very confident	10%
Somewhat confident	31
Not too confident	36
Not at all confident	18
No opinion	5

Some members of Congress maintain that the Constitution of the United States requires President Clinton "to obtain prior express congressional authorization before he may order United States armed forces to make war in Iraq." Do you favor or oppose President Clinton having to get congressional authorization before he takes any military action in Iraq?

Favor	73%
Oppose	23
No opinion	4

All in all, do you think the current situation in Iraq is worth going to war over, or not?

Yes, worth going to war	57%
No	36
No opinion	7

Interviewing Date: 2/24/98
CNN/*USA Today*/Gallup Poll
Survey #GO 121733

Thinking about the way this confrontation with Iraq was resolved, would you say that

Bill Clinton mostly backed down, or mostly got what he wanted?

Backed down 28%
Got what he wanted 56
No opinion 16

And would you say that Saddam Hussein mostly backed down, or mostly got what he wanted?

Backed down 32%
Got what he wanted 57
No opinion 11

Thinking about the new weapons inspections agreement, looking ahead, do you think it is more likely that Saddam Hussein will comply with the terms of the agreement, or that he will violate the terms of the agreement?

Comply with terms 13%
Violate terms 82
No opinion 5

How likely do you think it is that the United States will take military action against Iraq within the next year over the weapons inspections issue—do you think such military action by the United States will definitely happen, probably happen, probably not happen, or definitely not happen?

Definitely happen 14%
Probably happen 54
Probably not happen 26
Definitely not happen 3
No opinion 3

Do you favor or oppose using military force now to remove Saddam Hussein from power?

Favor 61%
Oppose 35
No opinion 4

~

Asked of half sample: Do you think Kenneth Starr should continue his investigation into the allegations surrounding President Clinton and Monica Lewinsky, or should he stop the investigation now?

Continue 37%
Stop now 59
No opinion 4

Asked of half sample: In your view, should the investigations into the allegations surrounding President Clinton and Monica Lewinsky continue, or should the investigations stop now?

Continue 32%
Stop now 65
No opinion 3

Interviewing Dates: 3/6–9/98
CNN/USA Today/Gallup Poll
Survey #GO 121850

Thinking about a few news sources, please say whether you think the news and information reported by each one tends to have a liberal bias, a conservative bias, or whether it tends to be fair and impartial:

National network television news?

Liberal bias 33%
Conservative bias 17
Fair and impartial 38
No opinion 12

National cable television news?

Liberal bias 25%
Conservative bias 15
Fair and impartial 36
No opinion 24

Local television news?

Liberal bias 22%
Conservative bias 23
Fair and impartial 47
No opinion 8

Weekly news magazines?

Liberal bias 28%
Conservative bias 14
Fair and impartial 30
No opinion 28

The Internet?

Liberal bias 17%
Conservative bias 4
Fair and impartial 24
No opinion 55

Radio news?

Liberal bias 25%
Conservative bias 17
Fair and impartial 36
No opinion 22

Local newspapers?

Liberal bias 28%
Conservative bias 27
Fair and impartial 36
No opinion 9

National newspapers such as the New York
Times, *the* Wall Street Journal, *and* USA
Today*?*

Liberal bias 29%
Conservative bias 18
Fair and impartial 30
No opinion 23

~

We have some questions about the North Atlantic Treaty Organization, also known as NATO—the military alliance of Western Europe and the United States that has existed since the 1940s. As you may know, NATO is committed to defending its members against a military attack by any other nation, including Russia. Which, if any, of the following countries do you think should be allowed to join NATO:

Poland?

Yes, allowed 65%
Not allowed 16
It depends (volunteered) 2
No opinion 17

Hungary?

Yes, allowed 58%
Not allowed 20
It depends (volunteered) 2
No opinion 20

The Czech Republic?

Yes, allowed 55%
Not allowed 24
It depends (volunteered) 2
No opinion 19

If NATO is expanded to include Poland, Hungary, and the Czech Republic, would you favor or oppose further expansion to include each of the following countries:

Slovenia, formerly part of Yugoslavia?

Favor 45%
Oppose 31
It depends (volunteered) 2
No opinion 22

Slovakia, part of the former Czechoslovakia?

Favor 49%
Oppose 28
It depends (volunteered) 1
No opinion 22

Romania?

Favor 52%
Oppose 25
It depends (volunteered) 2
No opinion 21

The Baltic States—that is, Lithuania, Estonia, and Latvia?

Favor 50%
Oppose 26
It depends (volunteered) 2
No opinion 22

How in your view does the NATO military alliance affect U.S.-Russia relations these days—does it make U.S.-Russia relations much better, somewhat better, somewhat worse, or much worse?

Much better... 8%
Somewhat better... 51
Somewhat worse... 16
Much worse 4
No effect (volunteered) 17
No opinion... 4

~

From everything you've heard or read about this issue, or from what you personally believe, what do you think was the nature of the relationship between President Clinton and Monica Lewinsky—in other words, can you describe the type of relationship you believe they had?

Sex; sexual... 20%
Intimate; lovers; an affair;
   more than friendship................................... 14
Just friends... 6
Professional; work relationship..................... 6
Nothing; no relationship............................... 5
Their business; not my business;
   not anyone's business.............................. 4
Don't care; don't want to know.................... 4
Personal relationship 3
Not sexual... 2
Inappropriate; improper................................. 1
Flirting 1
Other... 19
No opinion... 15

~

If you had to choose between the following two proposals in order to deal with the long-term problem of Social Security, which would you choose— providing more revenue by increasing Social Security taxes on people who are working today, or cutting expenditures by reducing Social Security benefits for people who currently receive them?

Increasing taxes 57%
Reducing benefits... 21
Neither; both (volunteered............................ 17
No opinion... 5

For each of those proposals, please tell me if in general you would favor or oppose it:

Increasing Social Security taxes on people working today?

Favor... 46%
Oppose... 49
No opinion... 5

Reducing Social Security benefits for people who currently receive them?

Favor... 16%
Oppose... 80
No opinion... 4

◆ ◆ ◆

Interviewing Date: 3/16/98
CNN/*USA Today*/Gallup Poll
Survey #GO 122072

Since the start of this year, would you say you have lost respect for President Clinton, or not?

Yes, lost respect... 46%
No 51
No opinion... 3

Paula Jones says that Bill Clinton made a sexual advance toward her while he was governor of Arkansas, and Clinton says he did not. Whom do you tend to believe more— Paula Jones, or Bill Clinton?

Jones 43%
Clinton 45
No opinion... 12

If Kathleen Willey's story is true, would you consider Bill Clinton's actions toward her to be an act of sexual harassment, or not?

Yes, harassment.. 63%
No 26
No opinion... 11

◆ ◆ ◆

Interviewing Dates: 3/20–22/98
CNN/*USA Today*/Gallup Poll
Survey #GO 122065

*I'm going to read off some personal charac-
teristics and qualities. As I read each one,
please tell me whether you think it applies or
does not apply to Bill Clinton:*

An effective manager?

Applies... 72%
Does not apply................................... 23
No opinion.. 5

A nice guy?

Applies... 70%
Does not apply................................... 22
No opinion.. 8

~

*Which of these statements do you think best
describes the condition of morals in the
country today—there is a moral crisis in this
country; there is a major problem with
morals in this country, but it does not represent a crisis; or moral conditions in this
country do not represent a major problem?*

Moral crisis.. 49%
Major problem but not crisis 41
Not major problem 8
No opinion.. 2

~

*Please say if you have a favorable or unfa-
vorable opinion of this person, or if you have
never heard of her:*

*Former White House volunteer Kathleen
Willey?*

	March 20–22, 1998	March 16, 1998*
Favorable	18%	23%
Unfavorable	40	29
No opinion	19	25
Never heard of	23	23

*Based on one-night poll

*Overall, which of the following statements
best describes your view of Bill Clinton's involvement with Kathleen Willey—Clinton did
something illegal, he did something immoral
but not illegal, or he did not do anything seriously wrong?*

Illegal... 12%
Immoral but not illegal 44
Nothing seriously wrong 36
No opinion.. 8

*If you were convinced that Bill Clinton made
an unwanted sexual advance toward Kathleen
Willey in the White House and lied about it
under oath, what action do you think Congress
should take toward Clinton—impeach him and
remove him from office, express formal disapproval of his actions but not remove him from
office, or take no formal action?*

Impeach and remove him 34%
Express formal disapproval 52
Take no formal action.................................. 11
Other (volunteered) .... *
No opinion.. 3

*Less than 1%

*Overall, which of the following statements
best describes your view of Bill Clinton's involvement with Monica Lewinsky—Clinton
did something illegal, he did something immoral but not illegal, or he did not do anything seriously wrong?*

Illegal... 13%
Immoral but not illegal 48
Nothing seriously wrong 32
No opinion.. 7

*If you were convinced that Bill Clinton had sex-
ual relations with Monica Lewinsky and lied
about it under oath, what action do you think
Congress should take toward Clinton—impeach him and remove him from office, express
formal disapproval of his actions but not remove him from office, or take no formal action?*

Impeach and remove him 37%
Express formal disapproval 48
Take no formal action.................................. 12

Other (volunteered) 1
No opinion 2

As you may know, a woman from Arkansas named Paula Jones is suing Bill Clinton, claiming that while governor of Arkansas Clinton made sexual advances toward her in a hotel room, which she declined. Do you think that Paula Jones's description of that incident is completely true, mostly true, mostly false, or completely false?

Completely true 4%
Mostly true 39
Mostly false 30
Completely false 17
No opinion 10

In your view, should the investigations into the sexual allegations involving Bill Clinton continue, or should they stop now?

Continue 38%
Stop now 61
No opinion 1

Next, we have a question about the way the White House has responded to all of the sexual allegations against Bill Clinton. Do you think the White House has gone too far or has not gone too far in attacking the credibility of the women who have made sexual charges against Clinton?

Gone too far 43%
Not gone too far 48
No opinion 9

Thinking about how Bill Clinton should respond to the sexual allegations, which of the following statements comes closer to your view—he should not address these matters publicly because they are mostly personal and not relevant to his duties as president, or he should address these matters publicly to allow Americans to judge whether or not his behavior as president was appropriate?

Should not address publicly 47%

Should address publicly 50
Other (volunteered) 1
No opinion 2

Comparing yourself to Bill Clinton, would you say your own personal moral standards are higher than Clinton's, lower than Clinton's, or about the same as Clinton's?

Higher 69%
Lower 3
About the same 22
No opinion 6

Thinking about sexual harassment, in terms of the number of women who face sexual harassment in the workplace, would you say sexual harassment these days is a major problem or a minor problem?

Major problem 50%
Minor problem 43
Not a problem at all (volunteered) 1
No opinion 6

Do you think that people in the workplace are too sensitive or not sensitive enough to the problem of sexual harassment?

Too sensitive 53%
Not sensitive enough 37
About right (volunteered) 4
No opinion 6

Asked of women: We'd like to ask about your chances of suing someone if you felt you were being sexually harassed. As a result of the recent events in the news about sexual harassment, would you be more likely or less likely to file a lawsuit against someone who sexually harassed you, or have your chances of suing someone not changed?

More likely 18%
Less likely 29
Not changed 49
No opinion 4

~

Which one of the five movies nominated this year for best movie would you like to see win

the Oscar award for Best Picture of the Year?

As Good As It Gets 8%
The Full Monty 2
Good Will Hunting 11
L.A. Confidential 4
Titanic 58
None; other (volunteered) 4
No opinion 13

◆　◆　◆

Interviewing Date: 4/1/98
CNN/USA Today/Gallup Poll
Survey #GO 122382

Kathleen Willey has said that Bill Clinton made a sexual advance toward her in the White House, and Clinton says he did not. Whom do you tend to believe more— Kathleen Willey, or Bill Clinton?

Willey 40%
Clinton 46
No opinion 14

◆　◆　◆

Interviewing Dates: 4/17–19/98
CNN/USA Today/Gallup Poll
Survey #GO 122406

Do you approve or disapprove of the way Newt Gingrich is handling his job as Speaker of the U.S. House of Representatives?

Approve 45%
Disapprove 46
No opinion 9

Do you think it is better for the country to have a president who comes from the same political party that controls Congress, or do you think it is better to have a president from one political party and Congress controlled by another?

Same party 40%
Different parties 42
No difference (volunteered); no opinion 18

Since the start of 1995 when Republicans took control of Congress, in general would you say the Republican Congress has been a success, or a failure?

Success 58%
Failure 30
No opinion 12

Please say whether each of the following phrases applies or does not apply to the Republican party:

Can bring about the changes this country needs?

Applies 56%
Does not apply 37
No opinion 7

Is able to manage the federal government effectively?

Applies 61%
Does not apply 31
No opinion 8

Please say whether each of the following phrases applies or does not apply to the Democratic party:

Can bring about the changes this country needs?

Applies 56%
Does not apply 38
No opinion 6

Is able to manage the federal government effectively?

Applies 55%
Does not apply 38
No opinion 7

〜

Do you completely agree, mostly agree, mostly disagree, or completely disagree with the statement that there is too much power concentrated in the hands of a few big companies?

Completely agree.. 35%
Mostly agree 41
Mostly disagree 16
Completely disagree 5
No opinion 3

Thinking now about mergers between large corporations, that is, when two large companies join together and become one very large company, which comes closer to your view— the government should generally allow mergers like these to happen, or the government should do more to stop mergers like these?

Allow mergers 40%
Stop mergers... 51
No opinion.. 9

Asked of half sample: Still thinking about corporate mergers, when two large companies merge and create one very large company, do you think the result is usually good for consumers or bad for consumers?

Good.. 33%
Bad... 54
Mixed (volunteered) 8
No opinion.. 5

Asked of half sample: Still thinking about corporate mergers, when two large banks merge and create one very large bank, do you think the result is usually good for consumers or bad for consumers?

Good 30%
Bad 58
Mixed (volunteered) 7
No opinion.. 5

~

Do you consider the amount of federal income tax you have to pay as too high, about right, or too low?

Too high 66%
About right 31
Too low.. 1
No opinion.. 2

Here are two questions about the Internal Revenue Service, also known as the IRS, which is the federal agency that collects taxes. Which of the following statements concerning IRS power do you agree with more— the IRS has been given about the right amount of power to do the job it is charged with carrying out, or the IRS has been given more power than it needs to do the job it is charged with carrying out?

Right amount 29%
More than it needs 68
Too little (volunteered).................................. *
No opinion.. 3

*Less than 1%

Still thinking about the power the IRS has been given to do its job, do you think the IRS generally uses its powers responsibly, or frequently abuses its powers?

Uses responsibly.. 34%
Frequently abuses 62
No opinion.. 4

~

We have some questions about the allegations being reported in the news concerning President Clinton. As I read each one, please say whether you think it is definitely true, probably true, probably not true, or definitely not true:

The allegation that Bill Clinton made unwanted sexual advances toward Kathleen Willey in the White House?

Definitely true.. 13%
Probably true 35
Probably not true 27
Definitely not true 12
No opinion.. 13

In your view, should the investigations into the allegations involving Bill Clinton continue, or should they stop now?

Continue 35%
Stop now.. 64
No opinion.. 1

Thinking about these investigations, in your view should President Clinton and his aides in-

voke "executive privilege" to protect the White House decision-making process, or should they drop the claim of executive privilege and answer all questions being investigated?

Invoke executive privilege 29%
Drop executive privilege 66
No opinion.. 5

Overall, which of the following statements best describes your view of Bill Clinton's actions which are currently being investigated by Independent Counsel Ken Starr—Clinton did something illegal, he did something unethical but not illegal, or he did not do anything seriously wrong?

Illegal... 24%
Unethical but not illegal 47
Nothing seriously wrong 24
No opinion.. 5

~

Here are two statements which people sometimes make when discussing the environment and economic growth. Which of these statements comes closer to your own point of view—protection of the environment should be given priority, even at the risk of curbing economic growth; or economic growth should be given priority, even if the environment suffers to some extent?

Protection.. 68%
Economic growth 24
No opinion.. 8

~

Thinking now about the stock market, if you had a thousand dollars to spend, do you think investing it in the stock market would be a good or bad idea?

Good idea 65%
Bad idea... 28
It depends (volunteered)................................. 4
No opinion.. 3

◆ ◆ ◆

Interviewing Dates: 5/8–10/98
CNN/*USA Today*/Gallup Poll
Survey #GO 122847

If Vice President Al Gore were the Democratic party's candidate and House Speaker Newt Gingrich were the Republican party's candidate,whom would you be more likely to vote for—Gore, the Democrat; or Gingrich, the Republican? [Those who were undecided were asked: As of today, do you lean more toward Gore, the Democrat; or Gingrich, the Republican?]

Gore 62%
Gingrich... 32
No opinion.. 6

~

As you may know, Congress is considering several proposals regarding the tobacco industry. As I read some of these, please say whether you favor or oppose each one:

Increasing federal taxes on cigarettes by $1.10 a pack over the next five years?

Favor... 59%
Oppose.. 39
No opinion.. 2

Classifying nicotine as a drug so that it can be regulated by the same government agency that regulates prescription drugs?

Favor... 50%
Oppose.. 47
No opinion.. 3

Requiring the tobacco companies to pay penalties if teen smoking is not reduced by a certain date?

Favor... 47%
Oppose.. 50
No opinion.. 3

Limiting the amount of money tobacco companies have to pay each year as the result of lawsuits against them?

Favor.. 41%
Oppose.. 54
No opinion... 5

Putting severe restrictions on the advertising and sale of cigarettes to minors?

Favor.. 87%
Oppose.. 12
No opinion... 1

If a federal tax increase on cigarettes is passed, how would you most like the government to use that additional revenue—spend it on anti-smoking programs, spend it on other government programs aimed at children and the elderly, use it to reduce taxes, or use it to reduce the national debt?

On anti-smoking programs............................. 13%
On programs for children and the elderly 46
To reduce taxes.. 21
To reduce national debt 16
All; none; other (volunteered) 3
No opinion... 1

~

As you may know, recent scientific developments in DNA testing may now allow the military to identify the body of the Vietnam soldier buried in the Tomb of the Unknowns [at Arlington], formerly known as the Tomb of the Unknown Soldier. Do you, personally, favor or oppose the U.S. military's plan to remove that body and attempt to identify him?

Favor.. 56%
Oppose.. 38
No opinion... 6

~

Asked of half sample: Which of the following statements comes closest to your view about the ability of ordinary citizens to own guns— there should be no restrictions on owning guns, there should be minor restrictions on owning guns, there should be major restrictions on owning guns, or all guns should be illegal for everyone except police and authorized persons?

No restrictions 9%
Minor restrictions 32
Major restrictions 43
All guns illegal except for police 15
Mixed; other (volunteered)........................... 1
No opinion... *

*Less than 1%

~

In the Middle East conflict, do you think the United States should take Israel's side, take the Palestinians' side, or not take either side?

Israel's side.. 15%
Palestinians' side 2
Not take either side............................... 74
No opinion... 9

In your view, has the United States put too much pressure, or not enough pressure, on Israel to make compromises with the other side in order to settle the Middle East conflict?

Too much.. 24%
Not enough 49
Right amount (volunteered)........................... 6
No opinion... 21

And has the United States put too much pressure, or not enough pressure, on the Palestinians to make compromises with the other side in order to settle the Middle East conflict?

Too much.. 21%
Not enough 54
Right amount (volunteered)........................... 4
No opinion... 21

~

Asked of half sample: Do you think that a cure for cancer will be found within the next fifty years?

Yes 84%
No 11
No opinion 5

Asked of half sample: Looking ahead ten years from now, do you think scientists will have found a cure for cancer by then, or not?

Yes 64%
No 31
No opinion 5

~

There is a new prescription drug on the market called Viagra. Without telling me the answer, specifically, do you know what this drug is used for, or not?

Yes 64%
No 33
No opinion 3

~

Which of the following statements do you agree with more concerning the controversy over allegations involving Bill Clinton [and Monica Lewinsky]—it is mostly the result of a right-wing conspiracy which is out to get Bill Clinton, or it is mostly the result of Clinton's own behavior?

Right-wing conspiracy 33%
Clinton's own behavior 55
Neither; other (volunteered) 7
No opinion 5

Asked of half sample: Now we have a few questions about the Whitewater investigation. Which of the following statements best describes your view of Bill Clinton's actions in these matters—Bill Clinton did something illegal, he did something unethical but not illegal, he did not do anything seriously wrong, or are you unsure? [Those who were unsure

were asked: From what you have heard or read, which way do you lean? Do you think Bill Clinton probably did something illegal, probably did something unethical but not illegal, or probably did not do anything seriously wrong?]

Illegal 29%
Unethical but not illegal 42
Nothing seriously wrong 24
No opinion 5

Asked of half sample: Still thinking about the Whitewater investigation, which of the following statements best describes your view of Hillary Clinton's actions in these matters— Hillary Clinton did something illegal, she did something unethical but not illegal, she did not do anything seriously wrong, or are you unsure? [Those who were unsure were asked: From what you have heard or read, which way do you lean? Do you think Hillary Clinton probably did something illegal, probably did something unethical but not illegal, or probably did not do anything seriously wrong?]

Illegal 31%
Unethical but not illegal 30
Nothing seriously wrong 32
No opinion 7

Asked of half sample: Do you generally think that Bill Clinton is honest and trustworthy?

Yes, honest and trustworthy 44%
No 51
No opinion 5

Asked of half sample: Do you generally think that Hillary Clinton is honest and trustworthy?

Yes, honest and trustworthy 54%
No 40
No opinion 6

◆　　◆　　◆

Interviewing Dates: 6/5–7/98
CNN/*USA Today*/Gallup Poll
Survey #GO 123254

Do you approve or disapprove of the way Bill Clinton is handling race relations?

Approve 67%
Disapprove 19
No opinion 14

~

Asked of half sample: I'm going to read a list of countries, some of which have and some of which do not have nuclear weapons. As I read each one, please tell me whether you think possession of nuclear weapons by that country would pose a serious threat to the United States, or not:

Russia?

Yes, threat 46%
No 53
No opinion 1

Great Britain?

Yes, threat 7%
No 90
No opinion 3

China?

Yes, threat 57%
No 41
No opinion 2

India?

Yes, threat 26%
No 69
No opinion 5

Pakistan?

Yes, threat 43%
No 52
No opinion 5

Israel?

Yes, threat 24%
No 74
No opinion 2

Brazil?

Yes, threat 11%
No 84
No opinion 5

Iraq?

Yes, threat 84%
No 14
No opinion 2

Iran?

Yes, threat 80%
No 19
No opinion 1

~

When a person has a disease that cannot be cured and is living in severe pain, do you think doctors should be allowed by law to assist the patient to commit suicide if the patient requests it, or not?

Yes 59%
No 39
No opinion 2

~

Concerning the presidential election in the year 2000, if Vice President Al Gore were the Democratic party's candidate and Elizabeth Dole were the Republican party's candidate, whom would you be more likely to vote for— Al Gore, the Democrat; or Elizabeth Dole, the Republican? [Those who were undecided were asked: As of today, do you lean more toward Al Gore, the Democrat; or Elizabeth Dole, the Republican?]

Al Gore 46%
Elizabeth Dole 48
No opinion 6

And if Hillary Rodham Clinton were the Democratic party's candidate and Elizabeth Dole were the Republican party's candidate, whom would you be more likely to vote for— Hillary Clinton, the Democrat; or Elizabeth Dole, the Republican? [Those who were undecided were asked: As of today, do you lean

more toward Hillary Clinton, the Democrat; or Elizabeth Dole, the Republican?]

Hillary Rodham Clinton 40%
Elizabeth Dole 55
No opinion 5

~

Please say if you have a favorable or unfavorable opinion of William Ginsburg, the former attorney to Monica Lewinsky, or if you have never heard of him?

Favorable 19%
Unfavorable 45
No opinion 9
Never heard of 27

~

I am going to read you a list of institutions in American society. Please tell me how much confidence you, yourself, have in each one— a great deal, quite a lot, some, or very little:

The church or organized religion?

Great deal 34%
Quite a lot 25
Some 26
Very little 12
None (volunteered) 1
No opinion 2

The military?

Great deal 33%
Quite a lot 31
Some 25
Very little 8
None (volunteered) 1
No opinion 2

The U.S. Supreme Court?

Great deal 24%
Quite a lot 26
Some 34
Very little 12
None (volunteered) 1
No opinion 3

Banks?

Great deal 16%

Quite a lot 24
Some 43
Very little 14
None (volunteered) 1
No opinion 2

Public schools?

Great deal 16%
Quite a lot 21
Some 40
Very little 20
None (volunteered) 2
No opinion 1

Newspapers?

Great deal 14%
Quite a lot 19
Some 44
Very little 20
None (volunteered) 1
No opinion 2

Congress?

Great deal 10%
Quite a lot 18
Some 48
Very little 20
None (volunteered) 2
No opinion 2

Television news?

Great deal 15%
Quite a lot 19
Some 40
Very little 24
None (volunteered) 1
No opinion 1

Organized labor?

Great deal 11%
Quite a lot 15
Some 45
Very little 22
None (volunteered) 2
No opinion 5

The presidency?

Great deal 25%

Quite a lot	28
Some	29
Very little	15
None (volunteered)	2
No opinion	1

The police?

Great deal	26%
Quite a lot	32
Some	30
Very little	10
None (volunteered)	1
No opinion	1

The medical system?

Great deal	16%
Quite a lot	24
Some	40
Very little	18
None (volunteered)	1
No opinion	1

The criminal justice system?

Great deal	9%
Quite a lot	15
Some	40
Very little	32
None (volunteered)	3
No opinion	1

Big business?*

Great deal	11%
Quite a lot	19
Some	43
Very little	23
None (volunteered)	2
No opinion	2

*Asked of half sample

Small business?*

Great deal	25%
Quite a lot	31
Some	34
Very little	9
None (volunteered)	**
No opinion	1

*Asked of half sample
**Less than 1%

Business and industry?*

Great deal	18%
Quite a lot	33
Some	38
Very little	7
None (volunteered)	1
No opinion	3

*Asked of half sample

~

Which comes closer to your opinion concerning the investigation being conducted by Independent Counsel Ken Starr—Clinton is trying to obstruct and delay the investigation, or Clinton is trying to cooperate with the investigation?

Obstruct and delay	57%
Cooperate	35
No opinion	8

When it comes to the investigation into President Clinton's involvement with Monica Lewinsky, do you think Independent Counsel Kenneth Starr is mostly trying to find out the facts, or mostly trying to damage President Clinton politically?

	June 5–7, 1998	Jan. 24–25, 1998
Find out facts	38%	38%
Damage Clinton politically	57	48
Neither; other (volunteered)	2	2
No opinion	3	12

~

Do you think the United States should return to the military draft at this time, or not?

Should	16%
Should not	81
No opinion	3

In your view, would the U.S. military be better off today with the draft, or without the draft?

With draft	26%
Without draft	69
No opinion	5

If a draft were to become necessary, should young women be required to participate as well as young men, or not?

Should.. 54%
Should not 44
No opinion.. 2

If a draft were to become necessary, should gay men be included, or not?

Should.. 77%
Should not 21
No opinion.. 2

~

Asked of half sample: Do you think the drinking water which comes from the tap in your home is safe to drink or not safe to drink?

Yes, safe 68%
Not safe... 30
No opinion.. 2

Asked of half sample: Do you think the drinking water supply in the United States is safe to drink or not safe to drink?

Yes, safe 64%
Not safe... 32
No opinion.. 4

Asked of half sample: How would you rate the job being done by state and federal governments in protecting the safety of public drinking water—very good, somewhat good, somewhat poor, or very poor?

Very good.. 20%
Somewhat good 49
Somewhat poor..................................... 18
Very poor... 11
No opinion.. 2

Asked of half sample: Does the drinking water in your home come directly from your own underground well, or does it come from a municipal water system?

Own well 22%
Municipal water system......................... 77
Other (volunteered) 1

No opinion...................................... *

*Less than 1%

Asked of half sample: What kind of water do you normally drink at home—straight tap water, tap water which has been filtered, or bottled water?

Tap water... 53%
Filtered water....................................... 24
Bottled water 22
Other (volunteered) 1
Don't drink water (volunteered).................... *

*Less than 1%

Asked of half sample: Have you ever received a notice or heard a community alert concerning safety problems with your drinking water supply?

Yes... 21%
No 79

~

Some people say our nation is moving toward two societies, one black, one white—separate and unequal. Do you agree with this, or not?

	Total	Whites only	Blacks only
Agree	25%	23%	45%
Disagree.....................	71	74	47
No opinion.................	4	3	8

In general, how do you think people in the United States feel about people of other races? Do you think only a few white people dislike blacks, many white people dislike blacks, or almost all white people dislike blacks?

	Total	Whites only*	Blacks only*
A few whites...............	63%	61%	50%
Many whites	31	34	40
Almost all whites........	3	3	5
None (volunteered).....	1	**	1
No opinion.................	2	2	4

*Aggregated results based on surveys conducted June 5–7 and April 17–19, 1998
**Less than 1%

And do you think only a few black people dislike whites, many black people dislike whites, or almost all black people dislike whites?

	Total	Whites only*	Blacks only*
A few blacks	58%	52%	57%
Many blacks	33	38	32
Almost all blacks	5	6	4
None (volunteered)	**	1	1
No opinion	4	3	6

*Aggregated results based on surveys conducted June 5–7 and April 17–19, 1998
**Less than 1%

Over the past year, do you think that relations between blacks and whites in this country have improved, remained about the same, or have gotten worse?

Have improved	33%
Remained the same	52
Gotten worse	15
No opinion	*

*Less than 1%

How closely have you followed President Clinton's initiative on race relations, which he launched last year—very closely, somewhat closely, not too closely, or not at all?

Very closely	6%
Somewhat closely	28
Not too closely	45
Not at all	20
No opinion	1

How effective do you think President Clinton's initiative on race will be at improving race relations in this country—very effective, somewhat effective, not too effective, or not effective at all?

Very effective	5%
Somewhat effective	43
Not too effective	31
Not effective at all	14
No opinion	7

~

Do you have any children now attending school, Kindergarten through Grade 12, or not?

Yes	31%
No	69

Asked of parents of school-age children: Thinking about your oldest child, when he or she is at school—do you fear for his or her physical safety?

Yes	37%
No	62
No opinion	1

Also asked of parents of school-age children: Now, thinking about all of your school-age children if you have more than one, for each of the following please say whether it is something you have already done specifically as a result of recent news about school violence, something you would consider doing, or something you would not consider doing:

Cautioned a child not to get involved in confrontations with other students?

Have already done	65%
Would consider doing	21
Not consider doing	13
No opinion	1

Limited a child's participation in school activities outside the classroom?

Have already done	10%
Would consider doing	17
Not consider doing	71
No opinion	2

Instructed a child in self-defense?

Have already done	33%
Would consider doing	39
Not consider doing	26
No opinion	2

Contacted a child's school to discuss safety issues?

Have already done 24%
Would consider doing 44
Not consider doing 31
No opinion 1

◆ ◆ ◆

Interviewing Dates: 6/22–23/98
CNN/*USA Today*/Gallup Poll
Survey #GO 123479

Do you approve or disapprove of the way Bill Clinton is handling relations with China?

Approve 40%
Disapprove.. 37
No opinion 23

If China were to attack Taiwan, do you think the United States should use its military forces to help defend Taiwan, or not?

Yes... 42%
No 46
No opinion 12

~

As you may know, last week the U.S. Senate defeated the tobacco bill it had been considering. Do you personally feel the Senate should or should not have passed that tobacco bill?

Should.. 36%
Should not 44
Not familiar with bill (volunteered) 15
No opinion 5

Which of the following statements better describes your impression of what the tobacco bill before the Senate was designed to do—it was mostly an attempt to reduce the number of teenagers who smoke, or it was mostly a bill to provide money for government spending by raising taxes?

Reduce number of teen smokers 41%
Provide for government spending 50
No opinion 9

If no tobacco bill is passed this year by Congress, will that make you more likely to vote for a Republican candidate for Congress, or for a Democratic candidate for Congress, or won't the tobacco bill affect your vote one way or the other this November?

Republican candidate 7%
Democratic candidate..................................... 12
No effect 78
No opinion 3

~

Do you use a personal computer either at home or at work?

Yes, at home 18%
Yes, at work.. 17
Yes, both (volunteered) 27
No 38

Asked of computer users: As you may know, Microsoft Windows is software which acts as an operating system for personal computers. Do you use some version of Microsoft Windows on any of the computers you use at home or at work?

Yes, use 86%
No 14

Asked of Windows users: If you had a choice, would you keep the Windows system you currently use, or would you switch to a newer, upgraded version of Windows?

Keep current system 49%
Switch to new system 44
Switch to different operating
   system (volunteered) 2
No opinion 5

Also asked of Windows users: Which comes closest to your view about upgrading your operating system—it is too complex and time-consuming, and you would prefer not to change; it is difficult to upgrade but worthwhile in the long run; or it's not a problem?

Prefer not to change... 19%
Worthwhile in long run 25
Not a problem... 53
No opinion.. 3

Does the lawsuit that was recently filed against Microsoft by the federal government make you more likely or less likely to want to purchase and use Microsoft Windows products, or does the lawsuit have no effect on your views?

More likely 6%
Less likely... 6
No effect.. 84
No opinion... 4

~

As you may know, Princess Diana's gravesite in England will be open to visitors for the first time on July 1st. If you could, would you like to visit her gravesite, or is that something you would not want to do?

Would like to... 26%
Would not want to 72
No opinion... 2

~

Turning to the investigations into Bill Clinton being conducted by Independent Counsel Ken Starr, should Attorney General Janet Reno fire Starr and appoint another Independent Counsel, or should Attorney General Reno allow Starr to continue his investigations?

Fire Starr... 39%
Allow Starr to continue 49
No opinion... 12

~

How important would you say religion is in your own life—very important, fairly important, or not very important?

	June 22–23, 1998	Jan. 16–18, 1998
Very important..............................	62%	59%

Fairly important 25   29
Not very important....................... 12   12
No opinion.................................... 1   *

*Less than 1%

At the present time, do you think religion as a whole is increasing its influence on American life, or losing its influence?

	June 22–23, 1998	Jan. 16–18, 1998
Increasing influence......................	37%	48%
Losing influence	56	48
Same (volunteered).......................	4	1
No opinion	3	3

Do you happen to be a member of a church or synagogue?

	June 22–23, 1998	Jan. 16–18, 1998
Yes..	70%	67%
No	30	33

Did you, yourself, happen to attend church or synagogue in the last seven days, or not?

	June 22–23, 1998	Jan. 16–18, 1998
Yes..	40%	39%
No	60	61

Would you describe yourself as "born again" or evangelical?

	June 22–23, 1998	Jan. 16–18, 1998
Yes..	44%	49%
No	48	43
No opinion	8	8

Do you believe that religion can answer all or most of today's problems, or that religion is largely old-fashioned and out of date?

	June 22–23, 1998	Jan. 16–18, 1998
Can answer	63%	67%

Out of date	20	20
No opinion	17	13

Which of the following statements comes closest to describing your views about the Bible—the Bible is the actual word of God and is to be taken literally, word for word; the Bible is the inspired word of God but not everything in it should be taken literally; or the Bible is an ancient book of fables, legends, history, and moral precepts recorded by man?

Actual word	33%
Inspired word	47
Fables and legends	17
No opinion	3

Asked of half sample: Do you agree or disagree with the following statement—"A wife should submit graciously to the servant leadership of her husband"?

Agree	26%
Disagree	69
No opinion	5

Asked of half sample: Do you agree or disagree with the following statement taken from the Bible—"A wife should submit graciously to the servant leadership of her husband"?

Agree	35%
Disagree	60
No opinion	5

~

I would like to read you the top movies recently voted by the American Film Institute as the best movies ever made. For each one, please tell me if you have, or have not, ever seen it either in the movie theater, on video, or on television?

	Have seen
The Wizard of Oz	94%
Gone With the Wind	85
The Godfather	76
Star Wars	74
It's a Wonderful Life	70
Casablanca	65
Singin' in the Rain	63
The Graduate	61
The Bridge on the River Kwai	59
Lawrence of Arabia	50
Schindler's List	49
Citizen Kane	45
Some Like It Hot	40
On the Waterfront	32
Sunset Boulevard	27

Now, thinking of all the movies just mentioned, which one do you personally think is the best movie?

	Total	Rank	AFI ranking*
Gone With the Wind	27%	1	4
The Wizard of Oz	11	2	6
Schindler's List	9	3	9
The Godfather	8	4	3
Star Wars	8	5	15
It's a Wonderful Life	8	6	11
Casablanca	6	7	2
The Bridge on the River Kwai	4	8	13
Citizen Kane	4	9	1
Lawrence of Arabia	2	10	5
Singin' in the Rain	2	11	10
The Graduate	1	12	7
On the Waterfront	1	13	8
Some Like It Hot	**	14	14
Sunset Boulevard	**	15	12
No opinion	9		

*American Film Institute 100 Years/100 Movies
**Less than 1%

~

Asked of half sample: When thinking about the causes of homosexuality, do you think it is always due to the way a person is born, it is always due to factors such as upbringing or environment, or do you think it depends on the person?

Way a person is born	18%

Upbringing or environment 12
It depends on person 63
No opinion 7

~

Have you, yourself, smoked any cigarettes in the past week?

Yes 28%
No 72

◆ ◆ ◆

Interviewing Dates: 7/7–8/98
CNN/*USA Today*/Gallup Poll
Survey #GO 123690

Do you approve or disapprove of the way Bill Clinton is handling foreign affairs?

Approve 56%
Disapprove 34
No opinion 10

What is your overall opinion of China—very favorable, mostly favorable, mostly unfavorable, or very unfavorable?

Very favorable 6%
Mostly favorable 38
Mostly unfavorable 36
Very unfavorable 11
No opinion 9

~

How would you rate economic conditions in this country today—very good, somewhat good, somewhat poor, or very poor?

Very good 29%
Somewhat good 50
Somewhat poor 15
Very poor 5
No opinion 1

~

If you were convinced that Bill Clinton lied under oath about his involvement with Monica Lewinsky, would you favor or oppose

an effort to impeach Clinton and remove him from office?

Favor effort 45%
Oppose effort 50
No opinion 5

If you were convinced that Bill Clinton participated in attempts to get Monica Lewinsky to lie under oath about her involvement with him, would you favor or oppose an effort to impeach Clinton and remove him from office?

Favor effort 48%
Oppose effort 45
No opinion 7

Asked of half sample: How interested would you, personally, be in hearing the tapes made by Linda Tripp—very interested, somewhat interested, not too interested, or not at all interested?

Very interested 11%
Somewhat interested 18
Not too interested 14
Not at all interested 56
No opinion 1

Asked of half sample: How interested do you think most Americans would be in hearing the tapes made by Linda Tripp—very interested, somewhat interested, not too interested, or not at all interested?

Very interested 41%
Somewhat interested 29
Not too interested 15
Not at all interested 11
No opinion 4

All in all, what would you rather see—a continuation of the investigations into the Monica Lewinsky matter to determine once and for all what happened and how involved Bill Clinton was; or a complete stop to the investigations into the Monica Lewinsky matter, letting Bill Clinton serve out the rest of

his term without a determination of what really happened and how involved he was?

Continuation 35%
Complete stop 63
No opinion 2

~

We have some questions about raising children in the United States today. We are interested in your opinions on these issues regardless of whether you, personally, ever had children or not:

Using a scale of one to ten, where one is very easy and ten is very difficult, how easy or difficult would you say it is to raise children to be good people these days?

One (very easy) 2%
Two 2
Three 3
Four 2
Five 11
Six 7
Seven 14
Eight 23
Nine 7
Ten (very difficult) 28
No opinion 1

Mean Rating: 7.5

Compared to twenty years ago, do you think it is harder or not harder to raise kids to be good people today?

Harder 89%
Not harder 10
No opinion 1

Asked of those parents with children ages 2–18: Have you, personally, taken any specific steps to shield your children from exposure to popular culture?

Yes, taken steps 75%
No 24
No opinion 1

Also asked of parents with children ages 2–18: I'm going to list several possible influences on children these days. For each one, please say whether it has had a very positive, somewhat positive, somewhat negative, or very negative influence on your own child or children:

Television?

Very positive 10%
Somewhat positive 34
Somewhat negative 36
Very negative 17
Neither (volunteered) 3
No opinion .... *

*Less than 1%

Movies?

Very positive 10%
Somewhat positive 40
Somewhat negative 34
Very negative 10
Neither (volunteered) 5
No opinion 1

The news media?

Very positive 5%
Somewhat positive 37
Somewhat negative 32
Very negative 15
Neither (volunteered) 9
No opinion 2

Advertising?

Very positive 6%
Somewhat positive 29
Somewhat negative 42
Very negative 16
Neither (volunteered) 7
No opinion .... *

*Less than 1%

Computers, including the Internet?

Very positive 28%
Somewhat positive 41

Somewhat negative.. 14
Very negative 7
Neither (volunteered) 7
No opinion... 3

Popular music?

Very positive 9%
Somewhat positive 31
Somewhat negative.. 37
Very negative 13
Neither (volunteered) 9
No opinion... 1

Also asked of parents with children ages 2–18: Here is a list of some people or groups that might provide support to some parents in raising their children. For each one, please tell me whether you think support from each one is an essential factor, or not an essential factor, in raising children to be good people today:

Extended family?

Essential... 87%
Not essential 11
No opinion... 2

Organized religion?

Essential... 79%
Not essential 20
No opinion... 1

Schools?

Essential... 92%
Not essential 8
No opinion... *

*Less than 1%

Friends and neighbors?

Essential... 86%
Not essential 13
No opinion... 1

Community groups such as the Girl Scouts and sports leagues?

Essential... 82%
Not essential 17
No opinion... 1

The government?

Essential... 44%
Not essential 54
No opinion... 2

Also asked of parents with children ages 2–18: As I read this list again, please say whether, as a parent, you get enough support from each one, or whether you would like more support from that area:

Extended family?

Yes, enough support...................................... 74%
No, would like more...................................... 23
No opinion... 3

Organized religion?

Yes, enough support...................................... 73%
No, would like more...................................... 25
No opinion... 2

Schools?

Yes, enough support...................................... 55%
No, would like more...................................... 41
No opinion... 4

Friends and neighbors?

Yes, enough support...................................... 76%
No, would like more...................................... 23
No opinion... 1

Community groups such as the Girl Scouts and sports leagues?

Yes, enough support...................................... 74%
No, would like more...................................... 22
No opinion... 4

The government?

Yes, enough support...................................... 37%
No, would like more...................................... 61
No opinion... 2

Also asked of parents with children ages 2–18: Do any of your children attend public school, in Kindergarten through Grade 12?

Yes 70%
No 30

◆ ◆ ◆

Interviewing Dates: 7/13–14/98
CNN/*USA Today*/Gallup Poll
Survey #GO 123792

I would like to ask you some questions about the media. As you know, people get their news and information from many different sources, and I would like to ask you where you get your news and information. I will read a list of sources, and for each one, please tell me how often you get your news from that source—every day, several times a week, occasionally, or never:

Newspapers?

	July 13–14, 1998	March 6–9, 1998*
Every day	50%	48%
Several times a week	13	13
Occasionally	27	29
Never	10	9
No opinion	**	1

*Asked of half sample
**Less than 1%

Local newspapers in your area?

	July 13–14, 1998	March 6–9, 1998*
Every day	53%	50%
Several times a week	15	12
Occasionally	22	26
Never	10	11
No opinion	**	1

*Asked of half sample
**Less than 1%

National newspapers such as the New York Times, Wall Street Journal, *and* USA Today?

	July 13–14, 1998	March 6–9, 1998*
Every day	4%	8%
Several times a week	11	6
Occasionally	26	28
Never	59	57
No opinion	**	1

*Asked of half sample
**Less than 1%

Nightly network news programs on ABC, CBS, or NBC?

	July 13–14, 1998	March 6–9, 1998
Every day	55%	56%
Several times a week	19	19
Occasionally	19	17
Never	7	7
No opinion	*	1

*Less than 1%

Morning news and interview programs on the national television networks?

	July 13–14, 1998	March 6–9, 1998
Every day	25%	25%
Several times a week	13	13
Occasionally	27	24
Never	35	37
No opinion	*	1

*Less than 1%

CNN News or CNN Headline News?

	July 13–14, 1998	March 6–9, 1998
Every day	21%	22%
Several times a week	16	16
Occasionally	33	34
Never	29	27
No opinion	1	1

Cable news programs other than CNN such as CNBC, MSNBC, or the Fox News Channel?

	July 13–14, 1998	March 6–9, 1998
Every day	14%	16%
Several times a week	11	11
Occasionally	34	33
Never	40	38
No opinion	1	2

C-SPAN?

	July 13–14, 1998	March 6–9, 1998
Every day	3%	3%
Several times a week	4	4
Occasionally	25	25
Never	65	65
No opinion	3	3

Public television news?

	July 13–14, 1998	March 6–9, 1998
Every day	16%	19%
Several times a week	9	10
Occasionally	33	32
Never	40	37
No opinion	2	2

Local television news from television stations in your area?

	July 13–14, 1998	March 6–9, 1998
Every day	57%	56%
Several times a week	15	17
Occasionally	19	17
Never	9	9
No opinion	*	1

*Less than 1%

National Public Radio?

	July 13–14, 1998	March 6–9, 1998
Every day	15%	20%
Several times a week	12	10
Occasionally	25	26
Never	47	43
No opinion	1	1

Local radio news from radio stations in your area?

	July 13–14, 1998	March 6–9, 1998
Every day	39%	38%
Several times a week	13	12
Occasionally	26	29
Never	21	20
No opinion	1	1

National network news on radio other than National Public Radio?

	July 13–14, 1998	March 6–9, 1998
Every day	10%	9%
Several times a week	6	6
Occasionally	26	30
Never	57	53
No opinion	1	2

Radio talk shows?

	July 13–14, 1998	March 6–9, 1998
Every day	12%	11%
Several times a week	9	5
Occasionally	21	25
Never	58	58
No opinion	*	1

*Less than 1%

Television talk shows?

	July 13–14, 1998	March 6–9, 1998
Every day	11%	11%
Several times a week	10	12
Occasionally	40	36
Never	39	40
No opinion	*	1

*Less than 1%

Discussions with your friends or family?

	July 13–14, 1998	March 6–9, 1998
Every day	27%	27%
Several times a week	26	23
Occasionally	41	42
Never	6	7
No opinion	*	1

*Less than 1%

Half-hour television entertainment news programs such as "Hard Copy," "Entertainment Tonight," and others?

	July 13–14, 1998	March 6–9, 1998
Every day	8%	10%
Several times a week	15	14
Occasionally	44	43
Never	32	32
No opinion	1	1

News on the computer using the Internet or an on-line computer service?

	July 13–14, 1998	March 6–9, 1998
Every day	7%	5%
Several times a week	6	6
Occasionally	17	18
Never	70	70
No opinion	*	1

*Less than 1%

And how often do you get your news from each of the following weekly sources of news—every week, several times a month, occasionally, or never:

Weekly news magazines?

	July 13–14, 1998	March 6–9, 1998
Every week	15%	13%
Several times a month	6	6
Occasionally	27	26
Never	52	54
No opinion	*	1

*Less than 1%

Television news programs on Sunday mornings?

	July 13–14, 1998	March 6–9, 1998
Every week	17%	18%
Several times a month	6	5
Occasionally	27	27
Never	50	49
No opinion	*	1

*Less than 1%

Television newsmagazine shows during the evening such as "60 Minutes," "20/20," "Prime Time Live," "Dateline NBC," and others?

	July 13–14, 1998	March 6–9, 1998
Every week	30%	30%
Several times a month	14	15
Occasionally	42	42
Never	14	12
No opinion	*	1

*Less than 1%

Next, I'm going to describe some stories involving journalists that have been in the news recently. For each one, please say whether you have heard or read anything about it before now:

That CNN broadcast a news story that was later printed in Time *Magazine concerning the use of nerve gas by the United States in the Vietnam War?*

Yes, have heard or read	71%
No	28
No opinion	1

That the Cincinnati Inquirer *newspaper admitted illegally obtaining information on the Chiquita Banana Company and paid Chiquita $10 million to settle the company's claims?*

Yes, have heard or read 27%
No 72
No opinion 1

That Boston Globe *columnist Patricia Smith was forced to quit her job after admitting she made up quotes in several columns?*

Yes, have heard or read 35%
No 63
No opinion 2

That New Republic *Magazine fired reporter Stephen Glass for fabricating all or part of twenty-seven magazine articles?*

Yes, have heard or read 26%
No 74
No opinion .... *

*Less than 1%

That New Yorker *Magazine editor Tina Brown resigned to start a company affiliated with Miramax Films?*

Yes, have heard or read 22%
No 77
No opinion 1

Asked of those who heard or read about the nerve gas story controversy: As far as you know, do CNN and Time *Magazine still stand behind the Vietnam nerve gas story they reported, have they retracted the story, or don't you know either way?*

Still stand behind story 6%
Retracted story... 42
Don't know; no opinion 52

In fact, CNN and Time *Magazine retracted the story they reported concerning the use of nerve gas in the Vietnam War. Do you think the misreporting involved in this story is an isolated incident, or does it reflect problems that are typical in today's journalism?*

Isolated incident 24%
Reflects typical problems 60

Neither; other (volunteered) 6
No opinion 10

~

From what you have read or heard, whose side do you favor in the United Auto Workers strike against General Motors—the company, or the union workers who are on strike?

	July 13–14, 1998	June 22–23, 1998
Company......................................	31%	28%
Union workers	42	51
Both sides equally (volunteered) ...	6	–
Neither (volunteered)....................	5	–
No opinion	16	21

~

Which of these statements concerning the Social Security system do you agree with more—it has some problems, but these can be dealt with gradually by Congress over the next few years; or it faces serious problems which must be dealt with by Congress in the next year?

Some problems 29%
Serious problems 67
It has no problems (volunteered)................... *
No opinion 4

*Less than 1%

In your view, which party would do a better job of dealing with the issue of Social Security—the Republican party, or the Democratic party?

Republican party.. 36%
Democratic party 43
Same; neither (volunteered) 12
No opinion 9

Next, I'm going to read a few changes that have been proposed as ways to keep the Social Security system operating in the next

century. Please say whether you would strongly favor, moderately favor, moderately oppose, or strongly oppose each one:

Allowing the federal government to invest a portion of the Social Security Trust Fund in the stock market?

Strongly favor.. 11%
Moderately favor 27
Moderately oppose 18
Strongly oppose.. 41
No opinion... 3

Allowing individuals to invest a portion of their Social Security savings in the stock market?

Strongly favor.. 29%
Moderately favor 37
Moderately oppose 12
Strongly oppose.. 17
No opinion... 5

Raising the retirement age at which people are eligible to receive their Social Security benefits to 70 years of age?

Strongly favor.. 10%
Moderately favor 17
Moderately oppose 18
Strongly oppose.. 52
No opinion... 3

Increasing the amount employers and employees pay in taxes to Social Security?

Strongly favor.. 13%
Moderately favor 22
Moderately oppose 27
Strongly oppose.. 35
No opinion... 3

Reducing Social Security benefits?

Strongly favor.. 4%
Moderately favor 9
Moderately oppose 20
Strongly oppose.. 65
No opinion... 2

Asked of those who are not retired: Do you expect to receive Social Security income when you retire?

Yes... 66%
No 31
No opinion... 3

Also asked of those who are not retired: When you retire, how much do you expect to rely on Social Security—as your main source of income, as a minor source of income, or not at all?

Main source 17%
Minor source.. 58
Not at all 23
No opinion... 2

Interviewing Date: 7/29/98
CNN/*USA Today*/Gallup Poll
Survey #GO 123693

If Monica Lewinsky says that she had an extramarital affair with Bill Clinton, and Clinton continues to say that no such affair ever happened, whom would you tend to believe more—Monica Lewinsky, or Bill Clinton?*

Lewinsky 48%
Clinton 44
No opinion... 8

*Based on one-night poll

If Monica Lewinsky says that Bill Clinton advised her to lie under oath, and Clinton says that he never advised her to lie, whom would you tend to believe more—Monica Lewinsky, or Bill Clinton?

Lewinsky 44%
Clinton 49
No opinion... 7

When Monica Lewinsky testifies before Ken Starr's grand jury, how likely do you think it

is that she will tell the truth—very likely, somewhat likely, not very likely, or not likely at all?

Very likely	23%
Somewhat likely	40
Not very likely	17
Not likely at all	17
No opinion	3

When Bill Clinton testifies in Ken Starr's investigation, how likely do you think it is that he will tell the truth—very likely, somewhat likely, not very likely, or not likely at all?

Very likely	31%
Somewhat likely	32
Not very likely	22
Not likely at all	12
No opinion	3

As you may know, Ken Starr had issued a subpoena which would have compelled Bill Clinton to testify before the grand jury, but withdrew it today when Clinton agreed to testify. Do you think Bill Clinton would have eventually testified in Ken Starr's investigation if Starr had not issued the subpoena, or has Clinton agreed to testify only because Starr issued his subpoena?

Would have testified	29%
Agreed because of subpoena	64
No opinion	7

As you may know, earlier in the year Monica Lewinsky testified under oath that she did not have sex with Bill Clinton. If Lewinsky now testifies that she did have sex with him, which of her two statements are you more likely to believe—what she said earlier (she did not have sex with Clinton), or what she says now (she did have sex with Clinton)?

What she said earlier	40%
What she says now	51
Neither; other (volunteered)	3
No opinion	6

◆   ◆   ◆

Interviewing Dates: 8/7–8/98
CNN/*USA Today*/Gallup Poll
Survey #GO 124014

I'm going to read off some personal characteristics and qualities. As I read each one, please tell me whether you think it applies or does not apply to Bill Clinton:

Tough enough for the job?

Applies	71%
Does not apply	28
No opinion	1

〜

I'm going to ask you about some scenarios that have not happened yet, but might happen in the future:

FORM A: *Suppose that Monica Lewinsky testifies before the grand jury that she had sex with Bill Clinton and there is physical evidence to support that fact. If Bill Clinton denies they had sex under oath in his own testimony, do you think Congress should or should not begin impeachment hearings that could remove Clinton from office?*

Yes, should begin hearings	44%
Should not	52
No opinion	4

FORM B: *Suppose that Bill Clinton publicly admits that he lied to the country about his relationship with Monica Lewinsky—that in fact he did have sexual relations with her and that he lied about it under oath in sworn testimony he gave last December. In that case, do you think Congress should or should not begin impeachment hearings that could remove Clinton from office?*

Yes, should begin hearings	41%
Should not	58
No opinion	1

If each of the following turned out to be true, how serious would you consider this matter—very serious, somewhat serious, not too serious, or not serious at all:

Bill Clinton had sexual relations with Monica Lewinsky?

	Aug. 7–8, 1998	Jan. 24–25, 1998	Jan. 23–24, 1998
Very serious	24%	34%	33%
Somewhat serious	25	26	26
Not too serious	25	19	21
Not serious at all	25	20	19
No opinion	1	1	1

Bill Clinton lied under oath about having sexual relations with Monica Lewinsky?

	Aug. 7–8, 1998	Jan. 24–25, 1998	Jan. 23–24, 1998
Very serious	49%	60%	63%
Somewhat serious	24	21	21
Not too serious	15	9	8
Not serious at all	10	7	6
No opinion	2	3	2

Bill Clinton participated in an effort to obstruct justice by getting Monica Lewinsky to lie under oath about their sexual relations?

	Aug. 7–8, 1998	Jan. 24–25, 1998	Jan. 23–24, 1998
Very serious	56%	66%	68%
Somewhat serious	23	17	17
Not too serious	10	8	7
Not serious at all	9	5	5
No opinion	2	4	3

Bill Clinton lied to the American public saying that he did not have sex with Monica Lewinsky?

Very serious	44%
Somewhat serious	22
Not too serious	19
Not serious at all	14
No opinion	1

◆   ◆   ◆

Interviewing Dates: 8/10–12/98
CNN/*USA Today*/Gallup Poll
Survey #GO 123694

Thinking about President Clinton, please say whether you strongly approve, moderately approve, moderately disapprove, or strongly disapprove of Clinton in each of the following areas:

The way Clinton is managing the government?

	Aug. 10–12, 1998	Jan. 30– Feb. 1, 1998
Strongly approve	34%	38%
Moderately approve	41	40
Moderately disapprove	14	11
Strongly disapprove	10	10
No opinion	1	1

Clinton's positions on major issues?

	Aug. 10–12, 1998	Jan. 30– Feb. 1, 1998
Strongly approve	30%	38%
Moderately approve	40	38
Moderately disapprove	17	14
Strongly disapprove	11	8
No opinion	2	2

The moral example Clinton sets for the country?

	Aug. 10–12, 1998	Jan. 30– Feb. 1, 1998
Strongly approve	12%	14%
Moderately approve	20	25
Moderately disapprove	20	19
Strongly disapprove	44	39
No opinion	4	3

Do you think Bill Clinton is honest and trustworthy enough to be president, or not?

Yes	55%
No	42
No opinion	3

We have two questions about the bombings of U.S. embassies in the African nations of Kenya and Tanzania last Friday [August 7]:

How much confidence do you have that the people responsible for those bombings will be caught—a great deal, a moderate amount, not much, or no confidence at all?

Great deal 23%
Moderate amount 40
Not much 24
No confidence at all 11
No opinion 2

If the United States determines that the government of a foreign country was in some way involved in those bombings, would you favor or oppose a U.S. military attack against that country?

Favor 48%
Oppose 45
No opinion 7

~

Do you consider yourself knowledgeable about the various matters involved in Ken Starr's investigation of Bill Clinton, or are you not that knowledgeable about these matters?

Yes, knowledgeable 61%
Not that knowledgeable 37
No opinion 2

Do you wish you knew more than you currently know about what happened between Bill Clinton and Monica Lewinsky, or do you wish you knew less than you currently know?

Wish you knew more 26%
Wish you knew less 61
About right (volunteered) 7
No opinion 6

Thinking about all of the various charges stemming from Bill Clinton's possible involvement with Monica Lewinsky, which of the following statements comes closest to your own view about your support for Clinton in this matter—even if all the charges are true, you would still support Clinton; your opinion of Clinton may depend on the final results of the current investigation; or you do not support Clinton and would not support him even if all the allegations were proven to be false?

Would still support Clinton 45%
Opinion depends on final results 27
Would not support him 25
None; other (volunteered) 1
Opinion depends on other things
  (volunteered) 1
No opinion 1

For each of the following matters, please tell me if you would prefer to see the formal investigation into those matters continue until the investigation is completed, or whether you would prefer that the investigation stop now:

The allegations concerning Bill Clinton and Monica Lewinsky?

Continue 43%
Stop now 56
No opinion 1

Bill Clinton's involvement in Whitewater and other financial dealings while he was governor of Arkansas?

Continue 52%
Stop now 45
No opinion 3

Fund-raising practices used by Bill Clinton and the Democratic party during the 1996 elections?

Continue 57%
Stop now 37
No opinion 6

◆ ◆ ◆

Interviewing Date: 8/17/98
CNN/*USA Today*/Gallup Poll
Survey #GO 124075

Now thinking about Bill Clinton as a person, do you have a favorable or unfavorable opinion of him?

	Total	Speech watchers*
Favorable	40%	39%
Unfavorable	48	53
No opinion	12	8

*Clinton's televised remarks on August 17 about Monica Lewinsky

As you may know, President Clinton testified today to the grand jury in Ken Starr's investigation of him. Just a few minutes ago he made a brief speech to the nation stating that he did have a relationship with Monica Lewinsky that was inappropriate and wrong, but that he did not lie in previous sworn testimony. Did you, personally, hear Clinton's speech to the nation on this subject this evening, or did you not happen to hear it?

Yes, heard it	64%
Did not	36

Asked of those who heard President Clinton's speech (64% of the sample): Are you personally satisfied or not satisfied with the explanation of the Lewinsky matter which Clinton gave tonight in his speech to the country?

Satisfied	53%
Not satisfied	39
No opinion	8

If you had to choose, which do you think would be better for the country—if Bill Clinton were to remain in office until the end of his term; or if Clinton were to resign now, and turn the presidency over to Al Gore?

	Total	Speech watchers*
Remain in office	72%	70%
Resign now	23	24
No opinion	5	6

*Clinton's televised remarks on August 17 about Monica Lewinsky

President Clinton explained that his relationship with Monica Lewinsky was inappropriate, but that he did nothing illegal. Do you believe Clinton when he says he did not do anything illegal?

	Total	Speech watchers
Yes, believe him	42%	41%
No	48	52
No opinion	10	7

In his speech tonight, Bill Clinton said this is a private matter that is nobody's business but his and his family's. Do you agree that this matter is only private, or is it something that concerns the public as well?

	Total	Speech watchers
Private matter	63%	58%
Concerns public	37	42
No opinion	*	*

*Less than 1%

As a result of what you have heard about Bill Clinton's testimony or speech today, have you lost confidence in Clinton as president, or not?

	Total	Speech watchers
Yes, lost confidence	33%	37%
No	65	61
No opinion	2	2

Thinking specifically about his testimony before the grand jury today, just your best guess—do you think Bill Clinton answered the questions put to him with the whole truth and nothing but the truth, or not?

	Total	Speech watchers
Yes	35%	36%
No	46	49
No opinion	19	15

Do you feel that Bill Clinton's speech and testimony today should end the Lewinsky matter completely, or do you feel further action against Clinton is needed?

	Total	Speech watchers
Should end matter	65%	61%
Further action needed	31	34
No opinion	4	5

In his speech tonight, President Clinton expressed regret and took responsibility for his actions, but did not apologize to the American public. Do you think that he should or should not have apologized to the American public as well?

	Total	Speech watchers
Should	58%	65%
Should not	37	29
No opinion	5	6

◆　　◆　　◆

Interviewing Date: 8/18/98
CNN/*USA Today*/Gallup Poll
Survey #GO 124094

I'm going to read some charges that may or may not be made against President Clinton. For each one, please say if you were convinced it were true, whether you think Bill Clinton should or should not be impeached and removed from office:

If you were convinced Clinton lied about having sex with Monica Lewinsky under oath when he was a witness in the Paula Jones case earlier this year?

Should	42%
Should not	55
No opinion	3

If you were convinced Clinton lied under oath in testimony before the grand jury in Ken Starr's investigation on Monday [August 17]?

Should	49%
Should not	46
No opinion	5

If you were convinced Clinton participated in obstruction of justice concerning his relationship with Monica Lewinsky?

Should	48%
Should not	49
No opinion	3

Now that Bill Clinton has admitted that he had an inappropriate relationship with Monica Lewinsky, which of the following best describes your own reaction to Clinton as a result of the events of the last few days—you support Clinton and are not disappointed with him personally as a result of the events of the last few days; you support Clinton but are disappointed with him personally; you used to support Clinton but no longer do; or you did not support Clinton even before the events of the last few days?

Support him, not disappointed	24%
Support him but disappointed	34
No longer support him	10
Did not support him	29
Other (volunteered)	1
No opinion	2

Thinking now about President Clinton's speech to the nation last night [August 17], overall do you think the speech did more good for the country or did more harm?

More good	45%
More harm	32
Neither; no effect (volunteered)	12
No opinion	11

Still thinking about President Clinton's speech last night, in general do you think he was completely open and honest about the Monica Lewinsky matter; or he told the truth on some matters, but tried to mislead the public on other matters?

Open and honest	29%
Tried to mislead public	61
No opinion	10

Now thinking more generally about the events of the last few days concerning President Clinton, Monica Lewinsky, and the Starr investigation, whom do you blame more for the fact that things have gotten to the point they have—Bill Clinton, or Ken Starr?

Clinton	39%
Starr	44
Both equally (volunteered)	6
The media (volunteered)	4
Neither; other (volunteered)	4
No opinion	3

Just answering based on your own personal impression, which of the following do you think is the main reason Hillary Clinton has stood by Bill Clinton through the entire Lewinsky matter—because she is committed to her marriage and loves her husband, likes being First Lady, or is committed to her husband's policies?

Committed to her marriage	40%
Likes being First Lady	34
Committed to husband's policies	16
None; other (volunteered)	7
No opinion	3

Finally, thinking about the upcoming elections for Congress in November, do the events of the last few days make you more likely to vote for a Republican candidate for Congress, more likely to vote for a Democratic candidate for Congress, or won't the Lewinsky matter affect your vote one way or the other this November?

Republican candidate	13%
Democratic candidate	12
No effect	71
No opinion	4

◆　◆　◆

Interviewing Date: 8/20/98
CNN/*USA Today*/Gallup Poll
Survey #GO 124115

How confident are you in Bill Clinton as a military leader—very confident, somewhat confident, not too confident, or not confident at all?

Very confident	29%
Somewhat confident	32
Not too confident	16

Not confident at all	20
No opinion	3

How worried are you that someone in your family will become a victim of a terrorist attack—very worried, somewhat worried, not too worried, or not worried at all?

Very worried	10%
Somewhat worried	22
Not too worried	38
Not worried at all	29
No opinion	1

As you may know, earlier today [August 20] the United States launched military attacks against terrorist facilities in the countries of Afghanistan and the Sudan. Do you approve or disapprove of those attacks?

Approve	66%
Disapprove	19
No opinion	15

In your view, are those attacks more likely to increase or decrease terrorist actions against Americans, either in the United States or abroad?

Increase	47%
Decrease	38
No effect (volunteered)	5
No opinion	10

Given the president's personal difficulties this week, is it legitimate or not legitimate for members of Congress to question the timing of this military action?

Legitimate	58%
Not legitimate	36
No opinion	6

If it turns out the U.S. military attack results in civilian casualties, which of the following statements would come closer to your view— civilian casualties are regrettable, but the United States was right to attack; or the United States should not have attacked unless it was certain there would be no civilian casualties?

Right to attack 65%

Should not have attacked 27

It depends on number of casualties
(volunteered) 1

It depends on other factors (volunteered) 1

No opinion 6

◆　◆　◆

Interviewing Dates: 8/21–23/98
CNN/*USA Today*/Gallup Poll
Survey #GO 124116

For each of the following areas, please say whether you have confidence in Bill Clinton to handle or deal with it, or not:

Congress?

Yes 65%

No 33

No opinion 2

The economy?

Yes 79%

No 20

No opinion 1

Foreign affairs?

Yes 69%

No 29

No opinion 2

Issues concerning families?

Yes 50%

No 47

No opinion 3

Asked of half sample: I'm going to read some personal characteristics and qualities. As I read each one, please say whether you think it applies or does not apply to Bill Clinton:

Honest and trustworthy?

Applies 31%

Does not apply 67

No opinion 2

Shares your values?

Applies 37%

Does not apply 61

No opinion 2

Cares about the needs of people like you?

Applies 62%

Does not apply 36

No opinion 2

Shows good judgment?

Applies 35%

Does not apply 64

No opinion 1

Can get things done?

Applies 76%

Does not apply 22

No opinion 2

Does a good job representing America to the world?

Applies 54%

Does not apply 44

No opinion 2

All things considered, are you glad Bill Clinton is president, or not?

Yes 56%

No 42

No opinion 2

~

Asked of half sample: I'm going to read some personal characteristics and qualities. As I read each one, please say whether you think it applies or does not apply to Al Gore:

Honest and trustworthy?

Applies 63%

Does not apply 25

No opinion 12

Shares your values?

Applies 52%

Does not apply 35

No opinion 13

Cares about the needs of people like you?

Applies... 59%
Does not apply.. 31
No opinion... 10

Shows good judgment?

Applies... 57%
Does not apply.. 29
No opinion... 14

Can get things done?

Applies... 47%
Does not apply.. 35
No opinion... 18

Does a good job representing America to the world?

Applies... 60%
Does not apply.. 29
No opinion... 11

Which of the following statements comes closest to your view of Al Gore—you think Al Gore is qualified to be president, and you would consider voting for him for president; you think Al Gore is qualified to be president, but you would not vote for him for president; or you do not think Al Gore is qualified to be president?

Qualified, would vote for him 34%
Qualified, would not vote for him.................. 22
Not qualified.. 36
No opinion... 8

~

We have some more questions about the matters concerning Bill Clinton and Monica Lewinsky. How closely have you followed the news about these matters—very closely, somewhat closely, not too closely, or not at all?

Very closely... 33%
Somewhat closely.. 50

Not too closely... 15
Not at all 2
No opinion... *

*Less than 1%

I'm going to describe some allegations being made about Bill Clinton. As I read each one, please say whether you think it is definitely true, probably true, probably not true, or definitely not true:

The allegation that Bill Clinton had sexual relations of any kind with Monica Lewinsky?

Definitely true.. 53%
Probably true 40
Probably not true 4
Definitely not true 1
No opinion... 2

As a result of the Monica Lewinsky matter, would you say that Bill Clinton betrayed the public's trust, or would you not say that?

Yes, betrayed trust... 57%
Would not say that... 41
No opinion... 2

Do you think Bill Clinton should or should not address the nation and further explain his relationship with Monica Lewinsky and what he has done about it over the past seven months?

Should 31%
Should not 67
No opinion... 2

In the remaining two and a half years of his term in office, do you think Bill Clinton will be a success or a failure as president?

Success 60%
Failure.. 33
No opinion... 7

In your view, will Bill Clinton mostly be remembered as president for his accomplishments, or for his involvement in personal scandal?

Accomplishments 23%
Involvement in scandal 71
Other (volunteered) 3
No opinion 3

Which of the following statements comes closer to your own view—Bill Clinton's personal life doesn't matter to you, as long as he does a good job of running the country: or Bill Clinton's personal life does matter to you, because the president's moral character is important?

Doesn't matter 57%
Does matter 41
Neither; other (volunteered) 1
No opinion 1

Now, turning to Hillary Clinton, if you had the opportunity to advise Hillary Clinton in the Monica Lewinsky matter, what would you suggest she do—publicly defend him [Bill Clinton] to help protect his presidency; stay with him in the marriage but not defend him publicly; or leave him on the basis of infidelity?

	Aug. 21–23, 1998	Jan. 30– Feb. 1, 1998
Defend him	32%	39%
Stay but not defend him	40	30
Leave him	18	19
No opinion	10	12

~

As you may know, Congress and the Justice Department are currently investigating the way Bill Clinton, Al Gore, and other White House officials raised funds for the Democratic party in 1996. Do you think Attorney General Janet Reno should or should not appoint an Independent Counsel to also investigate these fund-raising matters?

Should 53%
Should not 41
No opinion 6

~

As you may know, the United States recently launched military attacks against terrorist facilities in the countries of Afghanistan and the Sudan. Do you approve or disapprove of those attacks?

Approve 75%
Disapprove 18
No opinion 7

Asked of half sample: Would you generally approve or disapprove of future attacks by the United States using cruise missiles to attack terrorist groups or their facilities?

Approve 75%
Disapprove 19
No opinion 6

Asked of half sample: Would you generally approve or disapprove of future attacks by the United States using ground troops to attack terrorist groups or their facilities?

Approve 66%
Disapprove 29
No opinion 5

Shortly after it was announced that the United States had attacked terrorist facilities in Afghanistan and the Sudan on Thursday [August 20], President Clinton made a brief speech explaining the reasons why it was necessary to take this action at this time. How much do you trust Bill Clinton to provide an honest explanation for why he took this action—completely, mostly, not much, or not at all?

Completely 36%
Mostly 34
Not much 16
Not at all 11
No opinion 3

~

Turning for a moment to the federal budget, if the Republicans in Congress and President Clinton do not agree on federal spending

goals this fall, the federal government would have to shut down all of its nonessential services until a budget is passed. If that happens this fall, whom would you be likely to blame more for the shutdown—President Clinton, or the Republican leaders in Congress?

Clinton	27%
Republicans	56
Both equally (volunteered)	9
Neither (volunteered)	2
No opinion	6

~

Thinking about the U.S. stock market, do you think stock prices will go higher or lower in the next six months?

Higher	45%
Lower	38
Stay the same (volunteered)	5
No opinion	12

~

Thinking about the candidates in the 1996 election for president, if you could vote for president again, whom would you vote for—Bill Clinton, the Democratic candidate; Bob Dole, the Republican candidate; or Ross Perot, the Reform party candidate?

	Total	Registered voters	Regular voters
Clinton	46%	46%	44%
Dole	34	36	38
Perot	12	11	11
No opinion	8	7	7

~

As you may know, the one-year anniversary of the death of Princess Diana is coming up later this month. How would you describe the way you feel about her death—are you as upset as if someone you knew personally had died, or are you sad but not as upset as if it were someone you personally knew?

Upset	15%
Sad but not upset	75
Not sad (volunteered)	9
No opinion	1

From everything you've heard or read about the accident, how responsible do you feel each of the following factors was for Diana's car accident—extremely responsible, very responsible, not too responsible, or not responsible at all:

The photographers who were following Diana's car?

Extremely responsible	28%
Very responsible	43
Not too responsible	16
Not responsible	8
No opinion	5

The man who was driving Diana's car?

Extremely responsible	34%
Very responsible	40
Not too responsible	15
Not responsible	7
No opinion	4

Dodi Fayed, Diana's companion, who was in the car?

Extremely responsible	4%
Very responsible	10
Not too responsible	27
Not responsible	51
No opinion	8

Now, thinking about just two of these factors, who do you think was more responsible for the car accident—the photographers who were following Diana's car, or the man who was driving Diana's car?

Photographers following car	35%
Man driving car	55
Both equally (volunteered)	6
No opinion	4

◆ ◆ ◆

Interviewing Date: 9/1/98
CNN/*USA Today*/Gallup Poll
Survey #GO 124208

How likely do you think it is that there will be a recession in the country during the next twelve months—very likely, fairly likely, not too likely, or not at all likely?

Very likely	12%
Fairly likely	28
Not too likely	40
Not at all likely	15
Already in recession (volunteered)	*
No opinion	5

*Less than 1%

Turning to the stock market, as you may know, the Dow Jones Industrial Average, a key market indicator, fell by 513 points yesterday and gained 288 points today [September 1]. If you had a thousand dollars to spend, do you think investing it in the stock market would be a good or bad idea?

	Total	Stock-holders
Good idea	46%	60%
Bad idea	48	34
It depends (volunteered)	3	3
No opinion	3	3

How concerned are you, personally, about the direction the stock market takes in the next year—very concerned, somewhat concerned, not too concerned, or not concerned at all?

	Total	Stock-holders
Very concerned	22%	29%
Somewhat concerned	37	38
Not too concerned	25	26
Not concerned at all	15	6
No opinion	1	1

Asked of stockholders: Thinking about the past seven days, what changes, if any, have you made in your stock investments over the past week—have you put more money into the stock market, taken money out of the stock market, or kept the amount of money you have in the stock market?

Put more money in	6%
Taken money out	4
Kept money in market	86
No opinion	4

~

Thinking about the situation in Russia, in your view, should the United States continue to support Russian President Boris Yeltsin, or don't you think so?

Yes, continue to support	51%
Don't think so	35
No opinion	14

◆ ◆ ◆

Interviewing Date: 9/10/98
CNN/*USA Today*/Gallup Poll
Survey #GO 124288

Assuming that Congress goes forward with an investigation of the allegations contained in Ken Starr's report, do you think that members of the two parties in Congress will conduct this investigation in a fair and bipartisan way, or will they not be able to do this?

Yes, fair and bipartisan	49%
Not able to do this	47
No opinion	4

Thinking about Bill Clinton's personal response to the Lewinsky controversy, do you feel that Bill Clinton's apologies for his actions in the Lewinsky matter have or have not been sincere?

Yes, sincere	45%
No	50
No opinion	5

The Starr report may contain details of the sexual relations that occurred between Bill Clinton and Monica Lewinsky, which Ken Starr says would prove Clinton lied under

oath about their relationship. Do you think that those sexual details should be released to the public, or not?

Yes, should 26%
No 71
No opinion 3

◆ ◆ ◆

Interviewing Date: 9/11/98
CNN/*USA Today*/Gallup Poll
Survey #GO 124297

Which of the following statements comes closest to your view of Bill Clinton as a result of the Starr report—you feel less favorably toward Clinton and have lost confidence in his ability to serve as president; you feel less favorably but have not lost confidence in his ability to serve as president; or you do not feel less favorably and have not lost confidence in his ability to serve as president?

Less favorably, have lost confidence 34%
Less favorably but have not lost confidence ... 32
Not less favorably, have not lost confidence... 30
Other (volunteered) 1
No opinion 3

Next, I am going to read two different statements that have been made about the explicit sexual details contained in the Starr report. Bill Clinton's statement: "The Starr report is left with nothing but the details of a private sexual relationship, told in graphic details with the intent to embarrass." Ken Starr's statement: "In sworn testimony the president maintained that none of his sexual contacts with her [Monica Lewinsky] constituted sexual relations. In light of the president's testimony the evidence of his perjury cannot be presented without specific, explicit, and possibly offensive descriptions of sexual encounters." Which statement do you tend to agree with more—Bill Clinton's statement, or Ken Starr's statement?

Clinton's statement 50%
Starr's statement 43
Neither; other (volunteered) 4
No opinion 3

◆ ◆ ◆

Interviewing Dates: 9/11–12/98
CNN/*USA Today*/Gallup Poll
Survey #GO 124284

I'm going to describe some of the charges against Bill Clinton being investigated by Congress. As I read each one, please say whether you think it is definitely true, probably true, probably not true, or definitely not true:

The charge that Clinton lied under oath about having sex with Monica Lewinsky when he was a witness in the Paula Jones case earlier this year?

Definitely true... 51%
Probably true 35
Probably not true 6
Definitely not true 3
No opinion 5

The charge that Clinton lied under oath in testimony before the grand jury in Ken Starr's investigation?

Definitely true... 43%
Probably true 35
Probably not true 11
Definitely not true 4
No opinion 7

The charge that Clinton worked with Monica Lewinsky to conceal their relationship by concealing his gifts to her which were subpoenaed by investigators and by getting her to lie under oath?

Definitely true... 30%
Probably true 40
Probably not true 18
Definitely not true 6
No opinion 6

The charge that Clinton tried to help Monica Lewinsky obtain a job at a time when her testimony might have harmed him if she told the truth?

Definitely true... 29%
Probably true 41
Probably not true 17
Definitely not true 6
No opinion... 7

The charge that Clinton attempted to influence the testimony of his personal secretary?

Definitely true... 25%
Probably true 40
Probably not true 19
Definitely not true 8
No opinion... 8

The charge that Clinton lied to senior White House aides knowing that they would relay those false statements to the grand jury?

Definitely true... 35%
Probably true 42
Probably not true 12
Definitely not true 4
No opinion... 7

In his report to Congress, Ken Starr concluded that Bill Clinton committed acts which were not consistent with the president's constitutional duty to faithfully execute the laws. Do you agree or disagree with this conclusion?

Agree 49%
Disagree.. 46
No opinion... 5

As you may know, both Monica Lewinsky and Bill Clinton have testified before the grand jury in Ken Starr's investigation. Now that some of the statements made by Clinton and Lewinsky appear to conflict, whom do you tend to believe more—Bill Clinton, or Monica Lewinsky?

Clinton.. 34%
Lewinsky 49
Neither (volunteered) 10
No opinion... 7

Again, I'm going to read some of the charges in Ken Starr's report. For each one, if you were

convinced it were true, please say whether you think Bill Clinton should or should not be impeached and removed from office:

If you were convinced Clinton lied under oath about having sex with Monica Lewinsky when he was a witness in the Paula Jones case earlier this year?

Should be impeached and removed............... 38%
Should not be.. 60
No opinion... 2

If you were convinced Clinton lied under oath in testimony before the grand jury in Ken Starr's investigation?

Should be impeached and removed............... 50%
Should not be.. 46
No opinion... 4

If you were convinced Clinton worked with Monica Lewinsky to conceal their relationship by concealing his gifts to her which were subpoenaed by investigators and by getting her to lie under oath?

Should be impeached and removed............... 42%
Should not be.. 55
No opinion... 3

If you were convinced Clinton tried to help Monica Lewinsky obtain a job at a time when her testimony might have harmed him if she told the truth?

Should be impeached and removed............... 36%
Should not be.. 59
No opinion... 5

If you were convinced Clinton attempted to influence the testimony of his personal secretary?

Should be impeached and removed............... 42%
Should not be.. 55
No opinion... 3

If you were convinced Clinton lied to senior White House aides knowing that they would

relay those false statements to the grand jury?

Should be impeached and removed................ 41%
Should not be.. 56
No opinion.. 3

Which of the following statements comes closer to your own view about all of the charges against Bill Clinton which Congress is investigating—these charges are important indicators of Clinton's character and ability to serve as president, or these charges are not relevant to Clinton's character and ability to serve as president?

Important indicators 46%
Not relevant 50
No opinion... 4

Bill Clinton said under oath that he did not have sexual relations with Monica Lewinsky. Did Bill Clinton intend to lie when he said that, or did he intend to say something that was misleading but legally accurate according to the definition of sexual relations being used by those investigators?

Intended to lie... 46%
Misleading but legally accurate...................... 50
No opinion... 4

Thinking just about the Internet, have you personally read any of the actual Starr report on the Internet, or not?

Yes.. 12%
No 88

As you may know, President Clinton's attorneys released a rebuttal to Ken Starr's report. How much have you read or heard about the specific details contained in this rebuttal—a great deal, a moderate amount, only a little, or nothing at all?

Great deal 6%
Moderate amount... 20
Only a little... 35
Nothing at all.. 39
No opinion... *

*Less than 1%

Thinking about the graphic sexual details contained in the Starr report, in your view was it necessary that those details be released to the public, or could the public have understood the charges without those details being released?

Necessary to release details............................ 25%
Could have understood without details 72
No opinion... 3

In your view, has Bill Clinton apologized enough for this matter, or not?

Yes.. 64%
No 33
No opinion... 3

Does the Starr report contain any new details about Bill Clinton's behavior that make you feel the charges against Clinton are more serious than you felt before, or not?

Yes, more serious 27%
No 60
Less serious (volunteered).............................. 1
Not heard any details (volunteered) 7
No opinion... 5

If the reports of Clinton's sexual behavior are true, in your view would that make him unfit to be president, or not?

Yes, unfit.. 34%
No 63
No opinion... 3

Here is a different question about the possible impeachment of President Clinton. Do you think members of Congress should stick close to American public opinion when deciding what steps to take next, including the results of polls like this one; or should members of Congress do what they think is best regardless of what the American public thinks?

Stick close to public opinion 63%
Do what they think is best.............................. 34
No opinion... 3

◆ ◆ ◆

Interviewing Date: 9/13/98
CNN/*USA Today*/Gallup Poll
Survey #GO 124284

Regardless of whether or not you think Bill Clinton should be impeached, do you think Congress should or should not vote to censure Clinton—that is, pass a formal resolution expressing disapproval of his actions?

Should... 60%
Should not 36
No opinion... 4

Thinking about all of the charges against Bill Clinton that Congress is investigating, do you think these charges represent private matters only, or do they concern the public as well?

Private matters... 51%
Concern public 47
No opinion... 2

Regardless of how you feel about his political views, would you say you respect President Clinton, or don't you feel that way?

Yes, respect Clinton 43%
Don't feel that way 54
No opinion... 3

If you knew that Hillary Clinton had forgiven Bill Clinton for the Monica Lewinsky matter, how much would that affect your view of him—a great deal, a moderate amount, not much, or not at all?

Great deal 14%
Moderate amount... 11
Not much 22
Not at all 52
No opinion... 1

Do you feel that Hillary Clinton has or has not forgiven Bill Clinton for the Monica Lewinsky matter?

Yes, has forgiven him...................................... 38%
Has not.. 42
No opinion... 20

◆ ◆ ◆

Interviewing Dates: 9/14–15/98
CNN/*USA Today*/Gallup Poll
Survey #GO 124140

The following results are based on telephone interviews with 119 members of the House of Representatives or their designated spokesperson. The sample includes 62 Republicans and 56 Democrats.

Not including news accounts of the report, how much of the Starr report itself have you read so far? I'm just referring to the text of the Starr report which was released on Friday [September 11], not including footnotes and the boxes of corroborating material. Have you read all of the report, most of it, about half, less than half, or none of the actual report?

	Total	Republicans	Democrats
All of report	33%	44%	20%
Most of it	31	27	36
About half	14	15	14
Less than half	13	8	18
None	2	–	3
Not sure (volunteered)	7	6	9

When do you think the House of Representatives should make a final decision on whether or not to impeach Bill Clinton—next year after the 106th Congress is sworn in, or by the end of this year?

	Total	Republicans	Democrats
Next year	21%	18%	25%
By end of this year	52	58	45
It depends (volunteered)	13	13	12
It doesn't matter; no preference (volunteered)	2	3	–
Not sure (volunteered)	12	8	18

We know that many of your constituents will not have made up their minds, but, on balance, would you say more of your constituents support impeachment or oppose impeachment?

	Total	Repub-licans	Demo-crats
Support	52%	90%	10%
Oppose	30	3	61
Equally mixed (volunteered)	11	5	18
Not sure (volunteered)	7	2	11

How much attention will you pay to the opinion of your constituents when deciding whether or not to impeach Bill Clinton—a great deal, a fair amount, only a little, or none at all?

	Total	Repub-licans	Demo-crats
Great deal	39%	39%	39%
Fair amount	40	34	45
Only a little	8	10	7
None at all	5	8	2
Not sure (volunteered)	4	3	5
Refused	4	6	2

If your constituents want you to vote one way on impeachment but your conscience guides you to vote the other way, how would you vote—according to your constituents, or according to your conscience?

	Total	Repub-licans	Demo-crats
According to constituents	7%	6%	7%
According to conscience	67	71	62
It depends (volunteered)	8	5	11
Not sure (volunteered)	15	15	16
Refused	3	3	4

What do you think Congress should do with Ken Starr's report—hold hearings to investigate the charges contained in the report, or take no action on the report and end the investigation into these matters immediately?

	Total	Repub-licans	Demo-crats
Hold hearings	78%	92%	64%
End investigation	10	–	21
Other (volunteered)	3	2	4
Not sure (volunteered)	8	6	9
Refused	1	–	2

Thinking about the graphic sexual details contained in the Starr report, in your view was it necessary that those details be released to the public, or could the public have understood the charges without those details being released?

	Total	Repub-licans	Demo-crats
Necessary that details be released	49%	79%	16%
Public could have understood	43	11	77
Not sure (volunteered)	6	5	7
Refused	2	5	–

Not thinking specifically about how you would vote, but more generally—in your view, are any of the charges in the Starr report impeachable offenses, or are none of the charges impeachable?

	Total	Repub-licans	Demo-crats
Yes, any/some are impeachable	51%	79%	21%
None are impeachable	21	2	43
Not sure (volunteered)	25	14	34
Refused	3	5	2

If the House Judiciary Committee votes out Articles of Impeachment and a vote on impeachment is taken by the full House of Representatives, which of the following statements best describes where you currently

stand on that question—you currently support impeaching Bill Clinton; you are leaning toward impeachment, but you are waiting until the congressional inquiry into the charges has finished to decide; you are leaning against impeachment, but you are waiting until the congressional inquiry into the charges has finished to decide; or you currently oppose impeaching Bill Clinton?

	Total	Repub-licans	Demo-crats
Support impeaching Clinton	4%	6%	2%
Leaning toward impeachment but waiting	31	55	5
Leaning against impeachment but waiting	22	6	39
Oppose impeaching Clinton	13	–	29
Not leaning either way; totally undecided (volunteered)	15	11	20
Other (volunteered)	1	2	–
Not sure (volunteered)	8	10	3
Refused	6	10	2

Which of the following statements comes closest to where you stand on a resolution expressing formal disapproval of Bill Clinton's actions which would not result in his removal from office, such as a motion to censure Clinton—you currently support such a resolution; you are leaning toward such a resolution, but you are waiting until the congressional inquiry into the charges has finished to decide; you are leaning against such a resolution, but you are waiting until the congressional inquiry into the charges has finished to decide; or you currently oppose such a resolution?

	Total	Repub-licans	Demo-crats
Support resolution	7%	6%	9%
Leaning toward resolution but waiting	31	18	45
Leaning against resolution but waiting	12	14	9
Oppose resolution	22	34	9
Not leaning either way; totally undecided (volunteered)	12	10	16
Other (volunteered)	2	2	2
Not sure (volunteered)	7	6	7
Refused	7	10	3

Do you think that the response to the Starr report by Bill Clinton and his attorneys has been appropriate or inappropriate?

	Total	Repub-licans	Demo-crats
Appropriate	26%	3%	50%
Inappropriate	54	81	25
Not sure (volunteered)	18	13	23
Refused	2	3	2

◆   ◆   ◆

Interviewing Dates: 9/14–15/98
CNN/*USA Today*/Gallup Poll
Survey #GO 124310

Thinking about the elections in November, if your member of Congress does each of the following, would that make you more likely to support or to oppose your member of Congress in the November election, or would that make no difference to your vote:

Favors a formal censure of Clinton but did not favor impeachment?

	Total	Likely voters*
Support	30%	27%
Oppose	17	24
No difference	49	46
No opinion	4	3

*Based on 39% of the sample

Favors taking no formal action against Clinton?

	Total	Likely voters*
Support	20%	20%
Oppose	33	43
No difference	44	35
No opinion	3	2

*Based on 39% of the sample

Calls for Clinton to resign?

	Total	Likely voters*
Support	30%	41%
Oppose	34	31
No difference	35	27
No opinion	1	1

*Based on 39% of the sample

All things considered, are you glad Bill Clinton is president, or not?

	Sept. 14–15, 1998	Aug. 21–23, 1998
Yes	59%	56%
No	38	42
No opinion	3	2

How important do you think it is for the president to provide moral leadership for the country—very important, somewhat important, only slightly important, or not at all important?

	Sept. 14–15, 1998	Feb. 13–15, 1998
Very important	72%	65%
Somewhat important	18	22
Only slightly important	5	8
Not at all important	4	4
No opinion	1	1

The report which Independent Counsel Ken Starr formally submitted to Congress dealing with his investigation of Bill Clinton was released to the public last week. How much have you read or heard about the specific details contained in Starr's report to Congress—a great deal, a moderate amount, only a little, or nothing at all?

	Sept. 14–15, 1998	Sept. 13, 1998	Sept. 11–12, 1998
Great deal	23%	21%	14%
Moderate amount	37	33	32
Only a little	28	34	38
Nothing at all	12	12	16
No opinion	*	*	*

*Less than 1%

Asked of those who replied that Clinton can be an effective president during his remaining two years in office (58% of the sample): If Congress formally reprimands or censures Bill Clinton for the Monica Lewinsky matter, do you think Bill Clinton would be an effective president during his remaining two years in office, or not?

Yes, effective	84%
No	11
No opinion	5

What is your best guess about the future of Bill Clinton's presidency—do you think he will serve out the rest of his term in office, or he will be forced to leave office before the end of his term?

Serve out term	60%
Forced to leave office	33
No opinion	7

Next, if Congress considers voting to censure Bill Clinton for the Monica Lewinsky matter, what would you prefer it do—censure him only for the legal charges in Starr's report, censure him only for his improper relationship with Monica Lewinsky, censure him both for the legal charges and his improper relationship, or not censure him for either matter?

	Total	Likely voters*
Censure for charges	27%	29%
Censure for relationship	13	11
Censure for both	37	41
Not censure for either	19	17
No opinion	4	2

*Based on 39% of the sample

Still thinking about the Clinton investigation, in your view is Congress paying too much attention to the investigation, or is Congress paying the right amount of attention to the investigation?

	Total	Likely voters*
Too much	52%	43%
Right amount	42	51
Not enough (volunteered)	3	4
No opinion	3	2

*Based on 39% of the sample

Interviewing Date: 9/20/98
CNN/*USA Today*/Gallup Poll
Survey #GO 124367

As you may know, tomorrow [September 21] Congress will also publicly release about 2,800 pages of documents related to the Clinton investigation that Ken Starr turned over to Congress when he submitted his report. Do you think Congress should or should not release those documents to the public?

Should	46%
Should not	53
No opinion	1

The videotape of Bill Clinton's testimony will be released on Monday [September 21]. Do you plan to watch any of it on television, or not?

Yes	45%
No	50
No opinion	5

The videotape may be released Monday at the same time that President Clinton may be giving a speech to leaders of other countries at the United Nations. In your opinion, should the release of the videotape be postponed because of that, or should the videotape be released as currently planned?

Should be postponed	38%
Should be released	56
No opinion	6

As you may know, Monday is Rosh Hashanah, one of the major Jewish religious holidays. In your opinion, should the release of the videotape be postponed because of that, or should the videotape be released as currently planned?

Should be postponed	33%
Should be released	58
No opinion	9

As you may know, tomorrow [September 21] Congress will publicly release the videotape of Bill Clinton's testimony before the Ken Starr grand jury. Do you think Congress should or should not release the videotape of Clinton's testimony to the public?

Should	37%
Should not	62
No opinion	1

Interviewing Date: 9/21/98
CNN/*USA Today*/Gallup Poll
Survey #GO 124358

Based on what you know at this point, do you think that Bill Clinton should or should not be impeached and removed from office?

Should	32%
Should not	66
No opinion	2

You just answered that you think Bill Clinton should or should not be impeached and removed from office. How strongly do you feel about that—very strongly, or not so strongly?

Impeached, very strongly	28%
Impeached, not strongly	4
Not impeached, not strongly	15
Not impeached, very strongly	51
No opinion	2

Do you think Bill Clinton is honest and trustworthy enough to be president, or not?

Yes.. 49%
No 47
No opinion 4

Do you think it is definitely true, probably true, probably not true, or definitely not true that Bill Clinton lied under oath about his sexual relationship with Monica Lewinsky to the grand jury in the Ken Starr investigation?

	Sept. 21, 1998	Sept. 20, 1998
Definitely true...............................	48%	47%
Probably true................................	33	40
Probably not true	10	5
Definitely not true........................	4	2
No opinion	5	6

If you were convinced that Bill Clinton lied under oath about his sexual relationship with Monica Lewinsky to the grand jury in the Ken Starr investigation, would you think Clinton should or should not be impeached and removed from office?

	Sept. 21, 1998	Sept. 20, 1998
Should be impeached and removed	40%	39%
Should not....................................	56	56
No opinion	4	5

As you may know, the videotape of Bill Clinton's testimony in the Starr investigation was released to the public today [September 21]. Thinking about both the release and the contents of the videotape and documents from the Starr investigation, has what you've seen or heard about these matters made you feel less favorably toward each of the following than you did before, or not:

Bill Clinton?

	Total	Watched Videotape Yes	Watched Videotape No
Yes, less favorably	41%	45%	36%

No 51   51   51
No opinion................. 8   4   13

The Republicans in Congress?

	Total	Watched Videotape Yes	Watched Videotape No
Yes, less favorably	37%	38%	34%
No	50	54	46
No opinion.................	13	8	20

Independent Counsel Kenneth Starr?

	Total	Watched Videotape Yes	Watched Videotape No
Yes, less favorably	45%	42%	48%
No	43	50	34
No opinion.................	12	8	18

Now thinking more generally about the current situation involving Bill Clinton, Monica Lewinsky, and the Starr investigation, whom do you blame more for the fact that things have gotten to the point they have—Bill Clinton, Ken Starr, or the Republicans in Congress?

	Total	Watched Videotape Yes	Watched Videotape No
Clinton	43%	50%	32%
Starr	32	27	40
Republicans	16	15	17
All equally (volunteered)	4	4	3
None; other (volunteered)	1	1	2
The media (volunteered)	1	1	2
No opinion.................	3	2	4

Would you say the current situation has gotten out of hand in a way that does great harm to the country, or do you think the current situation is not really that bad?

	Total	Watched Videotape Yes	Watched Videotape No
Gotten out of hand......	68%	70%	65%
Not really that bad	29	27	32
No opinion.................	3	3	3

Asked of those who saw the Clinton video-tape on television (59% of the sample): Based on what you heard or saw of the videotape, did you feel that the investigators treated Bill Clinton fairly or unfairly?

Fairly 70%
Unfairly 27
No opinion 3

Also asked of those who saw the Clinton videotape on television (59% of the sample): How do you think Bill Clinton appeared on the videotape—more as someone guilty of no crime who was wrongly accused of one, or more as someone who is guilty of a crime and trying to hide something?

As wrongly accused 26%
As trying to hide something 62
Other (volunteered) 7
No opinion 5

Thinking about your own definition of sexual relations, do you think two people have had sexual relations only if they have had sexual intercourse, or two people can have what you would define as sexual relations without having sexual intercourse?

| | Total | Watched Videotape | |
		Yes	No
Only if intercourse	20%	20%	21%
Without intercourse	73	75	69
No opinion	7	5	10

◆ ◆ ◆

Interviewing Dates: 9/23–24/98
CNN/*USA Today*/Gallup Poll
Survey #GO 124403

I'd like you to rate Bill Clinton on a scale. If you have a favorable opinion of Clinton, name a number between plus one and plus five, where plus five is the highest position, indicating you have a very favorable opinion of Clinton. If you have an unfavorable opinion, name a number between minus one and minus five, where minus five is the lowest po-

sition, indicating you have a very unfavorable opinion of him. How far up or down the scale would you rate Bill Clinton?

Plus five 14%
Plus four 17
Plus three 18
Plus two 8
Plus one 6
Minus one 4
Minus two... 5
Minus three 7
Minus four 4
Minus five... 16
No opinion 1

Total favorable: 63%
Total unfavorable: 36

Thinking about Bill Clinton as a person, do you have a positive or negative opinion of him?

Positive 38%
Negative.. 55
No opinion 7

Do you approve or disapprove of the way Bill Clinton has handled the controversy over Monica Lewinsky?

Approve 30%
Disapprove... 66
No opinion 4

What is your best guess about the future of Bill Clinton's presidency—do you think he will serve out the rest of his term in office, or he will leave office before the end of his term?

Serve out term 77%
Leave office.. 21
No opinion 2

How much confidence do you have in Congress to do what is best for the country concerning the Clinton-Lewinsky matter—a great deal, a fair amount, not much, or none at all?

Great deal	9%
Fair amount	46
Not much	32
None at all	11
No opinion	2

Asked of half sample: As a result of the Monica Lewinsky matter, are you now less likely to believe Bill Clinton when he speaks about public policy matters, or has the Lewinsky matter not affected you this way?

Less likely to believe Clinton	36%
Not affected you	62
No opinion	2

Asked of half sample: As a result of the Monica Lewinsky matter, are you now less likely to believe Bill Clinton when he speaks about his own personal conduct, or has the Lewinsky matter not affected you this way?

Less likely to believe Clinton	55%
Not affected you	43
No opinion	2

In order to form your own opinion about the impeachment of President Clinton, do you feel you have all the facts and information you need, or do you feel you need more facts and information in order to make up your mind?

Have facts you need	72%
Need more	20
Have too much information (volunteered)	7
No opinion	1

Thinking about all of the charges against Bill Clinton that Congress is investigating, do you think these charges represent private matters only, or do they concern the public as well?

Private matters	52%
Concern public	45
No opinion	3

Still thinking about the Clinton-Lewinsky investigation, if Bill Clinton's version of events and Ken Starr's version of events appear to conflict, whom would you tend to believe more—Bill Clinton, or Ken Starr?

Clinton	37%
Starr	47
Neither (volunteered)	11
No opinion	5

Do you believe that President Clinton did or did not commit perjury in his testimony about Monica Lewinsky before the grand jury?

Did	66%
Did not	25
No opinion	9

~

As I read a list of issues being discussed today, please tell me how important each of the following is to your vote for Congress in November—extremely important, very important, somewhat important, or not important:

Health care, including HMOs?

Extremely important	28%
Very important	43
Somewhat important	21
Not important	5
No opinion	3

Tax cuts?

Extremely important	21%
Very important	39
Somewhat important	29
Not important	9
No opinion	2

Social Security?

Extremely important	33%
Very important	42
Somewhat important	20
Not important	4
No opinion	1

How Congress should handle the Clinton investigation?

Extremely important	17%
Very important	27
Somewhat important	26
Not important	26
No opinion	4

Moral values in the country?

Extremely important	29%
Very important	36
Somewhat important	24
Not important	9
No opinion	2

~

As you may know, the videotape of Bill Clinton's testimony in the Starr investigation was released to the public this week. Did you, yourself, happen to see any of the Clinton videotape on television, or not?

	Sept. 23–24, 1998	Sept. 21, 1998
Yes	66%	59%
No	34	41

Asked of those who watched the videotape on television: Approximately how much of the four hours of that videotape have you seen— less than 5 minutes, 5 to less than 10 minutes, 10 to less than 30 minutes, 30 minutes to less than an hour, an hour or more, or all of it?

	Sept. 23–24, 1998	Sept. 21, 1998
Less than 5 minutes	6%	4%
5 to less than 10 minutes	11	8
10 to less than 30 minutes	18	19
30 minutes to less than an hour	19	19
An hour or more	32	38
All of it	14	12

As you may know, removing a president from office involves two major steps in Congress. First, the House of Representatives must decide whether there is enough evidence to bring a president to trial before the Senate;

this step is called impeachment. Next, the Senate must conduct a trial to determine whether or not the president's actions are serious enough to warrant his being removed from the presidency. Would you prefer that the House of Representatives votes to impeach Clinton and the Senate votes to remove him from office; the House of Representatives impeaches Clinton but the Senate votes to keep him in office; or the House of Representatives decides not to impeach Clinton?

	Total	Likely voters*
House votes to impeach and Senate to remove Clinton	25%	30%
House votes to impeach but Senate to keep Clinton	10	8
House decides not to impeach	61	59
Other (volunteered)	1	1
No opinion	3	2

*39% of the sample

Interviewing Dates: 9/30–10/1/98
CNN/*USA Today*/Gallup Poll
Survey #GO 124440

The questions in this survey deal with what life will be like in the future. For most of the questions, we will ask you to think about life in the year 2025—that is, about twenty-five years from now when today's children will be adults:

Overall, in the year 2025 do you think the quality of life for average Americans will be better or worse than it is today?

Better	53%
Worse	42
Same (volunteered)	3
No opinion	2

Now, thinking about various income groups, do you think the quality of life for each of the following will be better or worse in the year 2025 than it is today:

The poor?

Better	35%
Worse	56
Same (volunteered)	7
No opinion	2

The middle class?

Better	43%
Worse	40
Same (volunteered)	14
No opinion	3

The rich?

Better	69%
Worse	17
Same (volunteered)	11
No opinion	3

Next, I am going to mention some specific aspects of life. For each one, please say whether you expect conditions in that area to be better or worse in the year 2025 than they are today:

Race relations?

Better	66%
Worse	26
Same (volunteered)	6
No opinion	2

Moral values in society?

Better	31%
Worse	62
Same (volunteered)	5
No opinion	2

The availability of good medical care?

Better	66%
Worse	29
Same (volunteered)	3
No opinion	2

The threat of terrorism?

Better	23%
Worse	70
Same (volunteered)	4
No opinion	3

The crime rate?

Better	35%
Worse	57
Same (volunteered)	6
No opinion	2

The quality of the environment?

Better	40%
Worse	54
Same (volunteered)	4
No opinion	2

Thinking about some institutions in society, do you think each of the following will have a larger influence or smaller influence in the daily life of Americans in the year 2025 than it has today:

The federal government?

Larger influence	55%
Smaller influence	38
Same (volunteered)	4
No opinion	3

Local government?

Larger influence	54%
Smaller influence	38
Same (volunteered)	5
No opinion	3

Organized religion?

Larger influence	49%
Smaller influence	43
Same (volunteered)	5
No opinion	3

Still thinking about the year 2025, do you think it will be easier or harder for people to:

Raise children to be good people?

Easier	22%
Harder	71
Same (volunteered)	6
No opinion	1

Afford medical care?

Easier 34%
Harder 62
Same (volunteered) 3
No opinion 1

Find and keep a good job?

Easier 35%
Harder 59
Same (volunteered) 4
No opinion 2

Next, we have some questions about what family situations will be like twenty-five years from now:

By 2025 do you think there will be more families or fewer families where both parents are employed?

More families 69%
Fewer families 28
Same (volunteered) 2
No opinion 1

By 2025 do you think single-parent families will be more common or less common than they are today?

More common 71%
Less common 25
Same (volunteered) 2
No opinion 2

In 2025, that is, about twenty-five years from now, do you think there will be more or less of each of the following:

Personal freedom?

More 37%
Less 56
Same (volunteered) 5
No opinion 2

Personal privacy?

More 17%

Less 79
Same (volunteered) 3
No opinion 1

Personal economic security?

More 41%
Less 53
Same (volunteered) 4
No opinion 2

Health and physical well-being?

More 63%
Less 31
Same (volunteered) 3
No opinion 3

Which of the following events, if any, do you think will have occurred by 2025:

A worldwide collapse of the economy?

Yes, will have occurred 49%
Will not 48
No opinion 3

An environmental catastrophe?

Yes, will have occurred 66%
Will not 31
No opinion 3

The emergence of a deadly new disease?

Yes, will have occurred 76%
Will not 21
No opinion 3

A military strike or attack using nuclear weapons?

Yes, will have occurred 48%
Will not 49
No opinion 3

Just your best guess, do you think the United States will or will not be involved in a full-scale war by the year 2025?

Yes, will 51%
Will not 46
No opinion 3

Asked of those who replied in the affirmative: Which country do you think the United States is most likely to become involved with in a full-scale war?

China 17%
Iran 6
Iraq 17
Russia 10
Arab countries 4
Middle East 18
Other 12
No opinion 16

By 2025 do you think humans will have made or received contact with alien life forms?

Yes 26%
No 68
No opinion 6

Asked of those who replied in the affirmative: Just your best guess, do you think those aliens are more likely to be friendly or hostile to humans?

Friendly 78%
Hostile 17
No opinion 5

In the year 2025 do you think Americans will be more religious or less religious than they are today?

More religious 48%
Less religious 47
Same (volunteered) 4
No opinion 1

Next, as I describe some practices, please say whether you think each one will be commonplace in the year 2025, or not:

Illicit drug use, such as marijuana and cocaine?

Yes, commonplace 64%
No 34
No opinion 2

Gay marriage?

Yes, commonplace 74%
No 22
No opinion 4

Physician-assisted suicide?

Yes, commonplace 68%
No 30
No opinion 2

Cloning of humans?

Yes, commonplace 37%
No 59
No opinion 4

Now thinking about these same practices, do you think that in 2025 each one will generally be legal or not legal in the United States:

Illicit drug use, such as marijuana and cocaine?

Legal 32%
Not legal 66
No opinion 2

Gay marriage?

Legal 69%
Not legal 28
No opinion 3

Physician-assisted suicide?

Legal 60%
Not legal 39
No opinion 1

Cloning of humans?

Legal 29%
Not legal 68
No opinion 3

Thinking about the ethnic and racial makeup of Americans, do you think that by 2025 whites will still be in the majority in the United States, or will Hispanics and non-whites be in the majority?

Whites the majority 33%
Nonwhites the majority 60
No opinion 7

In the year 2025 do you think there will be more peace among nations or more conflict among nations than there is today?

More peace 41%
More conflict 52
Same (volunteered) 5
No opinion 2

Next, I'm going to read some things that might or might not happen in the future. For each one, please tell me whether or not you expect it to happen in the next twenty-five years, that is, by the year 2025:

Cancer will be cured?

Yes 59%
No 40
No opinion 1

AIDS will be cured?

Yes 60%
No 38
No opinion 2

Most people will do their jobs from home?

Yes 52%
No 47
No opinion 1

Most people will be self-employed rather than work for a company?

Yes 34%
No 65
No opinion 1

The country will have elected a woman president?

Yes 66%
No 32
No opinion 2

The country will have elected a black president?

Yes 69%
No 29
No opinion 2

Most stores will be replaced by shopping on the Internet?

Yes 56%
No 43
No opinion 1

Space travel will be common for ordinary Americans?

Yes 29%
No 69
No opinion 2

People will routinely live to be 100 years old?

Yes 61%
No 37
No opinion 2

Cars will largely be replaced by mass transportation?

Yes 38%
No 60
No opinion 2

Finally, we have a few questions about what might happen to the world in the next century, meaning in the next 100 years:

How likely is it that civilization as we know it will be destroyed by a nuclear or other man-made disaster within the next century—very

likely, somewhat likely, somewhat unlikely, or very unlikely?

Very likely 19%
Somewhat likely 32
Somewhat unlikely 22
Very unlikely 26
No opinion 1

How likely is it that the Earth will be destroyed by an asteroid, ozone layer problem, or other environmental disaster within the next century—very likely, somewhat likely, somewhat unlikely, or very unlikely?

Very likely 14%
Somewhat likely 24
Somewhat unlikely 23
Very unlikely 37
No opinion 2

How likely is it that the world will come to an end because of Judgment Day or another religious event in the next century—very likely, somewhat likely, somewhat unlikely, or very unlikely?

Very likely 23%
Somewhat likely 16
Somewhat unlikely 16
Very unlikely 41
No opinion 4

◆   ◆   ◆

Interviewing Dates: 10/6–7/98
CNN/*USA Today*/Gallup Poll
Survey #GO 124563

Now suppose that the House of Representatives does decide to begin formal hearings into whether or not Bill Clinton should be impeached. The first step would be to determine what charges to consider. Do you think the House Judiciary Committee should consider only the charges stemming from Clinton's relationship with Monica Lewinsky, or any

charges that members of Congress believe should be investigated?

Only relationship with Lewinsky 30%
Any charges 50
None; neither (volunteered)........................... 16
No opinion 4

Do you think that the House Judiciary Committee should agree to end the hearings by a specific date, or allow the hearings to continue as long as the committee believes it is necessary to do so?

End hearings 69%
Continue 24
None; neither (volunteered)........................... 5
No opinion 2

From what you have heard or read, do you think that Congress has or has not been conducting its review of the charges against Bill Clinton in a fair and impartial manner?

Yes, fair and impartial 44%
Not fair and impartial 50
No opinion 6

Asked of those who replied "not fair and impartial" (50% of the sample): Whom do you blame more for the process being unfair—the Republicans in Congress, or the Democrats in Congress?

Republicans 36%
Democrats.. 5
No opinion.. 9
                                             50%

Next, comparing the charges against Bill Clinton today with the charges against Richard Nixon in the Watergate controversy, which do you think are more serious—the charges against Nixon or the charges against Clinton, or do you think the charges against both men are about equally serious?

Charges against Nixon..................................... 64%
Charges against Clinton................................. 10
Equally serious 23
No opinion 3

♦ ♦ ♦

Interviewing Dates: 10/9–12/98
CNN/*USA Today*/Gallup Poll
Survey #GO 124591

As you may know, the House of Representatives voted on Thursday [October 8] to hold hearings into the charges against Bill Clinton, in order to determine whether or not he should be impeached. Do you favor or oppose the decision to hold these hearings?

Favor	48%
Oppose	49
No opinion	3

~

Which of the following statements comes closest to how the Clinton impeachment issue will affect your chances of voting in the congressional elections this fall—you feel so strongly about the impeachment issue that you are certain to vote; the impeachment issue will not affect your chances of voting; or you are so upset with the impeachment issue that you might not vote at all?

	Total	Likely voters*
Certain to vote	34%	40%
Not affect voting	52	57
Might not vote at all	12	2
No opinion	2	1

*39% of the sample

In terms of publicly stating whether they will vote for or against impeaching Bill Clinton, do you think candidates for Congress should state their position now, prior to the election; or should they wait to state their position until Congress conducts its own investigation after the election?

	Total	Likely voters
State position now	51%	50%
Wait until after election	45	48
No opinion	4	2

Do you think the Republican party or the Democratic party would do a better job of dealing with each of the following issues and problems:

Taxes?

Republican party	41%
Democratic party	46
Same (volunteered); no opinion	13

Education?

Republican party	32%
Democratic party	54
Same (volunteered); no opinion	14

The environment?

Republican party	27%
Democratic party	59
Same (volunteered); no opinion	14

Foreign affairs?

Republican party	42%
Democratic party	43
Same (volunteered); no opinion	15

The economy?

Republican party	40%
Democratic party	50
Same (volunteered); no opinion	10

Health care policy?

Republican party	31%
Democratic party	57
Same (volunteered); no opinion	12

Crime?

Republican party	43%
Democratic party	39
Same (volunteered); no opinion	18

Social Security?

Republican party	33%
Democratic party	54
Same (volunteered); no opinion	13

Moral values?

Republican party.. 46%
Democratic party 34
Same (volunteered); no opinion 20

Impeachment proceedings against Bill Clinton?

Republican party.. 43%
Democratic party 40
Same (volunteered); no opinion 17

Here are some issues now being discussed in Washington. For each one, please tell me how important it will be to you personally when you decide how to vote for your member of Congress in November—will it be the top priority for you when you make your vote decision, a high priority, a low priority, or not a priority at all:

Taxes?

Top priority.. 32%
High priority 51
Low priority 11
Not a priority 4
No opinion.. 2

Education?

Top priority.. 40%
High priority 51
Low priority 5
Not a priority 3
No opinion.. 1

The environment?

Top priority.. 26%
High priority 47
Low priority 22
Not a priority 3
No opinion.. 2

Foreign affairs?

Top priority.. 21%
High priority 42

Low priority.. 29
Not a priority 6
No opinion... 2

The economy?

Top priority.. 35%
High priority 55
Low priority 6
Not a priority 3
No opinion.. 1

Health care policy?

Top priority.. 34%
High priority 49
Low priority 12
Not a priority 4
No opinion.. 1

Crime?

Top priority.. 36%
High priority 50
Low priority 11
Not a priority 2
No opinion.. 1

Social Security?

Top priority.. 34%
High priority 50
Low priority 12
Not a priority 3
No opinion.. 1

Impeachment proceedings against Bill Clinton?

Top priority.. 18%
High priority 25
Low priority 34
Not a priority 21
No opinion.. 2

~

As you may know, Serbian forces are attacking ethnic Albanian towns in a province of

Yugoslavia called Kosovo. Overall, how closely have you followed the situation in Kosovo—very closely, fairly closely, not too closely, or not at all?

Very closely	11%
Fairly closely	31
Not too closely	35
Not at all	23
No opinion	*

*Less than 1%

Based on what you have read or heard, do you think the United States and its Western European allies should or should not conduct military air strikes against the Serbian forces in Kosovo?

Should	42%
Should not	41
No opinion	17

~

Do you think the state of Nevada should or should not reinstate the boxing license of former heavyweight champion Mike Tyson, who was suspended from boxing last year?

Should	23%
Should not	70
No opinion	7

Do you think that boxer Mike Tyson should or should not be banned from professional boxing for the rest of his life?

Should	54%
Should not	40
No opinion	6

~

Are you a fan of professional baseball, or not?

Yes	47%
No	39
Somewhat of a fan (volunteered)	14

Asked of baseball fans: Who would you, yourself, say is the greatest baseball player in the game today?

Mark McGwire	36%
Sammy Sosa	11
Ken Griffey, Jr.	8
Cal Ripken, Jr.	6
Greg Maddux	2
Barry Bonds	1
Roger Clemens	1
Tony Gwynn	1
Randy Johnson	1
Mo Vaughn	1
Other	10
No opinion	22

~

Are you a fan of professional basketball, or not?

Yes	36%
No	54
Somewhat of a fan (volunteered)	10

Asked of basketball fans: As you know, there is currently a dispute between the professional basketball players' union and the owners which could lead to the cancellation of some regular season games. Which side in this dispute do you favor—the owners or the players?

Owners	36%
Players	44
Both sides (volunteered)	1
Neither (volunteered)	10
No opinion	9

Also asked of basketball fans: Who do you think are more concerned about the interests of the fans—the players or the owners, or are neither concerned?

Players	27%
Owners	13
Neither	57
Both (volunteered)	*
No opinion	3

*Less than 1%

Interviewing Dates: 10/23–25/98
CNN/*USA Today*/Gallup Poll
Survey #GO 124708

♦ ♦ ♦

Do you think the policies being proposed by President Clinton would move the country in the right direction or in the wrong direction?

Right direction 70%
Wrong direction 22
No opinion 8

~

Do you think the country would be better off if the Republicans controlled Congress, if the Democrats controlled Congress, or would the country be the same regardless of which party controlled Congress?

Republicans 24%
Democrats 22
The same regardless 48
No opinion 6

Compared to previous congressional elections, are you more enthusiastic about voting than usual, or less enthusiastic?

More enthusiastic 35%
Less enthusiastic 47
Same (volunteered) 16
No opinion 2

What effect, if any, will the Monica Lewinsky matter have on your vote for Congress in November—will your vote for a candidate be made in order to send a message that you support Bill Clinton, be made in order to send a message that you oppose Bill Clinton, or will you not be sending a message about Bill Clinton with your vote?

Message supporting Clinton 23%
Message opposing Clinton 19
Not sending message 52
Don't plan to vote (volunteered) 4
No opinion 2

Are you generally satisfied or dissatisfied with the way the candidates running in your area have conducted their campaigns this year?

Satisfied 52%
Dissatisfied 40
Mixed (volunteered) 2
No opinion 6

Overall, how negative would you say the tone of the campaigns in your area has been this year—extremely negative, very negative, moderately negative, only a little negative, or not at all negative?

Extremely negative 12%
Very negative 15
Moderately negative 39
Only a little negative 22
Not at all negative 8
No opinion 4

~

Asked of Republicans and those leaning Republican: I'm going to read a list of people who may be running in the Republican primary for president in the next election. After I read all the names, please tell me which of those candidates you would be most likely to support for the Republican nomination for president in the year 2000. And who would be your second choice?

	1st and 2d choices combined
Lamar Alexander	10%
John Ashcroft	7
George W. Bush	59
Elizabeth Dole	40
Steve Forbes	16
Newt Gingrich	12
John Kasich	9
Dan Quayle	22
Other (volunteered)	2
None; wouldn't vote (volunteered)	2
No opinion	6

Asked of Democrats: Next, I'm going to read a list of people who may be running in the Democratic primary for president in the next election. After I read all the names, please

tell me which of those candidates you would be most likely to support for the Democratic nomination for president in the year 2000. And who would be your second choice?

	1st and 2d choices combined
Bill Bradley	26%
Dick Gephardt	28
Al Gore	63
Jesse Jackson	23
Bob Kerrey	13
John Kerry	12
Paul Wellstone	4
Other (volunteered)	1
None; wouldn't vote (volunteered)	1
No opinion	8

Suppose the year 2000 presidential election were being held today. If Vice President Al Gore were the Democratic party's candidate and Texas Governor George W. Bush, the son of former president George Bush, were the Republican party's candidate, whom would you be more likely to vote for—Al Gore, the Democrat; or George W. Bush, the Republican? [Those who were undecided were asked: As of today, do you lean more toward Al Gore, the Democrat; or George W. Bush, the Republican?]

Al Gore	39%
George W. Bush	57
No opinion	4

~

Do you approve or disapprove of President Clinton's handling of the recent Middle East peace talks?

Approve	78%
Disapprove	12
Not familiar with talks (volunteered)	8
No opinion	2

~

Do you approve or disapprove of the federal budget that was passed by Congress last week?

Approve	50%
Disapprove	25
Not familiar with budget (volunteered)	21
No opinion	4

~

How would you prefer to see Paula Jones's sexual harassment lawsuit against Bill Clinton resolved—for the case to be resolved in court either by a judge's decision or through a trial; or for the case to be resolved in an out-of-court settlement in which Clinton would pay Paula Jones a significant sum of money and in exchange Jones would drop her lawsuit?

In court	45%
In out-of-court settlement	45
Neither; other (volunteered)	7
No opinion	3

~

Is there more crime in your area now than there was a year ago, or less?

More	31%
Less	48
Same (volunteered)	16
No opinion	5

Is there more crime in the United States now than there was a year ago, or less?

More	52%
Less	35
Same (volunteered)	8
No opinion	5

Thinking back further, is there more crime in your neighborhood now than there was five years ago, or less?

More	39%
Less	42
Same (volunteered)	9
No opinion	10

Is there more crime in the United States now than there was five years ago, or less?

More 56%
Less... 35
Same (volunteered)... 4
No opinion.. 5

Thinking about the media, from what you can tell, do television news and entertainment programs show more crime and violence now than they did five years ago, or do they show less crime and violence?

More 82%
Less... 11
Same (volunteered)... 5
No opinion.. 2

◆   ◆   ◆

Interviewing Dates: 10/29–11/1/98
CNN/*USA Today*/Gallup Poll
Survey #GO 124709

Do you think Congress should or should not impeach Bill Clinton and remove him from office?

Should impeach and remove him 27%
Should not 67
No opinion.. 6

Do you think Bill Clinton should or should not resign from office?

Should resign... 36%
Should not 61
No opinion.. 3

Do you think Congress should or should not censure Bill Clinton?

Should censure 40%
Should not 49
No opinion.. 11

~

Looking ahead for the next few years, which political party do you think would be more

likely to keep the United States out of war— the Republican party, or the Democratic party?

	Total	Likely voters
Republican party...........................	31%	37%
Democratic party	44	39
No difference (volunteered); no opinion..................................	25	24

Looking ahead for the next few years, which political party do you think will do a better job of keeping the country prosperous—the Republican party, or the Democratic party?

	Total	Likely voters
Republican party...........................	37%	42%
Democratic party	46	44
No difference (volunteered); no opinion..................................	17	14

~

Some people think that the government is trying to do too many things that should be left to individuals and businesses. Others think that the government should do more to solve our country's problems. Which comes closer to your own view?

	Total	Likely voters
Doing too many things	51%	58%
Should do more.............................	39	32
Mixed (volunteered); no opinion ...	10	10

Some people think that the government should promote traditional values in our society. Others think that the government should not favor any particular set of values. Which comes closer to your own view?

	Total	Likely voters
Should promote traditional values..	56%	59%
Should not favor any particular set	37	35
No opinion	7	6

In your opinion, is the federal government in Washington an immediate threat to the rights and freedoms of ordinary citizens like yourself, or not?

	Total	Likely voters
Yes, threat	26%	25%
No	69	71
No opinion	5	4

We have a few questions about NASA, the U.S. space agency. Do you approve or disapprove of NASA sending U.S. Senator John Glenn, a former astronaut, back into space this week on a space shuttle mission?

Approve	77%
Disapprove	16
No opinion	7

Do you think that NASA is sending John Glenn back into space mostly for the scientific value of conducting tests on human aging, mostly for the positive publicity created by his mission, or mostly as a political reward to Glenn for supporting the president?

Scientific value	35%
Positive publicity	45
Political reward	9
All equally (volunteered)	5
None; other (volunteered)	1
No opinion	5

In your view, is John Glenn too old to return to space on a shuttle mission, or not?

Yes, too old	15%
No	82
No opinion	3

◆ ◆ ◆

Interviewing Date: 11/2/98
CNN/*USA Today*/Gallup Poll
Survey #GO 124709

How much thought have you given to the upcoming elections—quite a lot, or only a little?

Quite a lot; some (volunteered)	52%
Only a little; none (volunteered)	48

Do you happen to know where people who live in your neighborhood go to vote?

Yes	73%
No	27

Have you ever voted in this precinct or election district?

Yes	65%
No	35

How often would you say you vote—always, nearly always, part of the time, or seldom?

Always	40%
Nearly always	26
Part of the time	16
Seldom; never (volunteered)	18

Do you, yourself, plan to vote in the election tomorrow, or not?

Yes	71%
No	25
Not sure (volunteered)	4

How certain are you that you will vote—absolutely certain, fairly certain, or not certain?

Absolutely certain	58%
Fairly certain	11
Not certain	2
Will not vote; unsure (volunteered)	29

Interviewing Dates: 11/13–15/98
CNN/*USA Today*/Gallup Poll
Survey #GO 124941

Just your impression, do you think the Starr report is a fair and accurate account of Bill Clinton's actions, or do you think it is an unfair and distorted account of Clinton's actions?

Fair and accurate	41%
Unfair and distorted	48
Other (volunteered)	3
No opinion	8

As you may know, the House of Representatives will hold hearings into the charges against Bill Clinton, in order to determine whether or not he should be impeached. Do you strongly approve, moderately approve, moderately disapprove, or strongly disapprove of the decision to hold these hearings?

Strongly approve 22%
Moderately approve.. 18
Moderately disapprove................................... 24
Strongly disapprove....................................... 35
No opinion.. 1

Assuming that the House Judiciary Committee holds hearings into the Clinton matter as scheduled, how important is it to you that the House of Representatives completes all action related to this matter by the end of this year—very important, moderately important, not too important, or not important at all?

Very important 58%
Moderately important..................................... 15
Not too important 12
Not important at all.. 14
No opinion.. 1

As you may know, a former White House employee named Linda Tripp secretly tape-recorded conversations she had with Monica Lewinsky in which Lewinsky allegedly discussed her relationship with Bill Clinton. Which comes closer to your opinion about those tapes—the tapes might be important evidence in these matters, and the public should eventually hear them; or the tapes recorded private conversations about a private matter and should not be made public no matter how important they might be as evidence?

Important evidence.. 25%
Private matter 72
Neither; other (volunteered) 2
No opinion.. 1

~

Do you think the policies being proposed by the Republican leaders in the U.S. House and Senate would move the country in the right direction, or in the wrong direction?

Right direction.. 43%
Wrong direction.. 40
No opinion.. 17

Do you think the Republican leaders in the U.S. House and Senate should promote policies that are more conservative or more moderate than the ones they promote now?

More conservative 36%
More moderate 55
No opinion.. 9

In general, do you think the political views of the Republican party are too conservative, too liberal, or about right?

Too conservative 39%
Too liberal 15
About right 41
No opinion.. 5

In general, do you think the political views of the Democratic party are too conservative, too liberal, or about right?

Too conservative 9%
Too liberal 37
About right 50
No opinion.. 4

Do you think the political views of the Republicans in Congress are too extreme or not too extreme?

Too extreme.. 47%
Not too extreme.. 48
No opinion.. 5

Do you think the political views of the Democrats in Congress are too extreme or not too extreme?

Too extreme.. 32%
Not too extreme.. 63
No opinion.. 5

In general, do you think the Republicans in Congress are too partisan and unwilling to compromise, or would you not describe them that way?

Too partisan... 56%
Not too partisan 40
No opinion... 4

In general, do you think the Democrats in Congress are too partisan and unwilling to compromise, or would you not describe them that way?

Too partisan... 40%
Not too partisan 56
No opinion... 4

In general, do you think the Republican party favors the rich, favors the middle class, or favors the poor?

Favors rich... 67%
Favors middle class 24
Favors poor.. 2
Favors none; all equally (volunteered).......... 4
No opinion... 3

In general, do you think the Democratic party favors the rich, favors the middle class, or favors the poor?

Favors rich... 20%
Favors middle class 43
Favors poor.. 28
Favors none; all equally (volunteered).......... 4
No opinion... 5

Thinking about their policies toward the government, do you think the Republican party wants the government to do too much, too little, or about the right amount?

Too much.. 31%
Too little 29
About right 36
No opinion... 4

Thinking about their policies toward the government, do you think the Democratic party wants the government to do too much, too little, or about the right amount?

Too much.. 39%

Too little 15
About right 43
No opinion... 3

All in all, do you think it is good or bad for the country that Speaker of the House Newt Gingrich has decided to step down and resign from Congress?

Good.. 67%
Bad... 21
No opinion... 12

Still thinking about this matter, would you like to see the Republicans in Congress elect leaders who will be more likely or less likely than Newt Gingrich was to compromise with Clinton and the Democrats?

More likely 65%
Less likely.. 27
Same (volunteered)... 2
No opinion... 6

~

In the last year or so, who would you say has been the winner in the confrontations between Iraq and the United States—Bill Clinton, or Saddam Hussein?

Bill Clinton... 37%
Saddam Hussein 53
Both equally (volunteered).............................. 2
Neither (volunteered) 6
No opinion... 2

Thinking about the U.S. missile attacks against Iraq which have occurred since the Gulf War, do you think those attacks have or have not achieved significant goals for the United States?

Have... 30%
Have not 66
No opinion... 4

If the United States attacks Iraq in the next few days, do you think those attacks will or

will not achieve significant goals for the United States?

Will 48%
Will not 42
No opinion 10

Which one of the following possible goals do you think should be the specific goal of any U.S. attack on Iraq at this time—to pressure Iraq into complying with United Nations weapons inspections, or to remove Saddam Hussein from power?

Pressure Iraq 25%
Remove Saddam 70
Other (volunteered) 3
No opinion 2

~

Do you use a personal computer on a regular basis, either at home, work, or school, or not?

Yes 56%
No 44

Thinking about Microsoft, the computer software company that produces Windows 95 and other products—do you have a favorable or unfavorable opinion of the Microsoft Corporation?

	Total	Computer users
Favorable	55%	69%
Unfavorable	17	17
No opinion	28	14

Now thinking about Bill Gates, the founder and CEO of Microsoft—do you have a favorable or unfavorable opinion of Bill Gates?

Favorable 56%
Unfavorable 18
Neutral; neither (volunteered) 16
Mixed (volunteered) 1
No opinion 6
Never heard of 3

As you may know, a lawsuit by the Justice Department against Microsoft is currently being tried in court. Based on what you know about the case, do you side more with the Justice Department or more with the Microsoft Corporation?

Justice Department 28%
Microsoft Corporation 44
Both; mixed (volunteered) 1
Neither (volunteered) 7
No opinion 20

~

Thinking about the new twenty-dollar bill, do you hate, dislike, like, or love the new bill?

Hate 12%
Dislike 23
Like 49
Love 6
Haven't seen it (volunteered) 3
No opinion 7

Do you agree or disagree with the following statements about the new twenty-dollar bill:

You wish they would go back to printing the old bill?

Agree 39%
Disagree 54
No opinion 7

You think the new bill doesn't look like real American money?

Agree 61%
Disagree 35
No opinion 4

~

As you may know, Monica Lewinsky's voice has not been broadcast by the media so far or heard by most Americans. Just your best guess, what do you think her voice probably sounds like—soft and sexy, high and childish, or deep and serious?

Soft and sexy 20%
High and childish 53

Deep and serious 17
Other (volunteered) 2
No opinion 8

◆　◆　◆

Interviewing Date: 11/19/98
CNN/*USA Today*/Gallup Poll
Survey #GO 124987

As you may know, Independent Counsel Ken Starr testified today [November 19] before the congressional committee investigating whether Bill Clinton should be impeached. Did you happen to see any coverage of those hearings on television today, or not? [Asked of those who replied in the negative: Have you heard or read anything today about what happened in today's hearings, or not?]

Saw on television 38%
Heard or read about hearings 6
No, not heard or read anything 56

Asked of those who have seen, heard, or read about today's hearings: Based on what you have heard about Ken Starr's testimony today, do you think it was a fair and accurate account of Clinton's actions, or do you think it was an unfair and distorted account of Clinton's actions?

Fair and accurate 46%
Unfair and distorted 41
Other (volunteered) 2
No opinion 11

Also asked of the aware group: Regardless of how you feel about him personally, how would you rate the job Ken Starr did today in presenting and defending his report to Congress—excellent, good, not so good, or poor?

Excellent 26%
Good 41
Not so good 9
Poor 12
No opinion 12

Also asked of the aware group: As a result of today's impeachment hearings, do you have more confidence or less confidence in the impeachment process in Congress?

More confidence 32%
Less confidence 42
No change (volunteered) 16
No opinion 10

Also asked of the aware group: From what you saw or heard of today's hearings, do you think today's hearings did or did not accomplish something worthwhile?

Yes, did accomplish 43%
Did not 49
No opinion 8

◆　◆　◆

Interviewing Dates: 11/20–22/98
CNN/*USA Today*/Gallup Poll
Survey #GO 124977

In determining what course of action to take in the Clinton investigation, Congress may face three major choices in the near future. As I read those choices, please tell me which you would prefer it take—Congress should continue to hold hearings on whether to impeach Bill Clinton; Congress should vote to censure Clinton and allow him to serve out his remaining two years in office, and stop holding hearings; or Congress should not hold hearings or censure Clinton, and should drop the matter altogether?

Continue hearings 29%
Censure Clinton 31
Drop matter 38
No opinion 2

Do you approve or disapprove of the way Independent Counsel Kenneth Starr is handling the current investigation into the charges against Bill Clinton?

Approve 36%
Disapprove 59
No opinion 5

I'm going to describe some allegations being made about Bill Clinton. As I read each one, please say whether you think it is definitely true, probably true, probably not true, or definitely not true:

The allegation that Bill Clinton lied under oath while president?

Definitely true	47%
Probably true	42
Probably not true	6
Definitely not true	2
No opinion	3

The allegation that Bill Clinton participated in an effort to obstruct justice while president?

Definitely true	28%
Probably true	31
Probably not true	24
Definitely not true	12
No opinion	5

As you may know, Independent Counsel Ken Starr testified on Thursday [November 19] before the congressional committee investigating whether Bill Clinton should be impeached. From what you saw or heard of that hearing, do you think that hearing did or did not accomplish something worthwhile?

Yes, did accomplish	27%
Did not	52
No opinion	21

What do you think the House Judiciary Committee should do now that they have heard testimony from Ken Starr—call other witnesses and investigate the matter more thoroughly, or wrap up the hearings and vote now on whether Clinton should be impeached?

Call other witnesses	25%
Wrap up hearings	68
Other (volunteered)	3
No opinion	4

From what you know about the way Ken Starr conducted his investigation into the Clinton-Lewinsky matter, do you think Starr acted more like a prosecutor or more like a persecutor?

Prosecutor	39%
Persecutor	53
Neither; other (volunteered)	1
Both (volunteered)	1
No opinion	6

As you may know, it was announced that a book by Monica Lewinsky will be published early next year. Would you personally be interested in reading that book when it comes out, or not?

Yes	7%
No	93
No opinion	*

*Less than 1%

Also, Monica Lewinsky will be interviewed on television by Barbara Walters early next year. Would you personally be interested in watching that television interview, or not?

Yes	37%
No	62
No opinion	1

~

Looking ahead, what would you say should be the number one priority for Congress next year?

Education	10%
Social Security	10
Leave president alone; return to government; settle this matter; get country back on track	9
Taxes	6
Health care	6
Budget	5
Economy	5
Middle East crisis	2
Do their jobs; listen to the people	2
Crime	1
Elderly	1
Medicare; Medicaid	1
Jobs; employment	1

Impeach Clinton 1
Homelessness; hunger 1
Focus on America; domestic issues 1
Morality; ethics............................... 1
Welfare reform 1
Y2K computer problem..................... *
Family issues.................................... *
Gun control..................................... *
Inflation .... *
National security............................ *
Other (volunteered) 18
Nothing (volunteered) 2
Everything (volunteered)............... *
No opinion...................................... 16

*Less than 1%

~

There is much discussion as to the amount of money the government in Washington should spend for national defense and military purposes. How do you feel about this—do you think we are spending too little, about the right amount, or too much?

Too little 26%
About right 45
Too much.. 22
No opinion...................................... 7

Now, I'm going to ask you about the three major branches of the military—the Army, the Air Force, and the Navy. Would you be willing to pay more money in taxes to support a larger Army?

Yes... 45%
No 52
No opinion...................................... 3

Would you be willing to pay more money in taxes to support a larger Air Force?

Yes... 52%
No 45
No opinion...................................... 3

Would you be willing to pay more money in taxes to support a larger Navy?

Yes... 45%
No 51
No opinion...................................... 4

Which branch of the armed services do you think should be built up to a greater extent— the Army, the Air Force, or the Navy?

Army... 20%
Air Force... 43
Navy 17
Other; none (volunteered) 11
No opinion...................................... 9

I am going to ask you several additional questions about government spending. In answering, please bear in mind that sooner or later all government spending has to be taken care of out of the taxes that you and other Americans pay. As I mention each program, tell me whether the amount of money now being spent for that purpose should be increased, kept at the present level, reduced, or ended altogether:

The U.S. space program?

Increased... 21%
Kept at present level 47
Reduced.. 26
Ended altogether............................. 4
No opinion...................................... 2

Improving medical and health care for Americans generally?

Increased... 77%
Kept at present level 16
Reduced.. 4
Ended altogether............................. 1
No opinion...................................... 2

Providing food programs for low-income families?

Increased... 44%
Kept at present level 42
Reduced.. 10
Ended altogether............................. 2
No opinion...................................... 2

Improving the quality of public education?

Increased	77%
Kept at present level	15
Reduced	5
Ended altogether	2
No opinion	1

~

What is your favorite way of spending an evening?*

Watching television	31%
Being with family, husband, wife	20
Reading	18
Dining out	15
Going to movies or theater	11
Resting, relaxing	10
Watching movies at home	7
Visiting friends or relatives	6
Entertaining friends or relatives	5
Listening to music	4
Going to bars; drinking	3
Using, working on computer or Internet	3
Staying at home	3
Playing cards, Scrabble, games, etc.	2
Participating in sports	2
Dancing	2
Going to church or club meetings	1
Sewing, knitting, crocheting	1
Household chores; cleaning house; ironing	1
Indoor hobbies (general)	1
Working	1
In-home workshop, home repair	**
Other (volunteered)	22
Nothing (volunteered)	**
No opinion	**

*Total may add to more than 100% due to multiple replies.
**Less than 1%

~

What is your favorite sport to watch?

Football	36%
Baseball	16
Basketball	12
Ice hockey	3
Golf	3
Ice skating; figure skating	3
Tennis	2
Auto racing	2
Soccer	2
Boxing	1
Bowling	1
Wrestling	1
Fishing	1
Gymnastics	1
Horse racing	*
Other (volunteered)	6
None (volunteered)	9
No opinion	1

*Less than 1%

~

What is your opinion about a married person having sexual relations with someone other than their marriage partner—is it always wrong, almost always wrong, wrong only sometimes, or not wrong at all?

Always wrong	76%
Almost always wrong	15
Wrong only sometimes	6
Not wrong at all	1
No opinion	2

There is a lot of discussion about the way morals and sexual attitudes are changing in this country. What is your opinion about this—do you think it is wrong for a man and a woman to have sexual relations before marriage, or not?

Yes, wrong	40%
Not wrong	56
No opinion	4

~

Everybody has fears about different things, but some are more afraid of certain things

than others. I'm going to read a list of some of these fears. For each one, please tell me whether you are afraid of it, or not:

	Afraid	Not afraid*
Snakes	56%	44%
Public speaking in front of an audience	45	54
Heights	41	59
Being closed in a small space	36	64
Spiders and insects	34	65
Mice	26	74
Needles and getting shots	21	79
Flying on an airplane	20	77
Thunder and lightning	17	83
Going to the doctor	12	88
Crowds	11	88
Dogs	10	90
The dark	8	92

*"No opinion"—at 3% or less—is omitted.

~

If you could live anywhere in the United States that you wanted to, would you prefer a city, suburban area, small town, or farm?

City	15%
Suburban area	25
Small town	36
Farm	24
No opinion	*

*Less than 1%

~

Asked of half sample: Can you imagine a situation where it would be all right for you to lie to someone who is close to you, either a family member or friend, or do you think it would always be wrong to lie to them?

Yes, all right	45%
Always wrong	54
No opinion	1

Asked of half sample: Can you imaging a situation where it would be all right for you to lie to someone who is not close to you, someone at work or in a business or store, or do you think it would always be wrong to lie to them?

Yes, all right	40%
Always wrong	57
No opinion	3

~

Suppose a young man came to you for advice on choosing a line of work or career. What kind of work or career would you recommend?

Computers	19%
Doctor; medical field	8
Military	2
Teaching	4
Business; self-employed; sales	7
Something he likes; it depends on the person; finish school	15
Lawyer; attorney	3
Police officer	1
Technology	3
Engineering	2
Something with people; helping others; social work	1
Government career	–
Clergyman	–
Banker	–
Dentist	–
Veterinarian	–
Other (volunteered)	20
Nothing (volunteered)	2
Anything (volunteered)	3
No opinion	10

Suppose a young woman came to you for advice on choosing a line of work or career. What kind of work or career would you recommend?

Computers	16%
Doctor; medical field	11
Nursing	4
Teaching	7
Business; self-employed; sales	5

Something she likes; it depends on
the person; finish school............................. 15
Lawyer; attorney... 2
Technology.. 2
Engineering 1
Something with people; helping
others; social work.................................. 2
Stay home; homemaker; wife, mother 2
Secretary; clerical 3
Actress .... –
Airline stewardess .... –
Beautician.. –
Department store sales clerk......................... –
Dietician; home economics .... –
Dressmaker; fashion .... –
Journalism .... –
Librarian .... –
Modeling .... –
Musician .... –
Other (volunteered) 14
Nothing (volunteered) 2
Anything (volunteered) 3
No opinion.. 11

~

*Please tell me how much you agree or dis-
agree with this statement: "There are clear
guidelines about what's good or evil that apply
to everyone regardless of their situation." Do
you completely agree, mostly agree, mostly
disagree, or completely disagree?*

Completely agree... 37%
Mostly agree... 46
Mostly disagree 12
Completely disagree 4
No opinion.. 1

*How much have you thought about each of
the following during the past two years—a
lot, a fair amount, only a little, or not at all:*

Your relation to God?

A lot.. 58%
Fair amount... 21
Only a little.. 14
Not at all 6
No opinion.. 1

Living a worthwhile life?

A lot.. 73%
Fair amount... 17
Only a little.. 6
Not at all 3
No opinion.. 1

Developing your faith?

A lot.. 50%
Fair amount... 21
Only a little.. 19
Not at all 8
No opinion.. 2

The basic meaning and value of your life?

A lot.. 69%
Fair amount... 20
Only a little.. 8
Not at all 3
No opinion.. *

*Less than 1%

*Do you rely more on yourself to solve the
problems of life, or more on an outside
power, such as God?*

More on oneself.. 54%
More on outside power.................................. 35
Both (volunteered).. 9
No opinion.. 2

*Did you receive any religious training as a
child?*

Yes.. 79%
No 21

*Would you want a child of yours to receive
any religious training?*

Yes.. 89%
No 9
No opinion.. 2

*Do you feel the need to experience spiritual
growth?*

Yes.. 82%
No 17
No opinion.. 1

◆ ◆ ◆

Interviewing Dates: 12/4–6/98
CNN/*USA Today*/Gallup Poll
Survey #GO 125317

In your opinion, which of the following will be the biggest threat to the country in the future—big business, big labor, or big government?

Big business.. 24%
Big labor 7
Big government 64
No opinion... 5

~

In the Middle East conflict, do you think the United States should take Israel's side, take the Palestinians' side, or not take either side?

Israel's side.. 17%
Palestinians' side 2
Not take either side....................................... 74
No opinion... 7

In the Middle East situation, are your sympathies more with the Israelis or more with the Palestinian Arabs?

Israelis 46%
Palestinian Arabs... 13
Both; neither (volunteered) 27
No opinion... 14

Do you think there will or will not come a time when Israel and the Arab nations will be able to settle their differences and live in peace?

Will... 40%
Will not... 56
No opinion... 4

~

Which of these statements do you think best describes the Social Security system today— the Social Security system is in a state of crisis, it has major problems, it has minor problems, or it does not have any problems?

State of crisis 15%
Major problems 55
Minor problems 23
No problems 5
No opinion... 2

In your view, which party would do a better job dealing with the issue of Social Security— the Republican party, or the Democratic party?

Republican party.. 33%
Democratic party 48
Same; neither (volunteered) 11
No opinion... 8

How much confidence do you have that President Clinton and Congress will be able to solve the financial problems facing Social Security—a great deal, a moderate amount, not very much, or none at all?

Great deal 17%
Moderate amount... 41
Not very much 28
None at all 13
No opinion... 1

Next, I'm going to read a few changes that have been proposed as ways to keep the Social Security system operating in the next century. Please say whether you approve or disapprove of each one:

Increase the amount employers and employees pay into the system each month?

Approve... 46%
Disapprove... 50
No opinion... 4

Allow the federal government to invest a portion of the Social Security Trust Fund in the stock market?

Approve... 33%
Disapprove... 65
No opinion... 2

Allow individuals to invest a portion of their Social Security savings in the stock market?

Approve	64%
Disapprove	33
No opinion	3

Gradually increase the age at which people become eligible to receive Social Security benefits?

Approve	35%
Disapprove	64
No opinion	1

Reduce Social Security benefits?

Approve	11%
Disapprove	87
No opinion	2

~

How often do you read the Bible?

Daily or more often	14%
Weekly	18
Monthly	18
Less than monthly	20
Rarely or never	27
No opinion	3

Asked of those who have read the Bible: Where do you do most of your reading of the Bible—alone, in a small group, or in a larger group such as a church congregation?

Alone	66%
In a small group	9
In a larger group	24
No opinion	1

Also asked of those who have read the Bible: To what extent—a great deal, somewhat, hardly at all, or not at all—has your reading of the Bible affected you in each of the following ways:

Has helped me to be more open and honest about myself?

Great deal	65%
Somewhat	25
Hardly at all	5
Not at all	4
No opinion	1

Has given me a new depth of love toward other people?

Great deal	61%
Somewhat	28
Hardly at all	4
Not at all	5
No opinion	2

Has helped me feel closer to God?

Great deal	74%
Somewhat	19
Hardly at all	3
Not at all	3
No opinion	1

Has led to the Bible being more meaningful in my life?

Great deal	68%
Somewhat	24
Hardly at all	4
Not at all	4
No opinion	*

*Less than 1%

Has helped me feel at peace?

Great deal	66%
Somewhat	26
Hardly at all	4
Not at all	3
No opinion	1

Has helped me find meaning in life?

Great deal	62%
Somewhat	28
Hardly at all	5
Not at all	4
No opinion	1

Has strengthened me to stand up against wrongs in society?

Great deal	62%
Somewhat	27
Hardly at all	5
Not at all	5
No opinion	1

How important would you say religion is in your own life—very important, fairly important, or not very important?

Very important	61%
Fairly important	25
Not very important	13
No opinion	1

Do you happen to be a member of a church or synagogue?

Yes	67%
No	33

Did you, yourself, happen to attend church or synagogue in the last seven days, or not?

Yes	42%
No	58

How often do you attend church or synagogue—at least once a week, almost every week, about once a month, seldom, or never?

At least once a week	35%
Almost every week	11
About once a month	15
Seldom	27
Never	11
No opinion	1

Would you describe yourself as "born again" or evangelical?

Yes	48%
No	46
No opinion	6

◆   ◆   ◆

Interviewing Date: 12/9/98
CNN/*USA Today*/Gallup Poll
Survey #GO 125379

In addition to a vote on impeachment, the House Judiciary Committee may also consider a resolution to censure Bill Clinton, that is, express formal disapproval of his actions. In your view, should the House Judiciary Committee vote for or against censure?

Vote for	55%
Vote against	38
No opinion	7

Next, we'd like you to think ahead to the actions the full House of Representatives might take after the Judiciary Committee has voted. Would you, personally, be angry or not angry if the full House of Representatives:

Votes to impeach Bill Clinton and send the matter to the Senate for trial?

		Impeachment View	
	Total	For	Against
Angry	47%	12%	70%
Not angry	50	88	26
No opinion	3	–	4

Votes to censure Bill Clinton but not impeach him?

		Impeachment View	
	Total	For	Against
Angry	29%	52%	16%
Not angry	68	44	81
No opinion	3	4	3

Votes against both impeachment and censure, and therefore takes no formal action against Bill Clinton?

		Impeachment View	
	Total	For	Against
Angry	42%	80%	22%
Not angry	54	19	73
No opinion	4	1	5

◆   ◆   ◆

Interviewing Date: 12/10/98
CNN/*USA Today*/Gallup Poll
Survey #GO 125380

I am going to read you four charges that have been made against Bill Clinton related to the current impeachment hearings. Regardless of whether you think Clinton should be impeached on any of the charges, please indicate if you think the charge against Clinton is or is not true:

The charge that Clinton committed perjury by providing false and misleading testimony to Ken Starr's grand jury?

True 71%
Not true...................................... 23
No opinion.................................... 6

The charge that Clinton committed perjury by providing false and misleading testimony as part of the Paula Jones lawsuit?

True 64%
Not true...................................... 27
No opinion.................................... 9

The charge that Clinton obstructed justice by trying to influence the testimony of Monica Lewinsky, his secretary, and others in the Paula Jones lawsuit?

True 50%
Not true...................................... 43
No opinion.................................... 7

The charge that Clinton misused and abused his office and impaired the administration of justice by making false and misleading statements to the public, his aides, and Congress?

True 63%
Not true...................................... 35
No opinion.................................... 2

Now, for each of those charges, I would like you to tell me whether you think that the offense is serious enough, if you were convinced that Bill Clinton had actually behaved in that way, to justify impeachment by the House and a trial by the Senate, or if you think the offense is not serious enough to justify impeachment:

The charge that Clinton committed perjury by providing false and misleading testimony to Ken Starr's grand jury?

Serious enough 40%
Not serious enough........................ 57
No opinion.................................... 3

The charge that Clinton committed perjury by providing false and misleading testimony as part of the Paula Jones lawsuit?

Serious enough 37%
Not serious enough........................ 60
No opinion.................................... 3

The charge that Clinton obstructed justice by trying to influence the testimony of Monica Lewinsky, his secretary, and others in the Paula Jones lawsuit?

Serious enough 40%
Not serious enough........................ 57
No opinion.................................... 3

The charge that Clinton misused and abused his office and impaired the administration of justice by making false and misleading statements to the public, his aides, and Congress?

Serious enough 47%
Not serious enough........................ 51
No opinion.................................... 2

Thinking again about the current impeachment hearings in Congress, how much of these hearings have you personally seen on television since they started on Monday [December 7]—have you seen some of the hearings on television as they were broadcast live, mostly seen excerpts from the hearings rebroadcast later on television news shows, or not seen any coverage of the hearings on television?

Seen live broadcasts 30%
Seen excerpts rebroadcast 47
Not seen coverage 23
No opinion.................................... *

*Less than 1%

And how much have you read about the im-peachment hearings in the newspaper since they started on Monday [December 7]—have you read most of the stories you have seen on the hearings, a few of the stories reporting on the hearings, just some of the newspaper headlines related to the hearings, or have you not read anything in the newspapers about the hearings?

Read most stories.. 16%
Read few stories 24
Read headlines... 26
Not read newspapers 34
No opinion... *

*Less than 1%

Interviewing Date: 12/11/98
CNN/*USA Today*/Gallup Poll
Survey #GO 125422

Rather than removing President Clinton from office, do you think Congress should or should not resolve this matter by voting to censure Clinton, that is, pass a formal resolu-tion expressing disapproval of his actions?

Should... 58%
Should not 38
No opinion... 4

Regardless of how you feel about impeach-ment, do you think that President Clinton has or has not committed perjury in relation to the Monica Lewinsky matter?

Has.. 67%
Has not.. 27
No opinion... 6

Do you think that Bill Clinton has given the public an adequate apology for his actions, or has he mostly been evading his responsi-bility for his actions in his public statements?

Has given adequate apology............................ 51%
Has been evading responsibility..................... 44
No opinion... 5

Bill Clinton has admitted that he gave false and misleading testimony, but has not admit-ted that he committed perjury. Do you think Clinton should or should not admit publicly that he committed perjury?

Should... 56%
Should not 38
No opinion... 6

As you may know, Bill Clinton made a state-ment about these matters in the White House Rose Garden this afternoon [December 11]. Have you read or heard anything about this afternoon's statement by the president, or not?

Yes, have read or heard 39%
Have not 61
No opinion... *

*Less than 1%

Interviewing Dates: 12/12–13/98
CNN/*USA Today*/Gallup Poll
Survey #GO 125423

Regardless of how you feel about impeach-ment, what is your best guess—do you think that eventually the full House of Representa-tives will or will not vote to impeach Clinton and send the case to the Senate for trial?

Will vote to impeach 54%
Will not vote to impeach 41
No opinion... 5

And what is your best guess about what the Senate would do if the House does in fact im-peach Clinton—do you think that the Senate would or would not vote to convict Clinton and remove him from office?

Would vote to convict 37%
Would not vote to convict 58
No opinion... 5

Thinking about the House Judiciary Commit-tee, do you approve or disapprove of the way each of the following has handled the current

investigation into the charges against Bill Clinton:

The Republicans on the House Judiciary Committee?

Approve 35%
Disapprove 58
No opinion 7

The Democrats on the House Judiciary Committee?

Approve 44%
Disapprove 46
No opinion 10

Now, thinking specifically about the chairman of the House Judiciary Committee, Henry Hyde—do you think the way he handled the impeachment hearings was fair or not fair?

Fair 50%
Not fair 32
Unsure; don't know enough to say;
   no idea (volunteered) 18
No opinion .... *

*Less than 1%

How important is it to you personally whether or not Bill Clinton is impeached and removed from office—very important, moderately important, only a little important, or not important at all?

Very important 53%
Moderately important 24
Only a little important 9
Not important at all 13
No opinion 1

How important is it to the country as a whole whether or not Bill Clinton is impeached and removed from office—very important, moderately important, only a little important, or not important at all?

Very important 65%
Moderately important 18
Only a little important 7
Not important at all 10
No opinion .... *

*Less than 1%

What consequences, if any, might occur if the full House of Representatives votes to impeach Bill Clinton and the Senate conducts a trial—do you think that while the Senate is conducting the trial, each of the following would or would not be seriously harmed:

The ability of the federal government to operate effectively?

Would 47%
Would not 48
No opinion 5

The nation's economy?

Would 48%
Would not 48
No opinion 4

The ability of the country to respond to foreign events and foreign policy matters?

Would 55%
Would not 41
No opinion 4

And now thinking more in the long run, which comes closer to your point of view—the country will be harmed in the long run if Clinton is not impeached; the country will be harmed in the long run if Clinton is impeached; or the country will not be harmed in the long run whether or not Clinton is impeached?

Harmed if not impeached 22%
Harmed if impeached 44
Not harmed 31
No opinion 3

Now, looking at your own personal reaction, if the full House of Representatives votes to impeach Bill Clinton and send his case to the Senate for trial, would you feel:

Angry or not?

Yes.. 41%
No 57
No opinion 2

Pleased or not?

Yes.. 31%
No 67
No opinion 2

Sad or not?

Yes.. 51%
No 47
No opinion 2

Suppose the full House of Representatives votes to censure Clinton but not to impeach him. Would you feel:

Angry or not?

Yes.. 28%
No 70
No opinion 2

Pleased or not?

Yes.. 46%
No 51
No opinion 3

Sad or not?

Yes.. 31%
No 67
No opinion 2

And, finally, suppose the full House of Representatives votes against both impeachment and censure of Clinton, and therefore takes no formal action against him. Would you feel:

Angry or not?

Yes.. 43%
No 56
No opinion 1

Pleased or not?

Yes.. 34%
No 65
No opinion 1

Sad or not?

Yes.. 35%
No 64
No opinion 1

Do you think that when members of Congress vote on impeachment, they have a duty to pay more attention to the people they represent, or to pay more attention to their own conscience?

To the people 70%
To their conscience... 27
No opinion 3

How closely have you been following the congressional impeachment proceedings against Bill Clinton—very closely, somewhat closely, not too closely, or not at all?

Very closely.. 25%
Somewhat closely... 52
Not too closely.. 20
Not at all 3
No opinion .... *

*Less than 1%

Have the congressional impeachment proceedings given you more respect or less respect for each of the following:

Congress?

More respect.. 34%
Less respect 53
Not affected respect (volunteered) 9
No opinion 4

The Republicans in Congress?

More respect.. 30%
Less respect 58
Not affected respect (volunteered) 9
No opinion 3

The Democrats in Congress?

More respect 30%
Less respect 53
Not affected respect (volunteered) 13
No opinion 4

◆   ◆   ◆

Interviewing Dates: 12/15–16/98
CNN/*USA Today*/Gallup Poll
Survey #GO 125463

Rather than removing President Clinton from office, do you think Congress should or should not resolve this matter by voting to censure Clinton, that is, pass a formal resolution expressing disapproval of his actions?

Should.. 54%
Should not 39
No opinion 7

As you may know, later this week the full House of Representatives will vote on whether or not to impeach Bill Clinton. If the House does vote to impeach Clinton and send the matter to the Senate for trial, do you think Bill Clinton should or should not resign and turn the presidency over to Al Gore?

Should.. 41%
Should not 55
No opinion 4

When the House votes on impeachment, some members also want to vote on a censure resolution as an alternative to impeachment. What would you prefer—that the House votes only on impeachment, or that the House votes on both impeachment and censure?

Only on impeachment 34%
Both impeachment and censure...................... 47
Not vote on either (volunteered) 13
No opinion 6

If the House of Representatives votes to impeach Bill Clinton, would the country face a serious crisis, a major problem but not a crisis, a minor problem, or not a problem at all?

Serious crisis... 20%
Major problem but not a crisis 35
Minor problem... 24
Not a problem at all 18
No opinion 3

~

Do you approve or disapprove of the way Congress is handling its job?

Approve 42%
Disapprove.. 52
No opinion 6

~

I'd like to get your opinion of some people in the news. As I read each name, please say if you have a positive or negative opinion of him or her as a person, or if you have never heard of him or her:

Bill Clinton?

Positive 46%
Negative.. 50
No opinion 4

Hillary Rodham Clinton?

Positive 64%
Negative.. 31
No opinion 5

House Judiciary Committee Chairman Henry Hyde?

Positive 31%
Negative.. 27
No opinion 23
Never heard of 19

~

Asked of half sample: Overall, would you say Bill Clinton is fit or unfit to be President of the United States?

Fit 62%
Unfit.. 36
No opinion 2

Asked of half sample: All things considered, are you glad Bill Clinton is president, or not?

Yes.. 62%
No 35
No opinion... 3

Do you approve or disapprove of the way each of the following is handling the current investigation into the charges against Bill Clinton:

The Republicans in Congress?

Approve... 38%
Disapprove.. 56
No opinion... 6

The Democrats in Congress?

Approve... 52%
Disapprove.. 40
No opinion... 8

The news media?

Approve... 32%
Disapprove.. 63
No opinion... 5

Hillary Clinton?

Approve... 67%
Disapprove.. 23
No opinion... 10

How closely have you been following the congressional impeachment proceedings against Bill Clinton—very closely, somewhat closely, not too closely, or not at all?

Very closely.. 26%
Somewhat closely... 49
Not too closely... 21
Not at all 4
No opinion... *

*Less than 1%

Asked of those who favor impeachment (36% of the sample): If the full House of Representa-tives votes this week not to impeach Bill Clinton, therefore ending the matter in Con-gress, would you find that outcome acceptable or unacceptable?

Acceptable... 36%
Unacceptable 63
No opinion... 1

Asked of those who oppose impeachment (61% of the sample): If the full House of Representatives votes this week to impeach Bill Clinton and send the matter to the Senate for trial, would you find that outcome accept-able or unacceptable?

Acceptable... 21%
Unacceptable 77
Neither; other (volunteered) 1
No opinion... 1

Also asked of those who favor impeachment (36% of the sample): Do you think that rea-sonable people can oppose impeachment even though you do not, or do you think that there is no reasonable justification for oppos-ing impeachment?

Reasonable people can oppose 55%
No reasonable justification for opposing........ 37
Neither; other (volunteered) 2
No opinion... 6

Also asked of those who oppose impeachment (61% of the sample): Do you think that rea-sonable people can support impeachment even though you do not, or do you think that there is no reasonable justification for sup-porting impeachment?

Reasonable people can support 40%
No reasonable justification for supporting 54
Neither; other (volunteered) 2
No opinion... 4

In your view, why do most Republicans in Congress support impeachment of Bill Clinton—because they are out to get Bill Clinton at all costs, or because they believe Clinton committed impeachable offenses?

Out to get Clinton 47%
Impeachable offenses 42
Neither; other (volunteered) 3
Both (volunteered)... 6
No opinion.. 2

In your view, why do most Democrats in Congress oppose impeachment of Bill Clinton—is it because they are out to protect Bill Clinton at all costs, or because they believe Clinton did not commit impeachable offenses?

Protect Clinton... 51%
Not impeachable offenses 36
Neither; other (volunteered) 6
Both (volunteered)... 4
No opinion.. 3

If the member of Congress from your district were to vote for impeachment, would this make you more likely to vote for your representative in the next election, less likely to vote for your representative, or would it not make much difference one way or the other?

More likely 19%
Less likely... 31
No difference.. 48
No opinion... 2

In your view, what is the impeachment controversy over Clinton's actions in the Monica Lewinsky matter mostly about—is it mostly about sex, or mostly about lying under oath and obstruction of justice?

Mostly about sex 28%
Mostly about lying under oath........................ 66
No opinion.. 6

Interviewing Dates: 12/19–20/98
CNN/*USA Today*/Gallup Poll
Survey #GO 125526

As you may know, the House has now impeached Clinton and the case will be sent to the Senate for trial. If the Senate holds a trial, what would you want your senators to do—vote in favor of convicting Clinton and removing him from office, or vote against convicting Clinton so he will remain in office?

Vote in favor of convicting Clinton 29%
Vote against convicting Clinton...................... 68
No opinion.. 3

Now thinking about the action taken by the House of Representatives this weekend, do you approve or disapprove of the House decision to vote in favor of impeaching Clinton and sending the case to the Senate for trial?

Approve.. 35%
Disapprove... 63
No opinion... 2

What would you want your member of the House of Representatives to do—vote in favor of impeaching Clinton and sending the case to the Senate for trial, or vote against impeaching Clinton?

Vote in favor of impeaching Clinton.............. 36%
Vote against impeaching Clinton 62
No opinion... 2

Do you think Bill Clinton should or should not resign now and turn the presidency over to Al Gore?

Should 30%
Should not 69
No opinion.. 1

In determining what course of action to take in the Clinton impeachment process, the Senate may face three major choices in the near future. As I read those choices, please tell me which you would prefer they do—the Senate should proceed with a trial on the articles of impeachment sent to them by the House of Representatives; the Senate should vote to censure Clinton and allow him to serve out his remaining two years in office, and not hold a trial; or the Senate should not

hold a trial or censure Clinton, and should drop the matter altogether?

Proceed with trial..31%
Censure Clinton...36
Not hold trial or censure Clinton.....................32
None; other (volunteered) .... *
No opinion.. 1

*Less than 1%

And what is your best guess about what the Senate will do now that the House had impeached Clinton—do you think that the Senate will or will not vote to convict Clinton and remove him from office?

Will...41%
Will not...49
No opinion..10

As of now, do you think Bill Clinton can be an effective president during his remaining two years in office, or not?

Yes, effective..72%
No..26
No opinion.. 2

Thinking about the same issue a little differently, we'd like to know whether you think his effectiveness has been harmed in any way. Do you think his effectiveness has been harmed a great deal, a moderate amount, not much, or not at all?

Great deal 24%
Moderate amount...35
Not much 27
Not at all 12
No opinion.. 2

~

Please tell me whether you have a favorable or unfavorable opinion of each of the following parties:

The Republican party?

Favorable 31%

Unfavorable..57
No opinion..12

The Democratic party?

Favorable 57%
Unfavorable..30
No opinion..13

Whom do you want to have more influence over the direction the nation takes in the next year—Bill Clinton, or the Republicans in Congress?

Clinton...60%
Republicans 31
Both; neither (volunteered) 6
No opinion.. 3

~

Based on what you know about Vice President Al Gore, do you think he is qualified to serve as president if it becomes necessary, or not?

Yes, qualified..63%
No..27
No opinion..10

~

Are you satisfied or dissatisfied with the way democracy is working in this country?

Satisfied...52%
Dissatisfied 44
No opinion.. 4

~

Regardless of whether you think Clinton should or should not be impeached, we'd like to know how you view the way the Republicans in Congress have handled the impeachment process. Do you believe the Republicans have abused their Constitutional powers, or the Republicans have properly exercised their Constitutional powers?

Abused powers 54%
Properly exercised powers..............................41

Neither; other (volunteered) 3
No opinion 2

Next, we have a question about Republican congressman Robert Livingston, who was in line to be the next Speaker of the House of Representatives. As you may know, this weekend Robert Livingston announced he will not serve as Speaker and he will resign from the House of Representatives because of his recent admission about having extramarital affairs. Does Livingston's decision to resign from Congress make you more likely to believe that Bill Clinton should resign as president, or does Livingston's decision not affect your belief about whether Clinton should resign?

More likely to believe
 Clinton should resign 14%
Does not affect belief about Clinton 84
No opinion 2

~

As you may know, the United States and Britain have carried out an air attack against Iraq over the past few days. Do you approve or disapprove of this attack?

Approve 78%
Disapprove 18
No opinion 4

Why do you personally think Bill Clinton ordered this military strike against Iraq—solely because he felt it was in the best interests of the country, or in part to divert public attention away from the impeachment proceedings?

Best interests 66%
Divert attention 25
Neither; other (volunteered) 7
No opinion 2

◆ ◆ ◆

Interviewing Dates: 12/28–29/98
CNN/*USA Today*/Gallup Poll
Survey #GO 125579

In general, are you satisfied or dissatisfied with the way things are going in the United States at this time?

Satisfied 50%
Dissatisfied 48
No opinion 2

In general, are you satisfied or dissatisfied with the way things are going in your own personal life?

Satisfied 86%
Dissatisfied 13
No opinion 1

~

As I read a series of statements, please tell me which you think is more likely to be true of 1999:

A year of economic prosperity, or a year of economic difficulty?

Economic prosperity 62%
Economic difficulty 34
No opinion 4

A year of full or increasing employment, or a year of rising unemployment?

Full or increasing employment 60%
Rising unemployment 35
No opinion 5

A year when taxes will rise, or a year when taxes will fall?

Taxes will rise 64%
Taxes will fall 27
No opinion 9

A peaceful year more or less free of international disputes, or a troubled year with much international discord?

Peaceful year 27%
Troubled year 69
No opinion 4

A year when America will increase its power in the world, or a year when American power will decline?

America will increase its power 60%
American power will decline 33
No opinion 7

A year when prices will rise at a reasonable rate, or a year when prices will rise at a high rate?

Rise at reasonable rate 70%
Rise at high rate 28
No opinion 2

A year when the federal budget is generally balanced, or a year when the federal government has a budget deficit?

Budget generally balanced 50%
Budget deficit 46
No opinion 4

A year of rising crime rates, or a year of falling crime rates?

Rising crime rates 42%
Falling crime rates 54
No opinion 4

~

Next, I'd like to get your overall opinion of some people who were in the news this year. As I read each name, please say if you have a favorable or unfavorable opinion of this person, or if you have never heard of him or her:

Bill Clinton?

Favorable 56%
Unfavorable 42
No opinion 2

Hillary Rodham Clinton?

Favorable 67%
Unfavorable 29
No opinion 4

Al Gore?

Favorable 57%
Unfavorable 28

No opinion 14
Never heard of 1

Attorney General Janet Reno?

Favorable 57%
Unfavorable 29
No opinion 9
Never heard of 5

Speaker of the House Newt Gingrich?

Favorable 38%
Unfavorable 51
No opinion 9
Never heard of 2

Independent Counsel Kenneth Starr?

Favorable 32%
Unfavorable 58
No opinion 6
Never heard of 4

House Judiciary Committee Chairman Henry Hyde?

Favorable 31%
Unfavorable 29
No opinion 20
Never heard of 20

Senate Republican Leader Trent Lott?

Favorable 29%
Unfavorable 25
No opinion 22
Never heard of 24

House Democratic Leader Dick Gephardt?

Favorable 46%
Unfavorable 22
No opinion 16
Never heard of 16

Monica Lewinsky?

Favorable 11%
Unfavorable 82
No opinion 7
Never heard of .... *

*Less than 1%

Linda Tripp?

Favorable 11%
Unfavorable 75
No opinion.. 8
Never heard of... 6

Paula Jones?

Favorable 16%
Unfavorable 72
No opinion.. 10
Never heard of... 2

Former White House volunteer Kathleen Willey?

Favorable 20%
Unfavorable 30
No opinion.. 23
Never heard of... 27

Federal Reserve Chairman Alan Greenspan?

Favorable 57%
Unfavorable 9
No opinion.. 17
Never heard of... 17

Secretary of State Madeleine Albright?

Favorable 64%
Unfavorable 14
No opinion.. 15
Never heard of... 7

~

How much trust and confidence do you have in our federal government in Washington when it comes to handling each of the following—a great deal, a fair amount, not very much, or none at all:

International problems?

Great deal 22%
Fair amount.. 54
Not very much 18

None at all 5
No opinion.. 1

Domestic problems?

Great deal 9%
Fair amount.. 52
Not very much 30
None at all 7
No opinion.. 2

As you know, our federal government is made up of three branches: an Executive branch, headed by the President; a Judicial branch, headed by the U.S. Supreme Court; and a Legislative branch, made up of the U.S. Senate and House of Representatives. How much trust and confidence do you have at this time in each of the following—a great deal, a fair amount, not very much, or none at all:

The Executive branch, headed by the President?

Great deal 24%
Fair amount.. 39
Not very much 23
None at all 12
No opinion.. 2

The Judicial branch, headed by the U.S Supreme Court?

Great deal 27%
Fair amount.. 51
Not very much 16
None at all 4
No opinion.. 2

The Legislative branch, consisting of the U.S. Senate and House of Representatives?

Great deal 13%
Fair amount.. 48
Not very much 30
None at all 7
No opinion.. 2

How much trust and confidence do you have in the government of the state where you live

*when it comes to handling state problems—a
great deal, a fair amount, not very much, or
none at all?*

Great deal 29%
Fair amount.. 51
Not very much... 15
None at all 4
No opinion 1

*And how much trust and confidence do you
have in the local government in the area
where you live when it comes to handling
local problems—a great deal, a fair amount,
not very much, or none at all?*

Great deal 23%
Fair amount.. 54
Not very much... 16
None at all 5
No opinion 2

*In general, how much trust and confidence
do you have in the mass media, such as newspapers, television, and radio, when it comes
to reporting the news fully, accurately, and
fairly—a great deal, a fair amount, not very
much, or none at all?*

Great deal 11%
Fair amount.. 44
Not very much... 35
None at all 9
No opinion 1

*Finally, how much trust and confidence do
you have in general in men and women in political life in this country who either hold or
are running for public office—a great deal, a
fair amount, not very much, or none at all?*

Great deal 7%
Fair amount.. 56
Not very much... 31
None at all 4
No opinion 2

INDEX

A

Abortion
    as act of murder, 157
    consider yourself pro-choice or pro-life, 159
    illegal to perform "partial birth" abortion, 157
    legal under any circumstances, 159
    as most important problem, 60
        trend, 61

Actress
    as career recommended for young woman, 239

Advertising
    influence on children, 189

Afghanistan
    approve of U.S. attacks against terrorist facilities in, 201, 204
    approve of using cruise missiles against terrorist facilities in, 204
    approve of using ground troops against terrorist facilities in, 204
    civilian casualties regrettable but U.S. was right to attack, 201–2
    legitimate to question timing of U.S. action, 201
    trust Clinton for honest explanation for actions in the Sudan and, 204
    U.S. attacks against, likely to increase terrorism against Americans, 201

AIDS
    cured by year 2025, 222
    as most important problem, 60
        trend, 61

Airline stewardess
    as career recommended for young woman, 239

Airplanes
    afraid of flying, 238

Albright, Madeleine
    as most admired woman, 2, 154
    opinion of, 155, 253

Alcoholism
    need to know if presidential candidate were an alcoholic, 36–37

Alexander, Lamar
    likely to support for Republican nomination, 65, 227
    opinion of, 64

Aliens (extraterrestrials)
    humans will have made contact with, by year 2025, 221
    likely to be friendly by year 2025, 221

"Ally McBeal"
    as funniest show on television, 61–62

"America's Funniest Home Videos"
    as funniest show on television, 61–62

Angelou, Maya
    as most admired woman, 2, 154

Annan, Kofi
    favor UN agreement with Iraq worked out by, 33

Arab nations
    Israel and, will be able to live in peace, 240
    likely to become involved with U.S. in full-scale war, 221
    See also Palestinians

Arafat, Yassar
    opinion of, 155

As Good As It Gets (movie)
    like to see it win Oscar, 175

Ashcroft, John
    likely to support for Republican nomination, 65, 227
    opinion of, 64

Asia
    impact of economic problems on U.S. economy, 157–58
    U.S. should help solve financial crisis in, 158

Auto racing
    as favorite sport to watch, 237

B

Baltic States
    allow them to join NATO, 171

Banker
    as career recommended for young man, 238

Banks and banking
    confidence in banks, 181
    good for consumers when two large banks merge, 176

Baseball
    fan of, 226
    as favorite sport to watch, 237
    greatest player in game today [list], 226

Basketball
    fan of, 226
    as favorite sport to watch, 237
    players or owners as more concerned about interests of fans, 226
    side with owners or players in dispute, 226

Bauer, Gary
likely to support for Republican nomination,
65
opinion of, 64
Beautician
as career recommended for young woman, 239
Bible
agree that "wife should submit to leadership of
her husband," 187
described as actual word of God, 187
how often do you read, 241
reading it has given me new depth of love, 241
reading it has helped me be more open, 241
reading it has helped me feel at peace, 241
reading it has helped me feel closer to God, 241
reading it has helped me find meaning in life,
241
reading it has led to Bible being more
meaningful, 241
reading it has strengthened me against wrongs,
242
where do you do most of your reading of, 241
Bilingual education
teach non-English-speaking students using
immersion or, 70–71
Blacks
country will have elected black president by
year 2025, 222
nonwhites with Hispanics as majority in U.S.
by year 2025, 222
See also Race relations
Blair, Tony
opinion of, 155
Bonds, Barry
as greatest baseball player today, 226
Bosnia
approve of presence of U.S. troops in, 157
See also Kosovo situation
Boston Globe
heard or read about columnist Patricia Smith
making up quotes in, 194
Bowling
as favorite sport to watch, 237
Boxing
as favorite sport to watch, 237
Bradley, Bill
likely to support for Democratic nomination,
66, 227–28
opinion of, 65
Brazil
possession of nuclear weapons as threat to
U.S., 180
possession of nuclear weapons as threat to
world peace, 79

The Bridge on the River Kwai (movie)
as best movie, 187
have seen, 187
Brown, Tina
heard or read about her resigning from New
Yorker, 194
Buchanan, Pat
likely to support for Republican nomination,
65
opinion of, 64
Budget, federal
approve of budget passed last week, 228
balanced in 1999, 3, 162, 252
blame Clinton or Republicans in Congress for
government shutdown, 204–5
confidence in Clinton or Republicans on
handling, 55–56
trend re deficit, 56
cut income taxes as priority for using budget
surplus, 162–63
expect it to be balanced, 162
if balanced in 1999, will stay balanced for
several years, 3–4
increase federal funds for public schools as
priority for using budget surplus, 163
increase spending on highway construction as
priority for using budget surplus, 163
as priority for Congress, 235
provide tax credits to parents for child care as
priority for using budget surplus, 163
provide tax credits to reduce pollution as
priority for using budget surplus, 163
reduce national debt as priority for using
budget surplus, 162
strengthen Medicare as priority for using
budget surplus, 163
strengthen Social Security as priority for
using budget surplus, 163
Budget deficit, federal
Clinton deserves credit for reduction in, 2
credit (prefer approach of) Clinton or
Republicans in Congress for reducing, 157,
162
economic conditions deserve credit for
reduction in, 3
as important issue in elections for Congress, 159
as most important problem, 60
trend, 60
Republicans deserve credit for reduction in, 2–3
as serious problem for country, 157
spending controls deserve credit for reduction
in, 3
tax increases deserve credit for reduction in, 3
use surplus federal money to pay down debt, 4

Bush, Barbara
    as most admired woman, 2, 154
Bush, George
    approval rating, 25
        trend, 25
    confidence more in Clinton or, to handle crises
        involving Iraq, 168
    Gallup analysis of volatility in job approval,
        22–23
    as most admired man, 1, 154
Bush, George W. (Texas governor)
    likely to support for Republican nomination,
        65, 227
    likely to vote for Gore or, in year 2000
        presidential election, 228
    opinion of, 64
Business and industry
    big business as biggest threat to country, 240
    business conditions as very good in your
        community, 48
        trend, 48
    as career recommended for young man, 238
    as career recommended for young woman, 238
    confidence in, 182
    confidence in big business, 182
    confidence in small business, 182
    See also Corporate mergers

C

Campaign financing and fund-raising
    Chinese officials attempted to influence U.S.
        elections, 167
    Clinton did something illegal, 167
    Gore did something illegal, 167
Cancer
    cured by year 2025, 222
    cure will be found in ten years, 179
    cure will be found within fifty years, 179
Careers
    choice [list] recommended for young man, 238
    choice [list] recommended for young woman,
        238–39
Cars
    replaced by mass transportation by year 2025,
        222
Carter, Jimmy
    approval rating, 24
        trend, 24
    Gallup analysis of volatility in job approval, 22–23
    as most admired man, 1
Casablanca (movie)
    as best movie, 187
    have seen, 187

Charles, Prince of Wales
    opinion of, 155
Child care
    provide tax credits to parents for, as priority
        for using budget surplus, 163
Children
    advertising as influence on, 189
    computers, including Internet, as influence on,
        189–90
    ease rated of raising them to be good
        people, 189
    easier to raise them to be good people by year
        2025, 219
    harder today than twenty years ago to raise
        them to be good people, 189
    if tax increase on cigarettes is passed, use
        revenue on programs for, 178
    movies as influence on, 187
    news media as influence on, 189
    popular music as influence on, 190
    support from community groups as essential to
        parents in raising, 190
    support from extended family as essential to
        parents in raising, 190
    support from friends and neighbors as essential
        to parents in raising, 190
    support from government as essential to
        parents in raising, 190
    support from organized religion as essential to
        parents in raising, 190
    support from schools as essential to parents in
        raising, 190
    taken steps to shield your children from
        popular culture, 189
    television as influence on, 189
    See also Public schools; School violence
China
    allegations are true concerning Clinton
        administration and, 75
    as ally or enemy of U.S., 83
        trend, 83
    approve of Clinton's decision to visit, 75,
        81, 86
    Clinton did something illegal in China matter,
        75
    Clinton should criticize its human rights
        policies while he's in China, 81–82
    Clinton's visit to, improved U.S. relations
        with China, 86
    Clinton's visit to, will (did) improve China's
        treatment of its citizens, 82–83, 86
    followed news on allowing China missile
        technology because of contributions to
        Democratic party, 75

China (*continued*)
    grant Most Favored Nation status to, 87
    Justice Department doing enough in
       controversy involving Clinton
       administration and, 76
    likely to become involved with U.S. in
       full-scale war, 221
    link human rights issues in, with U.S.-China
       trade policy, 83
    opinion of, 80, 188
       trend, 81
    possession of nuclear weapons as threat
       to U.S., 180
    possession of nuclear weapons as threat to
       world peace, 78
    relations with, handled by Clinton, 185
    U.S. military to defend Taiwan if attacked by,
       185
Chiquita Banana Company
    heard or read about *Cincinnati Inquirer*'s
       illegally obtaining information on, 193–94
Cigarette smoking and smokers
    if tax increase on cigarettes is passed, use
       revenue on anti-smoking programs, 178
    proposal to classify nicotine as drug, 177
    proposal to increase taxes on cigarettes, 177
    proposal to require tobacco companies to pay
       if teen smoking is not reduced, 177
    proposal to restrict advertising and sale to
       minors, 178
    Senate tobacco bill to reduce number of
       teenagers who smoke or raise revenue,
       185
    smoked any cigarettes in past week, 188
    See also Tobacco companies
Cincinnati Inquirer
    heard or read about its illegally obtaining
       information on Chiquita Banana Co.,
       193–94
Cities
    prefer to live in city, suburban area, small
       town, or on farm, 238
Citizen Kane (movie)
    as best movie, 187
    have seen, 187
Claustrophobia
    afraid of being closed in small space, 238
Clemens, Roger
    as greatest baseball player today, 226
Clergyman
    as career recommended for young man, 238
Clinton, Bill
    Afghanistan and the Sudan, trust him for
       explanation for actions in, 204

approval rating, 12, 17, 23, 72, 91–92, 109,
    126, 151–52
    by degree, 23, 100–101
    Gallup analysis, 22–23
    trend, 12–14, 17, 23, 72–73, 100–101,
       109–10, 126, 152
betrayed public's trust, 203
budget, confidence in Republicans or, on
    handling, 55–56
    trend *re* deficit, 56
budget deficit, credit for reduction in, 2
budget deficit, credit Republicans in Congress
    or, for reducing, 162
budget deficit, prefer Republicans' or his
    approach to reducing, 157
can bring about changes this country needs,
    160
can get things done, 202
cares about needs of people like you, 202
China, approve of his decision to visit, 75, 81,
    86
China, did something illegal in matter,
    75, *see also* Clinton administration
China, his visit improved U.S. relations with,
    86
China, his visit will [did] improve its treatment
    of its citizens, 82–83, 86
China, should criticize it for its human rights
    policies while he's in, 81–82
China relations handled by, 185
confidence in, 161, 199
confidence in, as military leader, 201
confidence in, to solve financial problems
    facing Social Security, 240
Congress dealt with by, 202
as conservative or liberal, 158
direction the nation takes, more influence than
    Republicans in Congress over, 160, 250
dissatisfaction with, as most important
    problem, 60
    trend, 60
does good job representing America, 202
economy handled by, 73, 202
    annual averages, 73
    trend, 73
education, confidence in Republicans or, on
    handling, 56–57
    trend, 57
as effective manager, 173
effective president in remaining two years,
    124, 250
family issues handled by, 202
faults worse than other presidents, 35–36
fit to be President of the U.S., 247

charge that he committed perjury before Starr's grand jury as true, 243

charge that he helped Lewinsky obtain job, 207–8, 208

charge that he influenced testimony of his secretary, 208, 208

charge that he influenced testimony of Lewinsky, his secretary, and others in Paula Jones lawsuit as serious enough for impeachment, 243

charge that he influenced testimony of Lewinsky, his secretary, and others in Paula Jones lawsuit as true, 243

charge that he lied to White House aides, 208, 208–9

charge that he lied under oath about having sex with Lewinsky, 207, 208

charge that he lied under oath before grand jury, 207, 208

charge that he misused office by false statements to public, his aides, and Congress as serious enough for impeachment, 243

charge that he misused office by false statements to public, his aides, and Congress as true, 243

charge that he worked with Lewinsky to conceal their relationship, 207, 208

charges against him as important indicators of his character, 209

charges against him represent private matters only, 210, 217

charges more serious against Clinton than charges against Nixon in Watergate, 223

confidence in his abilities to carry out duties, 15–16

committed perjury in testimony before grand jury, 217, 244

consider removing him from office if he had sex [with Lewinsky] in Oval Office, 104

consider removing him from office if he influenced Lewinsky to lie, 105

consider removing him from office if he lied about his relationship with Lewinsky, 104–5

consider removing him from office if he lies before grand jury, 107

controversy diverting him from Iraq crisis, 168

controversy mostly about sex or lying under oath, 249

controversy will harm his ability to serve in office, 161

country harmed in long run if he is not impeached, 245

did nothing illegal, 199

did something illegal, 173, 177

effectiveness as president, 124, 213, 250

enough cause to begin impeachment hearings against him, 42

favor effort to impeach and remove him if you were convinced he attempted to get Lewinsky to lie under oath, 7, 188

favor effort to impeach and remove him if you were convinced he lied under oath about involvement, 7, 188

favor his videotaping his grand jury testimony, 94–95

followed news about, 203

following congressional proceedings against, 246, 248

have facts needed to form your opinion about impeachment of, 217

heard allegations about his affair with White House employee, 5–6

heard or read about his statement in Rose Garden [Dec. 11], 244

heard speech stating that he did have inappropriate relationship with Lewinsky, 199

hiding something (engaged in coverup), 161, 167

Hillary has forgiven him, 210

how much of videotape of his testimony have you seen (plan to watch), 214, 218

if Hillary has forgiven him, would that affect your view of him, 210

important to country whether he is impeached and removed, 245

important to you whether he is impeached and removed, 245

intended to lie when he said under oath that he did not have sexual relations with Lewinsky, 209

investigation into allegations should continue or stop now, 176, 188–89, 198

investigation into charges against him as handled by Hillary Clinton, 248

investigation into charges against him as handled by Democrats in Congress, 248

investigation into charges against him as handled by news media, 248

investigation into charges against him as handled by Republicans in Congress, 248

investigators treated him fairly, based on videotape, 216

invoked "executive privilege," 176–77

journalists enjoy his troubles concerning allegations, 18

Clinton and Lewinsky/impeachment controversy
(*continued*)

Congress and impeachment controversy
(*continued*)

feel pleased if House votes to impeach Clinton and send case to Senate for trial, 245–46

feel sad if House takes no formal action against Clinton, 246

feel sad if House votes to censure Clinton but not impeach him, 246

feel sad if House votes to impeach Clinton and send case to Senate for trial, 245–46

following impeachment proceedings against Clinton, 148–49, 246, 248

hold hearings on charges against Clinton in Starr report, 120–21, 123–24, 130, 211

trend, 124

House Judiciary Committee should agree to end hearings by specific date, 223

House Judiciary Committee should call other witnesses or wrap up hearings, 235

House Judiciary Committee should consider only charges stemming from Clinton's relationship with Lewinsky, 223

House Judiciary Committee should vote for impeachment of Clinton, 149–50

House members' constituents support or oppose impeachment, 211

House should begin proceedings to impeach Clinton and remove him from office, 164

how much about impeachment hearings have you read, 244

how much of impeachment hearings have you seen on television, 243

how much of Starr report have House members read, 210

if Clinton admits that he lied about having sexual relations with Lewinsky, Congress should start impeachment hearings, 196

if Clinton denies he had sex with Lewinsky in his testimony, Congress should begin impeachment hearings, 196

if House Judiciary Committee votes out Articles of Impeachment, where do you stand, 211–12

if House votes not to impeach Clinton, would you find that acceptable, 248

if House votes to impeach Clinton, he should resign and turn presidency over to Gore, 247

if House votes to impeach Clinton, would country face serious crisis, 247

if House votes to impeach Clinton, would you find that acceptable, 248

if it censures Clinton, can he be an effective president, 213

if Senate holds trial, would you want your senators to convict Clinton, 249

if your member votes for impeachment, would this make you more likely to vote for him in next election, 249

impeach and remove Clinton, 229

impeach Clinton for his sexual advance toward Kathleen Willey, 173

impeach Clinton if he lied under oath, 173–74

impeach Clinton as priority for, 236

impeachment hearings accomplished something worthwhile, 234, 235

impeachment proceedings have given you more respect for, 246

important that House completes hearings into Clinton matter by end of year, 231

investigation into charges against Clinton handled by Democrats on House Judiciary Committee, 245

investigation into charges against Clinton handled by Republicans on House Judiciary Committee, 244–45

likely to support your member in November if he calls for Clinton to resign, 213

likely to support your member in November if he favors censure of Clinton, 212

likely to support your member in November if he takes no formal action against Clinton, 213

paying too much attention to Clinton investigation, 214

prefer that House votes only on impeachment or on impeachment and censure, 247

prefer that House votes to impeach Clinton and Senate votes to remove him, 218

prefer that Senate proceeds with trial of Clinton, censures him, or drops matter, 249–50

rate Starr's job in presenting his report to, 234

release Starr report, 119–20, 214

release videotape of Clinton's testimony, 214

stick close to public opinion when deciding to impeach Clinton, 209

think House will vote to impeach Clinton and send case to Senate for trial, 244

think Senate will vote to convict and remove Clinton, 244, 250

vote on impeachment according to House members' constituents (people they represent) or conscience, 211, 246

vote to censure Clinton, 126, 127, 210, 229, 242, 244, 247

vote to censure Clinton only for charges in Starr report or for improper relationship with Lewinsky, 213

Crime (*continued*)
    as most important problem, 60
        trend, 60
    as priority for Congress, 235
    Republican or Democratic party better at
        dealing with, 224
    television news and entertainment programs
        show more crime and violence now than
        five years ago, 229
    worry about being attacked while driving car, 146
    worry about getting mugged, 145
    worry about getting murdered, 145
    worry about getting sexually assaulted or
        raped, 146
    worry about home being burglarized, 145–46
Crime rate
    better in year 2025 than today, 219
    1999 as year of rising rates, 252
Criminal justice system
    confidence in, 182
Crocheting
    as favorite way of spending evening, 237
Crowds
    afraid of, 238
C-Span
    how often do you get your news from, 192
    trust accuracy of news from, 97
Czechoslovakia. *See* Czech Republic; Slovakia
Czech Republic
    allow it to join NATO, 171

D

Dancing
    as favorite way of spending evening, 237
Dark, the
    afraid of, 238
"Dateline NBC"
    how often do you get your news from, 193
    trust accuracy of news from, 98
Death penalty
    or life imprisonment for murder committed by
        man, 158
    or life imprisonment for murder committed by
        woman, 158
Debt, national. *See* National debt
Defense, national
    spending too little on, 236
    use surplus federal money to increase spending
        on, 4
Democracy
    satisfied with way it is working, 250
Democratic party
    Attorney General Reno should investigate
        fund-raising by Clinton and Gore for, 204

better than Republican party at dealing with
    crime, 224
better than Republican party at dealing with
    economy, 224
better than Republican party at dealing with
    education, 224
better than Republican party at dealing with
    environment, 224
better than Republican party at dealing with
    foreign affairs, 224
better than Republican party at dealing with
    health care policy, 224
better than Republican party at dealing with
    impeachment proceedings against Clinton,
    225
better than Republican party at dealing with
    moral values, 225
better than Republican party at dealing with
    Social Security, 194, 224, 240
better than Republican party at dealing with
    taxes, 224
better than Republican party at keeping
    country prosperous, 229
can bring about changes this country needs, 175
Chinese officials attempted to influence U.S.
    elections by donating to, 167
as conservative or liberal in its views, 231
continue investigation of fund-raising practices
    or stop now, 198
country better off if Republicans or Democrats
    controlled Congress, 227
favors rich, middle class, or poor, 232
followed news on allowing China missile
    technology because of contributions to, 75
manages federal government effectively, 175
more likely than Republican party to keep U.S.
    out of war, 229
opinion of, 250
vote for its candidate in elections for Congress,
    58, 112–14, 128, 133–34, 139, 141, 201
    generic ballots, 139
    trend, 58–59, 114, 128–29, 134
vote for its candidate in elections for Congress
    if no tobacco bill is passed, 185
vote for its candidate in elections for Congress
    if Republicans consider impeaching
    Clinton, 114
vote for its candidate in elections for Congress
    if Republicans vote for and Democrats
    against impeaching Clinton, 114–15
wants government to do too much, 232
Democratic presidential nominees
    likely to support [list], 66, 227–28
    opinion of, 65–66

more families where both parents are employed by year 2025, 220

satisfaction with future facing your family, 137

satisfaction with your family life, 137

single-parent families will be common by year 2025, 220

support enough to parents from extended family, 190

support from extended family as essential to parents in raising children, 190

trust accuracy of news from family, 98

visiting relatives as favorite way of spending evening, 237

"Family Matters"
as funniest show on television, 61–62

Farms
prefer to live in city, suburban area, small town, or on farm, 238

Fashion
as career recommended for young woman, 239

Figure skating
as favorite sport to watch, 237

Financial situation, personal
better off next year than now, 47
trend, 47-48
better off now than year ago, 46–47
trend, 47
changes in stock market have made you less confident about your own situation, 117
changes in stock market have made you shift money out of market, 117–18
more or less personal economic security in year 2025, 220
satisfaction with your family or household income, 137
satisfaction with your net worth, 138

Fishing
as favorite sport to watch, 237

Football
fan of, 10
as favorite sport to watch, 237
See also Super Bowl

Forbes, Steve
likely to support for Republican nomination, 65, 227
opinion of, 64

Foreign affairs
handled by Clinton, 188, 202
as most important problem, 60
trend, 61
as priority when you vote for your member of Congress, 225
Republican or Democratic party better at dealing with, 224

Foreign aid
as most important problem, 60
trend, 61

Foreign policy
harmed while Senate conducts trial of Clinton, 245

Fox News Channel
how often do you get your news from, 192
trust accuracy of news from, 97

"Frasier"
as funniest show on television, 61–62
replace "Seinfeld" on Thursdays with, 63

Freedom, personal
more or less, in year 2025, 220

Friends
all right to lie to friend, 238
entertaining, as favorite way of spending evening, 237
how often do you get your news from, 193
support enough to parents from neighbors and, 190
support from neighbors and, as essential to parents in raising children, 190
trust accuracy of news from, 98
visiting, as favorite way of spending evening, 237

"Friends"
as funniest show on television, 61–62

The Full Monty (movie)
like to see it win Oscar, 175

G

Gambling
need to know if presidential candidate has gambling problem, 37

Games
playing cards, Scrabble, games as favorite way of spending evening, 237

Gates, Bill
as most admired man, 1, 154
opinion of, 53, 155, 233

General Motors Corp.
favor company or union in United Auto Workers strike, 194

Gephardt, Dick
likely to support for Democratic nomination, 66, 227–28
opinion of, 65, 155, 252

Gingrich, Newt
approval rating as Speaker, 175
Gallup analysis of his public image, 142–44
good for country that he has resigned from Congress, 232

Gingrich, Newt (*continued*)
likely to support for Republican nomination, 65, 227
likely to vote for Gore or, 177
like to see Republicans elect leaders more likely to compromise with Democrats, 232
opinion of, 28, 64, 155, 252
trend, 28–29
Ginsburg, William
opinion of, 181
Girl Scouts
support enough to parents from, 190
support from, as essential to parents in raising children, 190
Glass, Stephen
heard or read about his fabricating articles in *New Republic*, 194
Glenn, John
approve of NASA's sending him back into space, 230
as most admired man, 154
NASA made right decision to allow him back into space, 158
NASA sending him into space for scientific value, for publicity, or as political reward, 230
opinion of, 155
too old to return to space, 230
The Godfather (movie)
as best movie, 187
have seen, 187
Golf
as favorite sport to watch, 237
Gone With the Wind (movie)
as best movie, 187
have seen, 187
Good Will Hunting (movie)
like to see it win Oscar, 175
Gore, Al
Attorney General Reno should investigate fund-raising by, 204
can get things done, 203
cares about needs of people like you, 203
Clinton should resign and turn presidency over to, 126, 131, 199, 247, 249
trend, 126, 131
does good job representing America, 203
fund-raising, did something illegal, 167
as honest and trustworthy, 202
likely to support for Democratic nomination, 66, 227–28
likely to vote for George W. Bush or, in year 2000 presidential election, 228
likely to vote for Elizabeth Dole or, in year 2000 presidential election, 180

likely to vote for Gingrich or, 177
opinion of, 27, 65, 155, 252
trend, 27
qualified to serve as president, 159, 203, 250
shares your values, 202
shows good judgment, 203
Government, federal
approve of way Clinton is managing, 197
big government as biggest threat to country, 240
blame Clinton or Republicans in Congress for shutdown, 204–5
as career recommended for young man, 238
confidence in Executive branch, 253
confidence in its handling of domestic problems, 253
confidence in its handling of international problems, 253
confidence in Judicial branch, 253
confidence in Legislative branch, 253
Democratic party wants it to do too much, 232
dissatisfaction with, as most important problem, 60
trend, 60
harmed while Senate conducts trial of Clinton, 245
influence larger in year 2025 than today, 219
programs proposed in State of the Union give government too much power, 162
Republican party wants it to do too much, 232
should promote traditional values, 229
support enough to parents from, 190
support from, as essential to parents in raising children, 190
as threat to rights of ordinary citizens, 230
trying to do too many things, 229
See also Government spending
Government, local
confidence in, 254
influence larger in year 2025 than today, 219
Government, state
confidence in, 253–54
Government spending
credit spending controls for reduction in budget deficit, 3
increase for food programs, 236
increase for medical and health care, 236
increase for public education, 237
increase for space program, 236
programs proposed in State of the Union cost too much, 162
spending too little on military, 236
use 1999 surplus to cut taxes, spend on government programs, or pay down debt, 4

willing to support larger Air Force, 236
willing to support larger Army, 236
willing to support larger Navy, 236
See also by program
The Graduate (movie)
as best movie, 187
have seen, 187
Graham, Billy
as most admired man, 1, 154
Great Britain
approve of U.S. and Britain's air attack against Iraq, 150, 251
if Americans and British launch air strikes against Iraq, then risk of dangerous chemicals and bacteria, 166
objective of British and American military action in Gulf should be Saddam's removal, 166
possession of nuclear weapons as threat to U.S., 180
possession of nuclear weapons as threat to world peace, 79
Great Britain, respondents in. *See* United Kingdom, respondents in
Greenspan, Alan
opinion of, 155, 253
Griffey, Ken, Jr.
as greatest baseball player today, 226
Guns and gun control
gun control as priority for Congress, 236
as most important problem, 60
trend, 61
no restrictions on ordinary citizens owning guns, 178
Gwynn, Tony
as greatest baseball player today, 226
Gymnastics
as favorite sport to watch, 237

H

"Hard Copy"
how often do you get your news from, 193
trust accuracy of news from, 98
Health
emergence of deadly new disease by year 2025, 220
like to lose weight, 158
more or less health and physical well-being in year 2025, 220
satisfaction with your health today, 137
trying to lose weight, 158
Health care
increase government spending for, 236

as most important problem, 60
trend, 61
as priority for Congress, 235
as priority when you vote for your member of Congress, 225
Republican or Democratic party better at dealing with health care policy, 224
with HMOs, as issue important to your vote for Congress, 217
See also Medical care
Health insurance
costs of Viagra covered by, 68
Heights
afraid of, 238
Highway construction
increase spending on, as priority for using budget surplus, 163
Hispanics
as majority with nonwhites in U.S. by year 2025, 222
Home economics
as career recommended for young woman, 239
"Home Improvement"
as funniest show on television, 61–62
Homelessness
as most important problem, 60
trend, 60
as priority for Congress, 236
Homemaker
as career recommended for young woman, 239
Homosexuality
born with, or due to other factors, 90–91, 187–88
trend, 91
homosexual behavior as morally wrong, 89–90
Homosexuals
gay marriage will be commonplace in year 2025, 221
gay marriage will be legal in year 2025, 221
include gay men in military draft, 183
need to know if presidential candidate were a homosexual, 38
Horse racing
as favorite sport to watch, 237
Household chores
as favorite way of spending evening, 237
Housing
satisfaction with your situation, 137
Human rights
Clinton should criticize China for its human rights policies, 81–82
Clinton's visit to China will [did] improve its treatment of its citizens, 82–83, 86
link human rights issues in China with U.S.-China trade policy, 83

Kerry, John
  likely to support for Democratic nomination, 66, 227–28
  opinion of, 66
Kevorkian, Dr. Jack
  opinion of, 155
"Kids Say the Darndest Things"
  as funniest show on television, 61–62
Knitting
  as favorite way of spending evening, 237
Kosovo situation
  have followed closely, 225–26
  U.S. and its allies should strike against Serbian forces, 226
  See also Bosnia

L

Labor, organized
  big labor as biggest threat to country, 240
  confidence in, 181
  favor company or United Auto Workers in General Motors strike, 194
L.A. Confidential (movie)
  like to see it win Oscar, 175
Latvia
  allow it to join NATO, 171
Lawrence of Arabia (movie)
  as best movie, 187
  have seen, 187
Lawyer
  attorney or, as career recommended for young man, 238
  attorney or, as career recommended for young woman, 239
Legislative branch
  confidence in, 253
Leisure time
  favorite way [list] of spending evening, 237
  satisfaction with amount of, 138
Lewinsky, Monica
  appropriate for Starr to call her mother as witness, 167
  believe her or Clinton if she said she had affair, 195
  believe her or Clinton if she says he advised her to lie under oath, 195
  believe her or Clinton now that statements conflict, 208
  favor her immunity agreement with Starr, 94
  feel sympathetic toward, 160–61
  interested in reading her book when it comes out, 235

  interested in watching Barbara Walters's television interview of, 235
  likely that she will tell truth when she testifies before grand jury, 195–96
  as most admired woman, 154
  nature of her relationship with Clinton described, 172
  opinion of, 18, 28, 155, 252
    trend, 18, 28
  as part of right-wing conspiracy to damage Clinton, 18, 164
  took first steps to establish relationship, 164
  Tripp's tapes of her conversations about Clinton might be important evidence, 231
  what does her voice sound like, 233–34
  See also Clinton, Hillary Rodham; Clinton and Lewinsky/impeachment controversy; Jones, Paula; Starr, Kenneth; Tripp, Linda
Liberals
  Clinton as conservative or liberal, 158
  Democratic leaders in Congress as conservative or liberal, 158
  Democratic party as conservative or liberal in its views, 231
  news report with liberal or conservative bias [media list], 170–71
  Republican leaders in Congress as conservative or liberal, 158
  Republican party as conservative or liberal in its views, 231
Librarian
  as career recommended for young woman, 239
Life, personal
  satisfied with way things are going in, 256
  thought about basic meaning of your life, 239
  thought about living worthwhile life, 239
  See also Quality of life
Lightning
  afraid of, 238
Lithuania
  allow it to join NATO, 171
Livingston, Robert
  his decision to resign from House makes you more likely to believe that Clinton should resign, 251
Lott, Trent
  opinion of, 155, 252
Lying
  all right to lie to family member or friend, 238
  all right to lie to someone not close to you, 238

M

"Mad About You"
    as funniest show on television, 61–62
    replace "Seinfeld" on Thursdays with, 63
Maddux, Greg
    as greatest baseball player today, 226
Magazines
    heard or read about Tina Brown resigning from *New Yorker*, 194
    heard or read about Stephen Glass fabricating articles in *New Republic*, 194
    how often do you get your news from, 193
    news reported with liberal or conservative bias, 171
    trust accuracy of news from, 98
Mandela, Nelson
    as most admired man, 1, 154
McCain, John
    likely to support for Republican nomination, 65
    opinion of, 65
McGwire, Mark
    as greatest baseball player today, 226
    opinion of, 154
McVeigh, Timothy
    Nichols as responsible as, for Oklahoma City bombing, 5
Media
    acted responsibly in Clinton-Lewinsky matter, 19
    concerned with accuracy in coverage of allegations about Clinton and Lewinsky, 18
    journalists enjoy Clinton's troubles concerning Lewinsky allegations, 18
    journalists enjoy Reagan's troubles concerning Iran-*contra* affair, 19
    as most important problem, 60
    trend, 61
    press should continue to cover sexual charges against Clinton, 42–43
    See also by type; News media
Medicaid
    as priority for Congress, 235
Medical care
    afraid of needles and getting shots, 238
    availability of, better in year 2025 than today, 219
    easier to afford by year 2025, 220
    increase government spending for, 236
    See also Health care
Medical field
    as career recommended for young man, 238
    as career recommended for young woman, 238

Medical system
    confidence in, 182
Medicare
    confidence in Clinton or Republicans on handling, 55
    trend, 55
    costs of Viagra covered by, 68
    as important issue in elections for Congress, 159
    as most important problem, 60
    trend, 61
    as priority for Congress, 235
    strengthen, as priority for using budget surplus, 163
    use surplus federal money to increase spending on, 4
Men
    most admired man [list], 1, 154
Mice
    afraid of, 238
Microsoft Corporation
    favor Justice Department forcing it to change Internet software packaging, 52
    following news about investigations of, 51–52
    government lawsuit against, makes you likely to use Windows products, 186
    keep Windows system or upgrade, 185
    opinion of, 52, 233
    opinion of Bill Gates, 53, 155, 233
    side more with Justice Department or, 233
    too complex to upgrade your Windows system, 185–86
    use some version of Microsoft Windows at home or at work, 185
    uses illegal business tactics, 52
Middle class
    favored by Democratic party, 232
    favored by Republican party, 232
    quality of life better in year 2025 than today for, 219
Middle East
    crisis as priority for Congress, 235
    favor U.S. military action against Iraq if it would turn Middle East countries against United States, 32
    likely to become involved with U.S. in full-scale war, 221
    peace talks handled by Clinton, 228
    See also Iran; Iraq; Israel; Palestinians
Military
    approve of U.S. attacks against terrorist facilities in Afghanistan and the Sudan, 201, 204

Military (*continued*)

approve of using cruise missiles against terrorist facilities in Afghanistan and the Sudan, 204

approve of using ground troops against terrorist facilities in Afghanistan and the Sudan, 204

better off today with draft, 182

build up Army, Air Force, or Navy, 236

as career recommended for young man, 238

civilian casualties regrettable in Afghanistan and the Sudan but U.S. was right to attack, 201–2

confidence in, 181

downsizing as most important problem, 60
trend, 61

gay men should be included in draft, 183

legitimate to question timing of U.S. action against Afghanistan and the Sudan, 201

return to draft at this time, 182

spending too little on, 236

strike against Serbian forces in Kosovo, 226

use U.S. forces to defend Taiwan if China attacks it, 185

willing to pay more taxes to support larger Air Force, 236

willing to pay more taxes to support larger Army, 236

willing to pay more taxes to support larger Navy, 236

women should be required in draft, 183

See also Iraq; NATO

Miramax Films

heard or read about Tina Brown resigning from *New Yorker* for, 194

Modeling

as career recommended for young woman, 239

Morals and morality

approve of moral example Clinton sets for country, 197

attention given to candidates' private lives, 163

importance of president's moral values on his ability to manage government, 163

important for president to provide moral leadership, 165, 213

important that president have high moral values, 165

moral crisis in this country today, 173

moral decline as most important problem, 60
trend, 60

moral values as issue important to your vote for Congress, 218

moral values better in year 2025 than today, 219

person must have strong moral values to be effective president, 165

prefer president who sets good example but whose views you do not agree with, 165

presidents held to higher standard now than in past, 165

as priority for Congress, 236

Republican or Democratic party better at dealing with moral values, 225

your standards higher than Clinton's, 174

See also Ethics; Lying

Mother Teresa

as most admired woman, 2

Movies

going to, as favorite way of spending evening, 237

have seen movies [list] voted as best ever made, 187

influence on children, 189

like to see win Oscar for Best Picture [list], 174–75

which is best movie ever made [list], 187

Music

influence of popular music on children, 190

listening to, as favorite way of spending evening, 237

Musician

as career recommended for young woman, 239

N

NASA (National Aeronautics and Space Administration)

approve of its sending Glenn back into space, 230

concentrate on unmanned missions or manned program, 147
trend, 147

decision to allow Glenn back into space, 158

increase government spending for space program, 236

rated, 147
trend, 147

sending Glenn into space for scientific value, for publicity, or as political reward, 230

space program's benefits justify its costs, 148
trend, 148

National debt

if tax increase on cigarettes is passed, use revenue to reduce, 178

reduce, as priority for using budget surplus, 162

National Public Radio

how often do you get your news from, 192

trust accuracy of news from, 97

Nuclear weapons (*continued*)
  likely that we will get into nuclear war in ten
    years, 79
    trend, 79
  military strike or attack using, by year 2025, 220
  possession of, by Brazil as threat to U.S., 180
  possession of, by China as threat to U.S., 180
  possession of, by Great Britain as threat to
    U.S., 180
  possession of, by India as threat to U.S., 180
  possession of, by Iran as threat to U.S., 180
  possession of, by Iraq as threat to U.S., 180
  possession of, by Israel as threat to U.S., 180
  possession of, by Pakistan as threat to U.S., 180
  possession of, by Russia as threat to U.S., 180
  U.S. national security threatened by countries
    with nuclear capabilities, 77
  world peace threatened by countries with
    nuclear capabilities, 78
  world peace threatened by possession of
    nuclear weapons by countries [list], 78–79
Nursing
  as career recommended for young woman, 238

O

Oklahoma City bombing (1995)
  See McVeigh, Timothy; Nichols, Terry
On the Waterfront (movie)
  as best movie, 187
  have seen, 187
Opportunity
  satisfaction with your opportunities to succeed
    in life, 137

P

Pakistan
  possession of nuclear weapons as threat to
    U.S., 180
  possession of nuclear weapons as threat to
    world peace, 78
Palestinians
  U.S. has put too much pressure on, to settle
    Middle East conflict, 178
  U.S. should take Israel's or Palestinians' side in
    Middle East conflict, 178, 240
  your sympathies more with Israelis or
    Palestinian Arabs in Middle East situation,
    240
Peace
  more peace or conflict among nations in year
    2025 than today, 222
  1999 as year free of international disputes, 251

Saddam Hussein represents threat to world
  peace, 165–66
world peace threatened by countries with
  nuclear capabilities, 78
world peace threatened by possession of
  nuclear weapons by countries [list], 78–79
Perot, Ross
  vote for Clinton, Dole, or Perot if you could
    vote in 1996 election again, 205
Poland
  allow it to join NATO, 171
Police and policemen
  confidence in, 146, 182
    trend, 146
  police officer as career recommended for
    young man, 238
Politicians
  confidence in men and women in political life,
    254
Pollution
  provide tax credits to reduce, as priority for
    using budget surplus, 163
Poor people
  favored by Democratic party, 232
  favored by Republican party, 232
  poverty as most important problem, 60
    trend, 60
  quality of life better in year 2025 than today
    for, 219
Popular culture
  influence of popular music on children, 190
  taken steps to shield your children from, 189
Poverty
  as most important problem, 60
    trend, 60
  See also Poor people
Powell, Colin
  as most admired man, 1, 154
Pregnancy
  teen pregnancy as most important problem,
    60
    trend, 61
Presidency
  better for country to have president from same
    party that controls Congress, 175
  Clinton's faults worse than other presidents,
    35–36
  confidence in, 181–82
  country will have elected black president by
    year 2025, 225
  country will have elected woman president by
    year 2025, 225
  importance of moral values or ability to
    manage government, 163

important for president to provide moral
leadership, 165, 213
important that president have high moral
values, 165
most presidents have had extramarital affairs, 35
person must have strong moral values to be
effective president, 165
prefer president who sets good example but
whose views you do not agree with, 165
presidents held to higher standard now than in
past, 165
Presidential candidates
increased attention given to candidates' private
lives, 163
need to know if he had child out of wedlock,
39
need to know if he had extramarital affair,
38–39
need to know if he had used drugs, 37–38
need to know if he has gambling problem, 37
need to know if he was not paying his debts,
36
need to know if he were an alcoholic, 36–37
need to know if he were a homosexual, 38
Presidential job approval ratings
Gallup analysis of volatility in, 22–23
Prices
1999 as year when prices will rise at
reasonable rate, 252
"Prime Time Live"
how often do you get your news from, 193
trust accuracy of news from, 98
Privacy, personal
more or less, in year 2025, 220
Problem, most important
facing country today [list], 60
trend, 60–61
Prosperity
Republican or Democratic party better at
keeping country prosperous, 229
Public schools
any children now attending Kindergarten
through Grade 12, 184, 191
confidence in, 181
enough support to parents from schools, 190
fear for your child's safety when at school,
184
increase federal funds for, as priority for using
budget surplus, 163
support from schools as essential to parents in
raising children, 190
use surplus federal money to increase spending
on, 4
See also School violence

Public speaking
afraid of, 238
Puerto Rico
become independent, remain territory, or be
admitted to U.S., 40–41

Q

Quality of life
better in year 2025 than today for average
Americans, 218
better in year 2025 than today for middle class,
219
better in year 2025 than today for the poor, 219
better in year 2025 than today for the rich, 219
Quayle, Dan
likely to support for Republican nomination,
65, 227
opinion of, 65

R

Race relations
better in year 2025 than today, 219
black people dislike whites, 184
effectiveness of Clinton's initiative on, 184
followed Clinton's initiative on, 184
handled by Clinton, 180
improved between blacks and whites in past
year, 184
as most important problem, 60
trend, 61
nation moving toward two societies, 183
new initiative needed to improve, 70
racism as most important problem, 60
trend, 61
state of, rated, 69
white people dislike blacks, 183
whites or Hispanics and nonwhites as majority
in U.S. by year 2025, 222
Racism
as most important problem, 60
trend, 61
Radio
confidence in, to report news fully, 254
how often do you get your news from local
stations, 192
how often do you get your news from national
network news, 192
how often do you get your news from talk
shows, 192
news reported with liberal or conservative bias,
171
trust accuracy of news from local stations, 97

Radio (*continued*)

trust accuracy of news from national network, 97

trust accuracy of news from National Public Radio, 97

trust accuracy of news from talk shows, 97

Reading

as favorite way of spending evening, 237

Reagan, Nancy

as most admired woman, 2

Reagan, Ronald

approval rating, 24–25

trend, 25

Gallup analysis of volatility in job approval, 22–23

journalists enjoy his troubles concerning Iran-*contra* affair, 19

as most admired man, 1, 154

Recession

likely during next twelve months, 206

as most important problem, 60

trend, 60

Religion

agree with Bible that "wife should submit to leadership of her husband," 187

Americans will be more religious in year 2025 than now, 221

attended church or synagogue how often, 242

attended church or synagogue in last seven days, 186, 242

can answer today's problems, 186–87

confidence in church or organized, 181

describe yourself as "born again" or evangelical, 186, 242

going to church as favorite way of spending evening, 237

guidelines about good or evil apply to everyone, 239

important in your own life, 186, 242

increasing its influence, 186

influence larger in year 2025 than today, 219

likely that world will end on Judgment Day in next century, 223

member of church or synagogue, 186, 242

need to experience spiritual growth, 239

postpone release of videotape of Clinton's testimony because of Rosh Hashanah, 214

received any religious training as child, 239

rely on yourself to solve problems, 239

support enough to parents from organized religion, 190

support from organized religion as essential to parents in raising children, 190

thought about basic meaning of your life, 239

thought about developing your faith, 239

thought about living worthwhile life, 239

thought about your relation to God, 239

want your child to receive religious training, 239

your sympathies more with Irish Catholics or Irish Protestants, 87–88

See also Bible

Reno, Janet

as most admired woman, 2, 154

opinion of, 155, 252

should fire Starr or allow him to continue, 186

should investigate fund-raising by Clinton and Gore, 204

Republican party

better than Democratic party at dealing with crime, 224

better than Democratic party at dealing with economy, 224

better than Democratic party at dealing with education, 224

better than Democratic party at dealing with environment, 224

better than Democratic party at dealing with foreign affairs, 224

better than Democratic party at dealing with health care policy, 224

better than Democratic party at dealing with impeachment proceedings against Clinton, 225

better than Democratic party at dealing with moral values, 225

better than Democratic party at dealing with Social Security, 194, 224, 240

better than Democratic party at dealing with taxes, 224

better than Democratic party at keeping country prosperous, 229

can bring about changes this country needs, 175

as conservative or liberal in its views, 231

country better off if Republicans or Democrats controlled Congress, 227

favors rich, middle class, or poor, 232

Gallup analysis of its public image, 144–45

manages federal government effectively, 175

more likely than Democratic party to keep U.S. out of war, 229

opinion of, 250

vote for its candidate in elections for Congress, 58, 112–14, 128, 133–34, 139, 141, 201

generic ballots, 139

trend, 58–59, 114, 128–29, 134

vote for its candidate in elections for Congress if no tobacco bill is passed, 185

vote for its candidate in elections for Congress if Republicans consider impeaching Clinton, 114

vote for its candidate in elections for Congress if Republicans vote for and Democrats against impeaching Clinton, 114–15

wants government to do too much, 232

Republican presidential nominees
likely to support [list], 65, 227
opinion of, 64–65

Republicans in Congress
abused their Constitutional powers in impeachment process, 250–51
blame them, Clinton, or Starr that things have gotten to this point, 215
blame them or Democrats for review of charges against Clinton not being fair, 223
budget, confidence in Clinton or, on handling, 55–56
trend *re* deficit, 56
budget deficit, credit Clinton or, for reducing, 162
budget deficit, credit them for reduction in, 2–3
budget deficit, prefer Clinton's or their approach to reducing, 157
as conservative or liberal, 158
direction the nation takes, more influence than Clinton over, 160, 250
dissatisfaction with, as most important problem, 60
trend, 60
education, confidence in Clinton or, on handling, 56–57
trend, 57
as extreme in their views, 231
government shutdown, blame Clinton or, 204–5
impeachment proceedings have given you more respect for, 246
investigation into charges against Clinton handled by, 248
like to see them elect leaders more likely than Gingrich to compromise with Democrats, 232
Medicare, confidence in Clinton or, on handling, 55
trend, 55
opinion of, 215
as partisan, 231–32
policies that are more conservative or moderate, 231
policies would move country in right direction, 231
as success or failure, 175

support impeachment to get Clinton or for impeachable offenses, 248–49
taxes, confidence in Clinton or, on handling, 54
trend, 55

Rich people
favored by Democratic party, 232
favored by Republican party, 232
quality of life better in year 2025 than today for, 219

Ripken, Cal, Jr.
as greatest baseball player today, 226

Romania
allow it to join NATO, 171

Russia
continue to support President Yeltsin, 206
likely to become involved with U.S. in full-scale war, 221
NATO alliance makes U.S.-Russia relations better, 171–72
possession of nuclear weapons as threat to U.S., 180
possession of nuclear weapons as threat to world peace, 78

S

Saddam Hussein
air strikes against Iraq would remove him from power, 168
backed down to resolve confrontation, 170
Clinton or, as winner in confrontations, 232
favor using force now to remove him, 170
goal to pressure Iraq into complying with UN inspections or remove him, 233
goal to reduce Iraq's weapons capacity or remove him, 31–32
if he places Iraqi civilians at attack sites, U.S. should attack anyway, 166
likely that he will comply with terms of weapons agreement, 170
objective of British and American military action should be his removal, 166
opinion of, 155
represents threat to world peace, 165–66
support attack on Iraq if goal is not to remove him from power, 169
United Nations should continue economic sanctions on Iraq until he complies, 166
worried that UN agreement will give him time to build weapons, 33–34
See also Iraq

Safety
contacted child's school to discuss safety issues, 184–85

involved in full-scale war by year 2025, 220–21

likely that U.S. will be attacked by country using nuclear weapons in ten years, 79

likely to become involved with Arab countries in full-scale war, 221

likely to become involved with China in full-scale war, 221

likely to become involved with Iran in full-scale war, 221

likely to become involved with Iraq in full-scale war, 221

likely to become involved with Middle East in full-scale war, 221

likely to become involved with Russia in full-scale war, 221

NATO alliance makes U.S.-Russia relations better, 171–72

1999 as year when America will increase its power in world, 251–52

possession of nuclear weapons by Brazil as threat to, 180

possession of nuclear weapons by China as threat to, 180

possession of nuclear weapons by Great Britain as threat to, 180

possession of nuclear weapons by India as threat to, 180

possession of nuclear weapons by Iran as threat to, 180

possession of nuclear weapons by Iraq as threat to, 180

possession of nuclear weapons by Israel as threat to, 180

possession of nuclear weapons by Pakistan as threat to, 180

possession of nuclear weapons by Russia as threat to, 180

put too much pressure on Israel to settle Middle East conflict, 178

put too much pressure on Palestinians to settle Middle East conflict, 178

Republican or Democratic party likely to keep U.S. out of war, 229

satisfaction with way things are going in, 25–26, 141, 251

trend, 26–27

take Israel's or Palestinians' side in Middle East conflict, 178

Unknown Soldier

favor attempt to identify Vietnam soldier buried in Tomb of the Unknowns, 178

USA Today

how often do you get your news from, 191

news reported with liberal or conservative bias, 171

trust accuracy of news from, 96

V

Vacation

changes in stock market have made you consider canceling, 117

Vaughn, Mo

as greatest baseball player today, 226

Ventura, Jesse

opinion of, 155

Veterinarian

as career recommended for young man, 238

Viagra (impotency prescription drug)

costs covered by health insurance, 68

costs covered by Medicare, 68

as good for society, 67

what is drug used for, 179

would like to try (asked of men), 67–68

would like your husband to try (asked of married women), 68

Vietnam War

CNN and *Time* misreporting on nerve gas as isolated incident, 194

CNN and *Time* stand behind nerve gas story, 194

heard or read about CNN broadcast concerning use of nerve gas in, 193

Violence

as most important problem, 60

trend, 60

television news and entertainment programs show more crime and violence now than five years ago, 229

See also Crime; School violence

W

Wall Street Journal

how often do you get your news from, 191

news reported with liberal or conservative bias, 171

trust accuracy of news from, 96

Walters, Barbara

interested in watching her interview of Monica Lewinsky, 235

War

more peace or conflict among nations in year 2025 than today, 222

Republican or Democratic party more likely to keep U.S. out of, 229